Marketing management and strategy

2ND EDITION

PETER DOYLE

University of Warwick

PRENTICE HALL

London ■ New York ■ Toronto ■ Sydney ■ Tokyo

Singapore ■ Madrid ■ Mexico City ■ Munich ■ Paris

First published 1994
This revised edition published 1998 by
Prentice Hall
A Pearson Education Company
Edinburgh Gate,
Harlow,
Essex, CM20 2JE, England

Typeset in 9/12 pt Stone Serif
by Goodfellow and Egan, Cambridge

Printed and bound in Great Britain by
T. J. International Ltd, Cornwall

Library of Congress Cataloging-in-Publication Data

Available from the publisher

British Library Cataloguing in Publication Data

A catalogue record for this book is available from
the British Library

ISBN 0-13-262239-4

6 7 8   02 01 00

Marketing management and strategy

**This book is dedicated to
Sylvia, Ben and Hugo,
with love.**

_____

Contents

Preface

This book explores the role of marketing in the modern organization. It presents an up-to-date review of the most important concepts and techniques managers need to analyze today's markets and to capitalize on the opportunities that are continually emerging. For most organizations, marketing is the single most important determinant of success. This is obviously true of businesses operating in the dynamic, globally competitive markets of the 1990s, where the ability to satisfy – or delight – customers is the only determinant of their ability to generate revenues. But marketing is increasingly recognized as central by managers in public sector and other, not-for-profit organizations. After all, no organization exists for its own sake, but rather its task is to meet the needs of those 'publics' it was created to serve.

Many managers still confuse marketing with selling. To them, the word 'marketing' conjures up images of the striking advertisements that they see on television, the latest in-store promotional gimmick, or the figure of the slick, smooth-talking salesman. But such images have little to do with the reality of developing successful marketing strategies today. Real marketing is the philosophy of management that recognizes that the success of the enterprise is sustainable only if it can organize to meet the current and prospective needs of customers more effectively than competition. Selling and marketing are contrasting in their approaches. Selling tries to push the customer to buy what the business has. Marketing, on the other hand, tries to get the organization to develop and offer what the customer will find is of real value. This way marketing seeks to build long-term, mutually beneficial partnerships between the organization and its customers.

As we arrive at the twenty-first century, marketing is becoming even more important. Gone are the stable markets of yesteryear; today's markets are fickle, fast moving and continually splintering as customers' wants change, technology advances and competitors find new ways of adding value and creating additional satisfactions for consumers. Organizations that do not focus on these continually changing markets are quickly beached by the stream of new products, new services and new positioning strategies being offered by their more alert competitors. No organizations are sheltered. Companies such as IBM, General Motors, ICI, GEC, Olivetti and Philips, which, not so long ago, were regarded as icons by managers in other firms, now struggle for their very survival. Hundreds of unsung, but often long-established companies disappear every year.

Marketing – the close analysis of customers and the search for new ways of adding value – offers the only opportunity for managers to keep their heads above these turbulent waters. In the chapters that follow, we look at how this should be done. We show how to develop a marketing orientation in the organization and how this impacts on the ultimate corporate goals of profit, growth and security. Then we examine how marketing strategies are developed and implemented through effective product, pricing, distribution, communications and service policies.

The target audience for this book are men and women who hold, or expect to hold, senior management posts in organizations. It is not written solely for marketing specialists. Marketing is so central to the success of an organization that it cannot be thought of as primarily a specialist discipline. Knowledge and concern for marketing are key responsibilities for all managers whatever their functional labels. The ultimate task of every manager is to contribute to developing products and services which meet the actual or potential needs of customers more effectively than competitors.

Two particular groups of readers were in mind when this book was planned. The first are middle and senior business executives working for companies competing in international markets. The second are those studying for MBA programmes who, I hope, will find the book a suitable text for their graduate marketing course. Teaching MBA and executive courses around the world, I have found that the requirements of executives and MBAs are no longer distinct and separate. All the top business schools now insist that MBA candidates have substantial business experience (the average age is over 30). Today's MBA students demand pragmatic, executive-orientated teaching materials and are not interested in impractical academic theorizing. At the same time, there has been a distinct shift among executives towards management texts which treat more seriously the complex and difficult issues of competing in a dynamic, international marketing environment. Teaching a high-level executive programme today is very similar in content and rigour to a good, graduate MBA class. Books which cover both audiences are now common in related disciplines, such as those by Tom Peters, Michael Porter, Kenichi Ohmae, Richard Pascale and Charles Handy. However, in marketing, there is as yet no such book available. It is hoped that this book will go some way to filling this gap.

The prime aim of this book is to provide a practical guide to marketing decision making and to developing a marketing strategy. It is written with the following objectives:

■ To appeal to executives across all the functional areas of the business. Effective marketing is fundamentally a multifunctional task. Today, all managers need to be drawn into contributing ideas for increasing their organization's marketing competitiveness.

■ To draw on multiple disciplines. Successful marketing requires managers to draw on findings and techniques from a number of fields, including finance, accounting, economics, management science and organizational behaviour.

- To reflect the key issues facing managers in today's markets. The 1990s brought new, additional priorities including responding to environmental pressures, the focus on time-based competition, the importance of the European Union and other regional markets, shortening product life cycles and the ever increasing importance of innovation.

- To present a global perspective. For today's major companies, the internationalization of markets and competition impacts on every aspect of their strategies. Therefore, unlike some books, this one does not have a special chapter on international marketing; instead the international perspective is reflected throughout the work.

- To provide an advanced treatment of marketing and strategy. The book is for current or potential senior executives. It assumes familiarity with the operations of the firm and the major institutions of the market. It focuses on those issues of most concern to senior executives. It avoids purely descriptive material and the treatment of lower-level management topics.

- To offer a practical, pragmatic approach. The book seeks to provide a guide on how to improve marketing performance. It includes concepts only when they provide managers with real insights on how to approach these important decisions. It is fairly ruthless in omitting abstract academic theorizing in order to allow more than usual scope for the detailed treatment of the most practical and relevant ideas and techniques.

- To provide an up-to-date review. The book incorporates the most recent thinking on markets, strategy and related disciplines.

 ## Second edition

The first edition appears to have met the main objectives set out for the work. It has been adopted by many leading business schools for their MBA programmes. These include the London Business School and the universities of Aston, Brighton, Buckinghamshire, Derby, Galway, Humberside, Liverpool, Luton, Newcastle, Norwich, North London, Oxford Brookes, Surrey, Teesside and Warwick, and University College Dublin.

It has also been widely used on company executive programmes, including Burmah Castrol, Cadbury Schweppes, Coats Viyella, Coca-Cola, KPMG, Novartis, Saatchi & Saatchi and Zeneca. I am grateful to the universities and companies that have adopted the book and I have used many of their suggestions in this updating.

The new edition has revised, updated and introduced changes in presentation to every chapter. More emphasis in particular has been given to relationship marketing, branding and financial aspects of marketing. In addition an entirely new chapter (Chapter 13) has been added on turnaround management, covering a set of tactical and strategic problems of great concern to many of today's top executives. The adaptations in the new edition reflect changes in the external environment, new perspectives on professional marketing and new insights from current academic work.

Besides the management literature, this book is influenced by several individual sources. One is the research that I have conducted with colleagues from many universities including Warwick, the London Business School, INSEAD, Stanford, Bradford, South Carolina and Hawaii. Among my past research colleagues, I would particularly like to acknowledge Professors Marcel Corstjens, David Cook, Ian Fenwick, Zeki Gidengil, Graham Hooley, Jim Lynch, John McGee, Paul Michelle, John Saunders, Vivienne Shaw, Veronica Wong and Arch Woodside.

My approach to teaching and research has also been influenced by other outstanding scholars, including Professors Ken Simmonds at the London Business School, Venkataraman Srinivasan at Stanford, Jean-Claude Larreche, Philippe Naert and David Weinstein at INSEAD, Michael Baker at Strathclyde, Robin Wensley at Warwick, Susan Douglas at New York University and the late Abe Schuchman at Columbia.

Most of all the book reflects what I have learnt from my consulting work over the last twenty years. In particular, the book is influenced by the co-operation of managers from the following client organizations:

American Home Products	Marks & Spencer
BMP DDB Needham	Nestlé
British Airways	Novartis
British Telecom	Ogilvy & Mather
British Steel	Philips
Burmah Castrol	Price Waterhouse
Cabinet Office	Rhône Poulenc
Cadbury Schweppes	Rover Group
Cargill	Saatchi & Saatchi
Coats Viyella	Sandoz
Coca-Cola	Sears
Dunhill	Shell
Electrolux	SKF
Gemini	J. Walter Thompson
Hewlett-Packard	Unilever
IBM	Volvo
ICI	Zeneca
KPMG	Zyma
3M	

I am grateful to Shirley Clarke, who provided, as always, excellent secretarial assistance. I also appreciate the help of Dr Veronica Wong, who kindly reviewed the entire work and provided insightful suggestions.

My deepest thanks are to my wife Sylvia and our sons Ben and Hugo, who provided me with the support, encouragement and inspiration to complete this work.

About the author

Peter Doyle is internationally recognized for his teaching and research in marketing and strategy. He is Professor of Marketing and Strategic Management at the University of Warwick Business School, where he also directed the School's MBA programme and executive courses. Previously he has held positions at INSEAD, London Business School, Bradford University, Stanford and University of Hawaii.

He has acted as consultant to many top international businesses including Coca-Cola, Shell, IBM, ICI, Unilever, Nestlé, Novartis, Royal Sun Alliance, Burmah Castrol, Hewlett-Packard, Marks & Spencer, British Airways and Saatchi & Saatchi. He has also acted as an advisor to such professional bodies as Britain's Cabinet Office, the Institute of Chartered Accountants, the Institute of Directors, the CBI, Japanese-American Institutes of Management Sciences, the Pacific Asian Management Institute, and the Singapore Department of Trade.

Peter Doyle has run executive programmes for senior managers throughout Europe, the USA, South America and the Far East. He has been voted 'Outstanding Teacher' on numerous university and corporate courses. In addition he has published five books and over one hundred articles in professional journals. He has a First Class Honours degree from the University of Manchester and an MBA and a PhD from Carnegie-Mellon University, USA. His research has twice led him to be awarded the President's Medal of the Operational Research Society and the Best Paper Award of the American Marketing Association and the European Marketing Academy.

Chapter 1

Management: objectives and tasks

This book is about the role of marketing and strategic management and how they contribute to the success of the firm. Marketing and strategic management are tools to enable the business to achieve its objectives. This chapter considers the objectives of the firm and of the managers who run it. The objectives of the firm are important because they govern the values of the organization, the direction it pursues, the capabilities it builds and the measures it uses to evaluate performance and incentivise staff.

This chapter shows how western managers tend to oversimplify when they set objectives for the business. This has led to unnecessary short-termism, reduced international competitiveness and heightened vulnerability. Managers need to set a balanced array of objectives covering more than just profitability and growth. Multiple objectives are necessary because in the long run the firm has to satisfy multiple stakeholders. A central task of management is to set goals which will satisfy the interests of all those parties on whom the firm's survival depends, including customers, shareholders, managers, employees and the community.

The chapter explores three issues. First, it examines critically the most common measures of business success used by managers. It shows how seeking 'excellence', or outstanding performance, on one single measure such as profits or growth invariably produces major problems in other areas. Instead, alternative approaches which achieve satisfactory performance across a balanced set of objectives are shown. Second, the concept of strategy and the criteria to judge potential alternative strategic options are explored. Finally, the firm's long-run competitiveness depends upon management's ability to build core competences. The last sections of the chapter discuss the type of organization that has to be built if the business is to create these capabilities and achieve international competitiveness.

Objectives and success

Companies use various criteria to judge the success of their business units and to motivate their managers. Each of these objectives has some merit. It is only when one is pursued to the exclusion of others that the limitations of these measures become strikingly apparent. Unfortunately, in recent years, there has been a growing tendency to stress unique measures of performance. One reason has been the increasing popular interest in business. This has encouraged journalists and commentators to seek to create league tables where companies are ranked, like football teams, in order of performance. Such rankings require single, apparently objective measures such as return on investment and capital growth. Managers now see themselves regularly and publicly rated in terms of 'success' against their competitors. A second reason has been the increasing number of books and articles on 'excellent' companies. The work which opened this floodgate was Tom Peters and Robert Waterman's *In Search of Excellence* published in 1982.[1] Typically these writers choose one or two measures of 'excellence', such as profitability or growth, identify the highest performers along these measures, and then extol other managers to follow the behaviour and practices of these companies.

The problem is, however, that it has become clear that the subsequent performance of these so-called excellent companies has been dreadful! For example, of the 43 outstanding US companies chosen by Peters and Waterman, only 14 were doing well five years later and only 5 ten years on. In fact, many had disappeared altogether – hardly a model of performance many managers would wish to emulate. Similarly, in the UK, the top-selling management publication, *Management Today*, identifies each year the country's best companies. Of 12 top companies identified between 1979 and 1990, only 5 survived to 1996! Of the five survivors only one could still be described as a high performer.[2]

What this shows is that outstanding performance on one or two measures is a very poor predictor of future success. As is explained below, the main reason is that each measure is strongly associated with one stakeholder group. For example, increasing shareholder value is beneficial for shareholders, but it can easily be inimical to managers, employees and the local community. Similarly, rapid sales growth often provides benefits for managers, but implies greater risk and reduced returns for owners and creditors. The more management seek exceptional performance on one measure of success, the greater these conflicts become and the more unstable the business.

Profitability

In western companies, profitability is by far the most important objective that senior managers are set (see Table 1.1). Sometimes they are set a target of an absolute measure of profits; more often it is a ratio such as earnings per share, return on investment or return on shareholder funds. The targets are normally determined on the basis of past performance and by comparison against other companies in similar lines of business. Performance against these profit objectives is measured at least annually and often quarterly or even weekly. Profitability is almost ubiquitous as the primary measure of corporate and divisional success, and forms the basis for the increasingly large bonus element in the compensation packages of senior executives. Table 1.2 shows a study of the goals of a large sample of American and Japanese executives. American senior managers were overwhelmingly geared to return on investment, with capital growth

Table 1.1 ■ Europe's largest companies, 1996

	Company	Country	Market capital-ization ($bn)	Sales ($bn)	Profit ($bn)	ROCE (%)	Employees (000s)
1	Royal Dutch/Shell	N/UK	103	95	10	14	106
2	Roche	Swi	67	12	3	9	61
3	Glaxo Wellcome	UK	42	9	3	29	47
4	BP	UK	41	52	4	11	67
5	Nestlé	Swi	40	48	4	17	213
6	Allianz	Ger	39		1		68
7	BT	UK	39	22	4	17	149
8	Unilever	N/UK	36	46	4	27	304
9	HSBC	UK	36		5	34	107
10	Sandoz	Swi	28	14	2	15	60
11	Siemens	Ger	27	58	1	2	394
12	SmithKlineBeecham	UK	27	10	1	20	52
13	UBS	Swi	27		2	10	28
14	BAT	UK	25	9	3	5	84
15	Daimler Benz	Ger	25	72	1	2	342
16	Deutsche Bank	Swe	23		2	12	65
17	Ericsson	Swe	23	17	1	15	74
18	Ciba	Swi	23	19	2	10	84
19	Astra	Swe	21	17	1	42	14
20	Nokia	Swe	21	7	1	29	28
21	Marks & Spencer	UK	19	11	1	22	42
22	Veba	Ger	19	46	2	6	129
23	Barclays	UK	19		3	36	96
24	BTR	UK	19	15	2	24	124
25	ABB	Swc/Swi	19	30	1	17	208

Source: Financial Times, 25 January 1996

for shareholders a poor second. By contrast, Japanese goals were more balanced, with return on investment, market share and new product development equally placed. The main reason why profits or earnings rank so highly in UK and US companies is that they are a key determinant of how the stock market values a company. This point is made clearly by the head of one leading stockbroker (see Box 1.1).

Despite the overwhelming popularity of measures of profit for judging business success, these indices have striking and well-known flaws and biases. First, profits in practice are easily and commonly manipulated by managers to produce misleading results. Different, and perfectly legal, methods of accounting for depreciation, stock valuation, research and development, foreign currency translations and especially different choices of accounting for acquisitions can change accounting losses into big

Table 1.2 ■ Rankings of objectives by American and Japanese senior managers

Objectives	Importance of objectives	
	USA	**Japan**
Return on investment	2.43	1.24
Capital gain for shareholders	1.14	0.02
Increase in market share	0.73	1.43
New product ratio	0.21	1.06

Note: Managers were asked to range importance of goals: 3 = most important, 2 = second most important, 1 = third most important, 0 = all the rest. Score equals mean for all participating managers in each country
Source: T. Kagono, J. Nanaka and N. Oikawa, *Strategic vs Evolutionary Management* (Amsterdam: North Holland, 1985)

BOX 1.1

The importance of profits

'At 8.15 each weekday morning, the security salesmen and analysts at my firm meet to consider the ideas that will be put to our 300 or so institutional customers during the day. Analysts give their recommendations for specific shares: buy, hold or sell. It is these recommendations, together with similar conclusions recorded at twenty or so other security houses, that collectively drive the share prices in the market. The single most important figure affecting the analysts' and hence the market's view is forecast earnings per share.'

Source: I. H. Davison, chairman of Alexanders Laing and Cruickshank

---

reported profits and vice versa. For example, Polly Peck, which was rated the most successful of British companies during the 1980s (prior to its collapse in 1991), was subsequently shown to have lost money in many of these years. For instance, rather than show a loss of £25 million in 1988, it chose to write off against reserves £170 million, so allowing it to state a profit of £155 million. Published profit figures are therefore dubious indicators of performance. Differences in legislation also create striking anomalies. For example, one company, SmithKline Beecham, showed its profit as £130 million in the UK but only £90 million in the USA. Carlton Communications showed its profits as $238 million in the UK, but according to the tighter US accounting rules they were only $133 million.[3]

Methodologically also, financial experts are familiar with a host of limitations surrounding conventional profit measures. Profitability is easily boosted by financing growth through debt rather than equity. Earnings per share rise, but the value of the shares drops due to the higher financial risk. For example, WPP, once the world's largest advertising agency, showed increasing earnings in the period up to 1991, while its share price fell from £8 to £0.60. Profits also fail to take into account the additional cash required to build them. Profit growth therefore can easily disguise an accelerating cash flow crisis.

Finally, and most important of all, profits are fatally flawed as a measure of the value of a business. Profits and ROI measure the past results of the business, not its future potential. Focusing on profitability as the primary objective invariably creates short-term management willing to sacrifice the business's long-term international competitiveness on the altar of short-term profits. Managers know that it is easy to boost current earnings by raising prices, cutting costs, reducing product development, brand support and curtailing investment. Often the board of directors can be fooled for a year or two into thinking such actions are producing a business 'turnaround'. In fact, most such profit improvement programmes are merely asset stripping. Rather than representing improved potential, sudden profit improvements often represent a destruction of the company's future. As Box 1.2 shows, such misunderstandings can influence national policies too.

Growth

Second to profits, growth of turnover or assets is a central objective for over four out of five firms.[4] Growth can be achieved internally or via acquisitions. When very high rates of growth are achieved, acquisitions invariably play the major role. Some companies have given an extraordinary priority to growth and size. Saatchi & Saatchi,

---

BOX 1.2

Long-term growth versus short-term profitability: the case of the UK

Over the last twenty years, manufacturing in the UK shows a remarkable paradox of record productivity growth with sharply declining international competitiveness.

Between 1979 and 1996, UK manufacturing output per person grew by 80 per cent, far outstripping productivity growth in Japan, the USA and the rest of Europe. Yet while world markets expanded, UK manufacturing output failed to grow. By contrast, despite slower productivity growth, manufacturing output jumped by 70 per cent in Japan and Italy, 55 per cent in the USA, 32 per cent in Germany and 17 per cent in France.

What explains this paradox? Productivity is measured by dividing outputs (numbers of cars, machine tools sold, etc.) by inputs (number of employees, amount of capital, etc.). UK companies focused on cutting inputs – denominator management. Overseas competitors focused on expanding outputs – numerator management. British managers sought to reduce costs and boost short-term profits. Their competitors looked to new marketing opportunities, invested in new products and technologies, and built competitive advantage. The result was that foreign companies expanded while employment in UK manufacturing contracted by over one-third (3 million employees) and the share of manufacturing in GDP fell from 32 per cent in 1973 to 20 per cent in 1996.

under the influence of Professor Theodore Levitt of the Harvard Business School, propogated what they called 'the law of dominance', which said that 'being the world's number one company is wonderful, two can be terrific, three is threatened and four is fatal'. Size became the overwhelming objective of the company and it pursued a hectic series of acquisitions in the 1980s to create the world's largest communications business.

Several explanations for the growth objective have been made. Many managers believe, like Saatchi & Saatchi, that there is a link between size and ultimate profitability. Unless a company becomes one of the biggest players, they believe that it will be vulnerable to stronger competitors. Others have shown the link between size and managerial salaries. Prestige and management perks are also correlated to the size of the business. Accounting procedures also encourage acquisitive growth. In many countries, accounting conventions allow the cost of the acquisitions to be excluded from the income statement, which has the effect of inflating profits and earnings per share and disguising the true cost of acquisitions. By contrast, internal growth is less attractive to these hypergrowth companies because it is slower and because investments have to be written off against the profit and loss statement.

Growth is a sensible objective but, taken to excess, the pursuit of size has proven even less robust as a strategy than profitability. The great majority of companies that pursue it prove to be very short-lived phenomena. In fact a computer model used to explain corporate failures in the 1980s found that very rapid sales growth was the best predictor of subsequent collapse.[5] It is easy to see why. Very rapid growth with its sudden, new challenges, hidden threats and organizational strains is virtually unmanageable. Further, excessive rates of growth invariably involve higher levels of financial risk as the company takes on more debt. Finally, given that the stock market values companies efficiently, then with bid premiums normally adding 50 per cent to the pre-bid share price, truly enormous improvements in the target company's performance must be achieved by the acquirer. In practice, many of these companies appear to make only the most cursory examination of potential synergies. Deals are often made on faith that rapid market growth, inflation and rising asset prices will make expensive purchases subsequently good value.

When these forecasts prove too optimistic, the real cost of the growth strategy becomes clear. Investors see a business which has extended beyond the capabilities of its management, highly geared and with a weakened capacity to compete in its core activities. Shareholder value often collapses. For example, the market value of Saatchi & Saatchi shares dropped from £7 to £0.20 over two years. Morale and employee motivation declines as savage cutbacks become necessary to meet interest rate obligations, and even creditors see their loans written off.

Shareholder value

Currently, the most intellectually respected business objective is shareholder value. This has considerable legal and conceptual merit. The company, it is argued, 'belongs to' its legal owners, who are its shareholders. The task of management is to enhance the value that these shareholders obtain. Shareholder value is increased in three ways:

dividends, appreciation in the value of the shares, and cash payments. Operationally, this means managing the business to generate cash rather than accounting profit. If the aim is to maximize shareholder value, the business should invest only if it can achieve a return greater than shareholders could obtain for themselves by investing the cash elsewhere. If a part of the business is worth more to another company than it is to its current management, then it should be sold forthwith and the receipts handed back to shareholders.

Management seeking to maximize shareholder value will normally pursue policies quite different from those geared to earnings or growth. Several studies have shown that policies to increase short-term earnings can decrease shareholder value.[6] Similarly, the stock market is quickly sceptical of companies planning acquisitive growth strategies, and the value of the acquirer's shares normally drops precipitously.

But again, seeking to maximize shareholder value runs into several practical problems as well as severe conflicts of interests among stakeholder groups. While it is a practical way to evaluate major acquisitions or divestiture options, it is hardly a viable means of assisting the operational decisions of management. For example, what price shall we charge next month? Shall a particular promotion be run? Even with major investment decisions there is a high degree of subjectivity in the shareholder value approach. Businesses rarely have planning horizons more than five years ahead, but only a small proportion of value can be attributed to estimated cash flows over this period. For example, Marsh,[7] comparing the value of ICI shares and its current dividend, showed that only 8 per cent of ICI's current market capitalization is attributable to the current year's dividend; only 29 per cent can be explained by the present value of the dividends expected over the next five years; and only 50 per cent by the value of the dividend expected over the next ten years. The bulk of the value of the business is thus its residual value. Unfortunately there is no reliable way of estimating this key figure, and different techniques will give quite different estimates of the shareholder value created. These practical difficulties of using the shareholder value approach no doubt account for the pervasiveness of profitability targets. Managers see profits as a usable proxy for shareholder value.

Shareholder value goals also make it difficult for British and US companies to compete, especially in manufacturing and high-growth areas. The cost of capital used to discount investment decisions in the UK, for example, has in the past been much higher than in Germany and Japan. This meant that the British company needed to see a profit which may be double that which its competitors needed to justify an investment decision. Put another way, a business in the UK which looked for an investment to pay for itself over four years, may have been competing with a business in Japan content with a ten-year payback period. Not surprisingly, companies seeking to maximize shareholder value are predominantly found in mature industries and in the service sector, where long-term investment, research and development, and technical training can be minimized. The community cost is, of course, to bias the economy away from manufacturing and high-growth areas. To employees this means lower real income growth and less security. It also makes managers taking the long-term view highly vulnerable to acquisition. Shareholder value in manufacturing can be released

BOX 1.3

Hanson Trust

Hanson claimed to put shareholder value as the top management priority. The growth strategy was to acquire poorly managed companies, introduce tight financial management and dispose for cash of businesses that did not fit. Lord Hanson's financial model was simple: set tight targets for return on capital employed, a ruthless budgetary process and a four-year 'payback' criterion for all capital expenditure projects above £500. This formula made Hanson a star performer for over a decade until 1987. By then it had become Britain's fifth largest company by stock market capitalization.

But after 1987, the lack of investment in new markets led to a relentless decline in the relative value of the company. By 1996 prospects were so bleak that it was decided to break the company up. It had become clear that shareholder value was a flag of respectability to a simple milking strategy. In the short run this could boost earnings, but in the long run it can only lead to stagnation and decline.

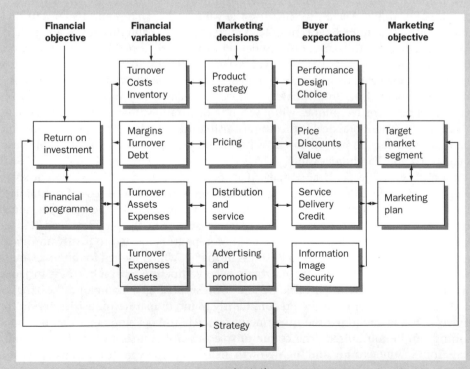

Figure 1.1 ■ Financial versus market orientations

by selling the business to an acquirer with a lower cost of capital or one willing sharply to curtail long-term investment. Hanson Trust (see Box 1.3) is an example of the dangers of relying on shareholder value.

Customer satisfaction

A fundamental problem with all three previous approaches is that they ignore the customer. Satisfied customers are, however, the source of all profits and shareholder value. Customers can choose from whom they buy, and unless the firm satisfies them at least as well as competitors, sales and profits will quickly erode. More companies are putting at the top of their agenda winning and retaining customers via increasing customer satisfaction. Companies like ATT, British Airways and Xerox now comprehensively and systematically survey customers on a regular basis to determine how satisfied they are. These scores are benchmarked against the customer satisfaction scores achieved by competitors. Xerox, for example, now places increasing customer satisfaction ahead of return on investment and to market share as key corporate objectives. The aim is to forge strong, enduring relationships with customers.

The fate of the leading US brewer Schlitz is a telling example of the results of orientating managers towards financial measures, rather than satisfying and retaining customers.

In the early 1970s, Schlitz decided on a programme to boost shareholder value. The firm shortened its brewing process by 50%, reduced labour costs, and switched to less costly ingredients. As a result, it became the lowest cost producer in the industry, its profits soared and its stock price rose to a high of $69 by 1974. Unfortunately, however, Schlitz's aggressive cost cutting campaign also degraded the quality of its beer. By 1976, the firm was receiving constant customer and dealer complaints and its market share was slipping badly. In 1978, a new management team attempted to get product quality back on track, but by then consumers had such a low opinion of Schlitz's beer that the company could not recover. By 1981, Schlitz's market share position had slipped from No. 2 all the way to No. 7, and its share price had dropped to a mere $5.[8]

Figure 1.1 contrasts the market-led business with the finance-led one and shows the nature of the trade-offs. The latter has as its central goal profitability or shareholder value. The key planning mechanism is the financial plan or budget. Assets, debts, costs and expenses are controlled to achieve the financial goal. The 'marketing decisions' of product, price, promotion and distribution are manipulated to control the financial variables. So in hard times, new product development, investment and promotion are likely to be curtailed to boost profits. Such policies, of course, have the downside that they trade off improved short-term financial performance for lower long-term market effectiveness. By contrast the market-led organization focuses primarily on satisfying customers. It defines the market segments to satisfy, researches the wants and expectations of these customers and then plans the products, pricing, promotion and distribution strategies which will most effectively match these expectations. Business decisions here flow back from an understanding of customers rather than from a financial requirement.

The market-led approach, which seeks market leadership through superiority in meeting customer needs, has often been associated with Japanese companies; the profit-led one with British and US ones. For example, a study of a matched sample of British, US and Japanese companies saw western companies overwhelmingly oriented to profit (Table 1.3).[9] Again the market-led approach can be taken to damaging extremes. Ultimately, customers would most prefer the highest quality, first-class service and rock bottom prices, but it would be foolish for a company to offer these. In practice, the firm has to negotiate a balance between the needs of its shareholders for profits and the desire of its customers for value.

Other objectives

These four goals are not an exhaustive list of alternatives. Some companies focus on *operational* objectives and see these as the drivers of financial and customer performance. Here managers identify those internal processes which the business must excel at to achieve high performance. These may cover measures of manufacturing excellence, quality and productivity. More recently, other companies have highlighted *innovation and learning* objectives. Success today is no guarantee of success tomorrow. Intense global competition means that companies must make continual improvements in their products and processes to stay at the forefront. Companies such as 3M have specific innovation targets – at least 25 per cent of any division's profits must come from products introduced within the last five years. Others set defined target improvement rates for internal operations such as on-time delivery, cycle time, defect rate and yield.

Service companies, in particular, often place satisfying *employees* as a key objective. They regard employees as the generators of both satisfied customers and shareholder value. Only if employees are satisfied and motivated by their jobs will they strive to satisfy increasingly discerning customers. Satisfied customers, who remain loyal to the business and spread positive 'word of mouth' publicity about it, are in turn the basis of continuing profits and enhanced shareholder value.

Interest groups have lobbied further goals: the community interest – local and national; environmental protection; advancing the causes of minority groups; enhancing relationships with suppliers; or simply minimizing risks.

In reviewing the evidence on company goals, at least three things seem clear. First, while any of these goals may be necessary at some point in the organization's history, if it is to survive, no single one is sufficient. Second, focusing on one goal involves trade-

Table 1.3 ■ How well does 'good short-term profits are the objective' describe your company?

Japanese	US	British
27%	80%	87%

Note: Based on a matched sample of ninety UK, US and Japanese companies

offs sooner or later with others. Maximizing short-run earnings will reduce the firm's long-run marketing competitiveness. Rapid growth leads to spiralling risks being absorbed by shareholders and creditors. The pursuit of shareholder value can erode the trust of employees and the local community as shareholder interests dominate. Third, the more sharply an organization focuses on one goal and seeks 'excellence' in it, the more extreme these conflicts become and the more likely a disequilibrium situation is created. Sometimes the break-up is quick and sudden; in others it is a longer-term decline as groups whose interests have been neglected withdraw organizational support. In both situations, history suggests that 'excellence' is a very dangerous concept.

Stakeholders' objectives and constraints

The fundamental problem of using any one of the above objectives is that they orientate management to a single perspective and to one group of stakeholders. Today, however, a business needs to adopt a multiple perspective and to satisfy different groups of stakeholders, which may include shareholders, employees, managers, customers, suppliers, creditors, the government and the community in which it operates. Where management focuses on one perspective, other interests are devalued.

A central task of top management is reconciling these diverging and partly conflicting interests. Figure 1.2 illustrates the expectations of the different stakeholders in a typical organization. In a well-balanced organization, reconciling these interests is not usually difficult. One reason is that stakeholders do not usually seek to maximize their interests; instead they usually look for satisfactory returns. In addition, expectations are normally incremental – people's demands are based on what they achieved in the past. Wage-earners or shareholders do not normally increase their demands upon the firm suddenly and radically.

Effectively, managers act in a *tolerance zone*. The tolerance zone is a performance band in which the firm is satisfying the interests of all its key stakeholder groups. As Figure 1.3 illustrates, performance falls outside this equilibrium zone and the viability of the firm and its management comes under threat under two circumstances. The first is when it fails to achieve minimum levels of performance. The second is when it achieves exceptionally high levels of performance on one or more of these objectives. The latter arises because maximizing on one eventually means minimizing on others. For example, Schlitz sought to maximize earnings per share and ended up minimizing on customer satisfaction.

The major stakeholders, the nature of their objectives and their areas of tolerance are as follows.

Shareholders

These are the most obvious stakeholders. They have invested in the enterprise with the expectation of rewards in terms of dividends, share appreciation and capital repayments. If dissatisfied, they can fire the executives and sell or close down the firm. While

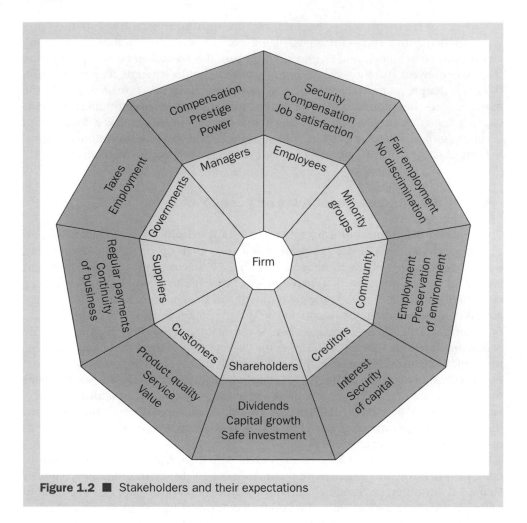

Figure 1.2 ■ Stakeholders and their expectations

legally their power to maximize shareholder value is absolute, in practice it is normally severely constrained. Today's shareholders are predominantly institutional investors rather than active owners. These institutions have a large portfolio of shares and will invariably sell the shares of a disappointing performer rather than seek to oust its management. Often the terms of their charters prevent these institutions playing an active role in the companies whose shares they hold.

The consequence is that companies rarely seek to maximize shareholder value and a substantial zone of tolerance is available. This is evidenced in both the relatively low priority that managers give to shareholder value (see Table 1.2) and the high bid premiums required to take over a company.

However, the power of shareholders can be activated if other stakeholder groups are not alert to their needs. If managers, employees or other groups are obtaining excessive

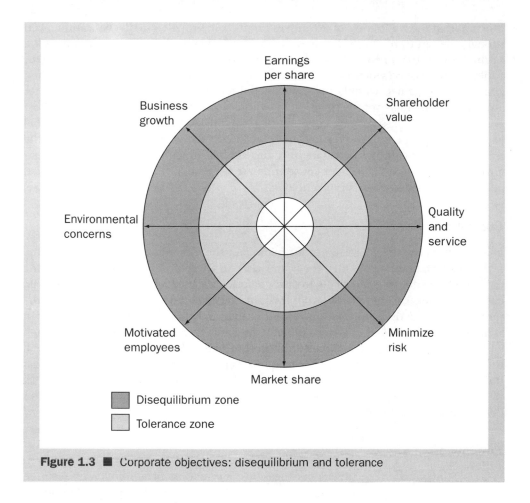

Figure 1.3 ■ Corporate objectives: disequilibrium and tolerance

rewards, so that the dividends or equity values become completely unacceptable to shareholders, then a disequilibrium situation is created. Then investors do step in and change the top management. Or, more commonly, an outside group bids for the company, taking advantage of its low valuation, and seeks to create greater value for its own shareholders.

Managers

Salaries and bonuses, perquisites and power are among the major motivators of senior executives. The separation of corporate ownership and control has unquestionably increased the power of managers.

Evidence of this is in the salaries of chief executives and senior managers, which have grown significantly faster than shareholder value over the last decade. It is also illustrated in the willingness of executives to invest in growth and diversification, even though the return has been less than the true cost of capital. But again executives are normally sensitive to the risks of maximizing their potential for personal gain. This zone of tolerance is evidenced in the premiums that executives normally obtain when changing companies. Unduly high managerial rewards create jealousy and pressures among other members of the coalition on whom the business's stability depends. Most company boards also have compensation committees which dampen managerial expectations. Similarly, the pressures to grow and diversify are also constrained by the need to increase earnings per share or return on investment, or to maintain interest-cover conventions. Where such constraints are breached, managers risk an eventual collision with other groups of stakeholders.

Customers

In a free enterprise system, customers are potentially the most powerful stakeholder group. If their expectations are not met, they can switch to alternative brands and so erode the company's revenue base and ability to satisfy all other stakeholder groups. Again, however, customers appear to have substantial tolerance levels. Customers are normally reluctant to incur the risks and costs of changing their existing repertoire of suppliers. In well-established markets it is very difficult for new entrants to succeed. Only when customer service and product quality fall substantially below those of competitors will the company's market share fall precipitously. Nevertheless, British and American postwar industrial history is replete with examples of where the excess pursuit of other stakeholder interests, the orientation to short-term profit, workers' reluctance to change, or diversification, has led to an erosion of customer support and a loss of markets.

Employees

Workers outside the executive ranks seek a combination of employment security, compensation and job satisfaction. As stakeholders, they are more dependent upon the firm for their livelihoods than shareholders and less able to control events than senior managers. Their power to achieve their goals depends upon their degree of organization, the tightness of the labour market for their special skills, and the recognition of managers and shareholders of the importance of motivated employees. Again workers are not maximizers. Consciousness of switching costs, uncertainty and interests outside their firm orientate them to accepting suboptimal returns from existing employers. However, a failure to meet their minimum expectations may create militancy; more certainly it will curtail the commitment of employees to provide high levels of quality and service to other stakeholders.

Creditors

Banks and other lenders have a legal right to specified interest and capital repayments. Having limited upside potential in their assets, creditors want the firm to be risk averse.

If the firm cannot meet its obligations to creditors, then they can liquidate the firm's assets to meet their claims. Normally, however, creditors are reluctant to do this and will defer repayments if they believe the business can be turned round. Only if the assets are at increasing risk are creditors likely to liquidate the business.

Other stakeholders with claims on the enterprise are suppliers, governments, the local community, minority groups and so on. The survival of the business depends upon the support, or at least the non-active opposition, of each of these. Again, for each of the groups there is a broad tolerance zone, within which passivity can be expected.

 ## Developing balanced objectives

Broadening the span of objectives means recognizing that 'excellence' is unlikely to be obtained on a single measure. Not surprisingly, those companies that have withstood the test of time – Unilever, Marks & Spencer, Procter & Gamble, Boeing, Mercedes-Benz, Siemens, 3M and Nestlé – are not outstanding on any single measure of performance. They recognize that maximizing profits today means sacrificing market position tomorrow; maximizing sales growth means eroding shareholder value. Rather they see the task as achieving a satisfactory level of performance across a multiple, competing set of criteria.

There are three mechanisms for developing a balanced set of objectives. Ideally, all three should be implemented, but each individually makes a contribution.

Balanced organizational representation

To prevent a company being captured by one interest group, the various stakeholders should be represented at the highest level. In Japan this is done with remarkable effect through the *kieretsu*. Each of the major Japanese companies sits in a web of strong, permanent relationships with its major creditors, suppliers, key customers and other important stakeholders. Internal and external stakeholders are bound together by complex and evolving ties of mutual benefit and commercial interest. All parties – customers, suppliers, employees – understand that they can all gain as the firm advances. The benefits of these negotiated and mutually agreed objectives are that each of the parties is willing to make long-term investments and to accept the occasional short-term economic sacrifices which are inevitable in a turbulent environment. Not surprisingly, major western companies such as Ford, IBM and Marks & Spencer are beginning to set up their own *kieretsu*-like structures.[10]

An alternative approach exists in Germany, Switzerland and some other countries of continental Europe with the use of supervisory boards or *Aufsichtsrat*. These, consisting of representatives of shareholders, management, trade unions, creditors and other stakeholder groups, supervise the management board (*Vorstand*) and check that its strategy is consistent with their own objectives. This structure sharply contrasts to American and British corporate boards, which in practice are dominated by one stakeholder group – senior managers. Not surprisingly, it is in these two countries that large firms have been prone to favour interests inimical to other groups and, as a result, to create crises for themselves. A two-tier board structure on the German model, with key interest groups represented on the supervisory board, would seem the most obvious way of representing their legitimate interests.

Defining the organization's mission

A second means of ensuring that the main interest groups are considered is through the company's mission statement. Most companies now have a mission statement which aims to spell out their central purpose and develop shared values. Marriott's mission goes:

> The mission of Marriott Hotels is to provide lodging and related services in a manner that builds strong, lasting, and satisfying relationships with customers, employees, owners, shareholders, and the communities in which it operates.

As Marriott illustrates, the major function of the mission statement should be to define the key stakeholders whom the corporation will seek to satisfy and, in broad terms, describe what strategy it will pursue to meet their objectives. The objectives written into the mission statement should contribute to motivating the loyalty of those on whom the success of the business depends, and encouraging management to evaluate their policies in the light of their stakeholders' expectations.

Figure 1.4 shows the mission statement of Marks & Spencer, rated by management guru Peter Drucker as the world's best-managed business. This mission statement clearly sets out the stakeholders whose expectations the company will seek to meet – customers, suppliers, shareholders, employees and the community. For decades this widely held mission has provided an equilibrium growth path for the business, enabling it to avoid the dangers of single-interest management. While in any particular year, Marks & Spencer had been beaten on any dimension by a range of competitors, over the long run none of them had been able to keep pace.

Creating the balanced scorecard

Broad objectives need to be refined into definite goals with specific measures of attainment if they are going to provide clear incentives for performance. In the past, these measures have been too focused on financial results. Today, management require a broader perspective which incorporates the interests of the various stakeholders and requirements for achieving long-term competitiveness.

For most businesses, the diverse objectives can be incorporated into four perspectives:[11]

■ Financial perspective – meeting the objectives of shareholders.

■ Customer perspective – meeting the needs of customers in highly competitive markets.

■ Operational perspective – achieving on the key levers which drive performance excellence.

Mission statement of Marks & Spencer plc

Our three great assets are:

1 The goodwill and confidence of the public.
2 The loyalty and devotion of management and staff throughout the system.
3 The confidence and co-operation of our suppliers.

The principles upon which the business is built are:

1 To offer our customers a selective range of high-quality, well-designed and attractive merchandise at reasonable prices.
2 To encourage our suppliers to use the most modern and efficient techniques of production and quality control dictated by the latest discoveries in science and technology.
3 With the co-operation of our suppliers, to enforce the highest standard of quality control.
4 To plan the expansion of our stores for the better display of a widening range of goods and for the convenience of our customers.
5 To foster good human relations with customers, suppliers and staff.

Figure 1.4 ■ Marks & Spencer mission statement

■ Internal perspective – meeting the expectations and building up the capabilities of employees whose skills determine the company's future.

The specific goals will depend upon the nature of the business: its industry, manufacturing configuration, type of customers and market dynamics. Figure 1.5 illustrates the type of scorecard which might be used. The balanced scorecard has the advantage of avoiding overloading managers with information, but giving them the multiple perspectives essential for the strategic development of the business. It is a positive sign that more and more far-sighted western companies have recently taken an interest in developing a balanced scorecard approach to reviewing business performance.

Developing a strategy

To meet their objectives, management need a plan or strategy. Rather than a single, comprehensive set of objectives and strategies, most companies have a *hierarchy* of interrelated strategies, each developed at a different level. Typically, there will be a corporate strategy for the whole company, individual strategies for each of the company's business units and, finally, a strategy for each market or product.

A strategy can be defined as a set of decisions taken by management on how the business will allocate its resources and achieve sustainable competitive advantage in its

Financial perspective

Goals	*Measures*
Survive	Cash flow
Succeed	Quarterly profits
Prosper	Return on shareholder funds
Recognition	Share price

Operations perspective

Goals	*Measures*
Technological	Competitive benchmarking
Manufacturing excellence	Productivity
Time-to-market	Benchmarking
Quality	Total quality

Consumer perspective

Goals	*Measures*
Satisfaction	Customer surveys
Responsiveness	On-time deliveries
Loyalty	Repurchases
Market share	Share growth

Internal perspective

Goals	*Measures*
Employees	Satisfaction surveys
Internal growth	Sales growth
Innovation	Number of new products
Development	Training days

Figure 1.5 ■ The balanced scorecard of objectives

chosen markets. Strategy, therefore, sets the *direction* of the business – in which products and markets it is going to invest its resources and efforts – and the *means* of getting there – how it is to create customer preference in these areas.

Some examples of strategic decisions are as follows:

■ ICI, one of the largest chemical companies, decided to make a series of acquisitions to build its Paints Division into the world's number one. It believed that economies of scale and global branding would provide sustainable competitive advantage.

■ Baske & Robbins, the ice-cream business owned by Allied Lyons, decided to build a major presence in Russia. Management believed they could offer quality and variety superior to that offered by domestic competitors.

- Marks & Spencer, Britain's largest retailer, decided to diversify into financial services. It believed that the Marks & Spencer brand name would encourage customer confidence and trust.

- McDonald's decided to broaden its traditional menu by adding pizzas. Management believed that this would strengthen the business by offering customers more choice and healthier eating.

Resource allocation

The two key dimensions of strategy are the resource allocation decision and the development of a sustainable competitive advantage. The resource allocation decision is the choice of which products and markets offer the best opportunities for investment. It is customary to set out the broad choices in terms of the growth direction matrix (Figure 1.6). A business can grow in four directions.

Market penetration is normally the least risky alternative, at least in the short run. Here the business sticks to its existing products and markets, and aims to grow through

	Current products	**New products**

Current markets	*Market penetration strategies*
	
	• Increase market share
	• Increase product usage:
	  – increase frequency of use
	  – increase quantity used
	  – new application
		Product development strategies
		
		• Product improvement
		• Product line extensions
		• New products for same markets

New markets	*Market development strategies*
	
	• Expand markets for existing products:
	  – geographic expansion
	  – target new segments
		Diversification strategies
		
		• Vertical integration:
		  – forward integration
		  – backward integration
		• Diversification into related businesses (concentric diversification)
		• Diversification into unrelated businesses (conglomerate diversification)

Figure 1.6 ■ Alternative growth directions

gaining market share or expanding the market for its products. ICI's paints business pursued an aggressive policy of gaining market share through acquisitions.

Eventually market share strategies will be constrained by the size of the market and the entry of new products. A second strategy then becomes *product development*. Here the company stays in its current market, but introduces improved products, product line extensions and new products. McDonald's introduction of pizzas is one example of this strategy.

The next level of strategy is *market development*, where the firm pushes its current products into new geographic markets or new segments of the market. Baske & Robbins' investments in Russia are an example of this strategy.

The final strategic option is *diversification*. This is typically the most risky option because it requires learning about both new markets and new products. There are different types of diversification, each with varying characteristics and levels of risk.

■ *Forward integration.* This involves moving 'downstream' to acquire operations previously undertaken by third parties such as wholesalers or retailers.

■ *Backward integration.* Here the company moves 'upstream' to take over functions previously done by suppliers.

■ *Concentric diversification.* Here the firm looks for new products or new markets which have synergies with its existing products or markets. The new activities can then lead to lower costs or enhanced marketing effectiveness. Marks & Spencer's move into financial services is an example.

■ *Conglomerate diversification.* This occurs when the products or markets have no relationships with the current products, technology or markets. This is likely to be the most risky form of diversification.

Sustainable competitive advantage

The resource allocation decision determines in which products and markets the business will compete. To win in these areas, the firm needs a sustainable competitive advantage. This is the capability to make target customers an offer which they perceive as providing superior value to the offers of competitors. The essence of business strategy is winning the choices of customers.

Customers buy from those competitors which they perceive as offering the best value. Perceived value consists of three elements: the perceived benefits offered by the company's brand; its price; and the other costs of owning it (Figure 1.7). A company can gain competitive advantage, therefore, through offering superior benefits, lower prices or a reduced cost of ownership. The product may command a premium price if it offers superior benefits with other ownership costs that are lower or at least competitive.

The perceived benefits are a function of the product's performance and design, the quality of the services which augment it, the staff which deliver it, and the image of the brand which the company succeeds in communicating. The price is the money

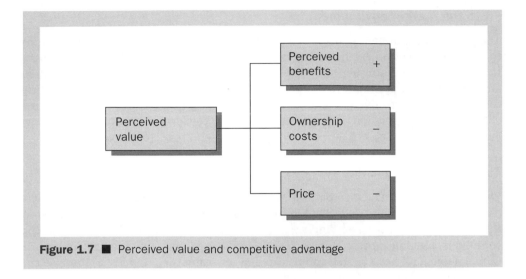

Figure 1.7 ■ Perceived value and competitive advantage

that the customer has to purchase the product. The other costs of ownership are those expenses which occur once the product is purchased. These may include installation, insurance, staff training, maintenance, energy consumption, trade-in value and the psychological costs of risking a switch to a new supplier.

A competitive advantage is of limited value if it is easily copiable. Management need strategies to sustain their advantage by building barriers to entry. Economists describe many types of entry barrier, including high capital requirements, scarce raw materials, scale economies, favourable locations, patents and licences. But the two most common barriers are the linked advantages of brands and core competences based on organizational effectiveness. The reputation of a successful brand, built upon long and successful use, gives customers confidence in the product or supplier and makes them reluctant to switch. The core competences of the business are the special technical and marketing skills built up by its staff, which, within an effective organization, are deployed to continually update, innovate, and enhance the value it offers to its customers. A business with strong core competences and an organization committed to success sustains its advantage with learning, change and constant improvement.

 ## Criteria for strategic success

Management are continually involved in proposing or approving strategic options. Decisions are made on new products, new markets, acquisitions, strategic alliances and a host of other strategic alternatives. Five factors determine whether a strategy will be likely to contribute to success.

Fit to the market environment

The primary determinant of whether a product or business will generate results is its fit to the needs of customers. If customers do not perceive an offer as having a competitive advantage – offering superior value – they will not buy it, or buy it in the desired amounts. Today's outstanding companies are those which customers see as meeting their needs most effectively. The needs of the market are shaped by the environment – changes in the population's demographic structure, the level of economic well-being, technology, politics, and changes in culture and values.

Timing: nothing fails like success

The problem for managers is that the environment and hence the needs of customers change. What provides an excellent fit to the market environment today will not do so tomorrow. In industry after industry – cars, consumer electronics, photography, computers, retailing, semi-conductors, earth-moving equipment – firms once thought impregnable have been broken and defeated by an inability to respond to the speed of change. Companies such as General Motors, Philips, Kodak, IBM, Sears, Texas Instruments and Caterpillar, which once totally dominated their markets, now struggle for survival.

As with evolution, the saying 'nothing fails like success' is almost inevitable. Paradoxically, the more successful a firm is today, the more vulnerable it is tomorrow. A firm which perfectly adapts its skills, assets, distribution channels and thinking to meet current opportunities and beat all current competitors risks becoming completely wrong footed when these opportunities disappear. For example, for over one hundred years Swiss companies dominated the watch market. Their success was due to focusing all their resources, skills and culture around precision engineering. Unfortunately, when electronics appeared, all the skills, assets, systems and values of the Swiss were counterproductive and most of these firms became extinct.

Many observers consider Microsoft's lead in the computer industry to be unassailable. But its founder and chairman, Bill Gates, says he is driven by a 'latent fear' that the company could become complacent and allow itself to be overtaken by nimbler competitors. It has happened to other large companies such as IBM, General Motors and Philips, he points out.

To maintain success – which history suggests is a very difficult task – management need continually to challenge the strategy and the mindset of the business. Companies like to continue doing what they have done in the past. But for many companies 'sticking to their knitting' becomes their epitaph.

Efficiency versus effectiveness

Efficiency and effectiveness are two concepts at the heart of strategy. The former reflects productivity; it is the relationship between outputs (e.g. production, profits) and inputs (e.g. labour, assets). Efficiency is internal to the firm, is easily measured and can often be improved quickly. In contrast, effectiveness is about satisfying customers' needs; it is externally determined and not easily measured, and achieving it is usually a lengthy process. However, effectiveness is much more important than efficiency to the survival and success of the organization.

Efficiency is concerned with costs; effectiveness with identifying opportunities to create markets. Peter Drucker conveyed the essence of the difference when he wrote 'Efficiency is doing things right. Effectiveness is doing the right things.' In many companies an obsession with efficiency and cost cutting is antithetical rather than complementary to effectiveness. The essence of effectiveness is innovation – finding new and better means of meeting the needs of customers. Focusing on reducing costs is a hopeless and retrograde effort if the business is producing products without market appeal. Management have to ensure that the primary focus of the organization is entrepreneurial rather than internal; efforts are put into making it effective before making it more efficient.

Speed and decisiveness

In today's dynamic and intensely competitive markets, speed and decisiveness are essential for strategic success. Time has become a competitive weapon. Companies that are fast to innovate, manufacture and distribute, and quick to respond to customer requirements, on average earn and sustain substantially higher profits and achieve bigger market shares than their slower-moving competitors.

However, strategic success requires more than speed; it also requires the decisive commitment of resources. The evidence suggests that fast innovators will fail to earn the rewards and achieve strong and lasting market positions unless they commit substantial marketing and promotional resources behind the product and aggressively seek to build market acceptance. Without this decisive commitment, they will be caught up and overtaken by competitors which follow in their slipstream. History suggests that smaller companies without access to sufficient resources should look to licensing or partnership agreements to lever the resources they need for successful entry.

Organizational effectiveness

Enduring international competitiveness depends first upon the core competences, or unique body of technical and marketing skills, possessed by the personnel of the firm. Second, it requires staff having the commitment to deploy these skills effectively. Effective deployment of core capabilities means orientating their application to opportunities in the market, to fast implementation and to achieving a position of leadership.

Business is essentially Darwinian in nature. Environmental forces – competition, changes in demographics, technology, new trading relationships, economics, etc. – result in the survival of those firms best fitted to the environment. Survival and fit depend upon the adaptability of the organization and management's ability to match strategy to this changing world (Figure 1.8).

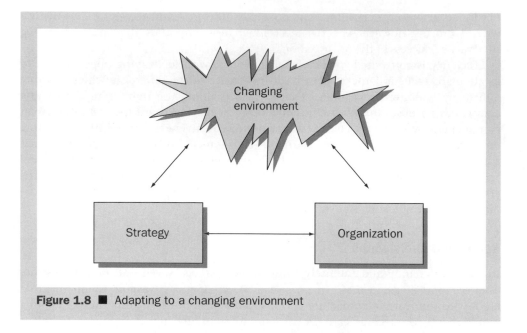

Figure 1.8 ■ Adapting to a changing environment

Strategic intent

To be a leader in today's globally competitive market requires two attributes – an ambitious intent and outstanding competences. Strategic intent refers to a conscious commitment of top management to focus the resources and energies of the organization on achieving a leadership position in the market.[12] Like an athlete competing at the top level, there is no chance of success unless an organization is totally dedicated to winning, and willing to make almost any sacrifice to get the prize. Organizations in which top management have not inculcated this shared vision of success do not succeed because they do not make the effort or develop the capabilities.

Companies such as Coca-Cola, Marks & Spencer, Canon, Boeing, Federal Express and Sony focus on enthusing their employees with this shared goal. Canon's long-term strategy was called internally 'Beat Xerox', Komatsu's was 'Encircle Caterpillar'. These were the rallying cries which stimulated their workforces steadily to close the gap, year after year, as they strived, ultimately successfully, to unseat the industry leader. Creating shareholder value generates little enthusiasm as an organizational goal. Why should workers make extraordinary efforts to satisfy a shifting body of faceless investors? The competitive challenge of working as a team to make it the number one can create this commitment.

Seeking leadership does not necessarily mean global dominance of major markets. For a smaller business it is more likely to mean seeking, at least initially, to become leader in selected niches, specific distribution channels or particular market segments.

But the concept of strategic intent is a recognition that companies with a small market share are exceedingly vulnerable. In an economic downturn, customers, distributors and retailers are likely to focus their buying on suppliers with a substantial share. The volume of a marginal supplier may become too small to support the required service levels and to generate the resources for investment in new products and markets.

Strategic intent is a long-term, shared vision stretching from a minimum of ten years up to an indefinite future. The skills and infrastructure needed to become the best are not acquired quickly and once acquired need to be continually adapted and enhanced. A practical problem is that few people can sustain the enthusiasm and commitment for a goal which may not be reached for ten or twenty years. Consequently, to operationalize strategic intent, top management set 'challenges' which are of much shorter duration, yet contribute to the ultimate goal. Hamel and Prahalad describe how Kamatsu's thirty-year strategy to overtake Caterpillar consisted of a series of almost annual targets. These included challenges to introduce specific new models, to enter new markets and to achieve cost reduction and quality targets. Such programmes have the effect of creating a sense of urgency in the business, developing necessary capabilities and providing milestones and review mechanisms and progress towards their ultimate long-term objectives.

These challenges, or short-run programmes, also allow strategy to be adapted incrementally. Strategic intent is a broad vision of where the company wants to be, not a detailed map of how to get there. Today's environment is too unpredictable to permit detailed long-term forecasts of markets, products and technologies. Through evolving challenges, top management fine tune strategy to the emerging opportunities and realities of the market and technological environment.

 ## Core competences

Without possessing the necessary skills, strategic intent is merely wishful thinking. To develop products which offer value superior to that of the best international competitors requires an organization with deep-rooted knowledge and learning ability. Creating superior value necessitates two sorts of knowledge: first, about what customers will value; and second, about the technological skills necessary to provide such values. The core competences of the organization are the unique bundle of skills it possesses which permit it to offer a sustainable competitive advantage.

For example, 3M's competence was founded originally on sticky tape. Over time it has built from this a unique bundle of skills in substrates, coatings and adhesives, and various ways of combining them. These core competences have allowed it to enter and excel in businesses as diverse as 'Post-it' notes, magnetic tape, photographic film, pressure-sensitive tapes and coated abrasives. Casio's core competences are in miniaturization, microprocessor design, material science and ultra-thin precision casings. These skills allow it to hold leading positions in calculators, pocket TVs, musical instruments and digital watches.

In the long run, success depends upon possessing superior core competences in the fields in which the organization operates. A company can, of course, look for short cuts

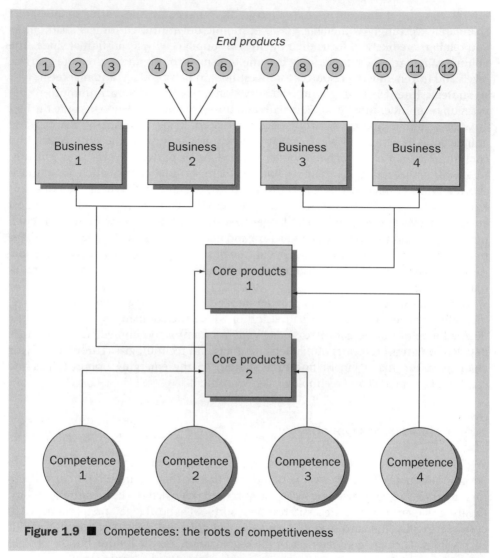

Figure 1.9 ■ Competences: the roots of competitiveness

Source: C. K. Prahalad and Gary Hamel, 'The core competence of the corporation', Harvard Business Review, May–June 1990, p. 81

to competitiveness by buying in products and technologies. Dozens of Japanese companies would be willing to supply computers, copiers or motors on an OEM private label basis. But as markets and technologies change, or if the supplier decides to enter the market itself, the company's product line together with all its investments in marketing and distribution may become quickly vulnerable. These core skills are hard to acquire because they take time, sacrifice and experience to develop.

Core competences provide the foundation for innovation and provide access to a wide variety of new products and markets. Prahalad and Hamel draw the analogy of a diversified corporation and a large tree (Figure 1.9). The root system that provides the nourishment, sustenance and stability is the core competences. One or more of these roots or core competences are applied in the development of core products. The core products are the components or sub-assemblies that form the foundation of a myriad of end products. These end products are usually grouped by the company, in terms of similarity of their markets, into business units. Returning to the analogy, the trunk and major limbs are the core products, the smaller branches are the business units and the leaves are the end products. For example, Honda's core competences lie in its specific design and development skills; these are then combined to produce various core engine products; in turn these lead to a huge and changing array of end products which are grouped into its motorcycle, car, lawnmower and outboard engine business units. As new market opportunities appear, it can reconfigure its core capabilities to create new business units and end products.

Many companies make the mistake of believing that their core competences lie in their portfolio of products and business units. But in today's fast-moving markets, products and businesses are temporary; the real foundation of the company is in its portfolio of capabilities.

Top management's task is to decide what the core capabilities should be. This will depend upon what skills have been inherited and what vision they have of the evolution of the firm's markets. What capabilities will provide the opportunity for market leadership? Coca-Cola saw distribution as the key – 'putting a Coke within arm's length of every consumer in the world'. NEC saw the convergence of computers and communications making competences in semiconductors a core capability. Once decided, developing these core capabilities requires a total organizational commitment and strategic investments far beyond what could be justified by conventional ROI criteria. Like products, core capabilities are not static, but depend upon continual learning and adaptation.

Organizational dimensions

Building these shared values and core skills depends upon the efforts of the people in the organization, and the strategy, structure and leadership provided by top management (Figure 1.10).

People

Creating strategic intent, core competences and competitive advantage depends totally upon the commitment, skills and initiative of the people who are working in the organization. Its people create the value and they are its most important assets. They should also be seen as appreciating assets, since their worth increases as they accumulate skills and experience. Unfortunately, too many western companies have seen employees as costs rather than assets. Personnel policies have been based on containment and control rather than on trust and empowerment. Still influenced by

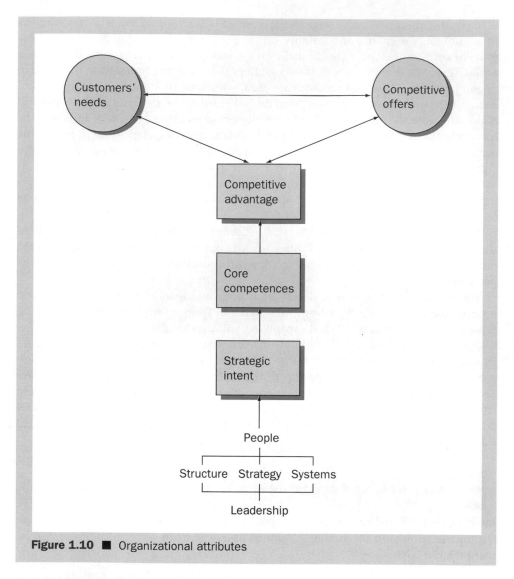

Figure 1.10 ■ Organizational attributes

discredited theories of 'scientific management' propogated sixty years ago, workers and even managers have been given narrowly defined, highly specialized jobs, with close supervision and disciplined by hierarchy, rules and regulations. The result, for most of the companies, has been workers and managers who are alienated, insecure and reluctant to take initiative.

Many Japanese companies after the war developed a different philosophy of managing people (Table 1.4). They realized that the route to competitiveness was to eliminate job insecurity, give people pride in their tasks, and empower them to take initiative in organizing their work to accelerate productivity, quality and innovation.

Table 1.4 ■ Western versus Japanese attitudes to employees

	Japanese	Western
People	Asset	Cost
Aims	Strategic intent	Financial performance
Philosophy	Initiative	Control
Direction	Challenges	Rules
Inspection	Self	Supervisors
Structure	Flat	Hierarchical
Jobs	Broad	Specialized
Decision making	Collective	Individualistic
Responsibility	Team	Individual
Employment	Permanent	Variable

Western companies are now seeking to apply these lessons. In the 1990s we are seeing the emergence of flatter organizations as decisions are pushed downwards, levels of supervision and control are eliminated, and workers are reorganized around self-managing teams. They are learning that these steps reduce overhead costs, increase speed of response and release the motivation pent up inside people who add value.

Structure

The business needs an organizational structure which meets three requirements. It should encourage people to make a wholehearted contribution, reinforce the development of core competences and strategic intent, and permit strategies to be tailored to defined markets.

Small business units are best for encouraging people to contribute. Small organizations simulate the advantages of working for a small company: bureaucracy is minimized, job definitions are broad and flexible, communications are good and everyone can see how they contribute to meeting the needs of customers. Unfortunately, the need to build and capitalize on core competences erodes the simplicity of an organization based upon small, autonomous business units. Different business units in a dynamic company would normally be based upon common core competences. Honda's car, motorcycle, power tool and outboard motor businesses, for example, rest upon shared design and development skills. Innovative businesses will be created out of new and different combinations of these core competences. If walls are built between units, information is not shared and people do not transfer between them, an organization will fail to leverage its competences and optimize its innovation capability. Completely autonomous business units are therefore neither possible nor desirable.

Not only do core capabilities have to be shared within a large organization, but, increasingly, strategic alliances require sharing skills across quite separate organizations. Pressures to accelerate innovation, the speed of change in markets and technology, and the high cost of developing new products and new markets are encouraging firms to share skills. Co-operative research, product licensing, co-marketing agreements and joint ventures are all rapidly growing. Structures are now created to facilitate the organization's learning of new marketing and technical skills.

Finally, structures have to reflect the market orientation. The market and sales teams have to be geared to markets rather than products or processes. In summary, organization structures are always unsatisfactory because they have to meet conflicting requirements. Shared values and common purpose have to be the glue to make them fly.

Strategy

The business also needs objectives and a strategy to provide direction and to guide the development of the structure and systems. The objectives should cover all the areas necessary for the survival of the business. They will cover marketing and financial perspectives, and internal and operational measures of efficiency and effectiveness.

The strategy will define the route that the business will seek to achieve these objectives. Strategy centres around decisions about marketing and innovation. The most important strategic decision is what markets to focus on. Next is the positioning decision – what competitive advantage should the firm develop to build leadership in these markets? These decisions then determine the core competences that the business needs to accumulate, the product range it will develop and the production and distribution infrastructures it must create.

Systems

Systems refer to how information moves around the organization. Information provides the links between customers and the business. Systems also share knowledge across business units and between functional areas. Management need to provide systems which meet three criteria. First, people require comprehensive information systems which give them a balanced picture of performance. If senior managers focus only on financial information, they will not attend to the marketing and human relations strategies upon which long-term competitiveness depends. Second, information should be widely accessible. If people from the different functional areas and diverse business units are to contribute and innovate, they need to be able to access all the information they require about customers, products and processes. Finally, information needs to be available fast. Today speed of response is fundamental to competitive advantage, and systems which provide fast and relevant information are the means to achieve it.

Leadership

The role of top management and, in particular, the chief executive is to provide the dynamic for organizational effectiveness. The first task is to articulate the vision of where the organization is heading. The chief executive's experience and values will allow him to define the areas where the company will compete and the core competences it must develop. Second, the leader has the crucial task of communicating these values and strategies to people throughout the organization. Today's leader has to be highly visible. He needs to inspire the workforce with the organization's aspirations and values. Third, the leader needs to be an orchestrator. He must create cohesion and direction from the multitude of talented and opinionated individuals within the company and stakeholders outside it. This requires organizational and political skills of a high order. The modern leader is a negotiator and a persuader rather than a dictator.

Summary

American and British firms have paid excessive attention to short-term financial performance. This has eroded the international competitiveness of their companies and often produced disaffected employees, customers and other stakeholders. Successful firms understand that survival depends upon balancing long- and short-term perspectives, and balancing the interests of shareholders with those of employees and other interest groups.

Ultimately, competitiveness depends upon the business's ability to satisfy the needs of customers more effectively than competition. Beating competitors depends upon developing within the organization a shared enthusiasm about 'winning' or strategic intent, and the core competences or skills to build superior products. Top management provide the leadership which motivates people, and develop the strategies, organization structure and systems to achieve these capabilities.

Questions

1. Why are profits an inadequate objective for the business?

2. Consider a business you know.

   (a) Rank its major objectives in order of importance.

   (b) What types of risk does this ordering suggest for the long-term success of the organization?

3. Should a company have a mission statement? What are its uses?

4. Consider a business with which you are familiar. What are the major environmental changes which could threaten its survival?

5. Why do so few western companies appear to have a long-term 'strategic intent'?

6. What are the major features which distinguish the leading Japanese from the leading western companies? What accounts for such differences?

Notes

1. Thomas J. Peters and Robert H. Waterman, *In Search of Excellence* (New York: Harper & Row, 1982).

2. Peter Doyle, 'What are the excellent companies?', *Journal of Marketing Management*, April 1992, pp. 101–16.

3. For an excellent review of how major companies employ creative accounting to camouflage their results, see Terry Smith, *Accounting for Growth*, 2nd edn (London: Random House, 1996).

4. James C. Collins and Jerry I. Porras, *Built to Last: Successful habits of visionary companies* (New York: Harper, 1994).

5. *Financial Times*, 'Clues that warn of collapse', 26 May 1991, p. 3. See also C. Pratten, *Company Failure* (London: ICA, 1991) for similar evidence.

6. T. Copeland, T. Koller and J. Murrin, *Valuation: Measuring and managing the value of companies* (New York: Wiley, 1995).

7. Paul Marsh, *Short Termism on Trial* (London: Institutional Fund Managers Association, 1990).

8. George S. Day and Liam Fahey, 'Putting strategy into shareholder value analysis', *Harvard Business Review*, March–April 1990, pp. 156–62.

9. Peter Doyle, John Saunders and Veronica Wong, 'A comparative study of British, US and Japanese marketing strategies', *Journal of International Business Studies*, October 1992, pp. 157–63.

10. 'Learning from Japan – American keiretsu', *Business Week*, 27 January 1992, pp. 38–44; 'Webb of interests', *Business Week*, 22 July 1996, pp. 14–16.

11. Adapted from Robert S. Kaplan and David P. Norton, *The Balanced Scorecard: Translating strategy into action* (Boston, MA: Harvard Business School Press, 1996).

12. The following section draws heavily from Gary Hamel and C. K. Prahalad, *Competing for the Future* (Boston, MA: Harvard Business School Press, 1996); George Stalk, Philip Evans and Laurence E. Shulman, 'Competing on capabilities: the new rules of corporate strategy', *Harvard Business Review*, March–April 1992, pp. 57–69.

Chapter 2

The customer-led business

The purpose of a business is to satisfy the needs of its customers. A business that fails to do this in a competitive economy will not survive because customers will go elsewhere. Businesses that are good at satisfying customer needs have the best opportunities to grow and prosper. Therefore, marketing – the task of creating and delivering products and services which customers will value, is the central task of management. Of course, this has also to be done in a way which makes a profit and which ultimately satisfies the requirements of its other stakeholders, such as employees, creditors and the society in which it operates.

This chapter discusses three issues. First, the theoretical roots of marketing, its key concepts and standard terminology are presented. These explain the central role that marketing plays in the efficient running of a competitive economy. Second, the characteristics of the successful customer-led business are shown, and these are contrasted with those of production and financially led businesses. Finally, a practical, step-by-step guide to transforming a business into a customer-driven organization is presented. Only by achieving such a change are companies likely to become, and remain, internationally competitive in the coming decade.

The theory of marketing

Marketing is largely a pragmatic subject and this book will not focus on academic theorizing. However, there are a number of reasons why it is useful for managers to have a basic understanding of the core concepts underpinning marketing. First, the theory provides a common terminology and framework for discussing marketing problems. Second, it introduces directions for managers to enhance the effectiveness of their marketing. Finally, it explains the economic and political significance of marketing and how it contributes to the general welfare.

Needs and products

The fundamental idea of marketing is that organizations survive and prosper through meeting the needs of customers. As Adam Smith showed over two hundred years ago, this is also the justification for free enterprise capitalism as a social and political system.[1] Smith showed that the drive of competing firms to make a profit, by providing customers with what they want, is ultimately in the interests of consumers because they obtain more and better products at lower prices. Companies that do this task well grow and prosper; those that do not go under. Marketing management is the task of facilitating this process by professionally identifying the needs of customers and developing those offers which give customers what they want.

Many people would quickly challenge this rationale for marketing and free enterprise. Nobody 'needs' a McDonald's hamburger or a Porsche sports car, they would argue. There are two types of response to this charge. The first is political and concerns an individual's freedom to buy and sell what he or she likes (subject to it not directly hurting others). If this freedom is to be restricted, then state officials will determine what companies may produce and what consumers may buy. This type of state socialism has proved to be both economically inefficient and injurious to individual rights. The second response relates to the nature of human psychology and behaviour. Social scientists would argue that marketing does not create needs – needs are more basic – but what marketing can do is influence how these needs are directed.

To see this important point, needs, wants and demands can be distinguished.[2] A *need* is a basic requirement that an individual wishes to satisfy. People have basic requirements for food, shelter, affection, esteem and self-development. Freud, Maslow, Herzberg and other social scientists have shown that these are not created by marketing, but are determined by human biology and the fundamental nature of social relationships.

While needs are broad, wants are narrow. A *want* is a desire for a specific product to satisfy the underlying need. An individual's basic food needs could be physically met for an expenditure of around £5 a week on bread, milk and a few vegetables. This might be all people need, but not surprisingly, it is not what they want. The teenager might want a Big Mac and strawberry shake, his father wants roast beef washed down with a 1976 Château-Lafite. In the China of Chairman Mao, the needs of its 1 billion people for clothes were met by identical plain, cheap cotton suits. But what the Chinese wanted were Levi jeans, Nike shoes, Lacoste T-shirts and pretty dresses. While needs are simple and few, wants are many and sophisticated. Wants are shaped by social and cultural forces, the media – and the marketing activities of firms.

A *demand* is a want for a specific product supported by an ability and willingness to pay for it. Many people want a Porsche, but few are able and willing to buy one. Companies therefore have not only to make products that people want, but they also have to make them affordable to a sufficient number. In summary, while companies do not create the need for food or social status, they do try to influence the demand by designing their products to be attractive, work well, be affordable and be readily available. They also try to communicate these features through advertising and other communications techniques.

A *product* is defined as anything that a firm offers to satisfy the needs or wants of customers. This can be a *physical* object such as a soft drink, car or breakfast cereal, but it can also be an intangible *service* such as a haircut, consultancy advice or holiday. The main point is that people never buy products for their own sake, but always for the needs and wants these products satisfy. People do not buy computers to look at, but rather to improve their decision-making capabilities. Cosmetics are bought because people hope they will enhance their looks. In designing and selling physical objects or intangible services, successful firms concentrate not on the product, but on enhancing their offer's ability to satisfy the needs and wants of customers. The key question is not what products the business makes, but rather which wants it seeks to meet. Then managers ask how they can redesign their products, augment them with other physical objects or service benefits, and communicate their offer more effectively so that they can better meet the needs of target customers.

Value and choice

What do the theoretical constructs tell us about how customers decide among alternative offers made by firms? First a customer has a *product choice set*. This consists of the number of alternatives that he or she considers when seeking to satisfy a certain need. A salesperson in an out-of-town hotel, considering how to meet a need for food, may have in his or her product choice set: eating in the hotel restaurant, going out for a hamburger, going to a pub, visiting the French restaurant nearby, or buying some snack food in a shop.

Choice is governed by the consumer's *need set*. The consumer might be influenced by a need for speed, service, convenience, perceived quality, ambience and reliability. Each of the product alternatives is subjectively weighed by the consumer against the choice criteria. The one which is rated best is perceived to have the highest utility. *Utility* is the consumer's estimate of the product's overall capacity to satisfy his or her needs. If the price of each of the alternatives were the same, the consumer would choose the one with the highest utility. But prices are not identical, so that in practice consumers do not choose the 'best' product, they choose the one offering the most *value*. Value is a combination of price and utility. While people prefer Porsches, they buy Fords. Buying the product with the highest utility would require giving up too many other products. Consequently, there are two ways of stimulating demand for a company's product – putting in qualities, features and images which enhance the utility it offers, or cutting the price.

Exchange and markets

Societies organize their economies to provide for the needs of their people. An economic system has three functions. First, it decides what is to be produced and in what quantities. Choices have to be made between guns and butter, roads and railways, Coke and Pepsi. Second, an economy determines how products are produced. It decides, for example, whether capital and the best brains go into the defence sector or the advertising industry. The third function of an economy is to determine who gets the highest incomes and the most products.

Societies have found two main alternatives for deciding these questions: economies based upon coercion, where the state makes the choices, and economies based upon exchange, where individual consumers and producers freely decide these questions through the choices they make. Exchange is the core concept which underlies marketing and the free enterprise system. *Exchange* is defined as the act of obtaining a desired product from someone by offering something in return. For exchange to take place there are two important conditions: (1) each party has to have something that might be of value to the other; and (2) each is free to accept or reject the offer. Then if the two parties agree on terms of exchange, the exchange process creates value, since normally both parties are better off than before the exchange. *Negotiation* is the process of trying to arrive at a mutually acceptable exchange. When an agreement is reached, a transaction takes place. A *transaction* is a trade of values between the two parties. This may be based upon *barter*, where, for example, one company may offer its oil in return for another's machinery. But barter is an inefficient means of exchange, and *money* transactions have long dominated the process. Customers exchange money for goods. In some cases neither money nor goods are traded; instead the marketer exchanges his or her product for a behavioural response in terms of respect, gratitude or political support.

The task of marketing in the exchange process is to seek to understand what the buyer wants to receive and what he or she is willing to pay. The marketer will also have a list of his or her own wants, such as a good price, a long-term contract and quick payment. A transaction takes place when an exchange is negotiated between the buyer and seller. Successful businesses prefer to move from transaction marketing to relationship marketing. *Transaction marketing* is a one-off negotiation. Here it pays both parties to seek to maximize their profits. But this changes if the parties are going to have a continuing relationship. *Relationship marketing* is a long-term, continuous series of transactions between parties. This occurs when each trusts the other to deal fairly, reliably and helpfully. When a good working relationship is built, negotiating time and costs are reduced and the pattern of transactions becomes more predictable and secure.

As discussed later in this chapter, relationship marketing – or creating customer loyalty – is becoming the central focus of marketing. Managers are realizing that taking a short-run profit-maximizing approach to customers does not pay off in the longer run. It pays to invest in quality, customer service and keeping existing customers happy. Satisfied customers – those who stay with the business over the years – tend to be much more profitable than new customers. First, this is because the firm does not have to incur the selling costs of acquiring new ones. Second, satisfied customers place more business with the firm, recommend it to others, and are less price sensitive. Studies by management consultants Bain and Company suggest that the annual profits generated from a customer who has been with a company for seven years are typically more than five times the amount it generates in the first year. Customers with a long-term relationship with a company are much more profitable than newly acquired ones.

In recent years, organizations have seen the advantage of generalizing relationship marketing to creating marketing networks. A *marketing network* consists of the company and those other organizations (suppliers, bankers, distributors, key customers) with which it has built long-term, dependable relationships. The Japanese *kieretsu* are an example of a marketing network. These longer-term partnerships seek to replace short-term adversarial relationships with co-operation based upon mutual trust, self-interest and commitment. While in the short run the company might buy cheaper through opportunistic sourcing, in the longer run it gains through forging a partnership where all parties commit to lowering costs, creating new products and developing systems which build competitiveness and market leadership.[3]

Exchange leads to the concept of a market. The creation of wealth leads to the division of labour – people are more efficient when they specialize in the production of one or a limited selection of products. This permits the development of expertise and economies of scale. Specialization creates the need for markets where specialized outputs can be exchanged (using money as the medium of exchange). The fields of economics and marketing define markets rather differently. For an economist, a market is a collection of both buyers and sellers who transact particular products. In marketing, however, the collection of sellers is termed the *industry* and the buyers are the market. A *market* is defined as all potential customers sharing a specific need or want who might be willing and able to exchange to satisfy that need or want.[4] Figure 2.1 illustrates how markets and industry interact. Sellers seek information about the needs and wants of potential customers, then develop, offer and communicate the benefits of their products to the market. If potential customers buy, then money is exchanged for the products.

In the modern free enterprise economy, there are literally millions of markets – markets for raw materials, components, labour, consumer goods, industrial products, money, distribution services and so on. All are linked together through the exchange process whereby parties freely trade products and services for money.

Markets and capitalism

Capitalism is based upon markets: buyers and sellers freely negotiating terms of exchange. As an economic system, capitalism has proved superior to state control or socialism in

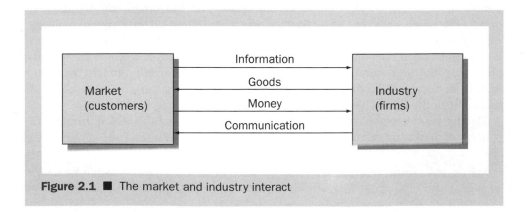

Figure 2.1 ■ The market and industry interact

three respects. First, it is consistent with individual freedom. If the state appropriates the right to decide what shall be produced and what prices will rule, it also must appropriate the rights to determine what occupations people will undertake, what they may earn and what they can do with their money. Economic freedom appears to be a necessary (though not sufficient) condition for political freedom.[5]

Second, empirically it has proved to be more efficient in allocating resources and increasing the aggregate wealth of societies. In a free enterprise system, the millions of prices are determined by the individual choices of consumers and producers. If too little of a product is produced, prices will rise. In the short term this efficiently rations the product to those consumers who most desire it and have the means to pay for it. In the long term, the higher prices encourage suppliers to boost production and overcome the shortage. Conversely, if too much of a product is produced, prices fall, stimulating demand and subsequently encouraging a curtailing of production and a switch of resources to more profitable products. Under socialism, prices do not reflect supply and demand so that queues and shortages are endemic in some areas, while gluts of unwanted products occur in others.

Third, capitalism encourages growth and innovation. Entrepreneurs receive big rewards for providing customers with better solutions to their needs and wants, and the economic system permits capital and skills to be rapidly transferred into these activities. By contrast, socialism provides no automatic incentives for satisfying customers and constricts the shift of resources into new areas.

While capitalism has worked better than socialism, it is not without its faults. There are four important weaknesses. First, its advantages break down if there is not strong competition between buyers and between sellers. Under monopoly, the price mechanism and exchange process do not operate efficiently to allocate resources and stimulate innovation. Second, because economic decisions are based upon changing expectations of benefit and profit, capitalism is economically unstable. There tend to be unpredictable cycles of boom and bust. Third, it leads to incomes which are very unequal. The most successful individuals can earn enormous incomes, while those who are ungifted or unlucky are unprotected. Finally, capitalism produces 'externalities' which can damage people who are not parties to the transactions. Thus a successful factory can earn high profits but pollute the neighbouring environment. These external costs are borne by others and there is no incentive for the producer to curtail such damaging externalities.

Consequently, even in the most capitalistic of economies the state must play a role. Its functions lie in encouraging competition, seeking to maintain economic stability, protecting the weak and underprivileged, protecting the environment from the 'selfish' concerns of producers and consumers, and undertaking those social tasks where the profit motive is inadequate.

Having completed the review of these important theoretical underpinnings, the concept of marketing can usefully be defined as follows:

Marketing is a social and managerial process by which individuals and groups obtain what they need and want through creating, offering and exchanging products of value with others.[6]

The customer-led business

The significance of marketing follows directly from the theory of exchange and markets. The task of marketing is to facilitate the exchange process and enhance the organization's ability to engage in mutually beneficial exchanges with customers. Marketing management seeks to attract and retain customers by offering them desirable products. This way the organization obtains the resources to meet the expectations of its own stakeholders – shareholders, employees and the community.

Marketing management consists of five tasks:

- *Identifying target markets*. Management have to identify those customers they desire to make exchanges with. Choice of target markets will be governed by the wealth they possess and the organization's capability to serve them.

- *Marketing research*. Management have to collect information on the current and potential needs of customers in the markets chosen, how they buy and what competitors are offering.

- *Product development*. The business must develop products (and/or services) which will meet needs and wants sufficiently to attract target customers to wish to buy.

- *Marketing mix*. Management will then have to determine the price, promotion and distribution for the product. This marketing mix is tailored to offer value to customers, to communicate the offer and to make it accessible and convenient.

- *Monitoring*. Since management will wish to build relationships which retain customers, they need to obtain feedback on customer satisfaction with the exchange and to modify the product and marketing mix as needs and competitive environments change.

Marketing management can be defined as the process of identifying target markets, researching the needs of customers in these markets and then developing the product, price, promotion and distribution to create exchanges that satisfy the objectives of the organization's stakeholders. Implicit in this definition is competitiveness. Customers have choices – normally there will be several competitors seeking to attract them – so the organization's ability to meet its objectives requires it to offer superior value to competition.

In economies based upon competition and free exchange, successful organizations must put the customer first. This obvious notion, however, has not been universally taken up. Many organizations operate under quite different philosophies. We will now look at four of the most common alternatives.

Production orientation

Some companies give primacy to their product rather than to the customer. There are two distinct variants of this philosophy. In high-tech companies, in particular, there is often a belief that developing technologically superior products is the route to success.

Here scientists make the product decisions. Little or no effort is made into researching whether the customer will want the features being developed, find the product attractive or be willing to pay for it. Generally the results are offers which are over-engineered, too costly to produce and insufficiently appealing to the market.

A second variant of the production concept is the view that success lies in producing the product more efficiently than competitors. Possessing the lowest cost is seen as the source of competitive advantage. Henry Ford epitomized this philosophy with his response to customers looking for novelty: 'they can have any colour of car they like – so long as it's black!' As Ford discovered, in affluent and rapidly changing markets an internal focus on production risks marooning the organization in the backwaters of low value-added products and declining markets.

Sales orientation

Production-oriented businesses often eventually make the transition to a sales orientation. Having produced products that are unappealing to customers, they see aggressive selling, advertising and sales promotion as the means to penetrate the market. But selling is not marketing – in fact, it can be just the opposite. As Levitt put it in his famous 'Marketing myopia' article:

> Selling tries to get the customer to want what the company has, marketing on the other hand, tries to get the company to produce what the customer wants.[7]

Another guru, Peter Drucker, put it equally clearly:

> Selling and marketing are antithetical rather than synonymous or even complementary. There will always, one can assume, be a need for some selling. But the aim of marketing is to make selling superfluous. The aim of marketing is to know and understand the customer so well that the product or service fits him and sells itself.[8]

While aggressive selling can sometimes fool the customer into buying a product once, it can never form the basis of a long-term relationship.

Financial orientation

Many companies today are neither product nor customer oriented, but instead focus on their financial assets. They see the task of management as generating the maximum amount of cash that can be produced from a given asset base. As the chief executive of Tomkins, one of these financially focused companies, explained, 'We regard our customers as the financial institutions, not the people who buy our company's products. We are in the business of buying companies rather than running them.'

Such companies can achieve high returns for a few years by exploiting the assets they inherit. But in the longer run they fail to satisfy customers, to build strong brands and to keep up with the changing marketing and technological environment.

Customer orientation

Today top companies recognize the primacy of being customer led. This business orientation is generally called the marketing concept.

The marketing concept states that a business is most likely to achieve its goals when it organizes itself to meet the current and potential needs of customers more effectively than competitors.

Figure 2.2 contrasts the customer orientation with the production and sales orientations. The last two 'sell what they make'. The customer orientation, on the other hand, works back from an appraisal of what customers want to how production and resources can be organized to meet these wants.

The rest of the chapter explores the key elements of the marketing concept defined above – business goals, meeting customer needs, organization and competitiveness. The five central components of the customer orientation are shown in Figure 2.3. At the centre is the focus on customer needs. Creating this focus requires organizational change and competitive advantage. At the top is the result – organizational success – which is derived from the effective customer focus.

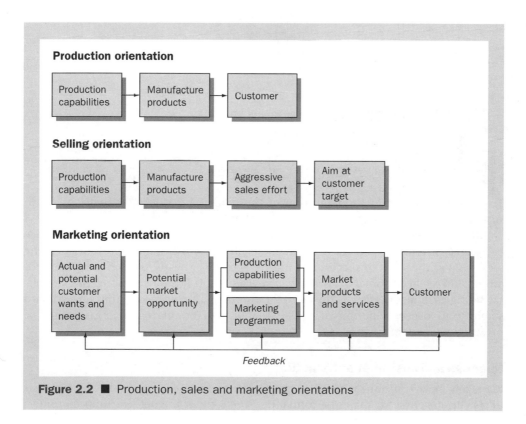

Figure 2.2 ■ Production, sales and marketing orientations

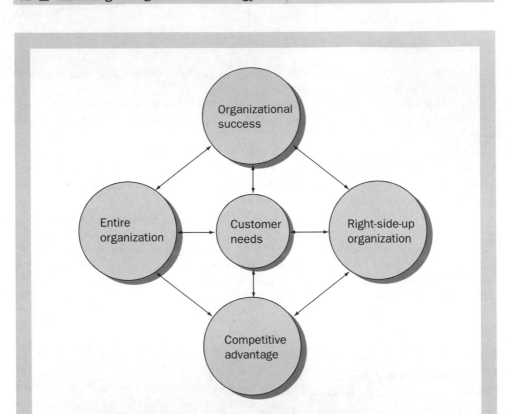

Figure 2.3 ■ The components of a customer orientation

 Success

The first component of the definition of the marketing concept is that it is about successfully meeting the goals of the organization.

All businesses have a range of financial and other stakeholder goals. The difference between a customer-led business and a financially led one is that the customer-led one sees profit as the result of successfully meeting customer needs. If a company does not attract and retain customers, it will not have a profitable business for long. Marketing – satisfying customer needs – is the central purpose of any business. Profit, growth and stability all depend upon management's ability to orientate the organization to meeting the needs of customers.

Success and customer satisfaction

Managers make a mistake when they gauge their company's performance on the basis of its current profit and sales performance. Profits today are derived from customers won in the past. Good profits today can temporarily mask sharply deteriorating customer performance. Similarly, sales growth may not lead to future profits if the new customers cost too much to attract or have no loyalty to the company. By looking at profits and sales alone, executives may only become aware of problems when sales and profits begin to fall away, and by then it is often too late.

Value – and tomorrow's sales and profits – are created by today's satisfied customers who want to continue doing business with the company. In the last few years there has been a lot of research into the value of satisfied customers and into what determines customer satisfaction (see Box 2.1). Today's top companies recognize that satisfied customers are highly valued assets. In contrast, dissatisfied customers can rapidly destroy the performance of the business.

A customer-led company recognizes that its only true assets are satisfied customers. Without satisfied customers the balance sheet's assets are merely scrap. The notion of customers as assets is not a philosophical point, but a hard, economic one. Companies can actually measure the lifetime value of customers (LVC) and estimate the potential revenues they will generate. The results can be staggering and should open the eyes of management to the profit implications of being customer led.

A supermarket group, for example, can estimate that an average family will spend £50 a week on groceries, or around £2,600 a year. This amounts to a lifetime expenditure of about £75,000 per family. Ford knows that a family's lifetime expenditure on cars could be around £150,000. But a good customer is worth more than this to a Safeway or Ford since a satisfied buyer tells on average another three to five other customers about the company. Thus the customer may be worth £300,000 to £500,000 potential lifetime revenue to the business. Satisfied customers are appreciating assets of great value.

By contrast, when a customer becomes dissatisfied with the quality of the firm's products or services, profitability can unravel very fast. Not only is the dissatisfied customer lost, but, on average, studies suggest that he or she tells fourteen others about the poor service.[9]

Consequently, it is crucial to measure customer satisfaction. Profits measure the results of past performance; customer satisfaction indicates what tomorrow's profits will be.

Focus on needs

The core idea of the customer-led company is that it focuses on needs not products. The central idea of marketing is the recognition that whatever product the company produces, the customer does not want it. The customer wants to meet a need, not purchase a product. This recognition is fundamental to the way the business defines and researches its markets, develops and prices its product range, communicates to its customers and organizes its employees.

A market is defined by a need not a product. Most managers, when asked what market they are in, respond by naming a product. We are in 'the cosmetics market' or 'computers' or 'the watch business'. But customers do not want cosmetics, computers or watches; they want to meet certain needs and seek products or services to satisfy

---

BOX 2.1

The ABC of customer loyalty

- *Loyal customers are assets.* A customer that generates a profit of £1,000 for a supplier in its first year is likely to generate a total profit of £50,000 if retained as a satisfied customer over ten years.
- *Loyal customers are more profitable.* They buy more of the company's products, take less of its time, are less sensitive to price and bring in new customers.
- *Winning new customers is costly.* It costs 3–5 times as much to find a new customer as to retain an existing one. These are the costs of researching, advertising, selling and negotiating with new prospects.
- *Increasing customer retention.* The average company loses 10 per cent of its customers annually. Studies show that increasing retention by as little as 5 per cent can increase a company's profits by 85 per cent.
- *'Highly satisfied' customers repurchase.* They are six times more likely to repurchase than customers who rate themselves just 'satisfied'. Highly satisfied customers tell others about the company.
- *Dissatisfied customers tell others.* On average they tell 14 others. So if losing a single customer represents the loss of an asset with a lifetime value of say £10,000, this might be only the tip of the iceberg. The total value lost might be 14 times as great.
- *Most dissatisfied customers don't complain.* While they tell their associates, only 4 per cent bother to complain to the company. For every complaint received, another 26 are likely to have problems and 6 will be serious ones.
- *Satisfactory resolution of complaints increases loyalty.* When complaints are resolved satisfactorily, these customers tend to be more loyal than those who never experienced a problem in the first place.
- *Few customers defect due to poor product performance.* Only 14 per cent defect for this reason. Two-thirds leave because they find service people indifferent or inaccessible.

them. A market is a group of potential customers with similar needs. IBM carved out a leadership position by defining its market, not as computers, but as managers wanting better information to make more profitable decisions. Buyers were much more ready to spend on better information systems than they were on computers. Scandinavian Airlines (SAS), under Jan Carlzon, carefully redefined itself as meeting the travel needs of business people rather than being in airlines. Charles Revson, founder of Revlon, put it more colourfully when he remarked, 'In the factory we make cosmetics, but in the store we sell hope.' Rolex defined itself as being in the status business not watches. The president of Black & Decker made a similar point: 'Last year one million quarter-inch drills were sold, not because people wanted quarter-inch drills, but because they wanted quarter inch holes.'

Once a company has defined its market in terms of customers, it must thoroughly research their needs. Often services are considered as important as the core product. When British Airways commenced its programme of customer research, it anticipated that the key requirements would be safety, on-time arrivals and schedule convenience. It was surprised to find four, rather secondary, factors valued most by customers:

■ Care and concern on the part of the staff that meet the customers.

■ Problem-solving capabilities of front-line personnel.

■ Flexibility in the interpretation of policies and procedures.

■ Recovery, or the ability of front-line people to make things right for the customer when they had somehow gone astray.

Increasingly, organizations in the public sector discover such findings. A National Health Service hospital recently surveyed its patients to determine the level of customer satisfaction. It discovered that patients rated clinical quality only fourteenth in their list of priorities. The top three concerns were length of wait, staff friendliness and physical surroundings.

The reason why such factors are rated so highly is that customer expectations are progressive. Once they have grown use to a benefit, it ceases to be a competitive discriminator. Customers expect all products and services to be safe and reliable – choice is now based on the additional features and services that competitors offer. The tasks are to determine what benefits are most valued and then to train and motivate staff to provide them and to monitor ongoing performance against these criteria.

Once the customer's needs are known, the company can then develop the range of products and services to meet them. It is useful to distinguish between the *core* product or service and the *augmented* or secondary products or services which surround the core. For a hotel, the core product is clean, comfortable accommodation. But since many hotels can meet this minimum requirement, differentiation and choice are based upon how effectively the hotel augments its core. Augmented products include personal service, restaurant, television, leisure facilities and so on. Airlines and hospitals find, not surprisingly, that they are being judged not by their core products, but by the quality of their augmented services.

Meeting needs also generates higher margins than selling products. If a salesperson tries to interest a customer in a £20,000 machine tool, the customer invariably perceives additional costs. The marketing approach is to focus on benefits not on products and costs. If the new machine saved £100,000 on labour, parts, material and power over its lifetime, the salesperson could demonstrate that the buyer would increase net company profits by £80,000.

Since successful marketing rates knowledge of the customer more highly than knowledge of the product, it often requires significant organizational changes. In the past, companies have often organized their businesses and sales along product lines; today they increasingly organize around markets. Rather than specialize in a specific product, they focus on a particular type of customer. This way they get to know the customer's business and needs, and can search with the customer for ways of enhancing performance.

The greatest opportunities lie in meeting needs that have not been met by competitors. Three types of need – or market – can be distinguished. *Existing markets* are those where customers are satisfied with existing products. When newcomers enter, they compete on price and promotion rather than offering new benefits. These markets approach commodity-like competition, margins are low and there are few differences between products.

Latent markets consist of customers with defined needs that have not yet been met by competitors. A company which develops a product or service to meet these needs has the opportunity, because of the absence of competition, to obtain a unique market position. These products may represent significant improvements over previous ones. For example, the personal computer was a breakthrough in the 1960s, video in the 1970s, the car telephone in the 1980s and internet browsers in the 1990s. There are lots of unmet needs. Pharmaceutical companies are looking for cures for cancer, AIDS and the common cold. Car manufacturers want to find engines which do not pollute and are more economical in fuel. Computer companies want speech-recognition technology.

The third are *incipient markets*. These are needs that customers have – but do not know they have until a product or service appears which triggers their recognition of certain needs or wants. Such markets appear more frequently than managers imagine. Customers are not professional innovators and, not surprisingly, are often myopic in imagining new solutions to their problems. High rates of technological change, in particular, make it difficult for customers to foresee the benefits that can be offered. Market research, therefore, often produces poor projections of the opportunities that new products represent. Examples of products meeting incipient needs are 3M's Post-it notes, the Sony Walkman, the Xerox machine and the fluorescent textliner. These products and services changed customer behaviour and created new markets when none previously existed.

Innovation – meeting latent or incipient needs, offers real opportunities for profit. Being customer led means being an innovator (see Box 2.2). There are few opportunities for profit in producing me-too products in existing markets. Growth and profitability come from identifying and meeting customer needs that have not yet been met. Without continuous improvement – finding new and better ways of satisfying customer needs – profit margins will be under continuous pressure. Customers expect prices to fall in real terms when products do not change, and competition normally ensures that this occurs. In the long run, no amount of efficiency improvement can compensate for a lack of customer focus and innovative thrust.

Organization

This is the third component of the marketing concept. Since marketing is what the business is all about, it has to be a central concern to all in the organization. That front-line staff have to be customer led is clear, but the marketing focus leads to a radical reassessment of the tasks and responsibilities of non-front-line personnel – those who serve in supervisory, middle and senior management ranks.

BOX 2.2

Customer needs and innovation

Federal Express and Milliken are two examples of companies that succeed through continuously generating innovative solutions to customer needs.

Fed Ex's customer satisfaction surveys showed that it provided excellent service, but it recently decided that it must do even better. It examined the entire package delivery and billing process from the customers' viewpoint. The result was Powership – a computer terminal given to thousands of the company's best customers. It creates address labels with routing instructions, and automatic billing that hits the screen when the package arrives. Fed Ex built more growth and increased customer loyalty and satisfaction by understanding customer needs better than customers did themselves.

Milliken, a leading textile manufacturer, sought new ways to provide value to its retail customers. Its customer taskforce found to its surprise that the biggest problem that retailers faced was not the cost of the items, but the cost of too many wrong items left unsold at the end of the season. Milliken's response was to drop its traditional once-per-season ordering system and allow retailers to make 'mid-flight course corrections' in a series of separate reorder stages throughout the season. To make this work, the company had then to re-engineer all its manufacturing and information processes to take out time and waste. The result was again higher customer loyalty, growth and secured margins.

Source: Boston Consulting Group, *Perspectives 1996*

Moments of truth

Jan Carlson's turnaround of Scandinavian Airlines was based upon focusing on what he termed the 'moments of truth'. He realized that customers prefer those suppliers who have an image for quality and service. Customers build up this image through the quality of their personal contacts with the company's products and staff. Each time the customer meets one of the company's sales people, service staff, agents or attendants, there is a 'moment of truth' where the customer can be won or lost by the quality of the service and personal contact he or she receives. To the customer the front-line staff *are* the company. In this sense a company is as good as its weakest employee. If at a moment of truth the company's representative responds inadequately, the customer does not say the representative does not care, he or she says 'the company does not care'.

The right-side-up organization

Consequently, front-line staff determine how customers perceive the organization. They need to be the most customer-oriented, best-trained and most highly motivated employees in the organization. Unfortunately, in many organizations the opposite is closer to the truth. This is illustrated in Figure 2.4. At the top of the figure is the hier-archical pyramid structure which still characterizes many organizations. At the base of this pyramid are the front-line personnel. Above them are the ranks of supervisors, middle managers and experts who control, co-ordinate and direct the front line. Today such traditional organizations are under pressure as never before. Three problems are crumbling these edifices. First, they result in excessive overhead costs: competitive pressures mean that few companies can afford to employ five to ten people to back up one front-line worker. Second, these organizations are too slow: customer require-ments are not solved immediately by the front line, but instead have to be passed upwards to co-ordinators and staff for study, consultation and decision. In an age of shortening product life cycles, such delays can be crippling. Finally, the lack of

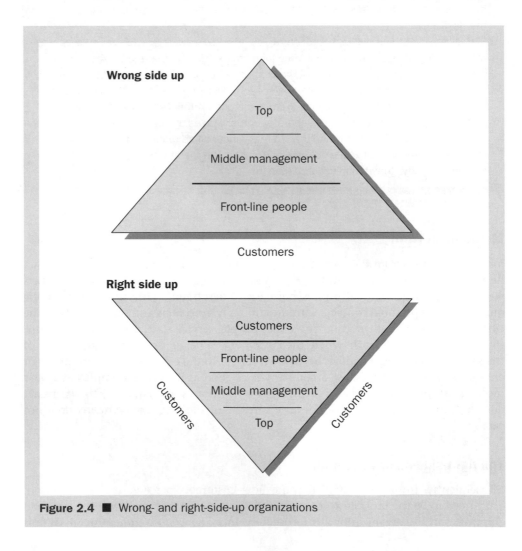

Figure 2.4 ■ Wrong- and right-side-up organizations

discretion and inferior status ascribed to front-line staff demotivates them and alienates them from both the company and its customers.

Today's leading companies are attempting to change dramatically by turning this pyramid upside down and flattening it (see the example of Pepsi Cola in Figure 2.5). By flattening it, they aim to take out layers of management and so slash overhead costs. By turning it upside down, they seek to create a customer-led business with front-line employees motivated and empowered to satisfy customers. These new organizations recognize first that everything should start from a customer perspective. Second, those employees closest to the customer are at the top of the organization. They should be empowered to exercise their freedom to act within their areas of competence – take responsibility, accept accountability, exercise initiative and deliver results. As far as possible they should see themselves as owner operators, recognizing that what is good for the customer is good for the company and good for them as individuals. Third, these companies see the primary role of staff, middle and senior management as helping the front line by providing the right products and resources and removing obstacles.

Measuring the performance of front-line staff in satisfying customers is normally fairly easy. Subjective impressions can be gained from customer complaints, from talking to customers, retailers and wholesalers, and from staff meetings. More comprehensive and objective measures can be obtained from formal customer surveys which poll customers about the quality of the product or service and the relationship they have with the company and its staff. This way front-line people learn whether they are doing a good job and where the problems are.

But how is the performance of non-front-line personnel evaluated? Since their task is to support the front line, the answer is clear – ask the front line. Those outside the front line need to be evaluated and rewarded on the basis of systematic feedback from their front line on the quality of the support they provide and the relationships they establish with them. When this is done, the company makes dramatic progress in being customer driven and empowering the front line. Middle management and staff positions cease to be hideaways for highly paid people who do not add value to the performance of the front line. Middle managers are incentivized to ask 'what can we do for the front line?' and so indirectly, 'what can we do for the customer?'

Competitive advantage

The fourth aspect of the marketing concept is competitiveness. The marketing concept requires more than being able to meet customer needs – it requires meeting them better than competitors. Customers choose those suppliers which offer the *best* value. If a company does not have a competitive advantage, it will lose market share or have to cut prices and profit margins to retain it. In the late 1980s, Swissair ceased to be the businessperson's favourite airline, not because it got worse, but because the competitors such as British Airways and SAS improved and then surpassed it in service.

It follows that companies must not only systematically monitor the level of customer satisfaction with their business, but also measure this against competitors.

Pepsi Cola – the right-side-up company

We will be an outstanding company by exceeding customer expectations through empowered people, guided by shared values

This requires

A consistent
customer focus
for our company which all of our people understand and feel passionate about

An
empowered organization
which is both motivated and supported to satisfy customers to the fullest
extent of their capabilities

A set of
shared values
which guides all of our decisions and actions

To make this a reality, we must turn the company 'right side up'. A 'right-side-up' company places the customer (anyone who buys or sells our product) at the top, thereby acknowledging everything starts with the customer.

Those employees closest to the customers are at the top of the organization. They must be empowered to satisfy customer needs. The rest of the organization's role is to help those closest to the customers by providing resources and removing obstacles.

Figure 2.5 ■ Pepsi Cola: the right-side-up company

Competitive benchmarking compares customer satisfaction with the products, services and relationships of the company with those of key competitors. Competitive benchmarking involves five steps:

1. Determine the critical success factors. Market research should identify the dimensions of quality and service most valued by customers.
2. Measure how customers perceive the business along these critical success factors.
3. Measure how customers perceive key competitors along these factors.
4. Measure the performance gap. How does the business compare with the best competitors? What are the strengths and weaknesses?
5. Produce action plans. Project teams need to be created to analyze the problem and determine how the gap can be closed.

Competitive benchmarking is important. It encourages management to focus externally on the customer and the competition. It destroys complacency and creates a sense of urgency. It should get everyone in the business involved and committed to a series of specific action targets providing for continuing improvement.

 ## Entire business

Finally, many managers make the mistake of thinking that becoming marketing oriented means making the marketing department the primary function in the business. But this is definitely not so. Marketing is a philosophy of business which places the customer, not the marketing department, at the centre. The marketing philosophy says that everyone's role is to focus on satisfying the customer. To avoid it being seen as a narrow functional task, some outstanding companies actually refuse to have a marketing department. For example, Marks & Spencer, which operates in seven countries, sells to another thirty, has a turnover of £10 billion and is widely regarded as Britain's best-managed company, has no marketing specialists at all. It believes that the central task of all its personnel – staff assistants, store managers, buyers and technical people – is to satisfy the customer. Marks & Spencer recognizes the words of Hewlett-Packard's chief executive, 'Marketing is too important to leave to the marketing department.' Peter Drucker explained it comprehensively:

> Marketing is so basic that it cannot be considered a separate function within the business, on a par with others such as manufacturing or personnel. Marketing requires separate work and a distinct group of activities. But it is first, a central dimension of the entire business. It is the whole business seen from the point of view of its final result, that is, from the customer's point of view. Concern and responsibility must therefore permeate all areas of the enterprise.[10]

The marketing department can play a useful role in companies as a facilitator and as a source of information and advice. But in most companies the really important 'marketing' decisions are crucially dependent on the work of other departments. Research and development often leads in developing new products; engineering and manufacturing determine product quality; distribution and service often report to operations. Marketing departments frequently control only the visible 'trappings' of marketing – advertising, promotions and packaging. Too many managers see these manifestations as the content of marketing. Real marketing depends upon cross-functional co-operation. This needs to be based on a deep understanding of and enthusiastic drive to being customer led throughout the entire business. Training and development in marketing thinking has to be company wide.

 ## Customers as assets

Loyal customers are assets (refer back to Box 2.1). Studies by consultants Bain & Company tried to measure the value of a loyal customer. If managers know the cost of losing a customer, they can evaluate the likely pay-off of investments designed to keep customers happy. For example, a customer that generates a profit of £1,000 for a supplier in its first year is likely to generate a total profit of £50,000 if retained as a satisfied customer over ten years. The Bain customer retention model (Figure 2.6) summarizes the typical pattern, demonstrating clearly the profitability of long-term customer relationships:

■ The cost of acquiring new customers can be substantial. A higher retention rate implies that fewer customers need to be acquired, so less marketing expenditure needs to be allocated to targeting potential customers.

■ Loyal customers tend to spend more.

■ Regular customers tend to place frequent, consistent orders and, therefore, usually cost less to serve.

■ Satisfied customers are the best advertisement for any business and are more likely to introduce new customers to the company through word-of-mouth recommendation.

■ Satisfied customers are often willing to pay premium prices to a supplier they know and trust.

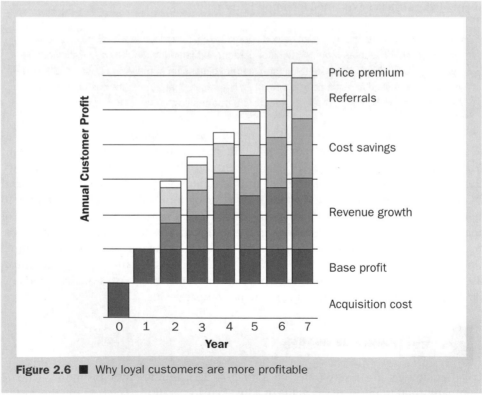

Figure 2.6 ■ Why loyal customers are more profitable

Source: Frederick F. Reichheld, *The Loyalty Effect: The Hidden Forces behind Growth, Profits and Lasting Value.* (Boston: Harvard Business School Press, 1996) p. 39

■ Retaining customers makes gaining market entry or share gain difficult for competitors.

■ The information collated and held on loyal customers through database management allows the company to communicate regularly with them.

Retention and satisfaction

The average company loses around 10 per cent of its customers annually. Bain's experience in the UK and the USA is that a 5 per cent increase in the retention rate increases

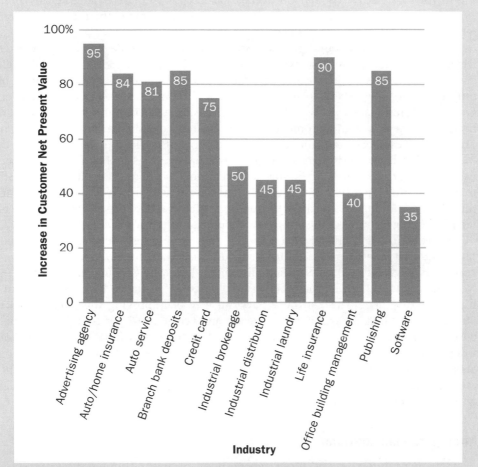

Figure 2.7 ■ Impact of a 5-percentage-point increase in retention rate on customer net present value

Source: Frederick F. Reichheld, *The Loyalty Effect: The Hidden Forces behind Growth, Profits and Lasting Value*. (Boston: Harvard Business School Press, 1996) p. 36

customer profits by between 20 and 85 per cent. Figure 2.7 suggests how this varies across different types of industry.

For the ongoing business, retaining customers is more important than creating a culture of 'closing the sale'. The key to raising the retention rate is creating highly satisfied customers. Studies show that customers who rate themselves 'highly satisfied' are six times more likely to buy again from the company than those who are just 'satisfied' (see Box 2.1). In other words, the relationship seems non-linear. Creating satisfied customers is not enough – customers rating themselves 'satisfied' are still often tempted away by competitors. Really to lock customers in, they have to be 'highly satisfied' or 'delighted' by the company's service. Such customers also tell others. Virgin Airways discovered that on average passengers who were delighted by their experience on its flights told four others. Delighting customers, then, both increases retention and generates new business.

If satisfied customers build profits, dissatisfied ones can erode them even quicker. Dissatisfied customers tell on average fourteen other people. So if losing a single customer represents the loss of an asset with a lifetime value of £50,000, this might be only the tip of the iceberg. The total value could be many times greater. Managers greatly underestimate the cost of dissatisfied customers. They think customers are happy because they get few complaints. But research suggests that only 4 per cent of dissatisfied customers complain. So for every complaint received there are likely to be 26 other dissatisfied customers, of whom 6 will have serious problems. For suppliers using third-party channels, the results are even more worrying, since it has been estimated that only 2 per cent of complaints made are actually received by the manufacturer. The rest are made to retailers, brokers or distributors. Dissatisfied customers can be rapidly eroding the value of the business without managers being aware of the problems.

Consequently, it is crucial systematically and continuously to measure customer satisfaction. It is also necessary to study dissatisfied customers and explore why customers have defected. Dissatisfied customers should be encouraged to complain. Not only does this indicate the problems, but it also offers the company the opportunity to rectify them. This can be a powerful way of improving the retention rate. Studies suggest that the company can retain an average of 62 per cent of dissatisfied customers if it responds to their complaints. If it responds very quickly, it can hold on to 95 per cent of these customers. British Airways, which has made major efforts in this area, found an even more striking pattern. It found that customers whose complaints are dealt with to the customer's complete satisfaction are 5–10 per cent more satisfied with the airline than those who have never had a problem.

Managerial implications

A company's future sales and profit depend upon its ability to forge successful long-term customer relationships. The basis of creating such loyalty is the company's ability to satisfy customers better than competitors. The first task of managers is to measure systematically and continually whether it is doing this. The second task is to put in place strategies to improve customer satisfaction. Executives do this by developing policies which deliver high value. This is achieved by offering products and services which are perceived by target customers as consistently superior or lower in cost, or both.

Superior value is based upon the company building core competences – specific knowledge and skills, which allow it to manage core processes more effectively than competition. The fundamental core processes centre around developing new products, managing operations and servicing customers. The value of the company's offer also needs to be communicated to target customers through brand-building programmes, which include advertising, public relations, sponsorship programmes and guarantees. In recent years, reflecting the increased attention to retaining key customers, companies have introduced a range of loyalty programmes. These include frequency marketing programmes, like those run by airlines, which reward customers who buy frequently. Another type of loyalty programme is the club concept, which offers customers who join special benefits such as discounts, interest magazines, newsletters or gifts. The Japanese video game company Nintendo enrolled over 2 million children in its Nintendo Club. Tesco, the British grocery retailer enrolled over 1 million members in the first six months when it launched its club card. Telephone help lines have been another rapidly growing medium to permit better communication between customer and company. In the USA, 83 per cent of all consumer goods companies carry freephone 'care line' numbers. Procter & Gamble prints a free telephone number on all its products and deals with 75,000 customers' calls a year. If 85 per cent of the complaints are handled to its customers' satisfaction, the benefit to the company annually was conservatively estimated at over half a million dollars, or a 20 per cent return on investment.

More generally, advances in information technology are making it possible for more and more companies to build economically, detailed databases on the behaviour and attitudes of their individual customers. This allows them to target offers and communications which are specifically tailored to be relevant to the needs and expectations of individual customers.

Finally, studies show that only 14 per cent of customers abandon a company due to product performance problems. Two-thirds defect to another supplier because they find service people indifferent or inaccessible. Such results highlight the importance of the selection and training of front-line staff and the development of customers as assets. In their 'moments of truth', front-line staff determine the future of the business.

Creating the customer-led business

Almost all top executives now claim that their companies are, or are to become, customer led. Hospitals, public sector organizations and non-profit bodies increasingly echo this claim. All now appear to see that a dedication to meeting the needs of customers is the critical requirement for survival and growth. Yet few companies, in practice, are truly customer led, and many which have tried to transform themselves have seen their initiative languish.[11] There are four main reasons for this failure:

- *Background of top executives*. Most companies are led by chief executives without training and development in marketing, and so lack the fundamental commitment to it. In some countries, notably the UK and the USA, their background is often in accounting, so that a financial orientation dominates their thinking. Short-term profitability and asset management take precedence over the customer. In others, such as Germany, an engineering background is at the fore and a production orientation often rules. In these companies, marketing issues receive insufficient attention at the top level, and this lack of focus then permeates down through the organization.

- *Misunderstanding marketing*. Many companies do not understand that marketing is a business philosophy which requires a complete change in attitudes and practices for everyone in the organization. Instead they see it as setting up a marketing department, harder selling, boosting advertising or upgrading the brochures. The business is then pushed towards a sales rather than a marketing orientation.

- *Lack of commitment*. Most chief executives underestimate the time and commitment involved in becoming customer led. Often they expect to see results after a year and the process completed in two. Unfortunately, changing the culture and the image of a company will generally take a generation of both employees and customers. Retraining staff from long-entrenched and deeply held attitudes and practices is an uphill task. Customers too have an image of the company built up over years of experience and observation, and it takes a disconcerting time for them to recognize a company's new reality. The commitment to achieve these changes will be massive both in the time and effort required from management and in the resources that have to be put into the retraining tasks.

- *Resistance to change*. Most truly customer-led organizations were born that way. Such companies as Marks & Spencer, Federal Express, Disney and Toyota had founders deeply committed to a customer orientation. As St Paul said, 'Faith is easier than conversion.' Non-marketing-oriented organizations resist change. They look back to distant days of success achieved without these new ideas. Non-marketing functions see the new philosophy as a threat to their power. Marketing departments often exacerbate these conflicts by seeking to appropriate control over the process and to enhance their power over resources. Overcoming such resistance requires sensitivity and leadership of a high order from the board.

Creating a customer-led business requires clarity of goals, an intense commitment over a long period and the active involvement of the entire workforce. The change process that is required can be divided into six stages (Figure 2.8).

Starting with the mission

Managers and staff must be motivated to commit to a revolutionary change in the culture and practices of the organization. They need to buy into an inspiring vision of the company – a shared goal worth putting all their energies and ideas towards achieving. At British Airways, chief executive Colin Marshall inspired change with the highly visible mission of making the airline the best in the world, 'the world's favourite

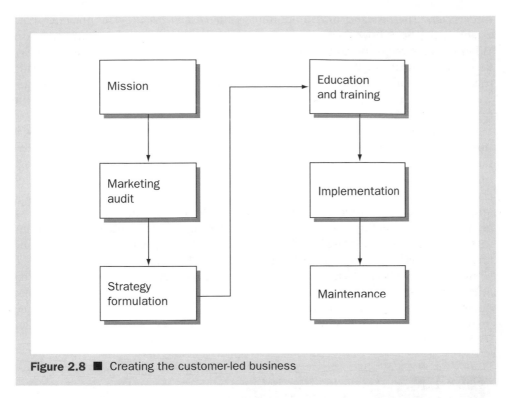

Figure 2.8 ■ Creating the customer-led business

airline'. Komatsu inspired the commitment of its workforce with its mission of 'encircling Caterpillar' – taking over as number one in the industry. People react best when they are given a clear, motivating challenge – a major competitive threat to beat off, or achieving a visible leadership role in the market. Top management have first to find, then to articulate, and finally to enthuse people around such a clear vision of winning the game.

Then management must connect winning with satisfying customers. This is an educational job of making staff see that being 'the best' results from being the preferred choice of customers – and that being the preferred choice means finding out what customers want, producing the quality solutions and delivering them to customers better than any competitor. This educational process is normally most effectively triggered by an executive workshop led by an outside professional. The goals of the workshop are to build a genuine understanding of the marketing concept and to create a common language and framework for taking it forward. The result of this initial phase should be a management team confident enough to articulate, lead and implement the customer revolution in their areas of responsibility.

The marketing audit

The second stage is collecting information to permit a detailed analysis of the current situation and to assess what needs to be done. Three types of audit need to be undertaken. The first and most important is the *customer audit*. The objective is to establish the base: how good is the company really at satisfying customers' needs? What does it need to do to improve its service to customers? What should be measured? To formulate a base for improving quality, management need to identify valid measures of 'quality'. These must be what customers define as quality – what customers want and expect from the company. Being customer oriented means making sure the business is really selling what the customer wants to buy.

The different customer-impinging processes will need to be evaluated separately. A hospital might separately measure its in-patient and out-patient operations. A manufacturer would measure its order processing, delivery and installation, customer usage of its products, and after-sales service. It will also want to benchmark against key competitors. Once the audit is designed, the company will collect data on a sizeable and representative sample of customers and potential customers. It will almost certainly employ an independent market research agency to conduct 'focus group' interviews, followed by a larger poll of customers. When these data are collected and analyzed, management have the information to move forward.

British Airways began its turnaround this way. Interviewers stopped hundreds of flyers at Heathrow, Gatwick and later other airports in the UK and overseas, and asked detailed questions of their flying experiences. The investigation focused on what criteria customers used to judge airlines and how BA and its competitors were rated. Armed with this detailed scorecard, chief executive Colin Marshall was able to identify what had to be done.

BOX 2.3

Importance of employee attitudes

Southwest Airlines, the Texas-based pioneer of low-cost air travel, has been the USA's only consistently profitable airline through the last twenty-five years. It has become an icon for many of today's managers seeking to achieve extraordinary levels of productivity and customer satisfaction.

Southwest's success is rooted in the enthusiasm of its employees. The company's mission is to deliver 'positively outrageous service'. Paradoxically, it believes that the best way of achieving this objective is to say that customers come second. The company's top priority is treating its employees well, out of a firm belief that if its people are happy, everything else will fall into place. Southwest has created a fun place to work, which in turn has resulted in the airline being a fun experience for passengers.

It does this by selecting prospective employees who have a sense of humour and commitment to service. A high-powered 'culture committee' of over 100 employees ensures that Southwest's spirit remains special. Birthdays, marriages and promotions are celebrated with champagne and cards from the CEO. Everyone is on first-name terms, rules are few and staff are encouraged to use their own initiative. As a result, Southwest is becoming America's fastest-growing and most profitable airline.

Second, the company must undertake a comprehensive assessment of its *competitive environment*. Customer needs and the technologies for meeting them will change in the years ahead. The trajectory of changes in demographics, the company's environment, its technology, markets and culture should be assessed. The management team have to determine whether the thrust of their product and marketing efforts looks right for the world they are moving into. Does the company have the wherewithal to be competitive over the next decade? Does it need radically to change its technology and markets?

Finally, the company should undertake an *audit of employee attitudes* and views. First, management need to know how employees feel about the company. If employees are not inspired by the company's mission and if they do not feel well treated by management, they are unlikely to extend themselves in treating customers with care, courtesy and commitment. Management will be in an unwinnable situation if employees feel insecure, frightened to take initiative and unrewarded for their efforts. Second, since a customer orientation requires teamwork, the company should explore cross-functional attitudes. How do R & D people feel about marketing and production staff? Are narrow functional perspectives hindering progress? Third, management should seek to elicit what employees think should be done to improve internal operations and attitudes, and to enhance external performance.

Strategy development

Once all this information is obtained, management have to develop a positioning strategy with the goal of obtaining high marks on the customers' scorecards. A positioning strategy has two components. The first describes what target markets the business is going to serve. Because different market segments have radically different customer wants, competitors and price expectations, it is usually necessary to choose a focus. Jan Carlson decided to focus SAS on business travellers. The publishers Prentice Hall chose to focus on the university textbook market. The second aspect of positioning strategy is the determination of what the business's differential advantage should be – how it can get target customers to prefer it to competitors.

Carlson made punctuality and reliability the differential advantage of SAS. Marks & Spencer chose quality and value for money. Volvo made car safety its selling point. The requirements of the differential advantage are two. First, it must offer an advantage that customers will truly value. The customer audit should have highlighted this dimension as a critical choice factor. Second, it must differentiate the business in the eyes of the customer.

Top management must hammer out a clear positioning strategy for the business. Positioning determines the targets, who the customers are it will seek to serve, and how the business will obtain the preferences of these target customers. The best vehicle for formulating such a strategy is an executive retreat. To make it effective, the workshop should be preceded by careful planning and preparation. Executives need to be assigned the tasks of summarizing the results of the three marketing audits, evaluating their implications and presenting the strategic options available. The chief executive needs to encourage a freewheeling debate about the strategy and how it might be implemented. Often an experienced facilitator will be useful to guide the discussion, to highlight the issues and to advise on 'making it happen'.

Education and training

Translating strategy into action usually requires a large-scale campaign of education and training of the workforce. For example, British Airways began by putting 37,000 people – virtually its whole workforce – through an intensive two-day workshop. This phase has four objectives. First, management have to communicate to everyone in the organization the 'putting customers first' message. Staff need to understand what the company is trying to achieve and why it is crucial for everyone's future. Second, employees need to be fed back the results of the marketing audits – how customers and staff judge the organization and how the competitive environment is changing. People need to know where the problems are, so that they can see what needs to be done to improve competitiveness. Third, the training session should be designed to involve employees in the change process. Staff need to be encouraged to consider how they as individuals can contribute to improving customer service. Fourth, the workforce have to be given the skills necessary to do the job properly. For example, British Airways staff were taught how to cope with the stress of customer contact, how to deal with the feelings generated by intensive customer service activities, and how to communicate effectively and assertively under pressure. The aim was to help staff become more personally effective and confident in their performance.

Implementation

The biggest problem in any change programme is achieving large-scale commitment and long-term follow-through. The best way of achieving this is not telling people what to do and how to do it, but rather empowering staff to identify the key tasks themselves, and encouraging them to get on with finding and implementing solutions. The tasks of management are to enthuse and facilitate the efforts of the front line to become customer driven, rather than to act as decision-makers and rule-enforcers. Two mechanisms are particularly useful for encouraging grass-roots commitment: quality circles and challenges.

A *quality circle* is a group of front-line people who meet on a regular basis to find better ways to do their work. Working effectively, quality circles can prove invaluable for investigating issues, problem solving and developing new methods for meeting customer needs. British Airways, for example, used quality circles as a fundamental part of its implementation strategy. It has 70 circles in the UK and over 40 in other countries. These circles have produced thousands of recommendations and ideas for improvement; hundreds of these ideas have been implemented and have resulted in dramatic improvements both in the quality of the service and in reducing costs.

Experience suggests that quality circles need to be encouraged to focus, and to avoid spending too much time on side issues such as the food in the company canteen or car parking problems. Their real focus should be on serving customers better. Giving them a clear customer mission is the best way of keeping them on track. Looking for new and better ways of scoring high marks on the customers' report card can give the group a sense of importance and a feeling that it is making a worthwhile contribution to the organization's success.

A second tool for achieving continuing commitment is the 'challenge'. A *challenge* is a task usually undertaken by a cross-functional team, to achieve a specific, measurable customer-related goal within a specified period. For example, SAS identified punctuality as a key want of its business customers. Carlson challenged his staff with making SAS the most punctual airline in Europe. The project was championed by a project team and became a rallying idea which captured the imagination of SAS staff, including the chief executive, pilots and ground staff. Within three months and with the expenditure of under £100,000, SAS achieved its objective. Successful companies like Marks & Spencer, Toyota and Microsoft run a continuous series of challenges to foster a sense of excitement, commitment and renewed enthusiasm that can carry forward the programme of becoming customer driven.

Maintenance

At some imperceptible point, the customer orientation programme ceases to be a change campaign and becomes the basic orientation of the organization. Then the company's strategy, structure, systems, people and leadership are integrated and totally focused on satisfying customers' profitably (Figure 2.9).

The customer-oriented company has a clear positioning strategy. Everybody knows its target market segments and the competitive advantages on which it seeks to focus. Its organization is flat and built around supporting the front line, whose responsibility is to provide quality products and services. People in this type of organization are highly responsive to customer requirements.

The support systems in the organization have also to be aligned to serving the customer. All job definitions – both front-line and staff positions – should describe how their work contributes to satisfying customers. New employees should understand from the beginning the total customer focus. The orientation and subsequent training programmes should re-emphasize this basic value. Information systems should regularly monitor how effectively the organization is scoring in meeting customer needs. Appraisal and reward systems need to provide feedback to employees about the effectiveness of their efforts. If top management want the organization to be customer driven, it does not make sense to appraise and reward people largely on the basis of short-term financial measures.

Finally, top management, and in particular the chief executive, must provide visible and consistent support for the drive to be customer oriented. They need to demonstrate their wholehearted commitment to the marketing concept and to use every occasion to preach the gospel of service to the customer.

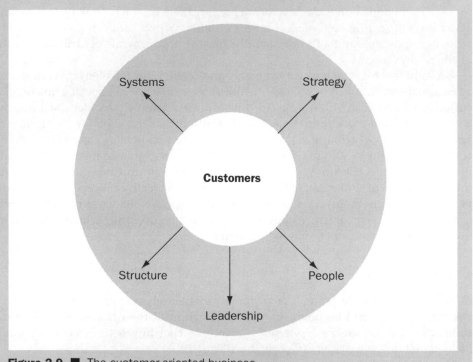

Figure 2.9 ■ The customer-oriented business

Summary

The marketing concept is not a theory of marketing, but a philosophy of business. It affirms that the key to meeting the objectives of stakeholders is to satisfy customers. In competitive markets this means that success goes to those firms which are best at meeting the needs of customers.

The top priority of business today is organizing to motivate employees to find new and better ways of satisfying customers. Marketing, in competitive, free enterprise markets, is both a central management task and an engine for economic progress. The tasks of the government are to encourage competition and to ensure that firms do not impose damaging environmental impacts upon others.

Questions

1. How, if at all, are marketing and democracy related?

2. What characteristics would distinguish a marketing-led company from production- and financially led companies?

3. Why is it important to obtain explicit feedback on customer satisfaction? Develop a short questionnaire which might be used to elicit such feedback for an organization with which you are familiar.

4. The 1980s and 1990s have seen a shake-out of middle management and a delayering of organizations. Why?

5. What are the main ways in which a company could search for developing a competitive advantage?

6. 'Most British companies are not marketing oriented.' What does this mean? How could they become marketing oriented?

Notes

1. Adam Smith, *An Inquiry into the Nature and Causes of the Wealth of Nations*, 1776.

2. These distinctions follow Philip Kotler, *Marketing Management: Analysis, planning and control* (Englewood Cliffs, NJ: Prentice Hall, 1997), pp. 9–10.

3. The practical approach to effective negotiation relationships is covered in Roger Fisher and William Ury, *Getting to Yes* (London: Hutchinson, 1982), and Roger Fisher and Scott Brown, *Getting Together* (London: Business Books, 1989).

4. Kotler, *op. cit.*, p. 8.

5. Milton Friedman, *Capitalism and Freedom* (New York: Macmillan, 1962).

6. For other definitions and a good introduction to marketing, see Michael J. Baker, *Marketing: An introductory text* (London: Macmillan, 1996).

7. Theodore Levitt, 'Marketing myopia', *Harvard Business Review*, July–August, 1960, pp. 45–56. See also Stephen King, 'Has marketing failed or was it never really tried?', *Journal of Marketing Management*, Summer 1985, pp. 1–19.

8. Peter F. Drucker, *Management: Tasks, responsibilities, practices* (London: Heinemann, 1974), p. 63.

9. The data presented here are based on studies reported in Karl Albrecht and Rom Zemke, *Service America* (Homewood, Il: Irwin, 1985), Lindon Silverman Goldzimer, *Customer Driven* (New York: Macmillan, 1989) and Frederick F. Reichheldan and Thomas Teal, *The Loyalty Effect* (Boston, MA: Harvard Business School, 1996).

10. Drucker, *op. cit.*, p. 65.

11. Nigel Piercy, *Market-Led Strategic Change* (London: Butterworth-Heinemann, 1992).

Chapter 3

Segmentation, positioning and the marketing mix

'Marketing' has two distinct meanings. The first, and most important, is as a philosophy for the whole business. It defines the primary goal of everyone in the organization as meeting the needs of customers. Marketing is the philosophy which integrates the disparate activities and functions which take place within the organization. Satisfied customers are seen as the only source of the firm's profit, growth and security. The second meaning of marketing is as a distinct set of activities and tasks which constitute marketing planning and decision making.

These marketing decisions and plans centre around four areas and they are the subjects of this chapter.

■ *Market segmentation.* Management have to segment the markets in which they operate, research the needs of customers in these segments, and study their characteristics, decision-making processes and buying behaviour.

■ *Selecting target markets.* The attractiveness of the different segments in terms of profit and growth have to be analyzed, and those offering the firm the best potential need to be chosen.

■ *Market positioning.* Once a segment is chosen, the firm has to seek to build a differential advantage which will make its offer preferred to those of competitors. It will then develop a marketing mix to implement this positioning strategy.

■ *Marketing planning.* Management will then develop a plan to implement the positioning strategy and build an organization capable of exploiting the potential of the market.

Figure 3.1 describes the main steps in market segmentation, targeting, positioning and planning. Whereas the philosophy of marketing refers to the whole orientation of the firm, marketing planning and decision making take place at a more disaggregated level. Marketing decisions are about how better to satisfy customers in individual market segments. These decisions and plans are therefore made by managers at the business unit, market or product planning levels of the firm.

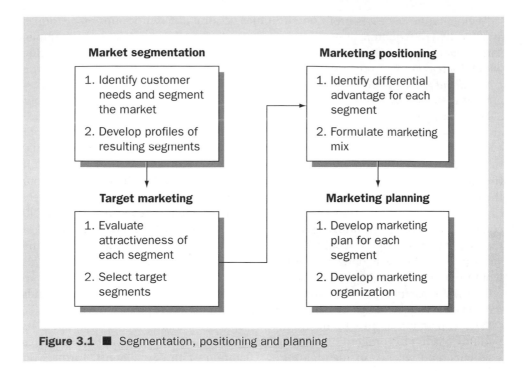

Figure 3.1 ■ Segmentation, positioning and planning

Market segmentation

A market consists of customers with similar needs. But customers in a market are never homogeneous. They differ in the benefits wanted, the amount they are able or willing to pay, the media they see and the quantities they buy. It therefore makes sense for marketers to segment the market and target one or more of these segments with specialized, tailored offerings. A market segment is a customer group within the market that has special characteristics which are significant for marketing strategy. In most markets the need for segmented offerings is obvious because a single product will not satisfy all the customers. For example, rich people want more luxurious hotel accommodation than poor; engineering offices need more powerful and sophisticated computing systems than secretarial offices; acute asthma patients need different drugs from mild or infrequent sufferers.

The current Nike catalogue carries 347 separate varieties of trainer. Philips produces 24 different irons and 13 kettles. The drug retailer Boots carries 240 varieties of shampoo and 75 kinds of toothbrush, not taking into account colour variations. That people have different tastes is fairly obvious. What managers often do not understand, however, is that it can pay to segment markets even when a single product is able to meet effectively the needs of the entire market.

Segmentation increases profit opportunities because different groups of customers attach different economic or psychological values to the solution offered. For example, some years ago a European chemical company developed a new patented herbicide which increased the productivity of any type of farm land. However, in practice, the *economic value to the customer* (EVC) of this innovation depended upon what the farmer grew. If the land was used for rough grazing, the EVC of the productivity improvement averaged only £5 per acre; for cereal products the EVC was £20 per acre; and for fruit and vegetables it was £50 per acre. Suppose the market consisted of 3 million acres split evenly between the three crops. If the company decides to sell the herbicide to the market as a whole, the price must be below £5 to give any advantage on grazing land. If the company charged £4 and its costs were as shown in Table 3.1, then the profit from the market would be £1 million. An alternative strategy would be to concentrate solely on the high-productivity fruit and vegetable farmers where it believed a price of £40 could be obtained. Even though the company would be focusing on only one-third of the market, this strategy would increase the profit potential to £35 million. The strategy with the most potential, however, would be a differentiated strategy. This would involve selling different versions of the product to each segment at prices to attract the separate types of customer. In this case the company would have brands covering the whole market, but still tap the value surplus in the premium segments.

The company's ability to maintain this strategy would depend first upon its building barriers to competition entering the market and, in particular, the high-price segments, and second on maintaining a separation of three segments. Farmers on premium land must continue to see the brand aimed at the low-value land as unattractive for them. In practice, the supplier would seek to do this by focusing its innovative effort to produce an even more superior product for the highest-value segment. Market segmentation is a spur to innovation by revealing hidden profit opportunities that can be won by better meeting the needs of specific high-value customer groups.

Core segmentation: an illustration

To demonstrate the central role of segmentation in building growth and profitability, the strategy of a modern airline can be shown. In the early days, airlines did not segment their market. But it soon became clear that passengers differ in their expectations. Business travellers valued convenience, comfort and service, while leisure passengers were more interested in low price. Table 3.2 illustrates the pricing and cost options for a carrier flying from London to New York using a 300-seater plane and anticipating an average load factor of 80 per cent. If it pursued an undifferentiated – one-class – plane, then management believed £250 to be the highest price chargeable to achieve 80 per cent occupancy. In this case the budgeted profit from the trip would be £5,200.

However, to the marketing management it was obvious that, while a price of £250 already begins to lose the business of low-budget travellers, business people and more affluent customers would be willing to pay much more for superior service and comfort. The result was that airlines moved to a differentiated strategy whereby they offered

Table 3.1 ■ Segmentation of agricultural chemicals

Strategy	Price (£)	Acres (m)	Revenue (£m)	Cost[1] (£m)	Profit (£m)
Undifferentiated	4	3	12	11	1
Focus	40	1	40	5	35
Differentiated					
– grazing	4	1	4	3.67	0.33
– cereal	15	1	15	3.67	11.33
– fruit	40	1	40	3.67	36.33
Total		3	59	11.01	47.99

[1]Variable cost per unit = £3; total fixed costs = £2m

Table 3.2 ■ Segmentation of airline passengers

Class	Passengers	Price (£)	Variable cost (£)	Revenue (£)	Variable cost (£)	Fixed cost (£)	Profit (£)
Undifferentiated strategy							
	240	250	20	60,000	4,800	50,000	5,200
Differentiated strategy							
Economy	144	250	20	36,000	2,880		
Business	72	500	40	36,000	2,880		
First	24	1,000	100	24,000	2,400		
Total	240			96,000	8,160	50,000	37,840

three levels of service on the plane – economy, business and first class – at very different price levels. As shown in Table 3.2, the first consequence is massively to enhance revenue and profitability. Second, the differentiated service better meets the needs of all customers by offering the values that the particular type of passenger prioritizes.

This example of airline segmentation is exactly analogous to the strategies pursued by most of the sophisticated marketing companies of today, as a few examples can demonstrate.

■ *Scotch whisky*. Until the 1980s Scotch was an undifferentiated market. Then Guinness-owned United Distillers, which sold the brand leader Johnnie Walker Red (priced at about £9 per litre), launched a deluxe version called Johnnie Walker Black at an 80 per cent price premium (£16 per litre), selling to status-oriented customers. Later it added Johnnie Walker Swing (£30), Premier (£70), Blue (£90) and Johnnie Walker Honour (£129). In a market which is static in volume terms, United Distillers' profits have exploded.

- *Credit cards*. Initially, credit cards operated in a largely undifferentiated market. Then American Express launched its Gold Card with a membership fee of £100, double that of its standard Green Card. Subsequently, it added a Platinum Card with a £300 membership fee. Amex substantially increased its profits by trading up its more affluent customers into higher-margin products.

- *Pharmaceuticals*. Pharmaceutical companies have become more adept at segmenting their markets and targeting offers that more precisely meet patient needs and capitalize on opportunities to add value. Glaxo, which is leader in the £3 billion a year asthma market, now segments patients into severe, moderate and variable sufferers. Prices range from £9 per month's treatment to £60 for the highly specialized products needed by acute patients.

- *Cars*. The market for cars is highly segmented. Mercedes Benz, for example, has twenty models from under £16,000 to over £90,000. Each model also has an extensive range of options: different-sized engines, different gears, sports equipment, air conditioning, etc. Every model is aimed at a specific target segment and the company encourages customers to trade up over time to higher-priced versions.

- *Others*. The list of markets where the leading players pursue segmented strategies is virtually limitless. It is pursued by the top hotel chains, restaurants, the railways, in marketing seats for the opera, by football clubs, in selling beer and wine, computers, educational programmes, electronics, etc. It is a feature of all consumer markets and more and more industrial and service markets. A price ratio of 1:10 from the lowest to the highest-priced offer in a segmented market is common.

Why segment markets?

Better matching of customer needs

Because the needs of customers differ, creating separate offers for each segment provides better solutions. For example, if an airline treated all passengers alike, business people would be unhappy with the level of service provided for the 'average' customer, and impecunious students would be unhappy about the average price they had to pay. Developing separate 'brands' for each segment allows a higher level of satisfaction for both.

Enhanced profits

Customers differ in their price sensitivities and, by segmenting the market, the marketer can raise average prices and substantially enhance profits. Experience shows that in most markets it is very difficult to raise prices to *all* customers by 5 per cent. However, it is often very easy to raise prices to *some* customers by 10 per cent or more. Price increases and profit margin enhancements are invariably best achieved via a segmentation strategy. Many production-oriented businesses fail to see this.

Three arguments are used to resist profitable segmentation. First, managers are discouraged by the additional costs of producing multiple, rather than single, product offerings. Second, they perceive the volume in the additional premium segment as small compared to their current mass-market offer. Third, they often argue that the additional brand would cannibalize sales from their current product.

What the managers fail to calculate is that the marginal revenue often vastly outweighs these negative factors. For example, after United Distillers launched its premium brands of Johnnie Walker Scotch, while they represented only 20 per cent of the volume of its mass Red Label brand, and did in fact cannibalize some of its sales, the much bigger margins on the premium brands were estimated as doubling the profits of the business.

Enhanced opportunities for growth

Segmentation can build sales growth. For example, if the airlines had not segmented their cabins, then the high-margin business travellers would have been creamed off by specialist airlines and the economy segment by charter and discount operators. Segmentation can also build profit growth by allowing the company to trade up customers to higher-margin products. American Express, Mercedes Benz and United Distillers all see their low-price offers as entry-level brands from which customers will be encouraged to move on to the premium ones, carrying margins two or three times higher.

Retention of customers

As an individual's circumstances change with age, family circumstances and income, his or her buying patterns change. For example, in the car market an individual's first car is usually a small, low-priced one; then with a family, a bigger car is needed. If he or she is successful in career terms, this may be followed by an expensive, status car. Finally, in retirement the individual may downsize again. By offering products appropriate to each family life cycle stage, the marketer can retain customers who would otherwise switch to competitive brands.

Targeted communications

It is difficult for a company to deliver a clear message to a broad, undifferentiated market. Effective communications require a demonstration that an offer will meet the relevant needs of the potential buyer. This is much easier to achieve if the marketer is targeting a homogeneous market segment.

Stimulation of innovation

Where the company pursues an undifferentiated marketing strategy, needs and prices are reduced to the lowest common denominator. Segmentation offers a clearer understanding of how needs and economic value to customers vary across the market. This is illustrated in Table 3.1. The average profit margin of only £1 in the undifferentiated market is insufficient to encourage investment in innovation. When the market is segmented, however, new profit opportunities appear. In certain segments the potential profit margin rises to £36 – an enormous reward for new targeted offerings.

Market segment share

Unless a brand is the biggest, or second biggest, in terms of share, it is unlikely to be profitable. Minor brands suffer from lack of scale economies in production and marketing, and pressures from distributors with limited space. These factors mean that they have higher costs and lower margins. Clearly, new or smaller companies are unlikely to achieve leadership in a total market, so they need to aim for leadership in a segment or distribution channel. By focusing, they can often achieve competitive production and marketing costs, and become the preferred choice of buyers in a specific segment.

It is generally share rather than size which determines profitability. It is invariably better to have 50 per cent of a £1 million market segment than 1 per cent of a £100 million market. The 1 per cent brand would not be the preferred choice of any customers or channels; it will have high marketing costs, lack scale economies and have to give big trade discounts to obtain distribution. By contrast, the 50 per cent brand will be the preferred choice of a segment of the market; it can focus its communications and be a 'must-stock' item to selected dealers. Segmentation offers the opportunity for smaller firms to compete with major ones.

Bases for segmentation

How should managers segment their markets so that tailored strategies can be developed? Unfortunately, segmentation is an art rather than a science. The task is to find the variable or variables which split the market into actionable segments. Segmentation variables are of two types: needs and profilers. Customer *needs* are the basic criteria for segmenting a market. The marketer will want to form segments made up of customers whose needs are homogeneous – who are seeking the same benefits – and so are likely to respond similarly to a particular marketing offer and strategy. The second type of segmentation variables are *profilers*. These are descriptive, measurable customer characteristics such as industry, geographic location, nationality, age and income. In general, these variables are complementary to each other. For example, a company marketing toothpaste divided the market into four need segments: one seeking low price, another prioritizing decay prevention, a third interested in bright teeth, and a fourth wanting a good-tasting toothpaste.[1] The problem with this need or 'benefit segmentation' is that, to analyze these segments and communicate to them, the marketer has to know who these people are: their profiles or customer characteristics. Table 3.3 shows the results of a market research study which linked needs to profilers describing the demographic, behavioural and psychological characteristics of the customers, together with competitors in each need segment.

Consumer and industrial markets generally differ in their sets of need and profiler variables. Some of the most common segmentation variables in each are described below.

Table 3.3 ■ Needs and profiles in the toothpaste market

Need segments	Profiles			
	Demographics	**Behaviour**	**Psychographic**	**Competitive brands**
Economy (low price)	Men	Heavy users	Value oriented	Brands on sale
Medical (decay prevention)	Large families	Heavy users	Conservative	Crest
Cosmetic (bright teeth)	Teenagers	Smokers	Active	Macleans Ultra Brite
Taste (good tasting)	Children	Spearmint lovers	Hedonistic	Colgate Aim

Source: Russell J. Haley, 'Benefit segmentation: a decision-oriented research tool', *Journal of Marketing*, July 1963, pp. 30–5

Consumer market segmentation

To find the needs of customers in a market, it is necessary to undertake market research. This will normally consist first of informal interviews and focus groups to identify what benefits customers seek and the extent of differences among them in their expectations. For example, are some giving the highest priority to low price, while others are emphasizing image or product performance? The next step will normally be administering a formal questionnaire to a large sample of customers to quantify these differences in requirements. There are a variety of statistical techniques such as discriminant analysis and cluster analysis to help in choosing the best variables for segmenting the market.[2] Often the market will be divided into quality, service, performance and economy oriented segments.

The next step will be to seek to link these differences in needs to profilers or consumer characteristics. The survey questionnaire should have collected data on both the needs sought and the characteristics of respondents. The most common profilers used in consumer market segmentation are as follows:

■ *Geographic*
  - Region of the country
  - Urban or rural area

■ *Demographic*
  - Age, sex, family size
  - Income, occupation, education
  - Religion, race, nationality

■ *Psychographic*
  – Social class
  – Lifestyle type
  – Personality type

■ *Behavioural*
  – Product usage: light, medium, heavy user
  – Brand loyalty: none, medium, high
  – Type of user: e.g. with meals, special occasions, etc.

Organizational market segmentation

The process of segmentation in industrial and other organizational markets is analogous to that employed in consumer markets. First management have to segment the market by benefits sought, then they have to describe the characteristics of these customers. The needs of organizational customers depend upon their strategy, their operating environments and the personal characteristics and relationships of the individual buyers within the organization. For example, a buyer in a static, commodity business is likely to be highly cost oriented. An organization in a dynamic, high value-added segment may be geared more to the performance-enhancing features of the product or the seller's speed of response.

The most common profilers in organizational markets are as follows:

■ Industry of end user (e.g. agriculture, aerospace, construction).

■ Organizational type (e.g. public or private sector).

■ Size of organization (e.g. big or small, national or multinational).

■ Geographical location (e.g. region, urban, rural).

■ Application (e.g. heavy or light use).

■ Usage (e.g. heavy or light user; loyal or non-loyal).

■ Purchasing organization (e.g. centralized or decentralized, purchasing policy and criteria, nature of decision-making unit).

In commodity-type markets, managers often make the mistake of thinking that all customers are the same, in their desire to get the lowest possible price. But such a view is invariably mistaken and costly. Studies by McKinsey and others have shown that even in these markets customers normally divide into three segments.[3] The first are *price-sensitive buyers* who are primarily concerned with the cost – and less so with the quality – of their purchases. Price is crucial because the product usually represents a major portion of their total product costs. Next is the *service segment* – customers who require the highest levels of quality and delivery performance. For them, price is secondary both to security of supply and to performance, as the product represents a relatively small, yet critical component of their total costs. Finally, *commitment-focused customers* value close, longstanding relationships through which superior product applications can be developed for their own products and processes. Such segmentation offers real opportunities to increase sales, achieve better profit margins and gradually reposition the business into more attractive markets.

Multilevel segmentation

Effective segmentation is not only about grouping customers according to need. Further opportunities lie in distinguishing the nature of the *decision-making unit* within any customer. In many situations there is not a single buyer whose needs have to be met, but several people whose needs may differ. There are often opportunities for the seller to target specific persons within any decision-making unit.

In consumer markets, a family's choices can be influenced by husband, wife or children, together with others outside the household who influence them. Each individual often has different buying criteria and roles in the buying decision. For example, in buying a new car the husband might initiate the process and be primarily influenced by economic factors; the children might affect the model choice and be motivated by performance; and the wife might be the main user and consider size and comfort as key factors.

Companies can often gain advantage by innovative strategies to target specific members of the decision-making unit. For example, Stew Leonard created the supermarket with the highest sales per square foot in the world. He noticed that mothers often had to take young children with them on their shopping trips. He redesigned his store with mini-shows, exhibits and Disney characters to appeal to young children and take the boredom out of shopping. Shopping became a fun experience for mothers with young families. Mothers drove with their young children for as long as two and a half hours to shop at Stew Leonard's.

In industrial markets, decision-making units and buying processes are even more complex, offering enormous opportunities for creative marketing. Typically a minimum of three parties can be involved in a purchasing process – the company's buyers, technical department and senior management. Each of these have different needs and purchasing criteria – normally price is the key factor for buyers, performance and specifications for technical people, and economic value (the impact on profits) for top management.

With a new, innovative industrial product or service it is often crucial to circumvent the control of the buying department so that the system economics can be demonstrated to top management. For example, a new machine might reduce labour costs in a production process by 50 per cent, offering a massive profit improvement for the customer, even though the machine costs 30 per cent more than those of the competitors. However, the customers' buying department would be deterred by the high price of the new machine. Many suppliers lack the sales expertise to overcome this problem, which requires attracting the interest of top management in the impact of the innovation on their return on investment. (This is discussed further in Chapter 8.)

Meeting customer needs and providing customer value require market segmentation. But meeting needs and providing value are not simple. They entail an understanding in depth of the customer's decision-making unit and buying processes. The supplier has to ask who influences the purchasing decision and what are the specific needs of each group. It then needs to assess the value and cost of meeting these various needs. Often this will require choices – should it focus on meeting the needs of professional buyers for lower costs, or on the needs of senior management for higher business performance? The choice will depend upon the skills of the company and the characteristics of its products or services. Finally, the supplier has to have the skills to communicate the benefits to the desired personnel within the buying centre.

Criteria for segmentation

To be a strategic tool, a segmentation scheme should meet five criteria:

■ *Effective*. The segments identified should consist of customers whose needs are relatively homogeneous within a segment, but significantly different from those in other segments. For example, an industrial marketer might identify the engineering and aerospace industries as separate segments, but if buyers in both industries purchase similar amounts at similar prices and have the same needs, it is not a useful segmentation scheme.

■ *Identifiable*. The business must be able to identify customers in the proposed segment. Some variables are harder to measure. For example, if a product is aimed at 'extrovert' customers, it would be difficult to identify and measure the size of this potential segment. To be useful, it is necessary to find some customer characteristics which link to the psychological profiles, such as age, media usage or nationality.

■ *Profitable*. The more segments identified, the greater the opportunity to target the offer precisely and to add value. Ultimately, each customer could be an individual segment. However, the greater the number of segments targeted, the higher the cost involved in separately targeting offers, and the greater the loss of economies of scale in manufacturing, marketing and distribution. Nevertheless, with the spread of CAD/CAM flexible manufacturing and with the growth of direct marketing techniques, more and more businesses are finding that narrower segmentation pays off.

■ *Accessible*. Customers in the segment should be capable of being reached and served effectively. For example, if it is decided to advertise a new industrial product to innovative buyers, and it is found that such buyers read the same journals as late adopters, then a substantial part of the advertising budget would be wasted. Such a segment is not amenable to separate communications.

■ *Actionable*. A company must be able to take advantage of the segmentation scheme that it develops. A small petrol station might divide its customers into several segments with different potential needs and spending power, but it would probably lack the staff, space and facilities to respond to these differences. By contrast, a large petrol station might have the opportunity to pursue such a differentiated strategy. For example, US stations provide both 'self-service' economy and 'full-service' premium offers to customers. With the latter, the attendant fills the tank and provides a check on the car's oil, tyres and windscreen, in return for a 20 per cent premium on the price of the petrol.

Dynamic targeting strategies

Choosing target market segments

After segmenting the market, the business must select those segments it aims to target. Five factors govern the attractiveness of the segment:

- Segment size.
- Segment growth.
- Profitability of the segment.
- Current and potential competition.
- Capabilities of the business.

In developing a segmentation strategy, management have several strategic choices.

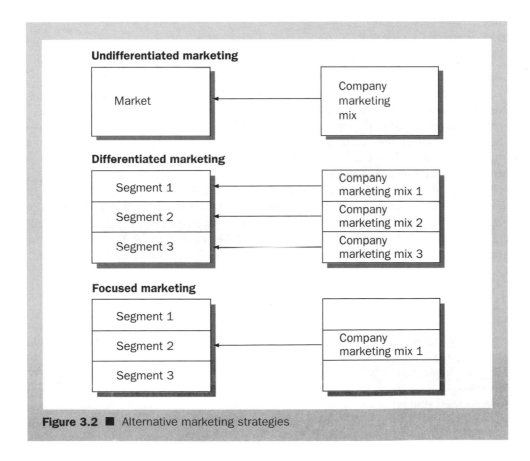

Figure 3.2 ■ Alternative marketing strategies

Undifferentiated marketing

Here the firm ignores actual or potential differences among segments, and targets one offer to the entire market (Figure 3.2). It designs a product and marketing mix which will appeal to the mass market. In the early days of their industries, Ford, Volkswagen, Coca-Cola, British Airways and Woolworths pursued this strategy. Coca-Cola, for example, had one drink, in one bottle size, with one taste, and sold at one price, which aimed to suit everyone.

The advantages of a single offer are economies of scale in production, distribution, advertising, marketing and inventories. However today, two factors make undifferentiated marketing strategies rarely optimal. First, as we have seen, customers are increasingly heterogeneous in their needs. They differ in benefits wanted, purchasing power, values, media and buying characteristics. For example, Coca-Cola is now sold in as many as nine varieties and six sizes of bottle and can: that is, it offers a total of up to 54 combinations. Second, even when needs are the same across segments, the value that customers attach to an offer varies and so, as has been shown, the opportunities for profitable product and price discrimination exist.

Differentiated marketing

As with undifferentiated marketers, differentiators seek to compete across the majority of the market, but here they do so with different offers. They develop different products and marketing programmes for each segment of the market. They seek to fine-tune their offers to the specific needs of each customer group and to capitalize on value differences by charging different prices. Thus an airline segments its cabin into different classes of customers; a whisky company sells higher-priced brands to Japan than it does to Spain; expensive laboratory equipment is targeted at the pharmaceutical industry rather than the jute industry.

Because differentiated marketing is better at satisfying disparate customers, it normally leads to higher average prices and greater sales volumes. But it also leads to higher costs of production, marketing, promotion and administration. Management have to choose the most profitable level of segmentation which balances the increasing revenue that segmentation offers against the increasing costs that it incurs.

Focused marketing

Here the company does not aim to compete in the majority of the market, but rather specializes in one segment, or a small number of segments. When the segment is small, the company is often termed a *niche* competitor. Small companies generally have no alternative but to pursue this strategy, since they lack the resources to compete across the market.

A focused strategy permits the firm to achieve efficient production, distribution and marketing through specializing its investments. It allows the business to build a strong reputation from its expertise in understanding the specific requirements of buyers in this segment. Also, by focusing, it can build a strong share, making it the preferred choice of buyers and distributors serving these customers. A well-focused strategy permits a competitor to achieve both low costs and high prices.

Focused strategies, however, do have dangers and limitations in the long run. First, by tying itself to the fortunes of one segment, the company incurs high risks. Jaguar's dependence on sales to the US luxury car market led to its collapse and acquisition by Ford, when this segment declined during the recession of the early 1990s. Second, if the segment is growing and profitable, it is likely to attract the attention of bigger competitors. This is a particular danger when product life cycles shorten and companies have to invest heavily in new product development. Larger competitors can often afford investments that smaller players cannot match, and they can transfer technologies from other segments to obtain leverage in cost and innovation.

Innovative segmentation

Market segments are not fixed. Instead continual opportunities for creating new profitable segments are being opened by changes in the environment and new knowledge. Environmental changes – rising incomes, demographic changes, fashion and new concerns – continually create new customer needs. New knowledge and technologies at the same time offer new opportunities to meet these needs. The potential profit and growth opportunities that these represent mean that looking for new ways to segment markets should be a top concern of managers.

For example, the airlines have conventionally segmented their cabins into economy-, business- and first-class customers. The economy class is the largest and lowest-margin segment. Recently, Virgin Airways noted that the economy class was in fact a very heterogeneous segment. While the average seat price was £300 on an Atlantic crossing, some last-minute and standby passengers were paying under £100, while other passengers were paying full-fare economy tickets costing almost £500. Yet all economy-class customers were in similar seats, receiving the same service. As a result, Virgin decided to segment its economy class, creating a new 'mid class' aimed at full-fare economy passengers. Virgin would make itself more attractive to this segment by offering a separate 'cabin', better food, a separate check-in and other service enhancements.

Creating new segments which add new customers or trade up current ones is a regular strategy pursued by expert marketers. Häagen-Dazs developed a premium segment for ice cream in the UK, selling at prices triple those for the mass market. Castrol developed a new segment in the US lubricant market, selling high-priced synthetic oil for drivers of high-performance, European cars. British Airports Authority recently segmented its long-term car park into tourist (£12 per day) and executive (£20 per day).

Segmentation over time

Opportunities for segmentation tend to increase as a market evolves. Industry-wide sales statistics suggest, erroneously, that a market grows or declines uniformly. For

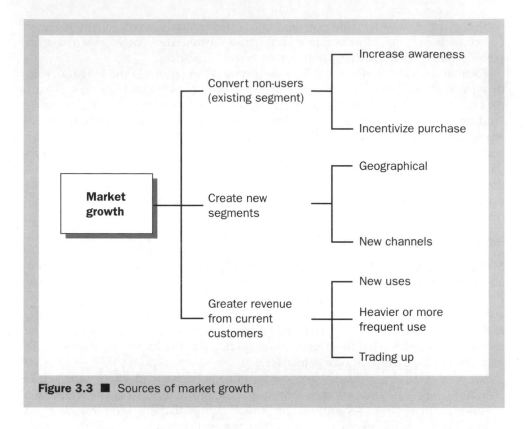

Figure 3.3 ■ Sources of market growth

example, industry statistics show that personal computer sales grew by 55 per cent per annum during the 1980s. Cigarette sales in northern Europe, on the other hand, declined by 3 per cent a year. But such broad trends are useless and even misleading for the firm. A market grows (or declines) in three ways (Figure 3.3). The most obvious way is by attracting new customers as they become aware of the product and are incentivized to purchase it. But more important to the long-term growth of the market is the attraction of new market segments, through the addition of different types of customer both nationally and internationally. For example, in the early years, the growth of the computer market was fuelled by more scientific customers being attracted, but then sales really boomed when a second segment – large business organizations – started using computers. Growth was further increased by the addition of a third segment – small businesses. Later, households and then students began to be attracted to the market. Figure 3.4 shows how a market grows by the addition of new market segments. The third way markets grow is by existing customers spending more on the product. This occurs when new uses are found for it, people become heavier or more frequent users, or they are encouraged to trade up to higher-priced models.

Consequently, even in growth markets the firm must change radically to grow. It must first shift resources out of maturing market segments into the new emerging

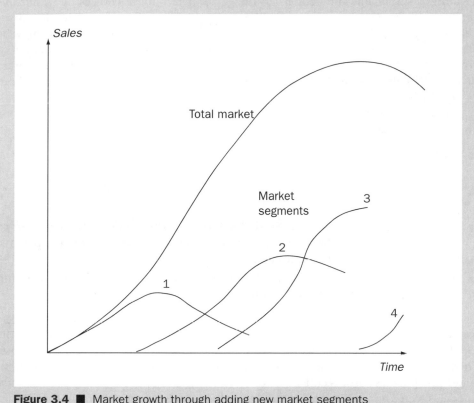

Figure 3.4 ■ Market growth through adding new market segments

ones. This means learning about the new customers and developing new products and distribution channels. Second, it must look to trade up existing customers, find new uses or encourage more frequent application of the product, by discovering new means of adding value. Unless management explore these two avenues, the firm will get trapped into declining, increasingly commodity-oriented segments. Analogously, creative marketers can still find buoyant growth segments even in mature or declining total markets. In today's highly fragmented markets, it makes more sense to talk about growing or declining companies than about growing or declining markets.

 Creating the differential advantage

The choice of target market segments determines where the business will compete. But other firms will also be seeking to compete in these segments, and customers will choose whom to support. The key task of management in competitive markets is creating a sustainable differential advantage to attract these choices. A *sustainable differential advantage* is a perceived difference which leads customers in the target segment to prefer one company's offer to those of others. The difference may be based upon a product which is perceived superior, has better service support, or offers a lower price. Where a firm creates a differential advantage, it achieves higher market share and higher profits, and has the ability to defend itself against an attack from competitors.

To be a sustainable differential advantage, any difference the firm obtains must meet four criteria:

■ *Customer benefit*. The difference must be seen by customers as offering some important benefit to them.

■ *Unique*. The benefit must be seen as not obtainable in a similar way from other companies.

■ *Sustainable*. The advantage must be difficult to copy. There must be some barriers to entry in the form of difficult to acquire skills, scale economies, branding or patents, to prevent the differential being rapidly eroded.

■ *Profitable*. The firm must be able to offer the product or service with a price, cost and volume structure which makes it profitable to produce.

Searching for a differential advantage begins with understanding what customers value. To a customer, value is the utility or total satisfaction he or she perceives the product offering, less the price to be paid for it, and less the other operating costs incurred over the life of the product. For example, a company chairman may have agreed to purchase an executive jet. In considering the options, the utility that any model is seen to offer would be influenced by the plane's size, the luxury of the fittings, range, speed, perceived image and so on. He will also take into account the price of the alternatives and what he can afford to spend. He is also likely to want to compare the other ownership and operating costs, such as maintenance, labour, insurance and depreciation. These ownership costs could easily exceed the price of the aircraft. The aircraft sales team will therefore need to research the factors constituting the prospect's utility function, his price of elasticity, and how important operating costs are rated in his buying equation.

The firm can create value for the customer by increasing the utility of the product (by offering features which are perceived as superior), by lowering the price, or by cutting other ownership costs. Higher ownership costs are normally a function of the product's design and so can be treated as part of the utility of the product. High ownership costs reduce utility; lower ownership costs act to enhance the attraction of the offer. The customer can then express his or her choice in the equation:

Value = Utility – Price

Besides offering superior value to the customer, the differential advantage must also be profitable to the firm. For the firm, the profit on a product can be expressed in the simple equation:

Profit = Price − Cost

These equations, expressing value to the customer and profit to the firm, show that there are three fundamental ways of creating a sustainable differential advantage. First, management can find ways of increasing utility without disproportionate increases in cost. Second, they can find ways of lowering costs without disproportionately lowering utility. Third, they can seek a new positioning in the market with different levels of both utility and price. The first two alternatives are discussed in this section and the last in the next section.

Drivers of utility

Utility is a traditional economist's word for the perceived satisfaction offered by consumption or ownership of the product or service. In much of the management literature it is often called 'quality'. Utility, perceived quality or customer satisfaction is always a combination of rational, economic factors and subjective image dimensions. In industrial markets characterized by professional buying, economic factors tend to dominate. Buyers choose sellers which they see as offering the most economic value. In consumer markets, the image conveyed by the brand will commonly play a major role. In services, the professionalism and empathy of the people representing the supplier often determine choice.

The factors which drive up the utility of an offer can conveniently be divided into four groups: product, service, personnel and image.

Product drivers

First, the physical product can be differentiated by design to make it perceived as better or cheaper to operate. The most important parameters for achieving a differential advantage are as follows:[4]

■ *Performance* – the level of the product's primary operating characteristics (e.g. speed, capacity, accuracy).

■ *Features* – the characteristics which are added to the primary function (e.g. a car can be augmented by sun roof, electric windows, stereo, air conditioning).

■ *Reliability* – the likelihood that the customer will have problems with the product.

■ *Conformance* – the degree to which the product's design and operating characteristics meet expected specifications.

■ *Durability* – the expected working life of the product.

■ *Operating costs* – the costs of operating the product over its life (e.g. installation, energy consumption, labour, insurance).

■ *Serviceability* – the facility with which a product can be repaired.

■ *Aesthetics* – how the product looks and feels to the buyer.

Services drivers

Services which augment the product have become increasingly important differentiators, as competition narrows product differences. The main service differentiators are as follows:

■ *Credit and finance*. Grants, loans, terms and conditions can add to the product's appeal.

■ *Ordering facilities* – the ease or efficiency with which customers can order the product.

■ *Delivery* – the speed and effectiveness with which the order is delivered to the customer. Generally people will pay more for a fast and reliable service.

■ *Installation* – the facility with which the product is put into working order for the customer.

■ *Training and consulting* – additional help and support offered to the customer.

■ *After-sales service* – the quality of its maintenance and back-up support.

■ *Guarantees*. Comprehensive guarantees may eliminate perceived purchase risks.

■ *Operational support*. A variety of services can be offered to reduce the customer's cost structure or enhance its marketing effectiveness.

Personnel drivers

Company personnel have become a valuable source of differential advantage, especially in service-oriented markets. High-quality personal service is difficult for competitors to copy because it is so dependent upon the hard-to-change culture of the company, and the skill of the management in empowering and motivating the front-line staff. The key attributes of people who add value through personal service are as follows:

■ *Professional*. They need the training to acquire the required skills and knowledge.

■ *Courtesy*. Customers expect politeness and consideration.

■ *Trustworthy*. Staff should be honest and credible.

■ *Reliable*. Customers want service which is accurate and consistent.

■ *Positive*. People want to deal with staff who believe they can overcome most practical difficulties.

■ *Responsive*. Staff should respond fast to customer requests and problems.

■ *Initiative*. They should be capable of using their initiative to solve customer problems and not have to refer small matters to superiors.

■ *Communication*. Personnel need to be able to understand customers and provide information to them effectively.

Image drivers

The image of the company or its brand should be a major source of differential advantage. Numerous experiments in many different product fields have shown that, while in blind product tests customers cannot differentiate between alternatives, once a well-known company or brand name is attached, they will not only choose this brand, but also be willing to pay more for it. A strong image gives the customer *confidence* in the product. This confidence value may be in the socio-psychological utility of the brand or in its economic performance.

Socio-psychological confidence is created when the customer perceives the brand as enabling him or her to make a positive personal or social statement. For example, young people see Coca-Cola, Levi jeans, Sony Walkman and Nike running shoes as consistent with the lifestyles they wish to express. Older people may turn to BMW cars, Rolex watches and Hermes scarves. *Economic* confidence is achieved when a brand or company name creates an image of reliability, performance or value. Many customers feel reassured by the Marks & Spencer label, the General Electric name or the Mercedes logo on a product.

The main approaches to creating value through image enhancement are as follows:

- *Reality*. The best way of creating confidence in a product is by the previous three factors – superior product performance, better services and top-quality personnel. Confidence, and consequently image, are based primarily upon satisfaction with using a company's product and services and dealing with its people. Without the reality of value being present, it is virtually impossible to create the image of it.

- *Advertising and related media*. These can articulate, clarify and reinforce the brand image or personality that the company wishes to present. Advertising and promotion can speed up the recognition of a company's real performance advantage. They can make customers aware of the offer, understand it and eventually try it. Other vehicles which help to convey and reinforce image are logos, colour, personal endorsements, exhibitions, public relations and events.

Cost drivers

It is crucial for management to look for ways of lowering costs without lowering utility. Some strategic thinkers postulate two alternatives open to the firm: competition based upon cost and competition based upon differentiation. But this choice is artificial. Today a company needs both low costs and utility-enhancing differentiation. Low costs permit the firm to create a differential advantage through either cutting the price to customers, or investing more in product, services, personnel or image improvements which offer them value, or both.

The first step is a cost analysis to determine the cost structure of the product or business unit. Most costing systems are poor at allocating costs realistically to individual business units, products and customers. Traditional accounting rules of thumb often give a misleading picture of the true profitability of the different businesses. More recently, activity-based costing has been introduced by more progressive firms to give a better picture.[5] Unless they allocate costs realistically, management lack the information rationally to improve efficiency.

Suppose a line of machine tools has the cost structure shown in Table 3.4 and generates a profit margin of 5 per cent. The company will want to assess the competitiveness

Table 3.4 ■ Profit and cost structure of a business

Revenue	100
Purchased materials	25
Manufacturing	15
R & D	5
Sales and distribution	15
Marketing	15
Central overheads	20
Profit margin	5

of its cost structure and how its costs could be brought down without sacrificing the quality of its product, service and image. Whether a company's costs are higher or lower than its rivals depends upon where it stands in relation to the following cost drivers:[6]

■ *Economies of scale.* Larger-volume competitors have the opportunity to operate at lower costs and to amortize fixed expenses such as R & D and advertising over a greater sales level.

■ *Experience.* Cost can decline over time due to learning that increases the firm's efficiency.

■ *Capacity utilization.* Firms operating their activities at full capacity will have lower costs.

■ *Linkages.* The level of certain costs can be influenced by other costs. For example, a company might spend more than competitors in purchasing high-quality materials, but this might be more than offset by lower manufacturing and service costs. Higher costs in one area therefore do not necessarily mean inefficiency.

■ *Interrelationships.* Where a product or a business unit shares costs (e.g. R & D, ordering processes) with sister units, costs can be reduced.

■ *Integration.* Vertical integration, where the firm undertakes tasks normally done by outside contractors (e.g. transportation), may lower total costs.

■ *Timing.* Being first in the market may give rise to a cost advantage. It is often cheaper to build a brand name at the start, and early experience may give subsequent cost advantage.

■ *Location.* Different operating bases also affect the relative cost of labour, management and materials.

■ *Institutional factors.* Tax rates, trade union practices, local content rules and government regulations can all affect the relative cost advantage of the business.

■ *Marketing strategy.* The utility-enhancing factors that the firm employs will also influence its costs. If it is adding multiple product features and value-added services, it will have higher costs which it anticipates recouping by higher prices or greater volume.

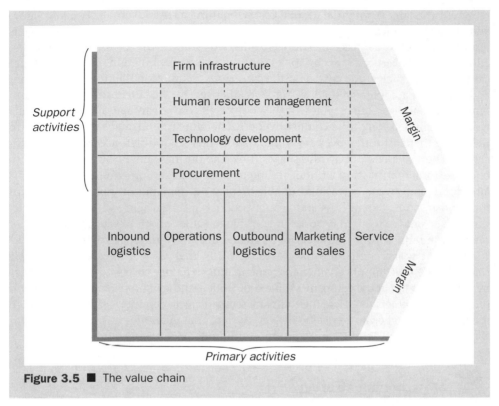

Figure 3.5 ■ The value chain

Value chain

One of the most useful tools for analyzing utility and cost drivers and the relationship between both is the value chain. The value chain describes how the activities of the business contribute to its tasks of designing, producing, delivering, communicating and supporting its product. The value chain of a business (Figure 3.5) consists of two types of activity which create value for customers. The *primary value activities* consist of bringing materials into the business, transforming them into products, distributing them, marketing and servicing them. The *support activities* underpin the primary activities by providing the purchased inputs, developing the technology used in the product and processes, hiring, developing and motivating the firm's personnel, and producing the infrastructure activities such as general management, finance and planning.

Each of the nine elements of the value chain can be a source of differential advantage. Management need to compare their value chain to those of their competitors. Managers can then analyze, first, whether costs can be reduced through cutting out non-value-adding activities. An analysis should reveal which value-added stages represent the largest potential of total cost. Obtaining a cost advantage in a key value-added stage can mean a significant competitive advantage, whether that advantage is used to support a low price or stronger differentiation. In the example of Table 3.4, cutting central overhead costs by 10 per cent suggests a profit margin increase of 40 per cent. However, such crude cuts make the dangerous assumption that these costs do not add value. In a company such as Marks & Spencer, for instance, the technical and buying skills in head office represent the company's core advantage, and arbitrary cuts would threaten its long-term competitiveness. Therefore careful analysis is necessary to judge whether cost differences are due to quality drivers or differences in relative efficiency. The value chain may also suggest how the business might be reconfigured to boost customer satisfaction without adding to costs. For example, Nestlé found that its large food plants were increasingly unable to meet the demands of supermarket groups for rapid response, small runs and greater product and packaging variety. By restructuring into smaller-focused factories, it was able to achieve both lower costs and higher satisfaction ratings from customers for its greater flexibility and speed of response.

In recent years, companies have extended this analysis to the concept of *supply chain management*. Supply chain management aims to reduce costs and increase quality by looking not just at the company's value chain, but at those of suppliers, distributors and ultimately customers too. Here the company seeks to create channel partners with which it can tailor a total customer value-delivery system that guarantees stringent standards for quality, on-time delivery and continuous improvement in costs and performance.

 ## Positioning strategy

It has been shown how a business can offer superior value by strategies which add value or reduce costs. The third way to enhance its competitiveness is through positioning itself more effectively. *Positioning strategy* is the choice of target market segments, which determines *where* the business competes, and the choice of differential advantage, which dictates *how* it competes.

A product or business unit may be inadequately positioned for three reasons. First, the segment in which it is targeted might have become unattractive because it is too small, declining, too competitive or otherwise unprofitable. Second, positioning might be inadequate because the quality and features that the product offers do not appeal to the segment to which it is targeted. Third, it might be wrong because the product's costs are too high to allow it to be priced competitively.

Figure 3.6 illustrates the structure of a typical market made up of four segments. Product X is inadequately positioned because it is too costly for the mass market and has insufficient perceived quality to appeal to the premium or luxury segments. The business has several repositioning options. The first two might be termed 'real' repositioning; the remainder are 'psychological' respositioning strategies.

■ *Introduce new brand.* After the declining price of personal computers in the 1990s threatened to oust IBM's high-priced machines from the market, the company

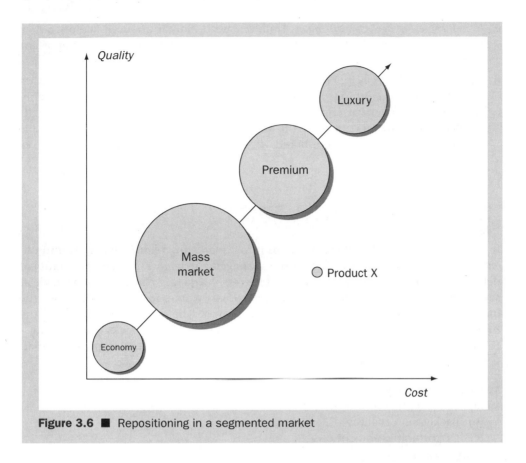

Figure 3.6 ■ Repositioning in a segmented market

introduced its own cheap 'clone' under the Ambra brand name and sourced from the Far East. The objective was to maintain a foothold in the booming mass and economy markets.

■ *Change existing brand.* Alternatively, a company may change its cost and utility combination to make it more appealing. In contrast to IBM, Compaq tried to solve the problem by cutting its prices and simplifying the features offered to hold on to a position in the mass market.

■ *Alter beliefs about the brand.* Chivas Regal Scotch whisky achieved some success in repositioning itself from the mass market to the premium segment, so rationalizing its higher price.

■ *Alter beliefs about competitive brands.* The Body Shop retail group succeeded in implying that the beauty and personal care products of competitors were not environmentally friendly.

■ *Alter attribute importance rates.* Volvo raised the importance of safety as an attribute in choosing a car, so enhancing the value of its differentiation.

■ *Introduce new or neglected attributes.* Unilever successfully introduced Radion, a new detergent which eliminated odours – a benefit previously not considered important by consumers.

■ *Find a new market segment.* When Dunhill diversified away from smoking accessories into the men's clothing market, rather than entering the already highly competitive segments it created a new luxury segment of very expensive, high-quality ready-to-wear suits. As the only 'typically British' competitor in this segment, it brought a unique brand with a strong appeal to affluent executives (especially Japanese!)

 The marketing plan

It is essential to formalize these decisions into a marketing plan. The plan communicates the objectives and strategy to the management team and permits a rational debate about the potential and chances of success. Marketing plans should be made at several levels in the business: for the company as a whole, for the divisions, for the business units, and at the product and market levels. The next chapter discusses the higher-level plans. This section summarizes the basic building blocks of marketing – the marketing plans for the individual products or target market segments. A marketing plan consists of seven integrated components:

1. Background analysis
   (a) Current performance
   (b) Background analysis
   (c) Opportunities and options

2. Marketing objectives
   (a) Marketing objectives
   (b) Financial objectives

3. Marketing strategy
   (a) Target market segments
   (b) Differential advantage

4. Marketing mix
   (a) Product
   (b) Price
   (c) Promotion
   (d) Distribution
   (e) Services
   (f) Staff

5. Action plans

6. Budget

7. Organizational implications

Background situation

The starting point of the plan assesses the health of the product or its position in a segment. It focuses on three questions. How well is it performing now? What factors have led to the current success or failure in the market place? Where is the business heading – do things look likely to improve or get wrorse? These questions are answered under the following headings.

Current performance

The two key measures of the health of the business at this level are marketing and financial results. Marketing performance is revealed in the sales and market share figures. Financial performance is shown by the performance of total profits, gross and net margins, return on capital employed and cash flow. These measures should be compared against major competitors and over the past five years. The results should be segregated by line of product and type of customer to exhibit the winners and losers in the portfolio. This section should conclude with a clear, unambiguous statement about whether current performance is good or bad, satisfactory or unsatisfactory.

Background

This section falls into two parts. The first accounts for current performance – how did we get here? The second seeks to project future performance on current assumptions about the environment and the policies of the business – where are we heading? Current performance has been determined by environmental changes affecting the market and by the effectiveness of past decisions taken by management. The background analysis should try and divide the explanation of current performance into these two components.

Environmental changes can again be split into macro- and micro-environmental changes. *Macro-environmental changes* refer to the broad shifts in economic conditions, demographics, technological, cultural and environmental forces which may have influenced performance either positively or negatively. For example, consumer durables and capital goods are strongly affected by the economic cycle.

Micro-environmental changes are those shifts which are specific to the market in which the business operates. In this section, the product or market manager will analyze the effects of changes in the behaviour of customers, distribution channels, competitive strategies, new products, prices and costs.

The environmental forces are largely outside the control of the firm. They are changes which the business must adapt to. The second set of factors which will have shaped current performance are the results of decisions that management took in the past. These include the objectives chosen, the strategies employed, and the product, price, promotion and distribution tactics. How appropriate were these decisions and how effectively were they implemented? Which of them were the critical factors in determining today's results?

The second part of the background analysis is to project a scenario of how the macro- and micro-environment of the business is likely to change, and to consider the implications. Then the appropriateness of the current goals and strategies of the business are assessed. The objective is to come to a conclusion about how bright the future of the business looks.

Opportunities and options

After describing the current situation and assessing the implications of the external and internal changes taking place, management should conduct a SWOT analysis. This requires listing and analyzing the main *strengths* of the business, its *weaknesses* and the likely *threats* and *opportunities* it will be facing in the future.

The next task is to identify clearly the key issues or options available to the business. Management will want to look at avenues which exploit the strengths and pursue the opportunities that have been identified. At the same time, they may wish to take action to counter the threats and weaknesses that have been perceived in the business. Options to be explored might be: shifting into a new market segment, adding new products, boosting service and quality levels, or diversification into other markets.

Marketing objectives

There will be two sets of objectives in the marketing plan: marketing and financial.

■ *Marketing goals*. The plan should have a clear sales goal. In addition, it is important to specify a market share target, since in high-growth markets adequate sales growth can disguise declining market share performance. Sales and share are the primary marketing objectives, but it is also useful to have intermediate goals covering customer satisfaction, loyalty, communications and distribution. These might include achieving target satisfaction scores, repurchase rates, certain awareness levels, target trial levels and aims for specific penetration levels among retailers and distributors.

■ *Financial goals*. The primary financial objectives will be profits, return on investment and cash flow. It is useful to break these down into convenient indices such as gross margin, return on sales, stock turnover and other managerial ratios which highlight important efficiency characteristics of the business.

It is important to set objectives because they can provide targets to stretch the endeavours of the management team and prevent complacency. They can also provide the means for evaluating the performance of a business and those who run it. To provide these benefits, however, the objectives need to meet certain criteria. First, they must be strategically relevant and consistent. For example, it would not generally make sense to have both ambitious sales growth objectives and high short-term cash generation targets for a new product. Second, the target should be reasonable. While it is important to set objectives which stretch management, they will not be motivating unless they are seen as attainable. Third, they should be measurable and unambiguous. For example, when the objectives are to be achieved should be made clear. Finally, they should be based upon reliable data. Many accounting systems allocate costs across products in ways which do not reflect their true loadings. For example, overhead costs often get allocated as a percentage of sales rather than as they are incurred. Such biases usually have the effect of undervaluing the gains made by successful products and disguising the true costs of poor ones.

Marketing strategy

The strategy to achieve the objectives is built around two cornerstones: the choice of target market segment or segments; and the choice of the differential advantage. These two comprise the positioning strategy of the business or the brand.

■ *Target market segment.* Here the plan will identify what types of customer the business is to aim for. The presentation will analyze their needs and profiles: what the customers expect, where they are, how and when they buy, and how they use the product.

■ *Differential advantage.* The plan will describe the competitors and their strategies, and present the company's own core strategy which will lead target customers to prefer and purchase its offer.

A clear statement of this positioning strategy is crucial because it defines all the ensuing decisions which implement the plan.

Marketing mix

The marketing mix is the set of marketing decisions that management make to implement their positioning strategy and achieve its objectives. These have popularly been termed the four Ps: product, price, promotion and place (i.e. distribution). Nowadays most managers would add two more decisions: service and staff. Each of these decisions is essentially a category under which a bundle of sub-decisions are needed. The main headings are as follows.

Product decisions	
■ Product variety	■ Product presentation
■ Product performance	■ Product packaging
■ Product features	■ Sizes
■ Product design	■ Brand name
Pricing decisions	
■ List price	■ Geographical pricing
■ Discounts	■ Payment terms
■ Allowances	■ Credit terms

Promotion	
■ Sales force	■ Consumer promotion
■ Advertising	■ Trade promotion
■ Public relations	■ Direct marketing
Distribution	
■ Channel selection	■ Distribution directness
■ Market coverage	■ Density of distribution
■ Channel variety	■ Dealer support
Services	**Staff**
■ Pre-sale services	■ Support staff
■ Point-of-sale services	■ Staff motivation
■ Post-sale services	■ Tasks and responsibilities

Action plans

These should specify the details of implementation. For each of the decisions, the action plan should state who is responsible, when it will be done, and how much it will cost. This is often done in the form of a calendar which schedules the necessary activities to achieve the results in the most effective manner.

Budget

The final step is to develop a budget which projects the revenues, expenditures, profits and cash flows over the planning period. Top management can then evaluate whether the plan is sufficiently ambitious, whether the expenditures are reasonable, and the nature of the risks involved.

 ## Market-centred organizations

To make a marketing strategy work, the business needs to put together an organization which encourages people to develop the necessary expertise and commitment. In the past, organizational activities have been structured around functions or divisionalized around geographical or production units. However, if the focus of the business is on marketing – meeting customer needs, implemented by clear segmentation and positioning strategies – a different type of organization is called for. The most obvious way of structuring activities is around customers, markets and market segments.

The problem with functional and other types of divisionally based organization is that they are not oriented to building up knowledge about customers; nor do they assign clear responsibility for meeting their needs. Building a market-centred organization requires the firm first to define its key customers or target market segments and then to organize product development, operations, marketing, sales and distribution around each of these segments. The aim is to build small, dedicated organizations committed to understanding and meeting target customer needs better than competitors.

For example, the Burton Retail Group initially had one women's wear business. Then to boost its market position it decomposed the market into six lifestyle segments. Each segment was given its own management board, and its own buying and marketing organization charged with developing a profitable positioning strategy. Each market-centred business unit developed its own shop formats, marketing plan, pricing and promotional platform. Similarly, Hewlett-Packard moved from a product-based division structure to one organized around market segments. It built new business units capable of selling any of the HP products, such as health care, financial services and engineering, to specific customer groups.

An organization can be market centred at several levels. The most complete form is the autonomous *market-centred division*, where the market segment forms the profit centre. At Burton's, for example, the market segment manager had total autonomy and profit responsibility. In this type of organization, production and R & D must become market focused or they will not be given any business by their internal customers. A less radical approach adopted by HP and many companies is to reorganize the *sales force* around market segments. A further step is to create a separate *marketing organization* for each of the major segments. These can research individual markets and develop appropriate strategies. Another increasingly popular option is *team-based* organizations, whereby personnel from manufacturing, R & D and marketing are assigned to task forces aimed at capitalizing on opportunities presented by specific markets.

Organizing around customers and markets can offer several advantages. First, it focuses managers and employees on what really counts – satisfying the needs of target customers. Second, the benefits increase as customers shift from buying commodity products to wanting value-enhancing solutions made up of several product and service elements. Third, it encourages innovation and value-added offerings, by creating expertise in the operations, problems and changing market environment of the buyer. Fourth, it stimulates teamwork and reduces functional conflict by providing a common focus through which specialized inputs can be directed.

Summary

Marketing has two meanings. First, it is a business philosophy which states that the central goal of the company must be to meet the needs of customers. Without this the firm cannot survive and prosper in competitive markets. The second idea of marketing is a distinct group of activities centred around market segmentation and positioning decisions.

Capitalizing on market opportunities requires several steps. First, it requires segmenting the heterogeneous markets open to the firm and understanding the needs of the separate customer groups. Segmentation is the key to marketing because it offers the firm the chance to meet customer needs more effectively and so build sales growth and profits. Market segments are not static, but offer continual opportunities for innovation and marketing creativity.

After choosing its target market segments, the business has to create a differential advantage. All segments are, or become, competitive and the firm must create a reason for preference. A differential advantage can be based upon an offer which provides higher utility or which is lower in price. To build a differential advantage, management need to understand what drives customer satisfaction and what drives the costs of meeting their requirements.

Finally, management must know how to put together marketing plans and market-centred organizations which are capable of translating strategy into actions.

Questions

1. The high street banks have traditionally not segmented their markets or developed discrete positioning strategies for the different segments. Do you think segmented offers would make sense for the banks? How could such a strategy be operationalized?

2. Is it possible for one petrol station to charge higher prices for petrol than its neighbouring competitors?

3. What are the benefits of market segmentation for the business?

4. A commercial vehicle business is seeking to 'reposition' its major product. What does this mean and how might it be done?

5. Show how the 'value chain' of a customer can be used to provide insights for segmentation and positioning.

6. What are the major components of a marketing plan for a product or target market?

Notes

1. Russel J. Haley, 'Benefit segmentation: a decision oriented research tool', *Journal of Marketing*, July 1963, pp. 30–5.

2. Peter Chisnall, *Marketing Research* (Maidenhead, UK: McGraw-Hill, 1995).

3. Louis L. Schorsch, 'You can market steel', *McKinsey Quarterly*, January 1994, pp. 111–20; V. Kasturi Rangan, Rowland T. Moriarty and Gordon S. Swartz, 'Segmenting customers in mature industrial markets', *Journal of Marketing*, October 1992, pp. 72–82.

4. David Garvin, 'Competing on the eight dimensions of quality', *Harvard Business Review*, November–December 1987, pp. 101–9.

5.   Robin Cooper and Robert S. Kaplan, *The Design of Cost Management Systems* (New York: Prentice Hall, 1991).

6.   Michael E. Porter, *Competitive Advantage* (New York: Free Press, 1985).

Chapter 4

Strategic market planning

Strategic market planning is concerned with adapting the organization to a changing environment. Organizations succeed when they meet the needs of customers more effectively than competitors. The problem is that the needs of customers change and competitors generally get better. As a result, successful companies decline if they do not continually change and adapt. To maintain success, organizations must have strategies to reposition themselves in the market, to move into new markets and to develop new products.

This chapter discusses how strategic market planning facilitates the company's ability to adapt to a changing and increasingly competitive world. It shows how accelerating and often unpredictable environmental change is requiring new techniques for strategic planning. It explores the components of an effective strategy and shows how strategic market planning is used, first at the corporate level and then at the level of the business unit.

Adapting to change

Success in business is achieved when management develop a strategy and an organization which optimally fit the environment within which the firm operates. In this situation it offers customers products and services which match their needs better than rival companies. Unfortunately, needs change and competitors develop new products and technologies which create added value. As a result, for most companies, success is a temporary phenomenon. Companies which were once held up as management icons, such as General Motors, IBM, GEC, Hanson Trust, Saatchi & Saatchi and PanAm, are, a few years later, struggling for their very survival. Their failure is due to the inability of their managements to adapt to change. Such companies are leapfrogged by new competitors with strategies and organizations better tuned to delivering value to today's customers.

Environmental changes are of two broad types: continuous and discontinuous. The former are those changes that are slow and fairly predictable. Demographic changes, increasing concern for the environment, and problems of growing congestion on the road are examples of such clearly discernible trends. With this type of change, affected organizations should have the time to adapt to the problems or opportunities that are being created. But today, change increasingly appears to fall into the discontinuous category. Many of the changes in the environment appear sudden, dramatic and unpredictable. Such an environment is fundamentally more difficult to plan for and to adapt to. In this world, flexibility has become a more important organizational strength than forecasting skill.

Strategic windows

When sudden environmental changes occur, they can trigger major developments in markets. These shocks are often termed *strategic windows* or *paradigm shifts*.[1] When a discontinuous change in a market occurs, the existing market leaders are ill-equipped to match the new requirements. New contenders can go through the open 'window' and displace the current players. In these situations, the major challenge facing the current leaders is to 'close' the strategic window before the new contenders can establish themselves. The task of the newcomers is to pass through the open window fast and effectively before it is closed against them.

The major causes of strategic windows opening are as follows:

■ *New technology*. A new technology can rapidly make obsolete the key strengths of current market leaders. For example, Ever Ready dominated the small battery market until Duracel used lithium technology to replace conventional zinc cells. The new batteries had operating lives two or three times those of Ever Ready, whose market share collapsed.

■ *New segments*. A new market segment offers a window to new players if the current competitors are not alert to its significance. The British motorcycle industry was destroyed in part by its failure to identify and capitalize on the sudden emergence of a leisure segment in the late 1960s – people buying motorcycles for fun rather than basic transportation. The rapid growth of the leisure market in the more affluent western countries provided a strategic window for Honda which it ruthlessly exploited to achieve industry dominance.

■ *New channels of distribution*. As a market evolves, the sudden emergence of new channels can create strategic windows. Pioneer's leadership in the hi-fi market was overturned when it failed to appreciate the move from traditional hi-fi distribution channels to discount and department stores. National Panasonic and Sony, as newcomers, were less tied to existing channels and were quick to capitalize on the trend towards the new types of outlet.

■ *Market redefinition*. As markets develop, the nature of demand sometimes changes from buying products to buying service systems. For example, Docutel initially dominated the market for automatic teller machines (ATMs). Then the banks began to look to integrate their electronic funds transfer systems. This opened the window to the major computer companies such as IBM and Burroughs, which could offer a total package (including ATMs). Docutel was ousted from the market because it lacked the new system capabilities.

- *New legislation.* New laws, regulations, privatizations and international agreements present strategic windows. The break-up of government monopolies in, for example, telecommunications has opened up long-protected markets to fierce, new competition from strong customer-oriented companies like Ericsson, Northern Telecom and Alcatel.

- *Environmental shocks.* Sudden, unpredicted changes in commodity prices, currency alignments, interest rates or political events can produce dramatic changes in market positions. In 1992 the sharp devaluation of the dollar and a tax on luxury cars brought back strong domestic US competition and ousted imports of high-priced European cars.

Lags in response to environmental change

Why have market leaders often reacted so slowly to events? Figure 4.1 illustrates the nature and causes of these delays in responding to strategic windows.[2] Four categories of lags can fatally delay change. First is the *observation* delay ($A_1 - A_0$). Often it is months before management notice that sales are sharply declining. Frequently they are monitoring trade orders rather than consumer off-take. For seasonal goods, trade reordering can lag sales performance by six months or more. Second is a *procrastination* period ($A_2 - A_1$). While the front-line management know that there is a major problem, they often lack the power to do anything about it. Power in these bureaucracies lies with senior management, who often have only a distant understanding of current marketing and technological issues. A lack of detailed knowledge adds to the delay and uncertainty.

Psychologically, too, people are averse to change. Change makes existing skills and assets obsolete, threatening careers and organizational power. As performance approaches the crisis level (A_3), management are forced to react. Normally, the response is *retrenchment* ($A_3 - A_2$). They seek to check losses by cutting costs and investment. But for a strategic window, retrenchment is exactly the wrong response: the problem is not efficiency but effectiveness. The company's losses are caused not by doing things wrong, but by doing the wrong things. It is stuck in yesterday's technologies, products or channels. Finally, with the failure of the retrenchment policy, if the business is to survive, a *power shift* ($A_4 - A_3$) is necessary, leading to the ousting of the management team responsible. If the new team are to be effective, they need a *shift in thrust* to invest in the new strategies which enable the business to adapt to the changed environment.

Reducing the lags in strategic response

Strategic market management is concerned with accelerating the shift in thrust necessary to adapt to environmental changes. In Figure 4.1 this means moving point A_4 (where the required management response is made) to the left. Each of the response lags needs to be truncated or eliminated. Four complementary sets of actions are required, each of which attacks one of the lags.

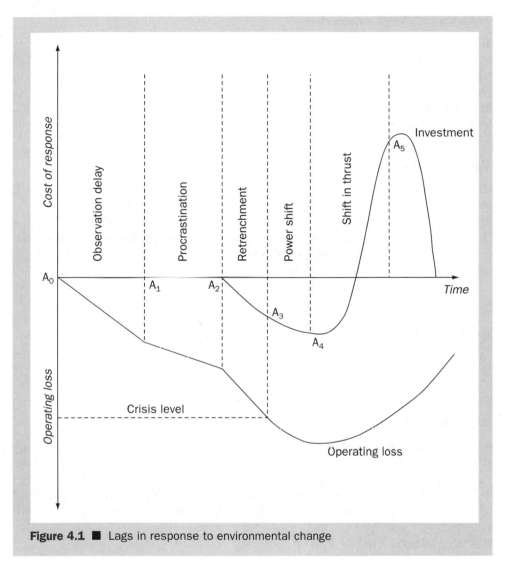

Figure 4.1 ■ Lags in response to environmental change

Source: adapted from H. Igor Ansoff, *Strategic Management*, London: Macmillan, 1979, p. 177

Effective management information systems

Observation delays are cut by quick feedback on customer behaviour. For example, modern retailers have scanning systems which alert management within hours to unanticipated changes in sales. The quicker strategic windows are flagged, the faster management can respond.

Enhanced strategic capabilities

To reduce procrastination, decisions have, as far as possible, to be devolved to managers close to the front line. Managers need to be customer rather than product led. They need broader horizons to scan the environment for signals of changes in technology, channels or customer expectations. Top management have to imbue an expectation of change and impermanence, and to encourage an aspirational culture which seeks to capitalize on opening strategic windows.

Corporate flexibility

Change threatens companies because revenues fall faster than costs. Consequently, one obvious move to cope with managing in a turbulent environment is to seek to restructure the business with the objective of making fixed costs variable. Where a company can buy in component products and services, rather than make them, it has a self-righting mechanism which reduces its downside risk. This is one of the reasons for the enormous growth in out-sourcing in recent years.

Flexibility can also be enhanced by diversifying the organization's portfolio of products or markets. This way it can spread its risks and not have all its eggs in one basket. The need for faster response also encourages organizations to find more dynamic, less bureaucratic leaders capable of making quick, dramatic moves. Finally, it also encourages companies to move beyond annual budgeting and planning systems to the new type of strategic market planning described below, which stimulates management to probe and respond to change.

Rapid power transfers

Radical changes in the company's markets and technological needs often make obsolete the competences of the existing management. When this power shift becomes necessary, it should be done quickly rather than endure further destabilizing delays. This is why a company requires a strong, independently minded board, with non-executive directors who can take the lead in bringing in a new executive team. Turbulent environments also make management development a key priority – having a pool of emerging talent able to take over the leadership of change.

 ## Evolution of planning systems

Leading companies have adapted their planning systems over the years, as their understanding of environmental change has grown (Table 4.1). The earliest planning systems were *financial* and based upon an annual budgeting cycle. They focused on controlling costs. The acceleration of growth and change in the postwar years led to more of an external focus and a greater concern with projecting trends and anticipating the opportunities being created. This was the era of *long-range plans*. Subsequently, the

Table 4.1 ■ Evolution of strategy and management systems

Characteristics	Financial planning	Long-range planning	Strategic planning	Strategic market management
Management focus	Budgets and control	Anticipate market growth	Respond to environmental changes	Capitalize on strategic windows
Assumptions	Long-run stability	Past trends to continue	New trends and discontinuities are predictable	Many changes will be sudden and unpredictable
Objective	Meet the budget	Predict the future	Think strategically	Create opportunities through change
Planning process	Annual	5 years, annual revisions	Annual revisions	Real time
When popular	Until late 1950s	1960s	1970s	After 1980s

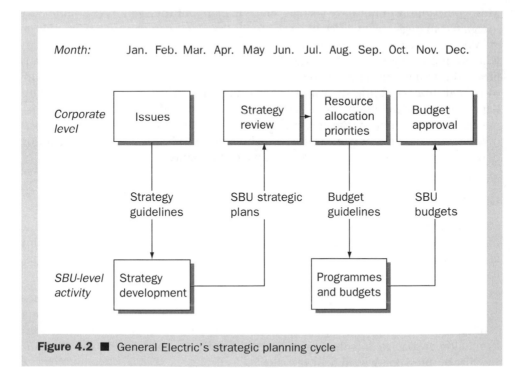

Figure 4.2 ■ General Electric's strategic planning cycle

energy crises of the 1970s appeared to trigger a new era of risk and unpredictability for organizations. *Strategic planning* was concerned with developing a detailed understanding of this new market environment, so that these new patterns could be predicted and responded to.

The new approaches to planning did not replace previous systems, but rather they augmented them. Budgets and long-term plans co-existed and integrated with the new strategic planning approach. All three approaches were usually based on the annual planning process. Long-range plans and strategies were generally updated in the first half of the year and these then provided the foundation for developing the operating plans and budgets for the individual businesses and markets. For example, General Electric's planning cycle is shown in Figure 4.2.

The current approach, termed *strategic market planning* or *strategic management*, differs in two respects from these earlier approaches. First, this new approach focuses much more directly on the firm's market opportunities and seeks to create change by identifying and exploiting strategic windows or paradigm shifts. Second, it recognizes that many changes must be agreed and pursued outside the normal planning cycle. It emphasizes reducing the lags in response to environmental change and using turbulence to the company's advantage.

The hierarchy of strategies

Most companies will not have a single strategic plan, but they will have a number of integrated strategies set at different levels. Typically, a large company will have a *corporate strategy* which sets the broad direction for the company as a whole. The company will normally consist of a large number of different businesses which are usually grouped into *divisions*. These divisions, which will be either regional groups or groups of related product businesses, will develop strategies for their areas of responsibility. Reporting into the divisions will be *businesses* – normally either country units or businesses providing a line of related products. Finally, each business will have a collection of individual products or markets, each of which needs to be planned. The description of product-market or *functional* plans was covered in Chapter 3.

Components of strategy

Strategic market planning can be defined as the managerial process of developing and maintaining a viable fit between the firm's strategy and organization and its changing environment. A well-defined strategy incorporates decisions about the following issues:

■ *Scope of the business.* Scope refers to the choice of products that the firm will produce, the markets it will serve, and the level of vertical integration it will pursue. Decisions on scope are based upon management's view of the organization's mission or strategic intent. They answer the questions: what business are we in; and what business do we want to be in?

■ *Objectives.* The strategy should also identify the firm's primary stakeholders, establish performance criteria and define what levels of attainment the firm will seek on these criteria.

■ *Strategic business unit identification.* Most companies operate with a diversity of products, technologies and market segments. Management need to structure the organization into identifiable business units with managers clearly accountable and responsible for their performance.

■ *Resource allocation.* A central strategic task is to allocate the resources of the firm among the business units and then among product-markets, functional departments and activities within each business.

■ *Developing sustainable differential advantage.* The most important strategic objective is to achieve a sustainable competitive advantage which makes the business the preferred choice for a significant number of customers.

■ *Effective functional strategies.* The competitive strategy needs to be activated and implemented by efficient and effective functional policies. These include policies for manufacturing, positioning, the product line, pricing, promotion and distribution.

■ *Synergy.* While the firm operates separate strategic business units, management should look for synergies: resources and capabilities which complement and re-inforce one another. Unless such synergies are identified and exploited, a business unit within a large successful company will have no advantage over small firms. Potential synergies may lie in umbrella brand names, shared distribution and logistics, or access to special development and managerial skills.

Corporate strategy

At the top of the hierarchy of strategic plans is the corporate plan. Companies differ in the extent to which they develop detailed strategic plans centrally. Goold and Campbell identified three broad styles.[3] *Strategic planning* companies have headquarter teams undertaking detailed planning. The centre takes the initiative in developing strategies to build long-run competitive advantage, to make individual businesses grow, and to identify and develop synergies among them. They generally have matrix structures, with centralized product managers responsible for developing global strategies. Companies which have these proactive centres include IBM, Cadbury-Schweppes, Unilever and Electrolux.

At the opposite end are the *financial control* companies. Here the centre is very small and does not get involved in the strategies of its business units. Instead headquarters sets stretching and tightly controlled profit and cash requirements for each of its businesses, which it runs like a holding company. Managers are held personally accountable for achieving the targets – how they do it is their responsibility. Such companies invariably have short time horizons, expect quick payback and grow via acquisition rather than internal development. Examples of these financially led companies are Hanson Trust, BTR and GEC.

Table 4.2 ■ **Role of headquarters in strategic market planning**

Characteristics	Corporate strategy and style		
	Strategic planning	Strategic control	Financial control
HQ strategic planning	Dominant	Balance	Minimal
Organizational structure	Matrix	Divisional	Holding company
Synergies among SBUs	High	Medium	Low
Managerial values	Collaborative	Personal responsibility	Personal accountability
Growth mode	Primarily internal	Mixed	Acquisition
Type of industry	Dynamic	Mixed	Mature
Investment payback	Long term	Medium	Short term

Strategic control companies fall in-between these two extremes. Primary responsibility for strategic planning is assigned to the operating unit, but the centre does take a view as to the long-term balance of its constituent businesses. Short-term constraints may be relaxed if the unit's longer-run opportunities look good. The centre will also evaluate the strategies of the businesses and withhold resources if it is unconvinced by them. Examples of such companies are Nestlé, ICI and Courtaulds. The three types of company are contrasted in Table 4.2.

None of these approaches demonstrates clear superiority. Largely this is because success depends upon many factors. Strategic planning is a highly effective vehicle for focusing on the creation of sustainable competitive advantage. But financial control may be superior in stimulating personal effort and accountability. A strong strategically oriented centre facilitates long-run growth, whereas financial control pushes ongoing results. In the short run, the latter will often be less risky and produce superior profits. The appropriate style will also depend upon the type of industry. In dynamic, resource-intensive industries such as electronics and pharmaceuticals, a focus on tight financial controls would quickly kill the business. But in mature industries, a priority for generating cash can provide the resources for a long-run acquisition-led growth strategy.

A corporate strategic plan consists of six main components (Figure 4.3).

Corporate mission

More and more organizations now write mission statements which seek to describe the purpose of the business and its essential character. A mission statement has four functions. First, it is meant to *motivate* employees by providing them with an external goal worth striving for. Second, it can provide a *shared sense of purpose* to people working in widely separated business units. It can provide a feeling of belonging to a family of like-minded people. Third, it gives a sense of *direction* by identifying those markets or tech-

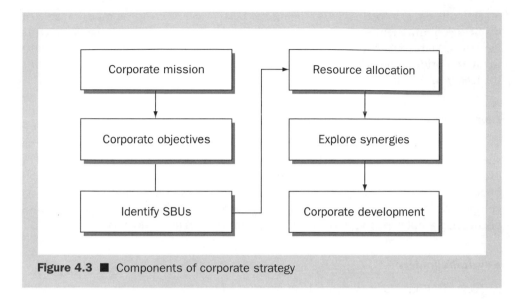

Figure 4.3 ■ Components of corporate strategy

nologies where management see the best opportunities. Finally, it identifies major *policies* which define how it should treat customers, employees, suppliers, distributors and other key stakeholders.

The components of the mission statement are as follows.

Definition of competitive scope

The scope of the organization defines what its business is, who its customers are, and what needs it will seek to meet. Competitive scope can be defined along a number of dimensions. *Industry scope* refers to the range of industries in which it will consider operating. Some companies, like Carlsberg or Glaxo, limit their scope to one industry; others, such as Hanson or Sweden's Procordia, will consider any industry where they see profit opportunities. *Customer scope* refers to the type of customers it will seek to serve. Dunhill, for example, focuses only on up-scale customers. *Vertical scope* defines the degree to which it will take direct responsibility for manufacturing its inputs and distributing its final products. *Geographical scope* refers to the number of countries or regions it will seek to operate in. Does the company seek to be a true multinational or to be a geographical niche player?

Strategic intent or vision

Increasingly, businesses see the mission statement as a means of inspiring employees. Maximizing profits or shareholder value is not a great motivator. Profit anyway is better seen as a result of a successful competitive strategy rather than as an actionable objective itself. Competitiveness – being the best – does seem to be more capable of inspiring commitment and enthusiasm if convincingly articulated. Companies such as Benetton, Marks & Spencer, Microsoft and Toyota have achieved outstanding commitment and pride among their workers by challenging them to make their organizations the leader in their fields.

Competences and competitive advantage

The mission statement should also define the organization's core values. These are the special skills it possesses which should allow it to offer superior value to customers. For example, 3M stresses innovation as its special competence; Marks & Spencer focuses on outstanding quality and value for its mass-market customers; Mercedes builds its competitor advantage around engineering excellence. Stating these core values encourages employees to prioritize building competences in these areas.

Key stakeholders

An organization's success depends upon the support of various groups. The most obvious ones are customers, employees and shareholders. But increasingly it depends on the endeavours, or at least the acceptance, of others including suppliers, the banks, distributors, the local community, national and supranational regulatory bodies. The mission statement should identify those groups central to the firm's long-term success, identify their requirements and state the priority that it believes should be attached to them.

Corporate objectives

The company's mission statement is broad and visionary. In contrast, the company's objectives should be specific and quantifiable and cover a defined time frame. Sometimes objectives are *top-down*, whereby headquarters defines what it wants and then tells each of the businesses what they need to contribute to the total goal. In others, they are *bottom-up*, whereby the corporate objectives are simply an aggregation of what the business units decide they will achieve. More generally, it is an interactive process which balances the ambitions of the centre with the greater knowledge in the units of what can be accomplished in their markets.

Many western companies make profits the central objective. This is a mistake which in the long run will erode the company's competitiveness. Profits are, of course, necessary to satisfy shareholders and to generate the resources to develop the business. But profits are tautological as a business objective, since they are a result of running the business efficiently and effectively. They measure the consequences of what managers have done, not how they have done it. Objectives should focus not on profits themselves, but on what generates them.

Marketing and innovation should be the foundation areas in setting objectives. It is the firm's performance in these areas that the customer pays for. If the company is not good at satisfying customers today and tomorrow, it will not make profits. In other areas – manufacturing, personnel and productivity – objectives and performance are important only to the extent that they enhance the attainment of the firm's ability to satisfy customers and foster innovation.

Management need to set a balanced array of objectives which cover all those areas which influence these two key measures of performance.

Six types of objective are needed:

■ *Market share objectives*. For those markets where the company has chosen to compete, it needs to build a viable position. In most market segments, unless a company is number one or number two, it will be a marginal and vulnerable supplier.

■ *Innovation objectives*. Without innovation in its products or services, its marketing approach, or its means of production, the company will be made obsolete by competitors. It therefore needs clear objectives in these areas: for example, 50 per cent of sales should be from products or services introduced in the last five years.

■ *Resource objectives*. Objectives are needed to attract the most valuable assets in the market: skilled employees, capital and physical facilities. These are marketing objectives. Companies compete to attract the best graduates. Retailers compete to gain the best sites. Their success in attracting the most valuable resources significantly influences their ability to meet their other goals.

■ *Productivity objectives*. A range of measures are needed to evaluate the efficiency with which these resources are employed. Unless people, capital and facilities are made productive, they will not generate enough value to be retained and renewed.

■ *Social objectives*. The social responsibilities of business can take two forms: being concerned about what the organization does *to* the community, and being able to do things *for* it. The first has been a major trend in the last decade. Communities are hostile to companies which produce negative environmental impacts. Organizations must identify these impacts and seek to minimize them. A more positive approach is making the skills and capabilities of the organization available to the community for helping to solve ongoing problems of education, unemployment and other social issues.

■ *Profit objectives*. Only after the above five core objectives are set can management define what profit it needs to achieve. These core objectives determine the capital needed and the risks involved. Profits are the necessary carrot to attract capital and to induce shareholders to share the business risks. Profit is therefore best seen as a constraint rather than an objective. It is the minimum return on capital needed for the business to survive and grow.

Defining strategic business units

When a company develops beyond a certain size, it needs to divide into separate business units to facilitate management performance. Each of these strategic business units (SBUs) then needs a definition of its business which specifies the arena in which it will compete.

Companies often define their businesses in terms of the *products* they produce. They say they are in the 'railways business', the 'agro-chemical business' or the 'slide-rule business'. But as Levitt showed in his classic 'Marketing myopia' article, this is a dangerous way to define a business.[4] Products are made obsolete by new technologies and changes in needs. To prevent the company being made obsolete, Levitt proposed that companies should define themselves in terms of the *customer needs* they served rather than the products they sold. So instead of railways the company should define its business as meeting customers' needs for transportation; rather than slide rules, a business should be defined as calculation.

While Levitt's criticism of product-defined businesses was undoubtedly correct, his alternative can often be unrealistically broad. It underestimates the challenges of acquiring the new technologies to meet the changing needs of customers. For example, Levitt's idea is that to continue to meet the transportation needs of its customers, the railways should have moved into 'cars, trucks, airplanes, even telephones'.

A better way of analyzing the strategic options is to define the business in terms of three dimensions:[5]

■ *Customer group dimension*. How many market segments will the business seek to serve?

■ *Customer need dimension*. How many customer needs will it meet?

■ *Technology dimension*. What technologies will it seek to master?

As Figure 4.4 shows, a business can compete in several ways. Business A meets a single customer need across multiple customer groups with a single technology (e.g. a business manufacturing steel rivets which it sells to the construction, mining, agriculture and aerospace industries). Business B sees its expertise as technology and industry

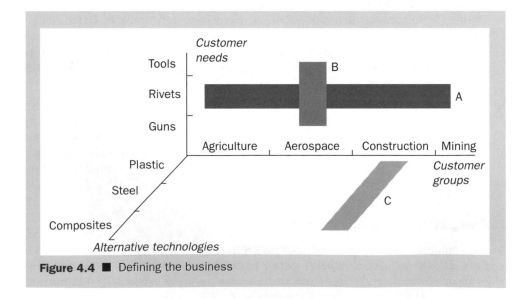

Figure 4.4 ■ Defining the business

knowledge, and meets multiple needs for a single technology and a single customer group (e.g. a business manufacturing steel rivets, riveting guns and other related tools, specifically for the aerospace industry). Business C serves a single need, in a single industry, but offers alternative technologies (e.g. plastic and steel rivets for the construction industry).

By mapping out its activities this way a business can assess the strengths and weaknesses of its position. Management can consider whether the core skills of the business are in technology, understanding specific customer needs, or knowledge of certain industries. They can look at the weaknesses inherent in their business definition. For example, competing in many customer groups (markets or industries) usually gives manufacturing cost advantages, but it fragments the sales and distribution activities. Meeting multiple customer needs risks uneconomic dispersion of technological and manufacturing resources. Management can also consider which is the best growth direction. Is it better to edge out into new technologies, new markets or new needs?

An SBU must be a sensible managerial entity. That is, it must be capable of being run as an independent business. Ideally an SBU should meet three criteria:

■ It should serve an *external* rather than an internal market. If the unit's output goes only to an internal customer, it is best treated as a cost centre.

■ It should have distinct *customers* and *competitors*. If two SBUs have the same customers and competitors, they are best managed together.

■ *Management* of the SBU must have control over the key factors that determine success in the market. If they were forced to share a pooled sales force and manufacturing activities, such control would be absent.

Resource allocation

A company has a portfolio of SBUs. Some of these SBUs will offer much more attractive growth and profit opportunities than others. The company therefore must agree appropriate objectives with each of the SBU managements. Some of the SBUs will be targeted for *build*, others for *growth, maintain, harvest* or *divest*. Not only will the SBUs differ in potential, but they will also differ in their cash flow characteristics. Some, with major new products or pursuing new market opportunities, are likely to require net cash investment. Others, with strong market shares and in mature markets, are likely to be substantial generators of cash. Top management have to ensure that cash is channelled into the appropriate SBUs.

The choice of SBU objectives and decisions about resource allocation depends upon two factors: the attractiveness of the market and the relative competitive strength of the SBU. It generally pays to set more ambitious objectives and prioritize resources to SBUs which are in attractive markets and which have a competitive advantage. *Market attractiveness* is a function of such factors as market size, growth, degree of competition, profit levels, government regulations and sensitivity to economic fluctuations. The SBU's *relative competitive strength* depends upon its market share, product positioning, cost competitiveness, technical skills, marketing and distribution capabilities, and organizational flexibility.

Drucker introduced portfolio planning thirty years ago. He found that most companies' products or markets could be broken into six types:[6]

- *Tomorrow's breadwinners* – new products which, while not yet profitable, can be expected to be in the near future.

- *Today's breadwinners* – well-established businesses which generate the bulk of the firm's profit and cash.

- *'In-between category'* – SBUs with a capacity to generate good results if drastic turn-around actions are taken.

- *Yesterday's businesses* – SBUs which were once strong but have now been made obsolete by changes in the market environment.

- *'Also-rans'* – products that, while not total disasters, never achieved what was forecast.

- *Failures* – SBUs which should have been eliminated long ago.

Drucker showed how companies allow resources and management time to be sucked into the last three categories, to the long-run detriment of those SBUs which are, or have the potential of, generating outstanding results. More recently, a number of rather more sophisticated portfolio planning techniques have become widely used for helping to set objectives and allocate resources across SBUs.

The BCG growth–share matrix

The Boston Consulting Group's growth–share matrix, developed in the early 1970s, probably became the most popular management technique ever. In the last two decades it became ubiquitous as a model for analyzing the company's portfolio of SBUs. The BCG matrix positions the firm's businesses in two dimensions, as shown in Figure 4.5.

The vertical dimension is the growth rate of the market, which is used by the BCG as a proxy variable for market attractiveness. High-growth markets are assumed to be more attractive because, being competitively non-zero sum, market share gains are often more easily obtained. Also market share gains in a growth market will be worth more in the future as the market develops. The mid-point between high and low market growth is arbitrary, but a 10 per cent annual growth rate is a popular figure.

The horizontal dimension is relative market share (ratio of SBU share to share of largest competitor), which is used as a proxy for relative competitive strength. This axis is plotted on a log scale so that the mid-point is 1.0, at which a firm's market share is exactly equal to that of its largest competitor. A relative market share of 0.1 means that the SBU's sales are only 10 per cent of the leader's; a share of 2 means that the SBU is the leader and has twice the sales of its nearest follower. High market share is assumed first to give the SBU a cost advantage. This occurs primarily through the experience curve, which suggests that firms with the greatest cumulative production experience obtain lower unit costs through greater learning and the ability to incorporate the latest technology and design. Costs may also be lowered by economies of scale in buying, production and marketing. A second advantage of a high market share is that

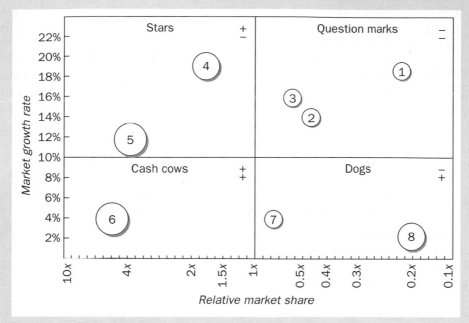

Figure 4.5 ■ The Boston Consulting Group's growth–share matrix

high brand recognition gives greater bargaining power with buyers, leading to potentially higher margins. Certainly there are many empirical studies which suggest a
correlation between market share and profitability. The most well known of these – the
PIMS study of over 3,000 SBUs in over 450 firms – shows that on average a difference of 10
per cent in market share is associated with a difference of about 5 per cent in pre-tax ROI.[7]

Figure 4.5 plots the positions of a company's SBUs. The size of the circles represents
the relative sales levels of the SBU. The matrix is divided into four cells, each of which
has broad policy implications and cash flow characteristics.

- *Cash cows*. The bottom-left quadrant consists of SBUs with high market shares operating in low-growth markets. Because they have a high market share, profitability
  should be good (+), and because investment requirements will be low, given the
  maturity of the market, cash requirements should be small (+). Consequently, cash
  cows should be generating the resources to support the company's development in
  other high-growth markets. These are what Drucker termed 'today's breadwinners'.

- *Stars*. A star is a market leader in a high-growth market. Profitability should be good
  (+), but investments to maintain the SBU's position are likely to be high (–). The
  stars should be the company's top priority for resourcing. In the future, when the
  market matures, they should become the company's cash cows.

- *Problem children*. These are businesses with low market share in high-growth markets (also called 'question marks' or 'wild cats'). They have high cash requirements because of their weak positions in resource-hungry markets. The company is often in a 'double or quit' situation. Whether it invests aggressively, seeking to overtake the leading competitors and become a star, depends upon three considerations. First, how much can the company afford to invest? Second, has the SBU the potential to create a real differential advantage capable of switching customers away from the market leader? Third, how aggressively and effectively could competitors respond to an attack? If a problem child's position cannot be improved, it will continue to absorb cash. As the market matures, it will become a cash-absorbing dog – a 'cash trap'.

- *Dogs*. These have low market shares in low-growth markets. Generally they are unprofitable, and if they require investment to maintain their position, they become cash users. Dogs often consume more management time than they are worth and the general recommendation is to divest from these businesses.

Portfolio analysis has three uses. First, a business can assess the *balance* of its portfolio. In the long term a company needs to maintain a balance between cash use and cash generation. If too many of its businesses are cash cows, then while it is rich in cash in the short term, it is vulnerable due to its lack of long-term growth potential. Such companies often become takeover targets for others anxious to employ their cash-generating ability. On the other hand, companies with a portfolio dominated by stars and problem children are likely to find themselves with insufficient resources to maintain market share. They risk taking on excessive debt, or if they are more prudent, they are likely to be caught up by better-financed competitors. In such a situation, a firm may decide to sell off some of its SBUs to generate resources.

Second, the portfolio provides a framework for strategic market *planning*. Over time SBUs are expected to change their positions in the matrix. Successful SBUs follow a life cycle. They generally start as problem children; then, if they are managed successfully, they are built into stars; eventually they become cash cows as the market matures; and finally they become dogs. The matrix provides a snapshot at one point in time. But management should also plan a moving picture of how the company's SBUs will develop over time so that market opportunities and cash-generating potentials are optimized.

Third, each SBU should have a clear *objective* appropriate to its portfolio position. Growth will be an appropriate objective for stars and selected problem children. Maintenance of sales is the likely objective for strong cash cows. Harvest will be the objective for weakening cash cows, some of the dogs and non-priority problem children. Divestment will be set for those dogs and problem children which are seen as having no potential.

Limitations of the BCG matrix

The BCG matrix became popular because it was easy to use and was intuitively appealing. Today, however, it has become somewhat discredited as managers have become more aware of its assumptions and limitations. The major weaknesses are as follows:

■ Market growth is an inadequate description of overall industry attractiveness. Factors such as low entry barriers, capital intensity and strong buyers can make even high-growth markets oversupplied, price oriented and unprofitable.

■ Market share is an inadequate proxy for relative competitive strength. Other factors such as location, degree of vertical integration and capacity utilization also affect relative costs. Price and margins are also influenced by product positioning and shared marketing, distribution and brand franchises.

■ The analysis is highly sensitive to how the market is defined. Do market share and growth refer to the total market or to the segments served? Is BMW's share 2 per cent of the total market or 30 per cent of the luxury car segment? Definitions of the market can be fairly arbitrary and different definitions will radically change an SBU's matrix position.

■ The model assumes that business units are independent. If two SBUs share facilities, divesting in the dog might weaken the star. In a highly competitive situation, harvesting a problem child might well allow the competitor to boost its profits. The additional cash that the competitor generates may allow it to attack the company's own star in another market.

Composite portfolio models

In an attempt to overcome the limitations of the BCG model, a number of alternatives have been proposed. The most well known are those of McKinsey, Shell and A. D. Little.[8] Although they differ somewhat from each other, all are similar in their thrust of replacing the two BCG dimensions with more comprehensive indices of market attractiveness and competitive strength.

The McKinsey approach positions the firm's SBUs in a 3 × 3 matrix according to their market attractiveness and the business's competitive strength. Market attractiveness, instead of just being based on growth, rates as many factors as appear relevant in the particular industry. In the example of Figure 4.6, nine factors are used. The managers involved have to select the most relevant factors, weight them by importance, rate an SBU on each factor, and then combine the evaluations to a summary measure. The second dimension is the business's competitive position. Again, as illustrated, a range of factors besides market share are identified and summarized.

The major application of this type of matrix is to help managers match the firm's strengths with the market opportunities available. The firm should invest and attempt to grow in the areas where it is strong and the market is attractive (in Figure 4.6 these are boxes 1, 2 and 3). Shell Chemicals, which uses a similar model that it calls the 'directional policy matrix',[9] assigns the following strategy recommendation to each of the nine cells:

1. *Leader.* This is the optimal position for an SBU, being in a strong position in a highly attractive market. The strategy is to give the top priority to enhancing or maintaining this position.

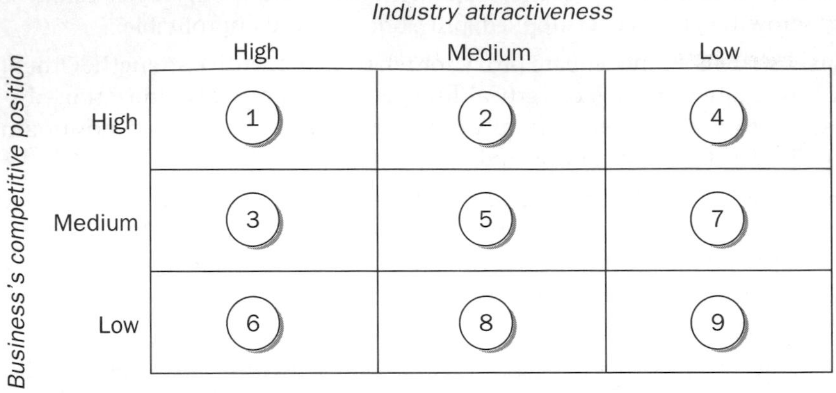

Variables that might be used to evaluate:

Business's competitive position		*Industry attractiveness*	
Size	Distribution	Size	Profitability
Growth	Technology	Growth	Technological sophistication
Relative share	Marketing skills	Competitive intensity	Government regulations
Customer loyalty	Patents	Price levels	
Margins			

Figure 4.6 ■ A composite portfolio model

2. *Growth leader*. Investment should be made to allow the product to grow with the market. Generally the product should be profitable and the growth self-supporting.

3. *Try harder*. This position might be vulnerable over time. Consideration should be given to investment to strengthen its competitive position.

4. *Cash generation*. These SBUs should be cash suppliers and should not require investment.

5. *Proceed with care*. Caution is required when investing in these businesses, since neither are they market leaders nor are their markets strikingly attractive.

6. *Double or quit*. Businesses here should be decisively partitioned into those to be abandoned and those selected for priority investment.

7 and 8. *Phased withdrawal*. Profit prospects are slight and the strategy should be a controlled switch of resources to other uses.

9. *Withdrawal*. These businesses will be losing money and their assets should be disposed of as quickly as possible.

Conclusions on portfolio models

Portfolio models reflect the fundamental strategic proposition that it makes sense for a company to invest in attractive markets where it has relative competitive strength. The idea that managers should have tools to formalize and structure their analyses is also appealing. The problem is that all such techniques require simplification if they are to be understood and applied. Not all possible variables and situations can be included in the models. The weakness of the BCG approach is that, by limiting its analysis to only two variables, it simplified the problems excessively and so limited its application to those areas where market share and growth were the overriding factors. The composite models, by including more variables that are likely to have an impact on future profitability, are more realistic and more widely applicable. The price to be paid is more subjectivity in the measures and greater ambiguity in the results.

None of the models gives much insight into implementation. Opportunities in a market are not given, but depend significantly upon the firm's creativity in identifying new segments and building growth opportunities. Similarly, the firm's competitive position can be enhanced by innovation and developing new capabilities.

Portfolio models a few years ago achieved exaggerated emphasis in strategic planning, but today, they risk being overly discredited. These models should never have been thought of as decision-making tools. Rather they are analytical techniques which can give managers important insights into the balance of their businesses, their relative strengths and the opportunities open to them.

Value-based planning models

Portfolio models give broad indications of which SBUs to invest in. However, they do not permit the evaluation of a proposed strategy for an SBU. Value-based planning is a resource allocation tool which attempts to measure the shareholder value that any proposed strategy is likely to create.

The components of the model are shown in Figure 4.7. The shareholder value created by an SBU strategy depends upon three factors: the cash flow it generates, the business's cost of capital (which is used to discount future cash flows to their present value), and the market value of the debt assigned to the SBU.[10] The core of the model is the cash flow generated by the strategy. This is determined by six 'value drivers': the rate of sales growth that the strategy is forecast to produce, the operating profit margin, the income tax rate, working capital investment, the investment in fixed capital and the duration of the value growth. The last, the duration of value growth, represents management's estimate of the number of years over which the strategy can be expected to produce rates of return that exceed the cost of capital. A strategy is worth pursuing from a shareholder point of view if it creates additional value, assuming other alternatives available would not generate even more value.

While analytically appealing and increasingly used (especially in acquisition studies), value-based planning has a host of practical problems. The major difficulty is the requirement to forecast detailed performance variables ten or more years ahead.

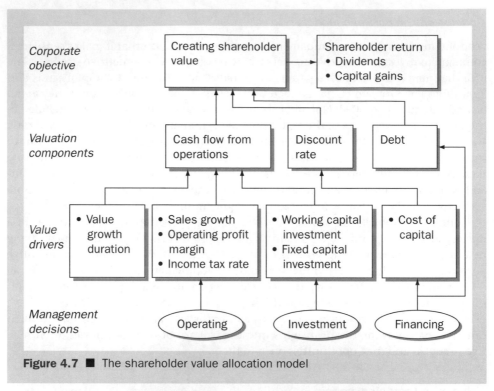

Figure 4.7 ■ The shareholder value allocation model

Source: reprinted with permission of The Free Press, a division of Macmillan, Inc., from *Creating Shareholder Value: The new standard for business performance* by Alfred Rappaport, p. 76. Copyright © 1986 by Alfred Rappaport

These include projections of sales volume, product mix, prices, cost, competitive actions and investment requirements. In most industries today, such long-term projections are mere guesses. No one can foresee what competitive conditions, demand, capacity and technologies will be like ten or twenty years ahead. The problem is that when such guesses are fed into the computer and the value estimates begin to be churned out, the numbers often begin to take on a life of their own. Managers accept the numbers as 'truth', losing sight of the often hopelessly unreliable assumptions behind them.

In addition, a number of important studies have shown how such financial planning models undervalue investment in holding on to current customers. An analysis often assumes that, if an investment is not made in a new product, the SBU will maintain its status quo. However, what the financial model does not often take into account is that, without the investment, current performance will deteriorate because customers will switch to more dynamic competitors which are investing in added value enhancements to their product lines.

Third, value-based planning only seeks to evaluate alternative strategies. It does not generate strategies. The best strategy will never emerge from the evaluation process if management fail to identify it. Truly creative strategies depend upon a detailed understanding of the changing market environment. Finally, the models assume that shareholders are the only stakeholders. However, any company aiming at long-term viability needs to consider balancing the partly conflicting objectives of its multiple stakeholder groups.

Exploiting synergies

Most resource allocation models treat the SBUs as independent. However, exploiting interrelationships between the businesses can generate powerful sources of competitive advantage. Synergy means that the whole is more than the sum of the parts. It means that two SBUs acting together will be superior to the same two SBUs acting independently. If larger companies fail to exploit synergies, then they have no advantage over their smaller competitors. Synergies can benefit the company by accelerating innovation, increasing sales of current products, decreasing costs or reducing the levels of investment needed to run the business.

Potential synergies exist throughout the value chain. First, sharing support activities such as procurement, technology development, human resource management and overheads can cut costs and enhance the quality of the personnel available. Next, each of the primary activities offers sources of synergy. Combining buying operations can produce discounts. Shared operations, outbound logistics and service can build experience and scale economies. Marketing and sales synergies are particularly important. One business unit can create leads for others. For example, American Express's credit card business allows its customer database to be used by its other divisions selling insurance, travel, magazines and other merchandise. Similarly, a brand franchise can be extended to create or enhance the performance of another unit. For example, the Cadbury brand name, originally based around confectionery, has been successfully used to launch a new ice-cream business. Finally, many potential synergies are knowledge based. The performance of one unit can be improved by the transfer of competences, knowledge or experience from other units within the firm. For example, the technical knowledge that Canon developed in the camera business was a crucial factor in its successful entry into the office copier business. The German subsidiary of Microsoft owed much of its success to following the marketing strategies proved earlier in the US division.

Synergies can be identified and exploited in various ways. Many companies group related SBUs into separate divisions which facilitate the sharing of primary and support activities. Others centralize or regionalize certain activities to enhance knowledge-based synergies. For example, a corporate R & D department is often better at discovering new technologies with potential applications across multiple businesses, than if each unit bore the burden of funding its own R & D efforts. Many companies have strong corporate-level co-ordinators to maximize the strength of the firm's accumulated marketing and technological knowledge, when competing in global markets. Company-wide management education and task forces also build networks and share knowledge to lever the performance of individual businesses. An example of how Toshiba exploits synergies is shown in Box 4.1.

It is important that the SBU managers buy into the search to exploit synergies. If head office dictates pooling and sharing schemes, the search for synergies can evaporate and turn into barriers to progress. Sharing facilities can introduce bureaucracy, limit the autonomy of managers and reduce a business's ability to respond quickly to changing market conditions. If the unit's management cannot control their own operations and sales, then they cannot be accountable for profit performance and can easily lose the incentive to be entrepreneurial and customer driven.

Corporate development

When the company aggregates the plans of its individual businesses, it will have a projection of corporate performance in terms of marketing, innovation and financial measures. Often there will be a *gap* between this projected performance and that desired by top management (Figure 4.8). In this case they have two alternatives: to reduce the objectives, or to seek to boost projected performance by reviewing the opportunities open to the businesses. The projected performance of the firm can be increased either by getting more from its current businesses, or by diversifying into new ones.[11]

Internal growth

Management should first assess whether higher performance can be achieved by the existing businesses. The first step is to review operating efficiency. The business units can be asked to look for specific levels of cost savings and economies. Second, opportunities to enhance marketing and innovation performance can be reappraised. This means systematically reviewing opportunities in the following areas:

- *Market penetration* – increasing market shares of current products in current markets.
- *Market development* – looking for new markets for current products.
- *Product development* – developing new products for existing markets.
- *Integration* – including backward integration to take over supply functions previously bought in; forward integration or taking over sales activities previously done by third parties; or horizontal integration, meaning acquiring competitive businesses.

External growth

If internal growth is insufficient to close the strategic planning gap, corporate management may turn to opportunities for diversification to boost performance. Success at diversification depends upon finding new markets which are attractive and where the firm has the capability to build a sustainable competitive advantage. The task of management is then to draw up a list of candidate industries which may meet these criteria.

Industry structure analysis provides the means for evaluating whether an industry is potentially profitable for the firm. The best-known model is that of Michael Porter, which shows that the profitability of the average firm in an industry depends upon five factors (Figure 4.9):[12]

BOX 4.1

Toshiba: exploiting internal and external synergies

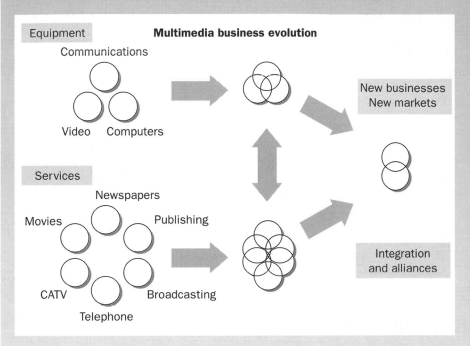

Toshiba sees its future in moving from producing electronic components and equipment (video, computers, semiconductors) to multimedia. It foresees an integration of electronic products with media services and software (newspapers, TV, movies, etc.) to create entirely new markets and businesses. By the year 2000 it anticipates the world multimedia market as worth 3 trillion dollars.

To exploit this opportunity, Toshiba assigns top priority to eliminating barriers between its operating divisions and specialist business units. It has also set up a range of international strategic alliances with leaders in adjacent hardware and software. These include IBM, Siemens, MCA, Time Warner and Thomson Multimedia. To catalyze this process Toshiba has set up a new Advanced-I Group of divisions reporting directly to the president, Mr Sato. The group has three objectives: first, to promote synergies between Toshiba's businesses to create new infrastructures, products and services; second, to concentrate development of key components and technologies; and third, to create external synergies by promoting strategic alliances which spread the development burden, encourage innovation and share ideas.

Source: *Financial Times*, 27 September 1995

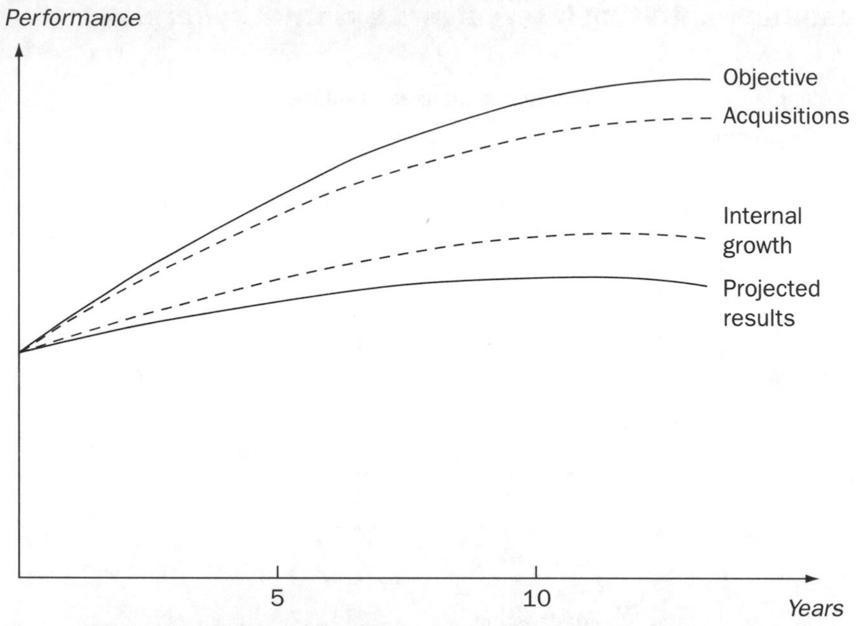

Performance

Objective

Acquisitions

Internal growth

Projected results

5　　　10

Years

Figure 4.8 ■ The strategic planning gap

■ *Competition among existing firms*. Industry profitability will be low if there is intense competition between the competitors in the industry. Competitive intensity tends to be high where there are a large number of competitors, if the market is stable or declining, if fixed costs are high, and where competitive products are perceived as very similar.

■ *Threat of new entrants*. Profits will be depressed if it is easy for new competitors to enter the industry. Barriers to entry which can keep profits high include high capital investment, patents, economies of scale, restricted distribution channels and brand loyalty.

■ *Threat of substitute products*. An industry's attractiveness is less if the product is easily substituted by alternative technology or the products of other industries.

■ *Strength of buyers*. If buyers are strong, they will have the bargaining power to squeeze the profits of producers. For example, the increasing strength of the major retail buying groups has been a major factor depressing the profits of grocery goods manufacturers.

■ *Strength of suppliers*. If raw material suppliers, utilities or trade unions are strong, they can depress the profits to be earned in the industry.

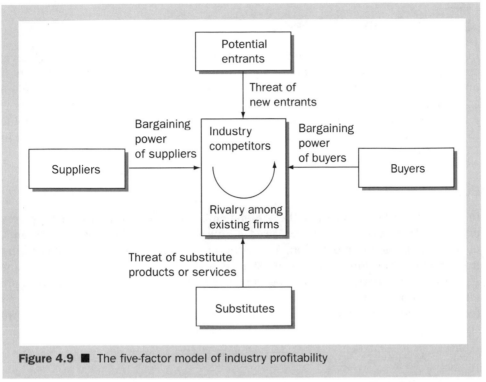

Figure 4.9 ■ The five-factor model of industry profitability

Source: reprinted with the permission of The Free Press, a division of Macmillan, Inc., from *Competitive Strategy: Techniques for analyzing industries and competitors* by Michael E. Porter, p. 4. Copyright © 1980 by The Free Press

The Porter model shows what determines the average profits in an industry. The company's ability to obtain profits above this average level depends upon its building a sustainable competitive advantage. This in turn depends upon the relative capabilities of the business. These capabilities are likely to be strongest where the firm diversifies into industries where there are some marketing or technological synergies with current businesses.

After an industry is selected, the company has to decide how to enter: should it develop a new business, should it acquire, or should it look for partners to develop alongside? The advantages of an acquisition are that it is fast and it removes a potential competitor. The disadvantages of acquisition are first that the bid premium often makes the route expensive. Second, it is unlikely that any acquisition will match the company's capabilities and facilitate synergies as effectively as a business developed internally. Partnerships and joint ventures can take many forms including licensing, franchising, joint sales companies and shared research and development. These provide an increasingly attractive route, offering the potential of a faster path into new markets than internal development and a less risky option than acquisition.

Business unit strategy

In the hierarchy of plans, the business unit strategy sits in between the high-level corporate plan and the detailed plans for individual products and markets. A business unit is responsible for a collection of closely related products or markets. While a corporate plan sets the broad direction for the company, the business plan details how a sustainable competitive advantage will be achieved, allowing the SBU to contribute to the corporate objectives. The key components in the business plan are shown in Figure 4.10.

Business mission

In highly diversified companies, the corporate mission statement may have to be very broad. Such missions are often viewed as meaningless 'motherhood' statements, devoid of content and motivation. As a result, many business unit managements find it desirable to develop their own mission, describing more specifically the unique scope of the business, its vision, specific competences and competitive advantages. Like the corporate mission statement, the functions are intended to encourage a feeling of pride in the business, a shared sense of purpose, to give it direction and to emphasize the major policies that should be pursued.

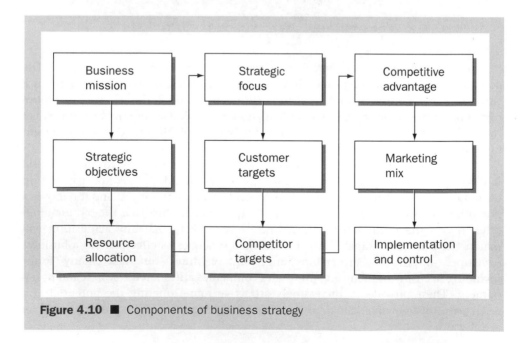

Figure 4.10 ■ Components of business strategy

Strategic objectives

The broad strategic objectives of the business unit will have been determined as part of the corporate planning process. In reviewing its portfolio of SBUs, the centre will have assigned resource priorities to each of them. The broad strategic choices are: growth, maintain, harvest, divest and for a new business, enter.

These broad strategic choices will then be translated into detailed marketing, innovation, resource, productivity, social and financial targets for the business over the planning period.

Resource allocation

An SBU will have its own collection of products and markets. Some of these will represent much better investment opportunities than others. Management will therefore have to decide which products and markets to prioritize. This is a micro-version of the corporate resource allocation process. Often SBU management find the same portfolio planning tools useful for assessing their choices. Management will determine the attractiveness of their individual target market segments and the relative strengths of their products within these areas.

The main point is that while corporate management may have assigned, say, a 'maintenance' objective for the SBU as a whole – implying limited growth and investment aspirations – within the SBU a variety of separate goals will be being pursued. Some product-markets will be geared for entry, others for growth, and others for harvesting or disinvestment. Management of the SBU need to exploit to the full the resources made available to them.

Strategic focus

Each of the major product lines within the SBU must then be strategically focused. There are two alternative ways of improving a product's profitability – a focus on increasing volume or a focus on improving productivity (more profit from the same volume). As Figure 4.11 shows, volume can be increased itself in two ways: expanding the market or greater market penetration. Productivity can be improved by cutting costs, raising prices or improving the sales mix (e.g. eliminating low-profit activities).

It is useful to consider these as alternatives because they do conflict. A focus on volume requires cash and investment; a focus on productivity should generate cash. Similarly, focusing on volume requires quite different marketing strategies (e.g. aggressive pricing, investment in distribution, range extension) from one geared to productivity. The choice of strategic focus depends primarily upon the strategic objective assigned to the product. If management see it as being of high growth potential, the focus is likely to be on volume; if they see its future as limited, the focus will be on productivity. Over time, a product is likely to evolve from volume to productivity: to move from being a cash user to a cash generator. As a product moves towards lower

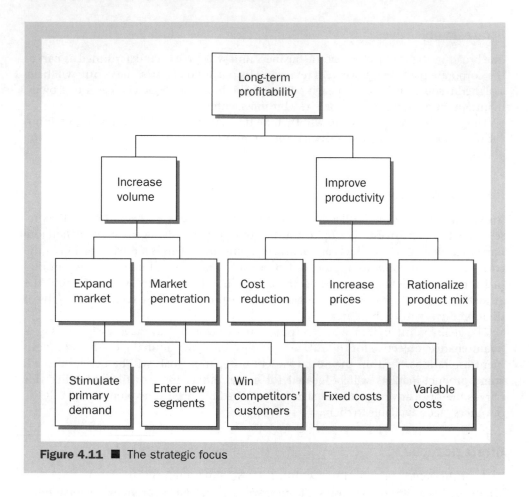

Figure 4.11 ■ The strategic focus

growth expectations, the task of management is to find new products and new markets to maintain momentum.

Customer targets

Choosing the right customers and responding to their needs effectively is the central thrust of strategy. In targeting customers, management need information to answer the following questions.

■ *Who is the customer and who should it be?* This is never an easy question to answer. Most businesses have at least two sets of customers. Branded consumer goods companies such as Unilever and L'Oreal have both shoppers and supermarkets as customers. It is necessary to motivate both if the brands are to sell. Similarly, banks have both borrowers and lenders as customers. The newly privatized UK telephone, gas and electricity utilities have to satisfy both subscribers and regulatory agencies. Each customer can have quite different concepts of value, want different things and behave quite differently, creating real conflicts for the organization. The selling requirements too may be quite different. Selling branded consumer goods to households requires classic consumer marketing skills. But selling these goods to supermarkets requires skills more akin to industrial marketing.

■ *What customer segments should be targeted?* Market segmentation is central to a successful strategy. Markets are not homogeneous, but are made up of different groups of customers, each with their own needs and price expectations. It will invariably be more profitable to develop separate offerings for each of the main segments of the market.

■ *Who makes the buying decision?* Most products and services – both consumer and industrial – are influenced by complex multiperson decision-making units. Different individuals in the buying organization or the household may be responsible for initiating the purchasing process, influencing the choice of supplier, making the decision and using the product (i.e. the consumer). One of the main reasons for IBM's initial success was its early understanding that different people in a company have to be sold to if the contract is to be won. The people who use the computer (usually accounting and financial staff) have to buy it. But top management also have to be convinced. And so do people who have to use the product as their information tool: that is, operating managers. A similar situation occurs in most fields. The marketer has to learn what each individual looks for, what they value most and how they can be reached.

■ *What do they buy?* Customers buy products or services not for their own sakes, but for the benefits they provide or the solutions they offer. Management have to get beyond a product focus to a fundamental understanding of the needs and problems faced by customers. They can then look to supply additional products or services which enhance customer satisfaction and add value.

■ *Where do they buy?* Carrefour became the biggest retailer in France by spotting the car-owning shopper's desire to avoid the hassle of high street congestion. First Direct developed an innovative telephone banking service in the UK by recognizing that customers did not want to spend time visiting bank branches, yet wanted up-to-the-minute information about their finances and quick transactions.

■ *When do they buy?* Many products and services are highly seasonal, so that planning has to be geared to a buying cycle.

Competitor targets

The company does not merely have to be good at meeting the needs of customers, it has to be better than competitors. Just as customers need to be analyzed and understood, so do competitors. Competitive analysis has taken on greater importance in the planning activities of many companies. One reason is the slower economic growth rates that have characterized the economies of the 1990s. As a result, more markets are zero-sum: a company can grow only by beating others. Second, in the last decade, more governments have been deregulating industries to provide fiercer competition for existing incumbents. Finally, the European Union has been successful in progressively eliminating barriers to trade between countries, bringing in a new era of competition in which only the strongest European competitors will survive.

Competitive analysis centres around five questions: who are the competitors, what are their objectives, what are their strengths and weaknesses, what should the strategy be towards them, and finally, what should be done to respond to competitor strategies?

Who are the competitors?

There is no easy or permanent answer to this question. Figure 4.12 defines four categories of competitors. *Direct competitors* are those offering similar products and services to the same customers. Two steel companies selling to the construction market are direct competitors. *Product competitors* sell the same product to two different customer groups. A steel business focusing on the car industry would not be directly competitive with one selling to the construction industry. *Indirect competitors* sell different products to the same industry. For example, the construction industry might use either steel or concrete in its projects. Steel and concrete are different products, but they may be strongly competitive. Finally, *implicit competitors* are a much broader set of competitors. A family might see a new car, a holiday or a major home improvement as alternatives for their limited budget.

A set of direct competitors is often called a strategic group. Porter observes how competitors in most industries fall into a small number of strategic groups.[13] Competitors within a strategic group focus on the same target market segments and pursue similar competitor strategies. Figure 4.13 illustrates the three major strategic groups within the UK food retailing sector. The biggest group is the premium sector of supermarket majors, with national coverage emphasizing image, shopping environment and differentiated products. At the other end are the low-cost retailers which compete directly on price. In between are local and regional firms which survive when they can meet specialized local requirements.

Research by Harvard's Michael Porter and the McKinsey Group[14] suggests that this picture can be generalized. They argue that competitors in a market can be categorized into three strategic groups based on the generic strategies they pursue.

■ *Cost leadership*. Firms in this strategic group seek to minimize production and distribution costs so that they can win market share by pricing lower than competitors. Examples of companies pursuing such a strategy are Aldi, Texas Instruments and Amstrad.

■ *Differentiation*. Firms in this strategic group seek to achieve high performance by producing products and services which offer superior value to target customers in terms of such dimensions as superior performance, features, design and brand image. Examples are Marks & Spencer, Siemens, Benetton and American Express.

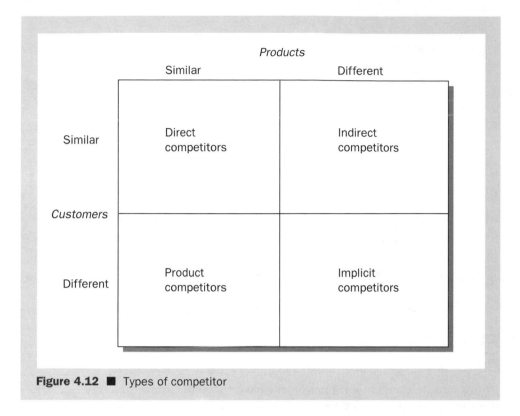

Figure 4.12 ■ Types of competitor

■ *Focus.* Firms in this strategic group specialize in a segment or region rather than in the total market. By obtaining superior knowledge, they pursue a cost leadership or differentiation strategy targeted to these particular customers. Examples of such companies are Bank of Scotland, London Cabs and Castrol Lubricants.

A company's ability to shift from one strategic group to another is limited by *mobility barriers*. These are entry barriers such as brand images, low-cost production, location advantages and customer loyalty. Consequently, a differentiated competitor may lack the cost structure to compete effectively in a low-cost strategic group. Similarly, a low-cost competitor is likely to lack the image and marketing skills to move easily into the differentiated group.

Most competitor analysis focuses on direct competitors or those within the same strategic group. This reduces the number of competitors to be analyzed to a manageable size. However, managers should be aware that indirect competitors with substitute products or services can be a major threat. Also competitors may develop over time the skills to shift into new, more attractive strategic groups. For example, Mercedes Benz did not see Toyota as a direct competitor in its strategic group. But in 1990, Toyota launched the Lexus, a new top-of-the-range car aimed directly at Mercedes customers. A weak competitor in the strategic group can also be transformed if it is acquired by a

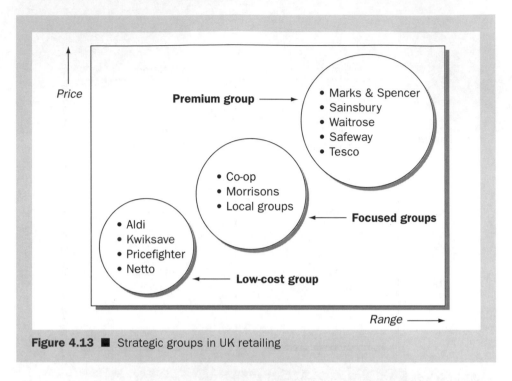

Figure 4.13 ■ Strategic groups in UK retailing

strong outside competitor. Management have to avoid 'competitive myopia'. They have to ask not only who are today's competitors, but who they may be tomorrow.

What are their objectives?

The next step is to interpret each competitor's objectives and to begin to assess the threat it represents. Does it have ambitious objectives aggressively to expand its market share? Two important factors shaping a competitor's objectives will be the composition of its portfolio of businesses and its current financial health. If this product is seen as a star in its portfolio, then the competitor is likely to be aggressive. On the other hand, if it has other, more attractive opportunities open, its top management may not wish to make major investments. The second factor shaping the threat that a competitor represents is its financial performance. If profitability and cash flow are weak, management are likely to be under greater pressure to restore profits and curtail expenditures than to seek market growth. Trade research and a close analysis of the company's financial statements are likely to provide enough information for making these assessments.

What are their strengths and weaknesses?

Does a competitor have the capabilities to be a significant threat? To answer this question, management need to evaluate the strengths and weaknesses of each competitor against the company's own profile. First, the dimensions should cover marketing strengths, including image among customers, market share, reputation for quality and service, effectiveness of communications, distribution and geographical cover. Second, financial strengths need to be evaluated, including profitability, cash flow and the amount of debt carried. Third, strength in operations should be measured, including costs, capacity, technical skills and on-time delivery. Finally, overall organizational capabilities are important, including corporate leadership, motivation of employees, flexibility and entrepreneurial skills. It is useful to get an independent view of these comparative ratings. For the marketing criteria it is crucial to establish how customers view the relative performance of competitors. Managers generally overestimate the reputations of their own products and people among customers, and underestimate those of key competitors.

What are the likely strategies?

An understanding of their objectives and relative strengths will suggest what strategies they are likely to pursue. A strategy which has been generating successful results to date is likely to be continued and developed. If a company has fully exploited opportunities in its current market segments, it is likely to shift its attention to new market segments or new geographical areas. Niche players in high value-added segments are particularly vulnerable to successful mass-market competitors seeking further growth and profit opportunities. Their access to substantial resources and scale economies can overcome in time the mobility barriers protecting smaller competitors. Finally, a company is likely to attack where it has relative strengths. A low-cost competitor is likely to attack a high-cost niche player, using price as a competitive advantage. An innovative company is likely to use differentiation as its weapon.

What should be done?

Finally, the company should consider how to respond to current or anticipated competitor strategies. Ideally the competitive analysis should allow the firm to develop a proactive approach to competition, but sometimes unanticipated moves require quick reaction.

A proactive competitive strategy consists of several components. First, and most important, it is crucial to seek to deal with those weaknesses which the SWOT analysis has shown put the company at a serious competitive disadvantage. At the same time, the company should seek to build up and promote those areas where it has competitive strengths. Such policies enhance the company's competitive position in its strategic group. Second, it should explore opportunities to boost mobility barriers which deter new competitors from entering the market. These might include maintaining high advertising levels to consolidate its image, broadening its product range to fill any gaps, seeking patent protection, controlling raw material sources or building scale economies. Third, the company can use market signals to influence or control competition.

Market signals can be either defensive or aggressive in intent. Defensive signals might include publicly explaining its moves and goals to assuage competitors. For example,

Sir Graham Day, chairman of Rover, announced that the company was seeking not to increase its market share, but only to improve margins. His objective was to dissuade competitors from price cutting in the UK market. Aggressive signals are used as threats to deter competition from attacking. A market leader might introduce a low-price fighter brand to threaten competitors entering its area. A multinational may respond to probes in its home market by a direct attack on its competitor's domestic market.

In attacking competition it is crucial to attack in areas where the company is at a comparative advantage. It is surprising how often companies fail to anticipate competitive reaction. For example, two new British airlines were started to attack the lucrative cross-Atlantic market: Laker and Virgin. Laker began by publicly signalling very ambitious market share objectives with low prices as its competitive advantage. Laker was small and very highly geared, and had virtually all its revenues coming from the one Atlantic route. By contrast, its rivals British Airways, PanAm, TWA and American Airlines were, at that time, giants with multiple profitable routes, which could easily afford to cross-subsidize temporary losses on the Atlantic route. Concerned about Laker's ambitions, they dropped prices and took business away from the airline, which quickly dropped below break-even into bankruptcy.

In contrast, Richard Branson's Virgin Airlines publicly signalled very small market share objectives and focused on quality rather than price to win a position. The result has been that competitors have allowed Virgin to gain share profitably. Virgin attacked on quality where it was relatively strong and successfully discouraged retaliation by astute market signalling.

Implenting the competitive intelligence system

Many of the largest companies have a section, usually within the marketing department, responsible for obtaining competitive intelligence. Other companies may assign small teams to monitor and become specialists on specific competitors. Their task is to collect data on a continuous basis from the field (customers, distributors, sales force, trade associations, etc.), published data (annual reports, press articles, etc.) and personal observation. They have to evaluate and analyze the information and then disseminate it throughout the company. Competitor evaluations should then feed directly into the strategic planning system.

Core strategy

A business's core strategy defines how it will seek to gain a sustainable competitive advantage. The three generic strategies – low cost, differentiation and focus – are useful to describe how strategic groups compete against each other for customers. But they do not help in answering the key question of how one firm can gain a competitive advantage against others within its strategic group – against its most direct competitors.

A core strategy is invariably based upon a combination of characteristics borrowed from all three generic strategies. Being the overall price leader with a poor product and inadequate service does not offer competitive value to customers. A competitive advantage for a business in the low-cost strategic group requires being competitive on price, but it also requires offering on top features which differentiate from and add value above those offered by competitors. It will also normally involve elements of focus, in that offers will be adapted to the differing requirements of major customers or customer groups.

Similarly, firms pursuing a differentiated strategy operate within price constraints. A differentiator can create added values by offering customers not only high-quality products, but also lower prices or better terms than the competitors within its strategic group. A major factor in Toyota's success with its Lexus model was that not only did it offer a car comparable to the best of its rivals, but its price was substantially lower.

To summarize, a firm's core strategy within its strategic group is based on a combination of five sets of attributes:

■ Price value (based upon low costs achieved by scale economies, experience, vertical integration, etc.).

■ Product differentiation (e.g. performance, design, features, reliability).

■ Service differentiation (e.g. finance, delivery, after-sales support).

■ Personnel differentiation (e.g. courtesy, reliability, responsiveness).

■ Image differentiation (e.g. confidence in the brand).

To design a specific combination of attributes that will create a competitive advantage requires market research covering the following five steps:

1. *Identify the attributes most valued by customers in the target segment.* This means listening to customers about what are, or might be, the key requirements.

2. *Rank the attributes in order of importance.* Customers should be asked to say what is most important: price, design, speed of delivery, etc.

3. *Score the business and its major competitors along these attributes.* Again these ratings have to be done by the customers in the target segment.

4. *Evaluation and strategy formulation.* After comparing the business attribute-by-attribute against its key competitors, the direction of the core strategy should be clear. If the business is fortunate enough to be superior across all the attributes, it is in a strong position. Price should not be a problem and a company has the choice of either raising prices to increase margins or maintaining price to increase market share. Most companies, however, will have a mixed picture of competitive strengths and weaknesses. The analysis will suggest where the business needs to reposition – which parts of the offer need to be improved, and how price may have to be realigned to enhance value.

5. *Monitoring competitive performance over time.* This exercise needs to be done on a regular basis, probably annually. The picture can shift over time as a result of changes in customer requirements, new technology and the changing structure of competition.

Implementation

After the business has developed its principal strategies for achieving its goals, it must work out how these are to be implemented. Implementation covers activities in four main areas.

First, the business has to co-ordinate *marketing mixes* for its major product lines. These decisions are normally made by the individual product or market managers, but top management will want to ensure that these are consistent with the objectives of the business and build the desired types of customer relationship.

Second, the business will want to produce *action plans* detailing what needs to be done over the coming year to implement the plan. These will assign responsibilities for conducting specific tasks to enhance and communicate the business's core strategy. They may cover programmes to reduce costs, to remodel certain lines, to train service personnel and to explore new geographical markets.

Third, the business will want *feedback and control* systems. These will include budgets which enumerate financial targets and which add benchmarks for monitoring developments and ensuring that the business is kept on track over the next year. The speed of environmental change is such that few plans will turn out as expected. Both new problems and new opportunities occur, and management need systems which will quickly identify those forces blowing the business on to a new course.

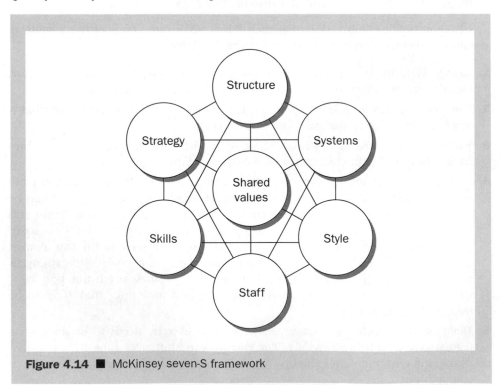

Figure 4.14 ■ McKinsey seven-S framework

Finally, the business needs periodically to review its *organization*. Strategy and systems are only two of the many factors which go into determining whether a business will be successful. 'Organization' means much more than the formal structure which appears on the company's organization chart. McKinsey identified seven characteristics which characterize the more successful companies.[15] The first three – *strategy, structure and systems* – it defines as the 'hardware' of success. The other four, which are often more vital, it calls the 'software' of success (Figure 4.14).

The first of these is *style*, which refers to the dominant pattern of behaviour and thinking of the management team. Thus top management at Marks & Spencer go out of their way to demonstrate to employees their detailed concern with the quality and value of the products on sale in the stores. The second element is *skills*, which means the specific capabilities possessed by employees that set the company apart from competition. *Staff* refers to the dominant culture of the people who work in the organization. For example, Hanson Trust has a predominantly 'financial culture'; at Unilever a marketing focus predominates. The final characteristic is *shared values*, which means the common values or goals which motivate people in the business. McKinsey believes that successful companies exhibit strongly held shared values that fit their strategy.

Summary

The most important reason for strategic market planning is to force managers to ask the right questions. General Eisenhower is said to have remarked, 'Plans are nothing, planning is everything.' This assertion is certainly true of marketing. Outcomes will rarely turn out as planned. The real value of planning is not to forecast events, but to encourage managers to explore carefully the real determinants of future success in competitive markets and to assess the business risks. As one executive at the space agency NASA put it, 'It's the risks that you don't consider that get you.'

Companies that do not undertake strategic market planning are usually fixated by production or financial priorities. Short-term problems displace the long-term strategic thinking necessary to build the capabilities required for maintaining and enhancing competitiveness.

Strategic market planning can also stimulate the ambitions of management. Looking to the future, marking out what looks to be required for being a winner and creating high aspirations almost invariably enhances performance. Companies that aim high usually achieve more. Well-thought-out and clearly communicated strategic plans provide a sense of direction and common endeavour to those working in the organization.

Drucker once wrote that planning is not necessary for success. In fact, he observed, success can be achieved by three different means: luck; having a genius run the business; and planning. The significance of planning is that it is the only route available to any company which will clearly increase the odds of success. Fortune and genius are attributes which are not, unfortunately, readily available to management.

Questions

1. Give an example of a company or an industry which has been subject to sudden environmental change. Identify what factors have hindered its speed of response to these changes.

2. Find an example of a company which has shown an ability to respond rapidly to environmental shocks or strategic windows. What explains this flexibility?

3. Discuss the relative advantages and disadvantages of the Boston and McKinsey portfolio techniques.

4. What are the components of a corporate strategic marketing plan?

5. What should be included in a review of a business's key competitors?

6. A large consumer goods company has one business unit focused on marketing Scotch whisky. Outline and comment on the components of a strategic marketing plan which would be suitable for such a business unit.

Notes

1. This section is adapted from Derek F. Abell, *Defining the Business: The starting point of strategic planning* (Englewood Cliffs, NJ: Prentice Hall, 1980).

2. From Igor Ansoff and Edward McDonnell, *Implanting Strategic Management* (Englewood Cliffs, NJ: Prentice Hall, 1990).

3. Michael Gould, Andrew Campbell and Marcus Alexander, *Corporate-Level Strategy: Creating value in the multibusiness company* (New York: Wiley, 1994).

4. Theodore Levitt, 'Marketing myopia', *Harvard Business Review*, July–August 1960, pp. 45–56.

5. Abell, *op. cit.*

6. Peter F. Drucker, *Managing for Results* (London: Heinemann, 1964).

7. Robert D. Buzzell and Bradley T. Gale, *The PIMS Principles: Linking strategy to performance* (New York: Free Press, 1987).

8. These are described in detail in many texts, including Roger A. Kerin, Vijay Mahajan and P. Rajan Varadarajan, *Contemporary Perspectives on Strategic Marketing Planning* (New York: Free Press, 1995).

9. D. E. Hussey, 'Portfolio analysis: practical experience with the directional policy matrix', *Long Range Planning*, August 1978, pp. 78–89.

10. Based on Alfred Rappaport, *Creating Shareholder Value: A new standard for business performance* (New York: Free Press, 1986). See also T. Copeland, T. Koller and J. Murrin, *Valuation: Measuring and managing the value of companies* (New York: Wiley, 1995).

11. This classic approach to corporate strategy is described in H. Igor Ansoff, *Corporate Strategy* (Harmondsworth: Penguin, 1968).

12. Michael E. Porter, *Competitive Strategy: Techniques for analysing industries and competitors* (New York: Free Press, 1980), pp. 126–56.

13. Porter, *op. cit.*, pp. 34–46.

14. Donald C. Waite, 'Deregulation and the banking industry', *Bankers Magazine*, January 1982, pp. 76–85.

15. Richard T. Pascall, *Managing on the Edge* (London: Viking Penguin, 1990), pp. 37–44.

Chapter 5

Market dynamics and competitive strategy

This chapter explores two related issues essential to developing marketing strategies. First, it examines how markets evolve over time – how they start, grow, reach maturity and eventually decline. This involves reviewing the limitations of the popular product life cycle concept and showing the comparative advantage of examining the broader underlying market dynamics which shape the behaviour of both customers and competitors. While there is no standard product or market 'life cycle', there are common evolutionary processes which influence markets over time.

Second, the chapter describes how an understanding of this process of change in a market should influence marketing strategy. By anticipating developments in buyer behaviour, competitive activities and emerging technologies, managers can reposition their businesses and proactively change products and marketing policies to strengthen their competitiveness and improve their financial performance. Finally, the chapter explores the strategic issues facing businesses in different competitive positions. It looks at the forces which should determine the different marketing strategies of the pioneers of the industry, those seeking to challenge the market leader, and those companies aiming at niche positions within the larger market.

 Cycles of confusion

The concept of a product life cycle has had a major impact on the marketing literature. Every textbook has a chapter on the subject and numerous articles have appeared on it. It has also influenced many of the popular management techniques, such as the Boston Consulting Group matrix and the McKinsey portfolio.

Figure 5.1 shows the popular representation of the theory.[1] The theory postulates that a product has a life cycle (usually described by an S-shaped sales curve) which can be divided into four stages: introduction, growth, maturity and decline. The slow introductory phase reflects the difficulty of overcoming buyer inertia and stimulating trial of a new product. Rapid growth then occurs as many new buyers are attracted once the product is perceived as successful. Saturation of the product's potential buyers is even-

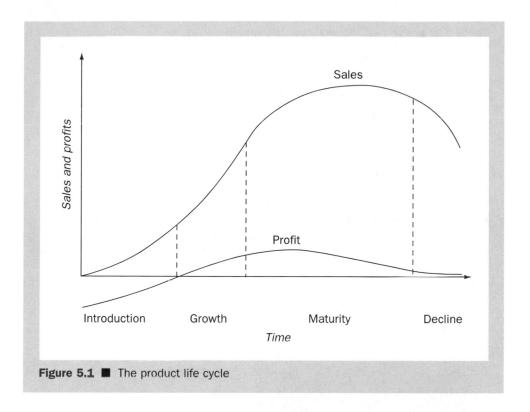

Figure 5.1 ■ The product life cycle

tually reached, causing the rapid growth to level out to the underlying rate of growth of the relevant target market. Finally, decline will set in as new substitute products appear.

From this product life cycle theory it has then been common to draw implications for marketing strategy, the marketing mix and the organization of marketing.[2] The main recommendations are summarized in Table 5.1. It is argued that in the introduction stage the strategic objective should be to develop the market aggressively, focusing on the most innovative customers and seeking to pre-empt competition. As the product moves into the growth stage, new competitors enter, the initial product has to be enhanced with features and line extensions, prices have to be cut and distribution intensified now that a mass market is emerging. As the market for the product matures, profit margins fall, competition is intense and the organization has to shift from a focus on marketing to one on efficiency and cost control. Finally, in the decline stage, the future is bleak and the business should seek to milk the product for cash. This cash is then pushed into new products and the product life cycle is repeated.

Despite the popularity of the product life cycle, there is unfortunately no evidence that most products follow such a four-stage cycle! Nor is there any evidence that the turning points of the different stages are in any way predictable. On the contrary, the shape of the sales curves appear to be completely idiosyncratic. One review of life cycles identified sixteen different patterns in addition to the S-curve. Some of the more

Table 5.1 ■ Product life cycle: implications for marketing

	Introduction	Growth	Maturity	Decline
Characteristics				
Sales	Low	Fast growth	Slow growth	Decline
Profit	Negative	Rapid rise	Falling margins	Declining
Cash flow	Negative	Moderate	High	Moderate
Strategy				
Objective	Aggressive entry	Maximize share	Boost profits	Milk product
Focus	Non-users	New segments	Defend share	Cut costs
Customer targets	Innovators	Early adopters	Majority	Laggards
Competitor targets	Few, pre-empt	Growing number	Many	Declining
Differential advantage	Product performance	Brand image	Price and service	Price
Marketing mix				
Product	Basic	Extensions and enhancements	Differentiation, variety	Rationalize range
Price	High	Lower	Low	Stabilizing
Promotion	High	High	Falling	Low
Advertising forms	Awareness	Brand performance	Loyalty	Selective
Distribution	Selective	Intensive	Intensive	Rationalize
Organization				
Structure	Team	Market focus	Functional	Lean
Focus	Innovation	Marketing	Efficiency	Cost reduction
Culture	Freewheeling	Marketing led	Professional	Pressured

common curves found in empirical studies are illustrated in Figure 5.2. Similarly, the turning point from maturity to decline can occur after a few months (e.g. the hula hoop) or not be evident after several generations (e.g. Scotch whisky). If the shape and length of the product life cycle are so irregular and unpredictable, the concept would appear to have little utility for market planning and decision making.

Part of the problem with the product life cycle concept is that it has never been properly defined. What does 'product' mean? Some studies use the total industry sales (e.g. computers), others use product forms (e.g. notebook computers), still others use brands (e.g. Apple Mac). Each 'product' has quite a different life cycle: one can be in long-term decline while another exhibits rapid growth.

To see the managerial implications of these differences, it is useful to show how they relate to one another (Table 5.2). Market analysis starts not with the product, but with the needs of customers. A *need* is a basic requirement of customers. For example, customers have needs for transportation, calculating power or energy. Such needs may

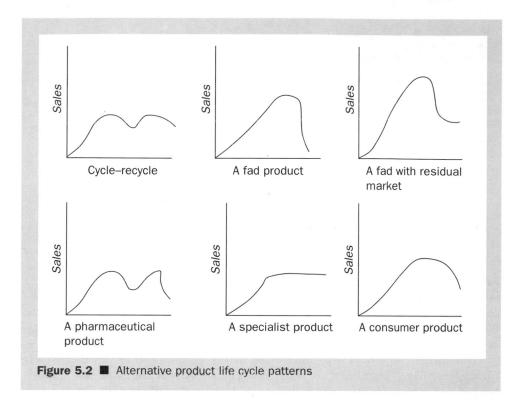

Figure 5.2 ■ Alternative product life cycle patterns

persist and grow over centuries, and indeed may never have a decline stage. Next, at one level of disaggregation, we have a *demand* for a specific solution to the need. This is sometimes called a demand-technology life cycle. For example, the demand for transportation was once met by a coach and horses, now it is met by a car. The electronic computer has replaced the mechanical comptometer. The life cycle of these broad product solutions, while shorter than the need curve, can be extremely long. Next is the *current technology* curve. While the demand curve represents a broad technological solution (e.g. internal combustion engine, electronics) beneath this curve are a whole series of incremental technological changes which make previous processes obsolete. For example, 16-bit technology replaces 8-bit; ceramic filters replace copper; fiber optic cables replace copper wire. Technology curves can be quite short and are certainly getting shorter.

At the next level of disaggregation, managers make choices. A *product* curve is a category of offer incorporating current technology. For example, companies offer four-wheel drive cars or a 16-bit personal computer. Next, line extensions or alternative *product forms* normally appear, such as open-top four-wheel drive cars or 16-bit notepad computers. Both product and product forms may exhibit short life cycles due to changing tastes and technology. Finally, there is the *brand* product life cycle. This is the distinctive offer of a specific business. The brand life cycle can be long or short

Table 5.2 ■ Alternative product life cycle concepts

Concept	Definition	Typical length	Examples
Need	Basic underlying requirement	Indefinite	Transportation, calculating
Demand	Specific solution to a need	Very long	Car, computer
Technology	Current state-of-the-art	Short	Composite engine, 16-bit computer
Product	Product with specific technology	Shorter	4-wheel drive car, 16-bit PC
Product form	Variant of product	Very short	Open-top 4-wheel drive, 16-bit notepad PC
Brand	Manufacturer's offer	Long	Honda Civic, IBM PC, Coca-Cola

depending upon the marketing strategy. Unilever believes that, by incorporating the latest technology and adapting the product and product form to changing market conditions, the brand can have an indefinite life. Brands such as Persil, Coca-Cola, Range Rover and many others last for generations because they change the technological, design and service content of the offer while still retaining the brand values.

For managers to talk of a product being at the declining stage can therefore be highly misleading. First, sales are often resuscitated by new uses and new markets. Second, for every declining product there are almost invariably rapidly growing technologies, product forms and brands. For example, total sales of tea have been declining for generations, but within this total, sales of some product forms such as herbal and instant teas have been showing explosive growth in recent years.

Weaknesses of the product life cycle

To summarize, for the following reasons, the product life cycle is not of much use for marketing strategy.

Undefined concept

There is no agreement about the level of aggregation that the concept is supposed to refer to. Needs, demands, technologies, product categories, forms and brands have quite different driving forces.

No common shape

However products are defined, there appears to be no standard curve. An S-shaped curve appears to describe only a minority of products. The actual sales development is shaped both by outside events and by the strategies of competitors.

Unpredictable turning points

While most products and brands do peak eventually, there is no way of predicting when the turning point will occur. For some it is a matter of months, for others it may be generations.

Unclear implications

Even where a life cycle pattern can be identified, the implications are not clear. For example, the growth phase may or may not be associated with high profit margins. If barriers to entry are low and industry competition is fierce (e.g. as in some areas of electronics), rapid growth can be accompanied by very low profits. By contrast, if there are low exit barriers and little competition, the decline stage can be exceptionally profitable (e.g. the foundry supplies business).

Not exogenous

The product life cycle is often the result of management actions rather than being caused by outside events. Many managers have been taught to think that the product life cycle is inevitable. When sales have plateaued, rather than looking to upgrade the technology and search for new opportunities, management have defined the business as a cash cow and sought to 'diversify' into other businesses. In these situations, the product life cycle becomes a self-fulfilling concept.

Foseco was the leader in supplying linings to steel refractories around the world – a £300 million a year business. The linings were fibrous boards installed inside the furnaces. A small competitor entered with a cheaper spray-based alternative. Foseco, with its strong reputation and marketing capability, could easily have responded to this threat by adopting the technology. In fact, it was given the opportunity to acquire the competitor. Instead management had identified their business as a 'cash cow' and so declined to invest. The result was that competitors rapidly took over the market. Spray linings became a high-growth business as the steel companies substituted from board. Foseco refractory profits collapsed. A few years later an ailing Foseco was acquired by Burmah Castrol.

Product oriented

The core concept of marketing is that the business should seek to meet the needs of customers rather than focus on selling its products. The product life cycle is a production rather than a marketing-oriented concept. By focusing on the product, managers fail to understand those factors which shape the business's ability to satisfy the needs of its customers in competitive markets. The fortunes of the company are tied not to its products, but to five other primary forces which determine its ability to maintain a competitive advantage. These forces are as follows:

■ The changing requirements of customers.
■ The objectives and strategies of competitors.

- The attractiveness of the market to new competitors.
- The emergence of new technologies which can replace existing solutions.
- The performance and power of those companies supplying resources, raw materials and components to the business.

These are the drivers which make the product obsolete. A product will die if the needs of its customers change, if competitors come up with better offers, if new technologies permit cheaper or superior solutions, or if suppliers to the firm choke off its ability to satisfy the market profitably. Therefore it is better to tune managers into concentrating on the causes of change rather than the consequences of it. That way they can more effectively anticipate developments in the market and create product strategies which adapt to these opportunities.

Market dynamics

Just as there is no uniform, predictable product life cycle, so there is no standard pattern of market evolution. However, there are common processes which shape markets. By analyzing these processes, managers can anticipate how markets and competition will develop. From this analysis they can develop strategies both to capitalize on these changes and to influence these forces of change. Such processes affect each of the following five 'actors' in the industry (Figure 5.3).

Customers

As a market evolves, certain changes can be anticipated among customers. First, the level of demand changes. Sales are a function of the number of buyers and the frequency with which they buy. In the initial stages, growth can be extremely rapid

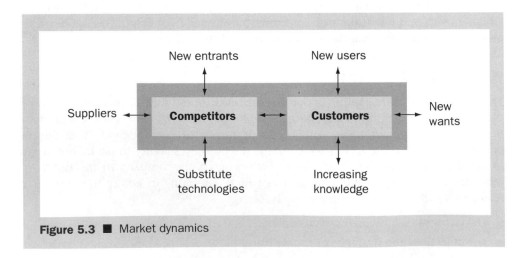

Figure 5.3 ■ Market dynamics

because of the number of new buyers being attracted to the market. Eventually this pool of available non-users diminishes, the market becomes saturated and sales slow as they become largely a function of repeat purchasing.

A second change to be anticipated is that customers' expectations will progress. The primary function of the product comes to be accepted as the 'norm' offered by all competitors. Customers look for additional attributes which add new benefits to the product. For example, in the early 1980s doctors hailed Squibb's revolutionary new hyper-tensive drug, Capoten, which eventually produced sales of over £1 billion a year. Subsequently, twenty competitors entered the market. The new products were not superior in the primary function of lowering blood pressure, but they began to offer additional desirable attributes such as lower dosage and fewer side effects. Today the market leader is Merck's Vasotec, which has the attribute that a patient needs to take it only once a day rather than the two or three times daily required by Capoten.

Finally, three factors cause customers to become increasingly price sensitive. First, customers become more knowledgeable and are willing to shop around. Second, there are more competitors to choose from. Third, as the market develops, more price-sensitive customer segments have to be penetrated to maintain growth. Innovative customers tend to be less price sensitive because they attach a high value to the new product; later customers have to be attracted by lower prices.

While evolutionary processes in the market push towards slower growth and falling prices, both can be postponed or forestalled by firms making product or market innovations. By innovative repositioning, the firm can meet new needs, offer new attributes or create new markets. Such innovations have fuelled resurgent growth and maintained high prices in many markets, such as those for bicycles, ice cream, alkaline batteries and industrial lubricants.

Competition

Evolutionary processes also lead to certain expected changes in the behaviour of current competitors in the market. First, the intensity of competition will initially be low because the rapid rate of growth makes competition a non-zero-sum game – all can grow. But later, as the market slows and firms have added to capacity, competition for customers becomes increasingly intense.

Second, during the latter part of the growth phase, the more aggressive competitors begin to pursue repositioning strategies which put them into direct competition with firms that were previously in different strategic groups. For example, until the mid-1980s, IBM and Apple did not compete head on. IBM dominated the mainframe market, Apple the emerging PC market. Then in 1984 IBM, concerned about the slowing growth in the mainframe market and the expanding purchases of PCs by its customers, launched its own PC. With this new direct clash between the two leaders, competition massively increased, producing a rapid shake-out of the weaker players.

A third change is that during the growth stage winning strategies begin to emerge and industry leadership tends to become established. The winners are those that have aggressively built market share in the early stages, moved down the experience curve and built economies of scale in operations and marketing. As the industry matures, they have lower unit costs and powerful marketing and distribution systems. The leaders then are hard to dislodge unless a competitor can introduce radically innovative products or marketing strategies.

New entrants

A market is pioneered by one or two companies. However, a rapidly growing market automatically attracts new competitors – often in large numbers. Sometimes there is an interval in which patents, lack of technical expertise and uncertainty about the market's potential act as barriers to entry. But this interval is now very short in most industries. Less than one year after Apple launched the first personal computer, it had ten competitors; eight years later it had five hundred. Speciality chemical companies expect their new products to be copied within six months.

Today all well-managed companies are scouring the environment for growth markets which might utilize their capabilities. As the market's potential becomes less uncertain, large firms will seek to enter the market. Sometimes they will establish their own businesses; more often they will acquire one or more of the pioneers. Not only do existing competitors have to compete with local entrants, but global competition increasingly becomes the pattern.

As the market enters its mature phase, the number of new entrants sharply reduces and companies begin the exit. Slow growth normally triggers a shake-out and the number of competitors declines. The survivors are increasingly those who have pursued the winning strategies of achieving high market shares, broad product lines and global markets. Consequently, managers in innovative businesses must appreciate that their lead time is always short and that soon they will be challenged both by small, nimble followers and by large, resource-rich giants. If they are to survive, their technological edge must be matched by strategy to build share rapidly and create a viable brand.

Substitute products and technologies

Over time, managers should expect substitute products and technologies to threaten their position in the market. A substitute is anything that meets the same customer need. Concrete can be a substitute for steel in building a bridge, high-fructose corn syrup can substitute for sugar, acrylic for nylon. Several factors increase the threat from substitutes as the market evolves.

First, competitors in adjacent industries are attracted by the growth and profit to be made in the market. For example, commercial banks once dominated the financial markets, but in the last decade they have lost share. On the commercial side, the banks have lost share to securities firms. On the retail side they have lost share to building societies and non-banks such as ATT and Marks & Spencer, which now offer services such as credit cards and investment funds. Second, needs in the market change, making old technologies less appropriate. For example, today's customers find making a special trip to a bank for a routine transaction a chore. A new bank, First Direct, attracted nearly half a million customers by offering telephone banking. Unlike old rivals, First Direct has no branches, all the functions and transactions are available through a seven-day, 24-hour telephone service. Third, progress in adjacent technologies is likely to threaten current solutions. For example, new plastics which are light and strong increasingly substitute for steel in car manufacturing. Finally, the government can influence the position of substitutes through regulations, quotas and subsidies. For example, environmental regulations are forcing the wind-down of many packaging and chemical products, and stimulating the creation of new substitutes.

In these situations, management have to decide whether to beat the emerging substitutes or to modify their strategies and incorporate the new products and technologies. The answer will depend upon an analysis of which alternative best meets the needs of customers, and of the trend in the relative price–performance ratios.

Supply relationships

Entrepreneurial firms depend upon suppliers and subcontractors to facilitate growth. During the initial stages of the market, obtaining suitable supplies may be a constraint on growth. Those early competitors that can access efficient suppliers or have the resources to integrate backwards can lever important competitive advantages.

Suppliers can limit the potential of a company to exploit its capacity for innovation. Porter suggests that a supplying group is powerful where the following conditions apply in the market:[3]

■ It is dominated by a few suppliers and is more concentrated than the industry it sells to.

■ It is not obliged to compete with other substitute products for sales to the industry.

■ The industry is not an important customer of the supplier group.

■ The supplier's product is an important input to the buyer's business.

■ There are high switching costs in moving away from the products of the supplier group.

■ The supplier group poses a credible threat of forward integration.

In general, supplier power diminishes as the market grows. Nevertheless control and power over suppliers can offer a sustainable competitor advantage. For example, Marks & Spencer's long-term relationship with its suppliers, its skill in influencing their design and processes, and its ability to negotiate strongly with them have been central to the company's sustained position as Europe's leading retail firm.

 The evolution of markets

These five key components described above are affected by evolutionary forces. For convenience, these developments can be divided into four phases.

The emerging market

A new market is triggered by an innovation. This innovation may be: a new product or a new service which is superior to earlier ones; a new marketing concept which creates a new set of customers; or a process innovation which dramatically cuts costs or increases the availability of a product.

For an innovation to succeed it has to offer benefits which customers perceive as superior to current solutions. The customers who perceive this benefit first and who can act on this perception are called *innovators*. Innovators are normally not price sensitive because they value the benefit highly and do not want to wait for competition to bring prices down. The central marketing task at this stage is to segment the market with the aim of identifying those buyers most likely to benefit from the performance or the promise of the new product. Typically, some potential customers will benefit hugely, while others perceive very little benefit at all. The former are the ones to target.

When Rolm (now part of Siemens) invented the electronic PABX (the telephone switching system used by an office or company), the primary benefit was that it allowed companies to economize on long-distance call costs. For the top 2 per cent of companies with very big long-distance call bills, the savings averaged over £100,000 a year. On the other hand, for most companies, with more modest long-distance bills, the savings were minimal. Rolm's initial strategy was therefore to identify and target the former segment. In launching a new product or service, a general rule in marketing strategy is that it pays to identify and target initially those customers for whom the perceived value will be greatest.

At the beginning, sales growth is normally slow, and buyers have to be informed about the innovation and persuaded of its benefits. Uncertainty, high switching costs and the lack of established distribution and service infrastructures also restrain buyers. Barriers to adoption are more easily broken down when the new product has the following characteristics:

■ It has a major performance advantage which is easily demonstrated.

■ The cost of switching into it is low.

■ The cost of product failures is limited.

■ Support requirements are small.

■ Buyers in the segment have the resources to change.

Once the innovators begin to adopt the product, the market may grow very fast, fuelled by the penetration of the large non-user group.

Competition is initially weak. The pioneer's main competition comes from the older technology. New entry is temporarily forestalled by barriers which include the following:

■ Patents.

■ Lack of technical know-how.

- Uncertainty about what customers want.
- Lack of expertise in sourcing supplies and parts.
- Shortage of risk capital.

Unfortunately for the innovator, such barriers to entry tend to crumble very rapidly. Movements of personnel, the spread of knowledge and the adaptability of aggressive, fast followers soon erode the leader's temporary monopoly. Within a year, there are likely to be several new entrants in the market.

The high-growth phase

The high-growth phase is characterized by the expansion of the market to new customer segments and new uses. These are stimulated by the spread of knowledge about the product beyond the innovator group, the reduction of uncertainty about standards and switching costs, and the inevitable decline in prices. As prices fall, the new product becomes increasingly attractive to customers who perceive only a modest advantage in it.

The number of competitors often grows strikingly high. For example, in the motor-cycle industry, at its peak, there were 136 manufacturers in the UK alone and an estimated 700 worldwide. They were attracted by the rapid growth and profitability of the market. In addition, development of a strong infrastructure of subcontractors and distributors facilitates entry. Prices generally fall rapidly as experience and scale economies lower unit costs, and competition increasingly forces most of these gains to be passed on to the customer.

In the later stages, as the growth rate begins to slow, competition for market share intensifies. The leading players begin to develop global ambitions and to broaden their product lines, pushing them into markets and segments occupied by other strong competitors. Companies which have not developed strong market positioning strategies or achieved low-cost structures begin to see their profit margins falling, and more are forced to exit the market.

The mature phase

Market maturity occurs when the number of new users and new uses dry up. The marketing focus then has to switch from attracting non-users and creating new uses to maintaining or gaining market share. Since current users are more experienced, price and service become more important. Difficulties in finding new uses for the product, and additional attributes to differentiate it at this stage of market, heighten the drift towards commodity status.

Competition has normally become fierce. There is excess capacity, the market is zero-sum and the in-roads of international competitors tend to increase the pressures on companies. Two other factors amplify these pressures on margins. Dealers become more powerful. They can play off alternative suppliers and may introduce their own brands. Second, it is harder for competitors to reduce costs because most of the scale economies and experience curve effects have already been obtained. The shake-out of marginal competitors then usually proceeds rapidly through amalgamations, takeovers and bankruptcies.

At the late stage of maturity, the market may consolidate around a handful of large competitors which effectively create barriers to entry. These barriers centre around the scale economies they possess, the high capital requirements, the advantage of established brand names and the implicit threat of sharp retaliation that newcomers may face. Markets that have matured into this oligopolistic pattern include the oil industry, the supermarket sector and the detergents business.

While internal competition in the industry may become more constrained, competition from substitute technologies is likely to grow over time. For example, continual improvements in plastics and composites add to the problems of steel producers seeking to maintain volume. Such companies then face the dilemma of a vain attempt to fight off the threat or a substantial investment in acquiring and adapting to the substitute technologies.

The decline phase

A new stage is reached when the market enters a period where volume looks set for permanent decline. This occurs when the pool of potential new users and new uses has dried up, when substitute products have demonstrated clear superiority or when buyers' needs change.

Characterizing the market as 'in decline' can be a dangerous mistake. Many markets have developed new sources of growth after entering what appeared to be the decline phase. Resurgent growth can be created by new products, new users and new uses. The motorcycle market declined by 50 per cent in the 1960s, then exhibited explosive growth as new younger customers bought motorcycles as a fun product rather than as a cheap form of transport. Nylon has been written off many times, but as Figure 5.4 illustrates, new uses have continually fuelled resurgent growth.

Even if the decline phase looks certain, the strategic implications are not clear. The usual recommendation from advocates of product life cycle theory, or portfolio concepts such as the Boston Consulting Group's matrix, is to divest from the market. But, in practice, such a view can be a costly oversimplification. Many markets in decline can be highly profitable and substantial cash generators for a very long period if managed properly (e.g. the cigarette market). Further, today there are many more declining markets than in the past. Slower world economic growth, rapid technological change and a fast-changing environment make the management of declining industries an important issue for most firms. The appropriate strategy depends upon how the evolutionary process affects the pattern of declining demand and the intensity of competition.

A market does not decline in a homogeneous pattern; rather the more innovative segments leave the market for new alternatives, leaving behind customer groups who are reluctant or unable to change. Often these remaining customer groups are conservative and price inelastic. This occurs where, perhaps because of habit, the product is

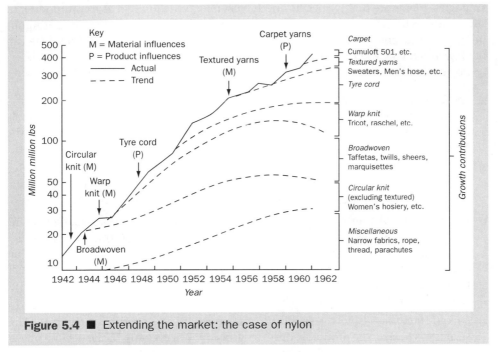

Figure 5.4 ■ Extending the market: the case of nylon

Source: Jordan P. Yale, 'The strategy of nylon's growth', *Modern Textiles Magazine*, February 1964, p. 33

perceived as important to them. Other factors may be a lack of acceptable alternatives, if it is not seen as a major cost element in the budget, or if past long-term advertising has built up strong brand loyalties. In these situations, the remaining competitors may be able to push up prices to offset the decline in volume.

Whether this is possible depends upon the intensity of competition. Factors which may damp down competition, allowing the survivors to earn reasonable returns, are as follows:

■ When there are only a small number of large, evenly balanced competitors remaining in the market.

■ If general agreement exists that the market will continue to decline, so that costly battles to win market share look unattractive.

■ If significant non-price differences exist between competitive products, so that they are not perceived as commodities.

■ If exit barriers are low, so that it is not too costly for competitors to leave the market as prospects decline.

■ If fixed costs are relatively low, so that total costs decline in line with volume.

In some markets (e.g. heavy chemicals) these conditions are clearly not present. Here fixed costs are high, there are major international competitors pursuing varying strategies, plants are highly specific and buyers regard the product as a commodity. In such markets the decline stage is often characterized by intensive competition, ruinous price wars and large losses. But in other markets (e.g. cigarettes), the decline stage can be slow and highly profitable for the remaining players.

Porter identified four strategic options available to the business in the decline phase:[4]

■ *Leadership*. The firm invests in acquisitions and other market share-building strategies to rationalize and dominate the market. This is a high-risk strategy justifiable only if management are convinced that the resulting market structure will allow the firm to recover its late investment.

■ *Niche*. The firm focuses on a segment which is more robust and price insensitive than the mass of the market. Again this may be a difficult strategy, since the remaining competitors are likely to target such a segment.

■ *Harvest*. Here the firm seeks to optimize cash flow rather than market share. Harvesting strategies involve cutting costs, raising prices and rationalizing the range of products, customers and channels. This strategy is most attractive if the firm has been a strong player in the market. If it has not been recognized as an industry leader, the harvesting strategy will normally lead to a rapid collapse of volume, thereby eliminating any gains to be obtained from the strategy.

■ *Divest*. Here the business is sold off to maximize its net investment recovery. This strategy is likely to be profitable only if a decision is made early in the decline phase. If left till later, or after the business has been harvested, there is not likely to be much interest in an acquisition.

Choosing the right strategy depends upon analyzing the strength of the firm's competitive position and assessing the evolutionary processes affecting the market. If the firm has a strong position and the decline phase is expected to be steady and without bruising price wars, the attractiveness of a leadership or niche strategy is enhanced. On the other hand, if the company has no marked advantage, if no robust niches are apparent, and if the products are seen as commodities, rapid exit may be the best alternative. The earlier the oncoming decline phase is recognized and the better the evolutionary characteristics are understood, the more options are available to management.

 ## Formulating marketing strategies

The marketing strategy that management should adopt depends upon three factors. First, what is its competitive position? Is it a market leader or a challenger? Second, what is its strategic objective? Is it seeking market dominance or merely to carve out a profitable niche? Third, at what stage is the market? Is it in its early growth stage or does it look to be in late maturity? The appropriate marketing strategy under these various circumstances is discussed next.

Strategy for the market pioneer

The pioneer is the company which initiates the market through a major new product (e.g. SmithKline's Tagamet), the introduction of a new marketing concept (e.g. Dell's development of mail order as a channel to sell computers), or the creation of a new process which dramatically cuts operating costs or enhances availability (e.g. Carrefour's hypermarche concept).

The pioneer has the opportunity to obtain significant *first mover advantages* which can translate into future market leadership and high returns. The main advantages are as follows:

■ *Demonstrable differential advantage.* Normally the innovation has clear and decisive advantages over the product or concept it replaces. For example, the new electronic Rolm PABX was demonstrably superior to earlier electro-mechanical versions. Subsequent entrants have the tougher job of proving that they are better than the pioneer which introduced the change.

■ *Higher prices.* The innovator segment is normally not price sensitive, allowing the pioneer to earn high margins. Later entrants have to offer lower prices because the market becomes more price elastic and because they have to create a differential advantage against the first mover.

■ *Switching costs.* Once customers have adopted a pioneer's product, they are often reluctant to change. The costs and risk of another change may make it relatively easy for the pioneer to hold on to its early customers.

■ *Economies of scale and experience.* Being first allows the pioneer to build scale economies and move down the experience curve ahead of potential rivals. With this cost advantage it can finance either aggressive pricing or additional marketing investments to boost its share of the market.

Certainly there is evidence that on average pioneers earn higher profits and achieve bigger market shares. The influential PIMS database of 3,000 strategic business units in 450 companies reveals that pioneers earn an average return on investment 35 per cent higher than late entrants. Also 70 per cent of the companies currently holding the leading share in their markets report being 'one of the pioneers'.[5] Other studies show that surviving pioneers in a market held on average a market share of 29 per cent when the industry reached maturity. This compares to an average of 17 per cent for early followers and 12 per cent for late entrants.[6]

But these average figures can be misleading. Some pioneers such as Apple, Glaxo, Carrefour, Denmark's Novo and Sweden's IKEA did extraordinarily well. Many others fail to exploit their innovations, are rapidly caught up by new entrants, and soon disappear. Being first is insufficient. Today there are two additional requirements. First, the pioneer needs to be *fast* into the main markets to exploit the innovation. Competitors can be exceptionally quick to copy winning formulas. Recently Glaxo, planning to launch its new product in South America, found that three local competitors had already copied its compound and launched it locally before Glaxo. The inventor entered as a me-too! Similarly, years after Federal Express had launched its revolutionary air courier system in the United States, it entered the European market. The result was a disaster: competitors like DHL and TNT had copied the Federal Express system and were already well-established in Europe.

Not only has the innovator to move fast to pre-empt competition, but it has to move in *big*. Unless the pioneer succeeds in expanding the market and obtaining significant levels of distribution, it will fail to exploit its strategic window and first mover advantages. If the pioneer succeeds only in establishing a small niche, the window remains open for new entrants to be first to capture the attention of the mass of customers. When this occurs, fast followers obtain the scale economies and capitalize on the innovation, giving them the opportunity to sweep aside the pioneer. This presents a real problem for smaller, innovative companies. Moving fast and big requires large resources to build capacity and invest in aggressive marketing efforts. To exploit their opportunity, small companies may have to look at licensing, joint ventures or co-marketing to leverage their resources. Small may be beautiful for making innovations, but it is not for exploiting them.

Management writers have often oversimplified the strategic options facing the pioneer. It is frequently presented as though the pioneer has a choice of aiming at a mass market or a niche. Correspondingly, the strategy choice is suggested as market penetration or market skimming. But these choices are artificial because they ignore how a market evolves. In practice, a successful pioneering strategy should systematically shift from niche to mass marketing and from what appears as a skimming strategy to one which might be termed penetration.

This is illustrated in Table 5.3, which contrasts the strategy desirable for a pioneer seeking to achieve market leadership, first at the early phase of the market and then at

Table 5.3 ■ Marketing strategy for the pioneer at the early and growth phase of the market

Strategy	Early phase	Later growth
Strategic objective	Rapid growth	Rapid growth
Strategic focus	Expand market: convert non-users, enter new segments	Expand and penetrate market: new users, new uses, new products
Customer targets	Innovators and early adopters	Later adopters, create new segments
Competitor targets	Pre-empt new entrants	Many
Core strategy	Perceived value	Matched to segment
Marketing mix:		
Product range	Narrow	Broad
Price	High	Varied and lower
Promotion	High	High (declining %)
Distribution	Selective	Broad

the later growth stage. At the beginning, the strategic objective of the pioneer should be rapid growth. The strategic focus will be to expand the market by encouraging non-users to purchase. The non-users to be targeted initially will be the innovators – those who first perceive a real benefit from the product and who have the resources to purchase. The competitive strategy is to pre-empt new entrants by exploiting as quickly as possible new market segments and emerging distribution channels. Initially the core strategy will focus on the superior performance of the product compared to previous products or technologies. Turning to the marketing mix, the range will be limited to a single or small number of products because the initial market segment will be a narrow one. Because early buyers are not normally price sensitive, the price should be relatively high. Promotional and advertising spend, however, will be very important to build up awareness and interest in the market. Again because of the initially restricted nature of the market, distribution will be relatively narrow.

As the market moves into the growth stage, the marketing strategy needs to change. The strategic objective is still fast growth, but the focus moves on to developing new market segments, finding new uses for the product and building market share. The target market must change from the innovators to the more typical segments which constitute the mass market. The business is now likely to have important competitors whose strategies need to be analyzed and understood if competitive advantage is to be maintained. The core strategy now becomes more complex: the company is now likely to have a variety of offers, each aimed at a target segment and each seeking to present an appropriate differential advantage.

The marketing mix should also change during the growth stage. The pioneer should broaden the product range to present attractive offers to the evolving market segments. Average prices will come down as the company seeks to penetrate the more price-sensitive segments of the mass market. However, the business should seek to introduce innovative new products in the range which can obtain premium prices and encourage customers to trade up. High advertising and promotional expenditures will still be necessary to support the company's market share aspirations. Finally, it should be seeking to broaden distribution channels to increase availability and service to its target customers.

As the market reaches maturity, the strategy should continue to evolve. Here the objective will normally shift to defending market share rather than aggressive growth. Recently marketing academics have found the writings of military strategists such as Clausewitz and Liddell-Hart illuminating for discussing the defensive options open to companies seeking to maintain the leadership positions they have built up.[7]

Offensive defence

This defensive strategy option operates on the military maxim that attack is the best form of defence. In marketing terms, this means the leader takes the initiative in setting an aggressive pace of innovation: being at the forefront in bringing out new products and new designs, adapting to the latest technologies and pioneering new segments and distribution channels. It means developing a broad product range and carrying items even if they are not profitable, in order to deny newcomers a foothold in the market. Normally, offensive defence is an option eminently suitable for a market leader. This is the policy of Honda in the motorcycle industry and the strategy being attempted by BT in defending its dominance of the British telecommunications market. The leader should have the means and experience to exploit this option. However, complacency, excessive short-term profit goals and a reluctance to invest often see the leader beginning to lag in marketing and technological innovation.

Position defence

The crudest defensive strategy is to seek to build an impregnable fortification to protect one's territory.[8] The weakness of this static form of defence is often illustrated by the calamity of the Maginot Line built by the French in a vain attempt to prevent a German invasion. When war came, the Germans simply went around rather than through it. In marketing terms, position defence means seeking to protect one's current products and technology. It is a form of 'marketing myopia'. Current products are always vulnerable to changing technologies and tastes. No amount of defensive advertising or pricing can prevent the product's obsolescence caused by the evolutionary forces in the market.

Flanking defence

A flanking defence can be used to support a position defence strategy. To protect against an attack directed at a weakly defended area (its exposed flank), the leader erects additional defensive outposts. In marketing terms, a common flanker defence is the launch of a fighter brand. If the leader's major brand is threatened by a competitor's new aggressively priced product, it can reply by launching a cheap brand which undercuts the new product. This prevents the newcomer from making progress in the market, while hopefully leaving relatively untouched the leader's major brand.

Pre-emptive defence

Whereas a flanking defence responds after an attack, a more aggressive strategy is to attack the potential challenger *before* it starts seriously threatening the company. For example, when it was learned that the Japanese intended to sell steel bearings in Europe, the market leader, Sweden's SKF, slashed prices on its matching range by 40 per cent, dramatically undercutting the challenger's expected prices. This strategy proved successful in maintaining market share, but it was extremely costly in eroding SKF's bottom line.

Sometimes, the leader will seek to avoid the cost of a massive pre-emptive defence by *market signals* – threatening huge price cuts if a competitor moves into its market. The company seeks to deter new entrants by making it clear that it will defend its position at all costs. For example, when a leading European supermarket group proposed to introduce its own-label colas, Coca-Cola responded by telling the company that it would reduce supply prices to the supermarket's competitors by 20 per cent in response. The group decided it could not afford to risk attacking Coca-Cola.

Counter-offensive defence

Generally, the leader will respond to a challenger which attacks it. It usually pays the leader to attack where the challenger is most vulnerable. For example, when Laker Airways began its attack on BA's profitable routes, the latter did not retaliate immediately. Laker was allowed to take out huge dollar loans to expand its fleet. Subsequently, when the dollar appreciated against other currencies, effectively increasing Laker's debt and interest obligations, BA slashed prices on Laker's most profitable routes. When Laker was bankrupt, BA restored prices to normal levels.

Mobile defence

A mobile defence involves the firm broadening or diversifying its market focus to strengthen its strategic defence capabilities. Generally this involves the company re-defining its business from a product to the underlying need. For example, ICI, the world leader in decorative paints, redefined its business as 'home adornment', implying a goal of developing product areas complementary and competitive to paints in meeting its customers' need for beautiful homes. The aim was to deter competitors in adjacent technologies from eroding its customer base.

Contraction defence

A leader sometimes has to recognize that it lacks the capability to defend its whole range of products against competition. It may decide to withdraw from those areas where it lacks comparative advantage and to refocus resources around certain core markets. For example, both General Electric and Heinz have announced that they will shift out of products where they do not hold brand leadership positions and refocus on brands where they are dominant.

Many companies do become too diversified. On the other hand, surrendering segments to competition does offer the latter a beach head, which in the longer run can be expanded to a general attack on the firm's core markets. These various defence options are summarized in Figure 5.5.

Market challenger

A market challenger is a company which seeks to wrest the leadership of the market from the current front runner. These challengers may be small entrepreneurial companies, or large businesses such as Unilever, Pepsi and Mercury. The appropriate marketing strategy will depend upon whether the challenger is attacking in the early or late phase of the market.

Attacking a market leader is difficult. Normally the leader's share superiority will mean it has lower unit costs, achieves higher trade prices and consequently possesses

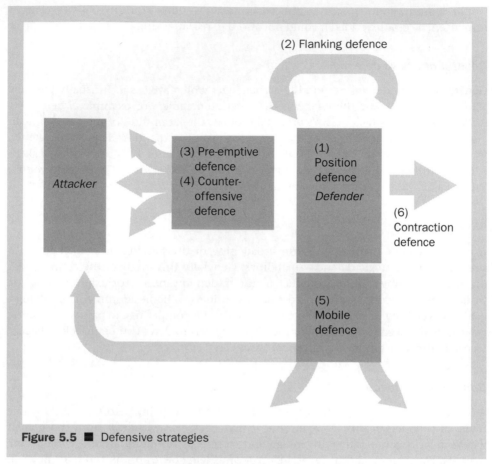

Figure 5.5 ■ Defensive strategies

Source: Philip Kotler and Ravi Singh, 'Marketing warfare in the 1980s', *Journal of Business Strategy*, Winter 1981, p. 36

much stronger profit margins.[9] The leader usually has the resources to pursue a punishing defence.

Attacking a market leader is easier when it is pursued at the early stage of a market's evolution. This is particularly the case where the pioneer has not aggressively expanded the market beyond the small innovatory niche. There are a number of reasons why the pioneer may react only weakly against a determined challenger. One is that it may lack the resources after the heavy R & D programme which preceded the launch. Second, the market is non-zero sum: there is room for both to grow. The challenger is not stealing the pioneer's customers, but rather attracting non-users to the market.

A challenger too has a number of advantages over the pioneer. The challenger can allow the pioneer to take the initial risks and then capitalize on its weaknesses and mistakes. Common errors made by the pioneer are as follows:

- *Marketing mistakes*. Often the pioneer cannot judge which target market segments will be most attracted to the new product. The challenger can take advantage of the pioneer's positioning misjudgements.

- *Product mistakes*. The pioneer's initial product is often discovered to have technical flaws and limitations. The challenger can identify these weaknesses and overcome them.

- *First-generation technology*. In markets characterized by rapid technological change, the challenger can enter with superior second-generation technology which leap-frogs the pioneer's advances.

- *Resource limitations*. Often the pioneer is a smaller company with limited financial resources and marketing expertise. Large, sophisticated companies entering later can swamp the pioneer's efforts by blanket promotion of their products.

At the early stage of the market, the two most effective strategies for the challenger are to seek new market segments or to seek new attributes.

New market segments

Markets grow mainly through the addition of new, discrete customer segments. Generally, only a small proportion of the market will have been penetrated in the early stages by the pioneer, so that focusing on non-users and new segments is a better strategy than seeking to get the pioneer's customers to switch. If the pioneer is still serving the specialist, innovative segment, then there is a window available to exploit the new, broader market segments. Generally this will require modified products, lower prices and different distribution channels.

In the 1960s, the 35 mm camera market was dominated by the industry pioneers – Germany's Rollei and Leica. The Japanese firm Canon observed that only photography specialists used these cameras; the rest of the market used cheap, low-quality alternatives from Kodak and others. Canon's strategy was to ignore the small specialist segment and tailor a simpler, lower-priced 35 mm camera for the mass of amateur, occasional photographers. Canon faced no competition. Within a couple of years it was outselling Rollei and Leica combined. Later, with its continually improving technical skills and marketing capabilities, it was able to take over leadership even in the professional segments.

In a rapidly growing market, the challenger should ask not only who is buying the product today, but also who might buy it tomorrow (Figure 5.6). By identifying the emerging market segments, the challenger can then become the pioneer. Even a late entrant can be the pioneer of an emerging mass market if the early entrants have not developed the new segments with the appropriate products and distribution channels.

New attributes

A second strategy for the challenger is to provide new attributes beyond those offered by the pioneer or market leader. A phenomenon of an evolving market is the accretion of attributes desired by customers. Initially the innovator creates a market by offering

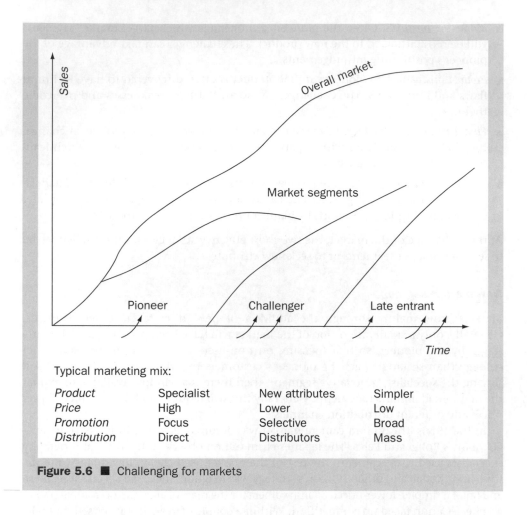

Figure 5.6 ■ Challenging for markets

the benefit which meets a latent need. This initial benefit can be called a core or primary attribute. For example, the first commercial computer provided a break-through in information-processing power. ICI's invention of beta-blockers signifi-cantly reduced the blood pressure and heart rate for patients with hypertension. However, soon many competitors were offering this primary benefit and it no longer appeared as a discriminator. Customers take it as a given for any supplier. If new attri-butes do not appear, the product becomes a commodity.

In practice, successful challengers develop additional attributes to augment the primary one. Computer manufacturers increase the power, reduce the size, make them more user-friendly and add services. Pharmaceutical companies develop drugs for hypertension which are smaller, longer lasting or faster acting. As each attribute gets matched by competitors, it ceases to be a discriminator. Customers' expectations are progressive – they continue to expect more. Thus the challenger can break into the market by innovating with a new attribute.

If a company seeks to mount a leadership challenge at a mature stage of the market, the strategic focus is different. Here the primary goal will be to attract customers from the leader, rather than to penetrate non-users. Again military analogies are being found useful. Kotler and Singh distinguished five attack strategies available for the challenger (Figure 5.7).[10]

Frontal attack

This is a head-on attack on the market leader. It means seeking to beat the leader by offering customers superior products or lower prices, or outspending it in advertising and promotion. This strategy normally fails because the leader is likely to have lower costs and better distribution, and is consequently in a good position to retaliate

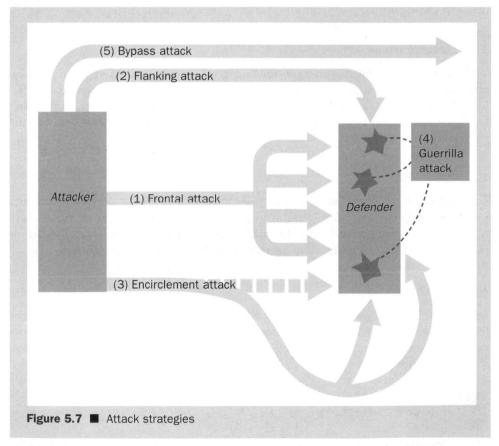

Figure 5.7 ■ Attack strategies

Source: Philip Kotler and Ravi Singh, 'Marketing warfare in the 1980s', *Journal of Business Strategy*, Winter 1981, p. 38

strongly. The military historian Liddell-Hart, after analyzing all the major battles from the Greek wars to the present day, concluded that only six of the 280 victories were the result of a frontal attack. The military view is that, for a frontal attack to succeed against a well-entrenched opponent, the attacker must deploy at least a 3:1 advantage in combat fire power. Frontal attacks make sense only if the leader has become seriously debilitated.

Flank attack

A flank attack differs from a frontal one in that it attacks where the leader is weak rather than where it is strong. While they are most common in the rapid growth phase, even in the mature stage two opportunities frequently occur which create the conditions for a successful flank attack. One is the emergence of new markets (e.g. overseas countries) or market segments not yet served by the leader. The second is the identification of new needs or attributes which are not effectively met by the market leader (e.g. low-calorie beer).

Encirclement attack

While a flank attack focuses on a specific target, an encirclement strategy launches an offensive on several fronts simultaneously. The challenger brings out a variety of offerings aimed at smaller or underdeveloped segments of the market. The attack does not challenge the leader's heartland, but focuses on specialized areas that it is not covering effectively.

Guerrilla attack

Smaller companies might not be able to finance any of the above strategies. An alternative is guerrilla attacks to surprise and wrong-foot the leader, with the objective of eventually seeking a stronger foothold in the market. Low-cost guerrilla attacks might include publicity stunts, special promotions and targeted efforts in a single geographic area.

Bypass attack

Rather than fight the leader, the bypass or leapfrog strategy aims to attack where the leader is unrepresented. This might mean choosing a country where the leader does not have an operation. Alternatively, it may mean developing a rival technological solution for the market.

Niche companies

All successful marketing is based upon the pursuit of niche markets. Markets are increasingly segmented and effective marketing centres on capitalizing on the differences in needs between segments by offering different products at different prices. Companies producing consumer goods, like Unilever and BSN, and those offering industrial products and services, like ICI and Alcatel, all pursue niche strategies. However, a niche company is something different. A niche company focuses on a single, narrow market segment. While larger companies pursue multiple niche strategies, a niche company pursues a single niche. Surviving as a niche company is considerably more difficult than surviving as a company pursuing a broad, multiple-niche strategy.

A niche company strategy is more viable in the early and growth stages of the market. As the market approaches maturity, it becomes much more difficult. At the outset a pioneer can aim either to be the market leader or to become a smaller niche player. The niche objective may be attractive to management for several reasons. First, pioneers often have limited resources to invest in capacity expansion and promotion. Focusing then on a specific segment of the market may appear the only viable alternative. Second, competition from the incumbents may be potentially so powerful that market leadership may appear unattainable. Third, the business may have special skills or competences which fit well with one segment of the market, but poorly with the mass market. For example, Hewlett-Packard possessed strongly based capabilities in the scientific and business market, but had little experience of consumer markets. This background dissuaded it from pushing first its electronic calculators then its personal computers into the growing mass market. Finally, many companies become niche players by default. They lack the foresight or skills to be credible as multiple niches.

A successful niche strategy is based upon offering superior value to customers in one segment of the market. Superior value can be based on either of two distinct strategies. First, the nicher can offer superior perceived 'quality' to customers in the target segment. This may arise from products with superior performance (e.g. Porsche), service (e.g. First Direct), personnel (e.g. Claridges) or image (e.g. Rolex). Superior quality is achieved when a nicher knows the requirements of customers in the niche better than its broadly based competitors, and has the skill to tailor its resources to meeting precisely the unique needs of this group. The second strategic option is to offer lower-priced solutions to the target niche. Many local companies pursue this strategy in their specific geographical areas. The local builder, accountant or repair shop will often undercut its bigger national rivals. Such companies often have lower overheads and higher labour productivity than their more bureaucratic competitors.

For a niche strategy to be viable there are several testing requirements:

■ *A separable niche.* The requirement of a distinct customer group with needs which differ from others is normally the easiest one. For example, people who buy luxury sports cars do not see a family saloon as a good substitute. A coatings company purchasing speciality chemicals will have different requirements from the run-of-the-mill blender.

■ *A separate cost structure.* More difficult is the requirement that the nicher is not penalized by a higher cost structure from operating in only a fraction of the market. Often the bigger companies have leverage in R & D, buying and scale economies which allow them to undercut the nichers in the specialized segment.

■ *Lack of strategic interest.* A small company has to hope that its niche is not of strategic interest to the major players. If giants like Toyota or Unilever do decide that it is strategically important to capture share in the niche, then they are likely to have the resources and capabilities to make it very tough for the smaller players.

■ *Lack of potential.* The major players are likely to be uninterested in a segment only if it is too small to be worth investment. For example, Car Bodies Limited has an 85 per cent share of the London black taxi market. The specialist requirements in London (especially the wheelchair access requirement) essentially prevents standard cars from being used as taxis. Because the annual volume is so small, it is not worthwhile for a major competitor to make the investment to produce a rival taxi. However, if the market grows, the niche is likely to attract competition.

■ *Cyclical stability.* A niche player has all its eggs in one basket. It is tough for niche players to survive for long in a market characterized by sharp cyclical swings. In a recession they have no other market to provide offsetting gains.

As the market develops towards maturity, the likelihood of these conditions being fulfilled diminishes. First, during the growth stage of the market, it is common for the market to be characterized by distinct strategic groups of competitors, each focusing on a single broad segment. For example, in the early days of the computer market, IBM dominated the mainframe, Dec led in minis and Apple led in PCs. In the 1960s, Ford and General Motors led in the mass car market, the Japanese were penetrating the low end, and specialists like Mercedes, BMW and Jaguar led the top end. As the market develops, certain segments mature, encouraging competitors in these areas to invade adjacent segments. For example, IBM invaded both the PC and the mini computer markets. Ford and GM tried to produce exclusive car marques.

Second, competitors which successfully penetrate the low-price end of the market eventually seek to move into higher value-added segments. For the last 25 years, the Japanese have moved 'up-market' in cars, cameras, chemicals and many other areas. A third reason why large companies develop multiple niche strategies is progress in management. Executives are learning how to restructure into networks of small businesses, each of which can be targeted as a niche. Each SBU has a separate marketing strategy and organization, but they have synergies in shared R & D, distribution and other scarce capabilities. For example, the giant engineering group ABB has 1,300 separate companies and 5,000 SBUs, each targeting specific niches but sharing certain key skills, resources and experience.

Over time niche strategies tend to become less viable. Famous niche companies like Aston Martin, Ferrari, Harrods, Financial Times, Perrier, Car Bodies, Foseco and Mont Blanc are now all part of large multiple-niche companies. Single-niche companies can have a long life. But their lifespan depends upon the strategic interest that their competitors have in the niche, and the strength of the barriers to entry that can be created.

Summary

Managers have to understand that markets are highly dynamic. Today customer requirements, competitive activity and technological solutions are impermanent and in constant flux. The product life cycle is too simple a model for predicting the nature of these changes. Instead management have to assess the six underlying evolutionary forces which shape the behaviour of markets.

Successful competitive strategies are based on anticipating these evolutionary forces and using them to advantage. Most pioneers need to appreciate that their advantage is shortlived and that the strategic window they create must be rapidly and decisively exploited and then vigilantly defended. Newcomers find the odds stacked against them when they attack an effective market leader. A successful leader is rarely overtaken by a head-on strategy. Instead success usually depends upon further innovation in identifying new market segments and additional attributes not yet identified or exploited by the leader.

Market evolution is characterized by competitors crossing into each other's strongholds. Competition increases both in intensity and scope. This makes it difficult for companies pursuing single-niche strategies. Over time, high-value niches become attractive to larger companies searching for new avenues of growth.

Questions

1. Give some examples of products that appear to have followed a product life cycle. Find some examples of products which have not. What are the underlying explanations of these differences?

2. An electronics company invents a major new home entertainment product. Discuss how the market is likely to change over the next five years. What implications do these changes have for the company's marketing strategy?

3. The cigarette market in western Europe appears to be slowly declining. What strategies would you recommend for a leading cigarette producer?

4. A small pharmaceutical company pioneers a major new heart drug. What strategic considerations should govern its approach to proceeding with the innovation?

5. Alpha Company dominates the market for the portable fire extinguishers maintained in hotels, offices and other public buildings. How could Beta Company, with half the sales of Alpha, challenge for market dominance?

6. Gamma holds a niche position making high-quality motors for garden mowers. Many major players such as Honda and Yamaha also operate in this sector. Discuss the problems likely to face Gamma in maintaining its niche position.

Notes

1. See, for example, P. Kotler, *Marketing Management* (Englewood Cliffs, NJ: Prentice Hall, 1997), 9th edn, p. 346.

2. See, for example, Theodore Levitt, 'Exploit the product life cycle', *Harvard Business Review*, November 1965, pp. 81–94; Robert D. Buzzell, 'Competitive behaviour and product life cycles', in John Wright and J. L. Goldstucker (eds.), *New Ideas for Successful Marketing*, (Chicago, IL: American Marketing Association, 1966), pp. 46–68.

3. Michael E. Porter, *Competitive Strategy* (New York: Free Press, 1980), pp. 27–8.

4. *Ibid.*, pp. 267–73.

5. Robert D. Buzzell and Bradley T. Gale, *The PIMS Principles: Linking strategy to performance* (New York: Free Press, 1987).

6. Peter N. Golder and Gerard J. Tellis, 'Pioneer advantage: marketing logic or marketing legend', *Journal of Marketing Research*, May 1993, pp. 158–70; Roger A. Kerin, P. Rajan Varadarajan and Robert A. Peterson, 'First mover advantage: a synthesis, conceptual framework and research propositions', *Journal of Marketing*, October 1992, pp. 33–52.

7. Carl von Clausewitz, *On War* (London: Routledge, 1908); B. H. Liddell-Hart, *Strategy* (New York: Praeger, 1967). For applications to marketing, see Philip Kotler and Ravi Singh Achrol, 'Marketing warfare in the 1980s', *Journal of Business Strategy*, Winter 1981, pp. 30–41; Al Ries and Jack Trout, *Marketing Warfare* (New York: McGraw-Hill, 1986).

8. The following draws heavily on Kotler and Singh, *op. cit.*

9. See Buzzell and Gale, *op. cit.*, pp. 8–15.

10. Kotler and Singh, *op. cit.*

Chapter 6

Building successful brands

Brands are at the heart of marketing and business strategy. Marketing is about de-commoditizing the company's offer. If a company's offer is perceived to be the same as those of competitors, then consumers will be indifferent and will choose the cheapest or most accessible. Companies that are forced to compete on price rarely make satisfactory profits. The purpose of marketing is to create a preference for the company's brand. If customers perceive one brand as superior, they will prefer it and pay more for it. Brand equity is the value of these additional cash flows generated for a product because of its brand identity.

Developing brand equity is a central issue for top management because it is a key determinant of corporate value. The average British and American company is valued by the stock market at around twice net balance sheet assets. However, companies with portfolios of strong brands are valued by the stock market at four times net assets.[1] Huge sums are now paid for brands. Nestlé paid £2.5 billion for Rowntree – six times net assets. Grand Met paid $1.2 billion for Heublein, largely to obtain the right to market the Smirnoff brand in the USA. Brand identities can be rented or licensed. Sunkist, for example, receives £10 million per year in royalties for allowing such companies as Cadbury-Schweppes, General Mills, Lipton and Ciba-Geigy to use its brand name.

Successful brands create wealth by attracting and retaining customers. When a company creates this type of customer preference and loyalty, it can build a strong market share, maintain good price levels and generate strong cash flows. This in turn drives up the share price and provides the basis for future growth. Brands are not just a feature of consumer markets; they are equally central in industrial markets, for services and retailers, and for organizations marketing a collection of skills.

The following sections begin with an analysis of brands from a marketing viewpoint: the characteristics of strong brands, how they are built and how they are reinforced. It is then shown how, by adding values for customers, successful brands create financial assets which generate sustainable cash flows for shareholders. The most common types of problem that managers face with brands are then explored. When should a firm try to extend a successful brand to a different market area? How can brands be revitalized and repositioned? What is the future of global brands? Under what circumstances does it pay to acquire brands or companies with strong brands? Finally, a key dilemma in branding is discussed – the conflict between long-term investment in building and reinforcing brands and the need to maintain short-term profit performance.

Products and brands

To understand the role of brands it is necessary to distinguish three concepts: a product, a brand and a successful brand. A *product* is anything which meets the functional needs of customers. This can be a *physical product*, such as a specific chemical compound, an industrial lathe or a watch. Alternatively, it can be a *service product*, such as a bank, courier or management consultancy service. At the most basic level, customers buy products to meet certain functional needs: a watch is bought to tell the time, a bank is used to save, transfer or borrow money.

Most suppliers will want to identify their own product and differentiate it from competitors' products. They do this by branding it. A *brand* can be defined as a specific name, symbol or design – or, more usually, some combination of these – which is used to distinguish a particular seller's product. A supplier will then normally try to create awareness and preference among customers for its brand. Awareness can be created by developing a striking presentation of the brand and spending sufficiently on advertising and promoting it. Creating brand preference, however, is more difficult. Many suppliers achieve high awareness, but are disliked by large sections of the market. These are *negative brands* – the brand name is a liability rather than an asset. In the past Woolworths, British Leyland, the Midland Bank and Skoda are examples of companies which achieved this dubious distinction.

The specific characteristic of a *successful brand* is that, in addition to having a product which meets the functional requirements of consumers, it has added values which meet certain of their psychological needs. These *added values* are elicited feelings of confidence that the brand is of higher quality or more desirable than similar products from competitors. Table 6.1 shows the leading brands as perceived by representative consumers in some major countries. The rankings are based upon a summation of customer brand awareness and brand preference.

A successful brand (S) can be seen as a combination of an effective product (P), a distinctive identity (D) and added values (AV).

$$S = P \times D \times AV$$

Product effectiveness can normally be measured in blind product-use tests against competitors. Distinctive identity is measured by prompted and unprompted brand awareness. Added values can be measured by perceptual research and brand preferences. The three characteristics of a successful brand are multiplicative rather than additive – each is essential. Without a good product it is impossible to create a successful brand. Similarly, unless differentiation and awareness can be developed, a good product will not leave the supplier's premises.

Table 6.1 ■ The world's most powerful brands

Europe	USA	Japan	UK
1 Coca-Cola	Coca-Cola	Sony	Marks & Spencer
2 Sony	Campbell's	National	Cadbury
3 Mercedes-Benz	Disney	Mercedes-Benz	Kellogg's
4 BMW	Pepsi Cola	Toyota	Heinz
5 Philips	Kodak	Takashimaya	Rolls-Royce
6 Volkswagen	NBC	Rolls-Royce	Boots
7 Adidas	Black & Decker	Seiko	Nescafé
8 Kodak	Kellogg's	Matsushita	BBC
9 Nivea	McDonald's	Hitachi	Rowntree
10 Porsche	Hershey	Suntory	Sainsbury

Source: Landor Image Power Survey (London: Landor Associates, 1991)

Companies can choose to focus their brand building at various levels.

■ *Company brand.* Companies such as Philips, Mercedes Benz and Heinz choose to make the company name the dominant brand identity across all or most of their products.

■ *Individual brand names.* At the opposite extreme, companies such as Unilever and Procter & Gamble have focused on individual brand identities for each of their products (Unilever: Persil, Surf, Whisk, Domestos, Fairy Liquid, Comfort, Radion, etc.) and avoid featuring the company name.

■ *Company and individual brand.* Companies such as Kellogg's (Kellogg's Cornflakes, Kellogg's Raisin Bran, etc.) choose a middle way, featuring both company and individual brand names.

■ *Range branding.* Some companies group families of products under separate range names. For example, Matsushita markets its electronic products under four brand families: National, Panasonic, Technics and Quasar.

Company brand names have the advantages of economies of scale in marketing investments and greater recognition, and they can often facilitate the introduction of new products. On the other hand, individual brand names permit finer segmentation of markets, limit cannibalization between the company's brands and reduce the risk of individual brand failures harming the company's overall reputation. Range branding and mixed strategies seek a balance between these two extremes.

The trend today is clearly away from companies launching new free-standing brands in the way Unilever and Procter & Gamble did in the past: the marketing costs are simply too great and the risks too high. Instead they are focusing on promoting the company as the umbrella brand or concentrating on a handful of strong 'pillar' brand names and using these as range brands or the core for line and brand extensions.

Added values

Added values – the subjective beliefs of customers – are at the heart of building successful brands. That such beliefs exist has been demonstrated on countless occasions. In tests where customers are presented with competitive products in an unbranded form, there is often no clear preference. But if a top brand name such as Marks & Spencer, the *Financial Times*, Sony or Cadbury is attached, a dramatic switch in preferences invariably occurs (see Box 6.1). Not only will people prefer the strong brand name, but they will actually be willing to pay a higher price for it.

Nor is the emotional impact of the brand limited to consumer goods. A classic study by Professor T. Levitt at the Harvard Business School clearly demonstrated that brand image has a significant effect on industrial buying decisions.[2] He found that the more powerful the brand name, the greater the chance of the industrial buyer giving the company a hearing for a new product, and the greater the likelihood of its early adoption. Further, the study showed that the stronger the technical background of the purchasing manager, the greater the influence of the brand.

Global marketing increases the importance of industrial brand names. For example, in the international construction market, US-trained engineers and consultants dominate as specifiers of the equipment and materials employed. For the big contracts in Asia and the Middle East, local suppliers often cannot compete because the specifiers are selecting the international brand names (e.g. Grace, Seka, MBT) that they are familiar with.

BOX 6.1

What's in a brand name?

Coke and Pepsi. A panel of consumers were asked to taste Coke and Pepsi. In *blind tests* (i.e. where the brand identity was concealed), 51 per cent preferred Pepsi and 44 per cent Coke. In the *open test* (where brand identities were shown), preferences were completely reversed: 65 per cent preferred Coke and only 23 per cent Pepsi. Such tests often provide striking illuminations of the power of brand names.

Toyota and General Motors. A joint venture plant in Fremont, California produced two virtually identical cars: one branded Toyota Corolla, the other GM's Geo Prizm. The production costs were the same – $10,300. However, outside the plant the Toyota retailed at a price 10 per cent higher than its twin; it depreciated more slowly, so that its second-hand value was almost 18 per cent higher than the GM model after five years; and its market share was more than twice that of the Geo. In five years, it is estimated that Toyota made $128 million more profit than GM from their joint venture. Many markets are like this – the power of the brand name is more important than differences in manufacturing costs or quality.

Sources: Leslie de Chernatony and Malcolm H. B. McDonald, *Creating Brands* (London: Heinemann, 1992); *The Economist*, 6 January 1996, p. 61

Sources of brand values

That most buying decisions are influenced by brand values which are additional to those based upon real performance differences cannot be in doubt. There are two reasons why this occurs. First, the task of choosing competing products on technical or rational grounds is too difficult, time consuming and expensive for most buyers. The sheer volume of decisions to be made every day, the pace of technical change, the number of competing alternatives and the bewildering variety of advertising and selling messages mean that buyers look for safe short cuts. Reputable brand names provide confidence and allow customers to cut through the risks and complexity of choice.

The second reason that added values occur is that brands are bought for emotional reasons as well as function. A Mercedes car is bought to make a personal statement as well as for a means of transport. Similarly, most watches tell the time with high reliability, so that functionality has little relevance to the choice process. People use brands to show off their lifestyles, interests, values or wealth. Customers choose brands which they perceive as meeting their 'needs'. But in today's affluent society, these needs, to borrow from Maslow's theory of motivation, are as likely to be about self-actualization or esteem, or to gain a sense of belonging, as they are to be basic physical or economic needs.

How added values occur

How is it that some brands have strong images while others do not? Brand values derive from five main sources:[3]

■ *Experience of use.* If a brand provides good service over many years of regular use, it acquires added values of familiarity and proven reliability. By contrast, a brand which is often unsatisfactory in use or where, through lack of reminders, the customer slips out of a regular usage pattern will fail to acquire these positive associations. The British motorcycle and car industries suffered declining brand images during the 1960s and 1970s as a result of their lack of reliability compared to their German and Japanese competitors.

■ *User associations.* Brands frequently acquire an image from the type of people who are seen as using them. Advertising and sponsorship are often used to convey images of prestige or success by associating the brand with glamorous personalities. In consumer tests, buyers will describe with great facility the types of people whom they perceive as drinking Carling Black Label, driving Volvos or buying a Rolex.

■ *Belief in efficacy.* In many cases, if customers have faith that a brand will work, it is more likely to work effectively for them. For pharmaceuticals, cosmetics and even complex high-tech products, faith in a brand generates satisfaction in use. Beliefs in efficacy can be created by comparative evaluations and rankings from consumer associations, industry endorsements and newspaper editorials.

■ *Brand appearance.* The design of the brand can clearly affect preference by offering cues to quality. Levitt describes an experiment with expensive laboratory technology.[4] Two designs of the same product were developed, one by engineers, the other by professional designers. When the two models were shown to a sample of laboratory directors – all with PhDs in electronics – the professional design was overwhelmingly chosen.

■ *Manufacturers' name and reputation*. In many situations a strong company name (e.g. Sony, Kellogg's, Hewlett-Packard) attached to a new product will transfer positive associations, so providing confidence and incentive to trial.

Measuring and planning added values

There are a variety of research methods for helping managers understand how consumers perceive brands. For industrial goods and services this is often straightforward, but for consumer goods, indirect or projective interviewing techniques are sometimes more useful. Consumers are often unwilling or unable to explain the inner feelings and motivations which drive their brand choices, so researchers approach these issues obliquely.[5] The most common projective techniques are as follows:

■ *Free association*. Customers are asked to provide spontaneously the words that come to mind when a brand, brand name or slogan is presented to them. This is followed by a discussion which seeks to discover why the brand creates these associations.

■ *Picture impressions*. Customers interpret scenes in which the brand plays a role. In one example, a man is shown reading a specific mail order catalogue, and his wife, standing nearby, is making a remark. The respondent is asked to imagine what the wife is saying about the catalogue. This technique recognizes that, while consumers are often constrained in talking about their own feelings, there are no such inhibitions in projecting these feelings on to others.

■ *If the brand were a person*. Respondents are asked to think of the brand as a person and describe its personality. The result is often a revealing picture of the brand's perceived personality and associations.

■ *Animals, activities and objects*. Customers are asked to relate brands to types of animal, car or tree. Again the particular association reveals how brands are thought of by customers.

■ *What is the brand user like?* Respondents describe typical users of various brands. The aim is to reveal hidden needs and motivations behind brand choices.

■ *Brand similarities and differences*. To identify choice dimensions, respondents are asked to identify how brands differ. A related approach is to ask consumers to rank pairs of brands according to similarity. Then, using computer-based scaling techniques, a map of a market can be derived. Figure 6.1 shows a brand map of the beer market as perceived by US consumers. The dots show the perceived positions of the brands, and the circles the preferences of consumers. The larger the circle, the greater the customer segment. The map reveals the strengths and weaknesses of the various brands, 'gaps' for new brands can be explored, and directions for repositioning existing brands can be suggested.

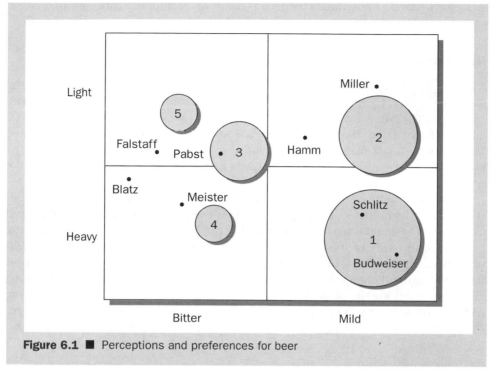

Figure 6.1 ■ Perceptions and preferences for beer

Source: Philip Kotler, *Marketing Management: Analysis, planning, implementation and control,* 7th edn, Englewood Cliffs, NJ: Prentice Hall, p. 448

Building on such measures of consumer perceptions, the manager will seek to formulate a *brand positioning strategy* – a plan of what image the brand should cultivate. For example, should it be seen as 'prestigious' (e.g. Rolls-Royce), 'value for money' (e.g. Marks & Spencer), 'environmentally friendly' (e.g. Body Shop) or 'high-tech' (e.g. Hewlett-Packard)? In developing the positioning concept, the manager will have two criteria in mind. First, he or she wants it to be *unique*: to differentiate the brand clearly from other competitors in the market – otherwise, why should customers select it? Second, the unique advantage must be considered relevant and *desirable* by the target market segment. Developing a positioning strategy involves four steps:

1. *Attribute research* – qualitative research of the type described above, into what attributes buyers use in considering alternative brands.

2. *Competitor research* – identifying how competitive brands are perceived along these attributes.

3. *Gap analysis* – exploring whether there are any need 'gaps': attractive positions which would allow the company to offer desirable added values superior to or not offered by competitors.

4. *Concept testing* – evaluating whether any resulting positioning concepts offer added values which are understood, believed and of perceived value to target customers.

Brand identity

A *brand image* refers to how the target market perceives the brand. A *brand identity* is the message sent out by the brand through its product form, name, visual signs, advertising, etc. The two are often different: what image people have of the brand can be quite different from the message that the company is seeking to communicate. Management should plan the brand's identity, since this is the key to acceptance in the market. To help managers plan and analyze a brand's identity, the dimensions of the brand need to be described.

Kapfferer introduced the concept of the brand pyramid, consisting of three tiers (Figure 6.2).[6] Its fundamental or genetic code is the brand core, which remains fixed over time. The middle tier of the pyramid is the brand style, which articulates the brand core in terms of the culture it conveys, its personality and its image or self-projection. The base layer of the pyramid comprises the brand themes, which are how the brand currently communicates through its advertising, press releases, packaging, etc. Themes include the physical appearance of the product (colour, logo, packaging), its reflection (e.g. type of spokesperson used to advertise the brand) and the relationship expressed (e.g. glamour, prestige). Brand themes are more flexible than the brand

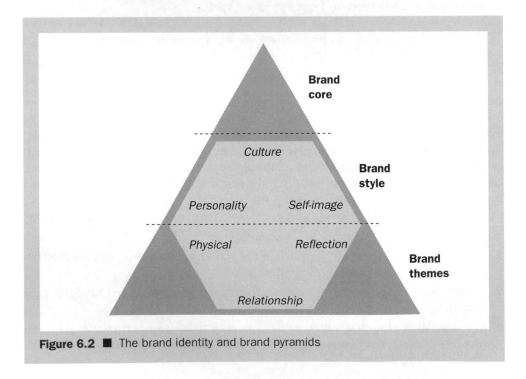

Figure 6.2 ■ The brand identity and brand pyramids

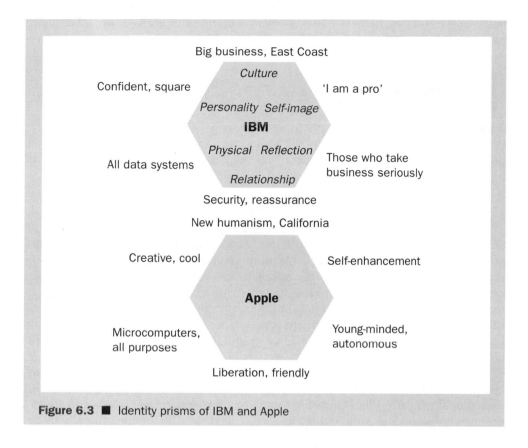

Big business, East Coast

Culture

Confident, square   'I am a pro'

Personality Self-image

IBM

Physical Reflection   Those who take

All data systems   business seriously

Relationship

Security, reassurance

New humanism, California

Creative, cool   Self-enhancement

Apple

Microcomputers,   Young-minded,
all purposes   autonomous

Liberation, friendly

Figure 6.3 ■ Identity prisms of IBM and Apple

style and brand core, and will change with fashion, style and technology. Kapfferer describes the set of brand style and themes as the identity prism. Figure 6.3 shows the prisms of the IBM and Apple brands.

Not only do identity prisms differ between brands, but so do brand cores. IBM's core might be 'professional systems for professional managers'; Apple's might be 'PCs for creative people'. Some brand cores are narrow; others offer much more scope for stretching across a broad range of products. For example, it is hard to see brand names like Persil, Land Rover and British Airways expanding far beyond their current product and market areas, whereas the Virgin brand name has been stretched – so far successfully – across an airline, radio stations, colas, record shops, insurance and financial products. Clearly, having a brand name which is both strong and stretchable is a considerable asset.

The concepts of the brand prism and brand pyramid are useful. First, they enable management and their agencies to understand the brand, its strengths and opportunities. Second, they help develop brand strategy and the formulation of the brand's positioning in the market. Third, they enable the brand team to develop consistency in the message being transmitted through packaging and design, advertising, below-the-line activities and through line and brand extensions. Finally, understanding the brand's core and style helps set the perimeters of brand extensions – how far the brand can be meaningfully stretched to other products and market segments.

How to build brands

A successful brand is one which customers perceive as offering superior value. A brand image can be thought of as being built up in four layers – a quality product, a basic brand which differentiates the product, and then augmented and potential layers of branding which enhance its values.[7]

A quality product

Since satisfactory experience in use is the major way in which brand values are acquired, having a quality product is the foundation upon which all other brand associations are built. New products are unlikely to succeed unless they score better than existing competitors in blind product-use tests. Since it takes time to build values of trust and confidence, existing brands in the market always have an advantage unless the new product offers demonstrably superior performance. Of course, if existing brands are not updated as superior technology and features become available, they will become obsolete.

However, having a superior product or service is only the starting point. Today, competitors quickly copy innovations, making functional advantages shortlived. For example, in the early 1980s the world's most profitable pharmaceutical product was a unique anti-ulcer drug from SmithKline, which generated £1 billion annually in net cash flow. Then its patent expired, generic versions of the drug were rapidly introduced by competitors, and profits quickly drained out of the product, forcing SmithKline into a merger with Beechams a few years later. Products cannot generate high sustainable profits unless the company can build barriers to competitive entry. In some markets, patents can keep competitors out for an extended period. In others, government regulations, monopoly of the resource base, control over distribution or scale economies can stop competition from eroding market share and profits. But these are exceptional restrictions. The most common barrier to competition is to build a brand which has values beyond those of functionality.

The basic brand

The 'basics' of the brand are the core elements upon which first differentiation and then the brand personality are built. They are the essential marketing mix elements: product features such as choice of brand name, design, packaging, logo and colour; price points; communications, including advertising, selling and sales promotion; and channel decisions such as type of outlet and mode of distribution. The brand elements should be tested against three criteria:

- Do they support product *performance*? (For example, does the pack keep the contents fresh? Is it easy to open? Is the distribution channel capable of efficient delivery and servicing?)

- Do they *differentiate* the brand, facilitating brand awareness and recall? (For example, is the brand name easy to remember? Is the advertising effective?)

- Do they contribute to the brand's *positioning* strategy? (For example, are the name, design and advertising consistent with the image the brand seeks to convey?) Brand features often signal desirable attributes to customers. With cars, a solid door closure sound implies good workmanship and a solid, safe body. In stereo, large speakers imply better sound. With detergents, suds indicate an effective cleaner.

The augmented brand

The basic brand delivers the core product to customers in an attractive way. But successful companies seek the competitive edge by enlarging the core product with supplementary products and services which enhance the customer's total purchasing and use experience. The company searches for ways to meet expectations beyond that required or even expected by the buyer. It is at this augmented level of added values that much of today's competition occurs. For example, when a customer buys a PC from Dell, he or she also obtains a toll-free hotline number to answer any problems in using the product on a day-to-day basis. When the customer phones, the Dell operator has on-line details of the enquirer's machine, any special features and what its service history has been. Besides offering a good product, Dell uses its 'direct relationship marketing' to forge a close, direct relationship with its customers, and offers them some of the best back-up services in the industry, all of which are designed to build brand loyalty.

The most common methods of augmenting the brand are services, unlimited guarantees and financial support. *Services* are particularly important. For example, an MBA programme is a service product offered by many university business schools. The core brand that most offer is an examined set of courses in professional management. Since the basic products are all similar, the top schools seek to augment their brands with extra services for their customers. These may include attractive hotel and restaurant facilities, social programmes for the student's spouse, a crèche, leisure facilities, foreign language tuition, overseas exchanges, career counselling, job placement and net-working associations. Prospective students choose the brand which they perceive is most likely to offer the best total solution to their needs of a satisfying educational and social experience, and a rewarding career afterwards.

Unlimited guarantees are becoming increasingly popular among the best companies. Xerox, Marks & Spencer and Federal Express, for example, offer customers the opportunity to return the product and get their money back, whatever the reason. Such guarantees are found to have a double benefit. First, they provide a competitive advantage from the security offered to customers. Second, unconditional guarantees can be a lever for a general upgrading of the quality of the supplier's product and service standards. Potentially expensive guarantees highlight to employees very directly the cost of poor quality and their responsibilities for satisfying customers. Paradoxically, run properly to challenge personnel to achieve excellence in product and service delivery, unconditional guarantees actually lower the supplier's total costs.[8]

Financial support can be a powerful and direct means of building customer loyalty. The supplier can offer distributors or end customers loans to finance their own business development. These loans are repaid not in cash, but in long-term supply contracts. Such arrangements are common in brewing, the oil industry, pharmaceuticals and the restaurant business. Besides tying the customer to long-term contracts, they facilitate the introduction of higher-priced brands by enabling the customer to write off its debt faster.

These augmented brand features offer differential advantages to customers and they have the additional advantage of being more difficult to copy. Some, like financial support, are expensive for competitors to match. Others, such as service and guarantees, depend upon the culture and commitment of the people in the organization. Such assets and core capabilities are more difficult to build and emulate than simple product features.

The potential brand

The final defensive ring to be built around the product is the potential brand (Figure 6.4). A brand achieves its potential when its added values are so great that the customers will not willingly accept substitutes even when the alternatives are substantially cheaper or more readily available. Here the psychological benefits – confidence, esteem, total satisfaction – make possible brand dominance, high profit margins and long-term brand loyalty. By these means brands such as Coca-Cola, McKinsey, Kellogg, Kodak, Gillette, Marks & Spencer and Levi have maintained brand leadership for over fifty years.

The major characteristics of brands which achieve their potential can be summarized as follows:

- *A quality product.* Since satisfactory experience in use is the major determinant of brand values, quality is the number one requirement. If quality is allowed to deteriorate or if the brand is surpassed by competitive products which work better, then its position will be undermined.

- *Being first.* Being first into the market does not necessarily bring success, but it does make the task less tough. It is easier to stake a position in the consumer's mind when the brand has no competitors to rival its claims. 'Being first' means first into the key markets, not first with the technology. For example, Texas Instruments brought out the first electronic watch, but Casio and Seiko were first to bring it to a mass market. TI developed the technology, but it was the Japanese who developed the first successful brands.

- *Unique positioning concept.* If the brand is not the innovator, it must have a unique positioning concept – a segmentation scheme, benefit proposition or augmented brand – which will distinguish it from the field of competitors. Swatch did this with its

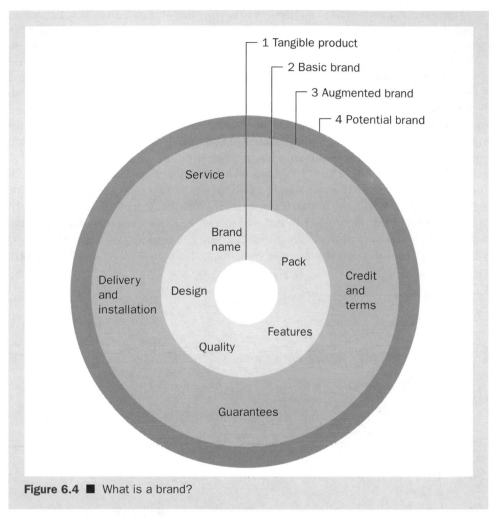

1 Tangible product

2 Basic brand

3 Augmented brand

4 Potential brand

Service

Brand name

Pack

Delivery and installation

Design

Credit and terms

Features

Quality

Guarantees

Figure 6.4 ■ What is a brand?

Source: adapted from Theodore Levitt, 'Marketing success through differentiation – of anything',
Harvard Business Review, January–February 1980, p. 86

youthful fashion concept in the watch market; Body Shop with its 'green' positioning in beauty care retailing; and Thermalite with its branding of basic building bricks.

■ *Strong communications programme.* A successful brand requires an effective selling, advertising or promotional campaign which will communicate the brand's function and psychological values, trigger trial and reinforce commitment to it. Without building awareness, comprehension and intention to buy, the brand will not leave the manufacturer's shelves.

■ *Time and consistency.* Brands are not built quickly. It often takes years to build up the added values. Brands require investment, which has to be maintained over their lives. First, cash is required to build brand adoption and use, then it is needed to maintain the brand's values and relevance in the changing environment. There are no short-term techniques for building sustainable brand equity, but the rewards can be momentous. Aaker estimated the profits from Procter & Gamble's Ivory brand name. Ivory has been the leading brand of household soap in the USA for over a hundred years. Over its life, Aaker calculated that around $400,000 was spent on advertising it. The total profits generated from Ivory he estimated as $2.5 billion.

Figure 6.5 illustrates the principles of building successful brands. Management must start with a quality product which meets the functional needs of customers. Next it must wrap around the product an attractive presentation which will differentiate it and enhance its appeal. Third, it should seek to augment its basic appeal with additional products or services to delight customers. The brand-building process starts when the customer tries the brand. If management have developed the brand properly, it should then be satisfactory in use and lead to a willingness to repeat buy. To get trial and repeat purchase, however, requires triggering mechanisms. This stimulus is provided by the firm's investment in advertising, selling, promotion, public relations,

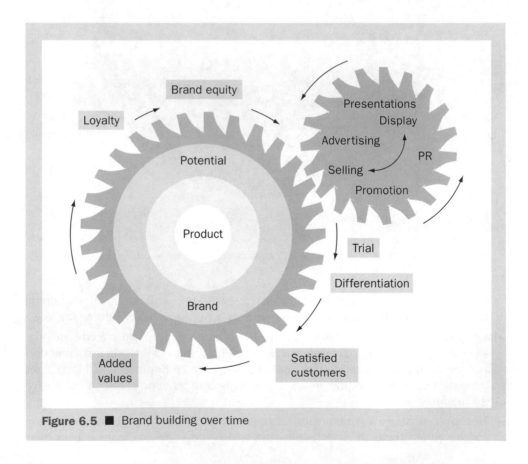

Figure 6.5 ■ Brand building over time

etc. The firm needs to communicate the values of the brand and then reinforce brand associations to start the wheel of usage experience and keep it turning. Through the combination of the stimulus of consistent communications and satisfactory usage experience, brand awareness, confidence and brand equity are built.

The acid tests of whether a brand is successful are three:

■ Has it captured the leading share in its market segment or distribution channel?

■ Does it command prices sufficient to provide a high profit margin?

■ Will the brand sustain its strong share and profit position when competitive and generic versions of the product hit the market?

The benefits of brands

Brands generate value for companies in four ways. First, strong brands usually obtain price premiums from either consumers or resellers. Second, strong brands obtain higher market shares. Third, because of customer loyalty, successful brands generate more stable and less risky earning streams. Finally, successful brands offer avenues for further growth.

Brands, market share and profits

A successful brand is one which customers want to buy and retailers want to stock – it achieves a high market share. Typically, a brand leader obtains twice the market share of the number two brand, and the number two brand obtains twice the share of the number three. The brand with the highest market share is always much more profitable. The well-known PIMS findings, based on detailed research into a sample of 2,600 businesses, found that, on average, brands with a market share of 40 per cent generate three times the return on investment of those with a market share of only 10 per cent (Figure 6.6).[9] Weak brands mean weak profits. For fast-moving consumer goods (fmcg) the relationship is even stronger (Table 6.2). Studies in the USA and UK indicate that, on average, the leading brand operates on a typical return on sales of 18 per cent, the number two brand has a return of only 3 per cent, and the rest are unprofitable.[10]

Brand leverage

Strong brands generate these exceptional levels of profit through a triple-leverage effect. The most obvious effect is through the higher volume that the brand achieves, which allows higher asset utilization and scale economies. The second source of leverage is through the higher prices that the brand obtains. Sometimes this price premium occurs at the consumer level, but more frequently it is earned at the retailer or distributor level. Because they have a strong consumer franchise, successful brands are more able to resist trade pressures on their margins. This, in turn, generates

Table 6.2 ■ Market share rank and return on sales for grocery brands

Brand rank	Return on sales (%)
1	17.9
2	2.8
3	−0.9
4	−5.9

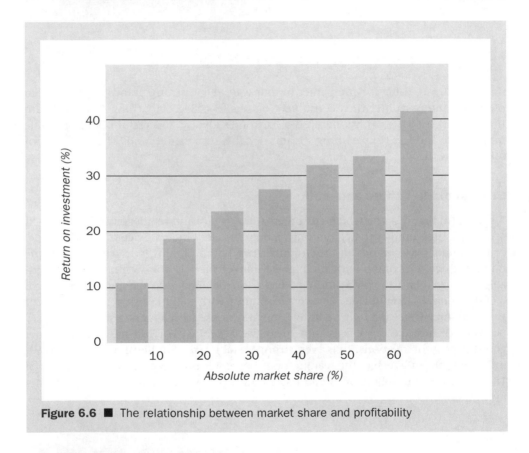

Figure 6.6 ■ The relationship between market share and profitability

superior earnings. On average, premium price brands earn 20 per cent higher return on investment than discount products.[11]

Finally, brand leaders also have lower unit costs. This may occur primarily in development, production or marketing, depending on the structure of the industry's value chain.

The impact of these three leverage advantages for a brand leader can be illustrated in a typical fmcg situation. For example, in the UK Coca-Cola has around three times the

Table 6.3 ■ Brand leaders: leverage on profitability

Brand	Unit market share (%)	Net sales (£m)	Gross margin (%)	Marketing expenses (£m)	Contribution to overheads and profit (£m)
Leader	60	170	60	25.5	76.5
Follower	20	50	52	8.5	17.5
Follower with 'equilibrium marketing budget'				12.8	13.2

market share of Pepsi. The problems this creates for the brand follower are illustrated in Table 6.3. In terms of unit market share, the leader is three times bigger than the follower. The spread at the net sales level, however, expands because the follower has to give away greater trade discounts. In addition, the leader will normally have some sourcing and operating advantages at the cost of goods level, which together with its price advantage significantly widen the gross margin. Finally, supposing the brand leader spends 15 per cent of its turnover, or £25.5 million, on marketing, advertising and promotion. Now, to have the same unit marketing costs, the follower would spend £8.5 million. Unfortunately, if the brand leader were outspending the follower by three to one, the follower's market share would fall even further. Invariably, to maintain its position, the follower is forced to spend more (in this example, it spends half as much as the brand leader). This leads to two 'laws' of brands – the bigger the brand, the more (in total) is spent on marketing; and the bigger the brand, the less (in unit cost terms) is spent on marketing! The end result is that the brand leader's market share advantage is substantially magnified at the profit level. Here a brand advantage of 3:1 results through leverage in a profit contribution advantage of nearly 6:1.

The value of niche brands

To be a successful brand does not necessarily mean being big in absolute terms. It is market share which is a key to profit, not absolute sales. Managers frequently do not understand this. Often they believe that obtaining a small share of a huge market would be attractive. After all, they say, 5 per cent of a £1 billion market means sales of £50 million. What they often do not understand is that a company with a tiny share rarely makes profit because its lack of strong customer franchise means weak distribution, poor prices and high costs. Being number one in a small niche market is invariably more profitable than being number five in an enormous market.

Brand loyalty and beliefs

The high failure rate of new products has enhanced the attractiveness of established brands. Strong brands, because they have a core of established and loyal users, have more predictable earnings streams. Because of their lower risk, companies with strong brand portfolios are valued more highly by investors. Brand loyalty provides two other benefits. First, it means lower marketing costs. New brands or unsuccessful ones must win new customers to survive. This hits the net margin because it is much more expensive in advertising, promotion and selling to win new customers than to hold existing satisfied ones. One study suggests that it costs six times as much to win new customers as to retain current users.[12] Second, strong brands can often override the occasional hitches and even disasters which destroy weaker brands. After samples of the leading brand of an analgesic, Tylenol, were poisoned, it was removed from retailers' shelves for several weeks. When distribution was resumed, consumers returned to the brand, ensuring a complete recovery of its market position.

The brand barrier

Today, competition can quickly copy advances in technology or product formulations. Competitors can easily reproduce a cigarette, a soft drink formula or a strategic consultancy. But what cannot be copied is the Marlborough, Coca-Cola or McKinsey brand personality. By focusing on building brand values, the company builds barriers to competitive attack.

A brand leader is in a strong position to fend off aggression. First, it has financial strength – almost invariably it will have the highest market share and highest profit margins. This should enable it to outgun competitors in terms of aggressive promotion and innovation. Second, the trade is always reluctant to add new brands if the existing brand leader satisfies customers. Third, the brand leader can exploit its superiority, as Coca-Cola does with its 'real thing' advertising. Without a major 'strategic window', only substantial underinvestment in quality and brand support is likely to dethrone a successful brand.

Avenues for growth

The product life cycle is a well-known phenomenon. The product reaches a peak and eventually dies as its markets mature and new technology replaces it. But the product life cycle refers to products, not to brands. There is no reason why a brand cannot adapt to new technologies and move from mature into new growth markets. Such repositioning explains the extraordinary longevity of many brand leaders – brands which have held their leading positions for generations.

Successful brands adapt by incorporating developments in technology, packaging, tastes and lifestyles. Coca-Cola illustrates how, by a subtle adaptation in product form and communications, it can keep a brand up-to-date to successive generations of teenagers. Johnson & Johnson's baby shampoo is only one of many examples of brands which have moved into new segments to continue growth. Strong brands can increasingly be rolled out geographically to new countries and form the basis for powerful regional or global brands. Finally, by brand extensions the brand name can often be used to enter new fields. For example, by extending its brand name into ice cream, Mars stimulated the growth of the European premium segment and quickly captured brand leadership.

Motivating stakeholders

Companies with strong brands find recruitment easier. People want to work with companies that exhibit success. Strong brands also widen share ownership by increasing awareness and understanding of the company. Finally, successful brands elicit community and governmental support. For example, in recent years, western governments have competed with inducements to attract the better-known Japanese companies to build their brands with them. They have learned that companies with portfolios of powerful brands offer the security and long-term employment prospects which start-up companies cannot match.

Multibranding, line and brand extensions

If a company is to progress beyond being a narrow niche player, it will have to broaden its product range and market coverage. Frequently a company will target several brands at the same broad market. In some cases it will extend the same name over the brand family; in others, it will choose to use independent brand names. *Line extensions* are new products introduced into the existing product category and under an existing brand name. Examples are new flavours, forms, pack sizes, etc. *Multibrands* are brands in the same product category, but with different brand identities. For example, Procter & Gamble pursues a multibranding strategy in detergents with its Tide, Bold, Dash, Cheer and Oxydol brands. *Brand extensions* involve using the same brand name, successfully established in one market or channel, to enter others. It is often termed brand *stretching* when the markets are very different. For example, the successful Porsche name has been used to develop a range of sunglasses, while the Yamaha name has been attached to pianos, hi-fi products and sporting equipment.

There are two reasons for the development of multibranding and line extensions. The first is the increasing segmentation of markets. In the earliest stage of the development of a market, a single product will often be sufficient. Demand is normally homogeneous and too small to warrant a company employing a range of products. Then, as the market develops new segments are added, consumer requirements fragment and new branding opportunities occur. As customer needs diverge, differentiated distribution channels evolve, providing a second stimulus to separate branding. In recent years, further momentum has been given to the growing range by the development of new flexible manufacturing techniques which have lowered the cost of product variety, and by new targeted marketing and advertising media which access specialized customer segments. Finally, aggressive competitors, particularly from Japan, now view multiple brands, innovation and creative market segmentation as powerful competitive strategies for today's affluent markets.

Two types of branding can be identified: horizontal and vertical. *Horizontal branding* is aimed at differentiating distribution channels rather than consumers. By giving different retailers or distributors specific brands, the manufacturer aims to increase distribution and market share. For example, Levi sells two varieties of its famous 501s: a cheaper line (orange tab) for discount stores, and a more expensive one (red tab) for department and speciality stores. Horizontal branding is often low cost because the brands may have only cosmetic differences. *Vertical branding* targets different customer groups with differentiated branding strategies. In this case the distribution channels may or may not be the same. In highly segmented markets, single brand strategies are rarely effective. For example, Amstrad, which built a leading position in the home computer market, found its brand image a major handicap in its efforts to penetrate the business segment. A separate brand identity with an image, sales and service system geared to the corporate market would have been a more effective means of attacking the new target market.

Vertical branding is more powerful than horizontal. Its major problem is often the cost of building distinct brand identities. Ford paid £1.5 billion to buy the Jaguar brand to provide an entry into the executive car market. Toyota invested substantially more to develop its Lexus brand. Thus, while vertical multibranding can generate significantly higher revenues, it offers fewer opportunities than horizontal multibranding for economies of scale and shared purchasing, marketing, distribution and service costs.

Today there is a growing use of line and brand extensions, umbrella brands and particularly the company name to front individual products, rather than multibrands. Most of the top brand names now are company brands – Coca-Cola, Sony, Mercedes Benz, Marks & Spencer and Cadbury. Brand extensions and corporate branding have grown for three reasons. First, the high failure rate of new products has encouraged companies to look to extensions to reduce the odds of failure. Attaching a successful brand name to a new product reduces the buyer's perceived risk. It may inherit brand values of 'prestige' or 'technical performance' from the original brand. The brand name may offer an implicit quality guarantee. In virtually all new product concept tests, the addition of an established brand name such as Cadbury or Sony will greatly increase the initial reaction, interest and willingness to try the product. Second, building a complete new brand is expensive. In the grocery market, for example, £20 million is probably the minimum required for developing a successful new product. In general, it costs less to launch a product when a well-known family brand name is behind it. Finally, companies look for economies of scale and scope in focusing resources around one umbrella brand. With too many brand names, promotional resources can be fragmented and the brands can be outgunned by competitors able to concentrate support around one name. For example, Electrolux operates five brand names in the UK white goods market: Electrolux, Zanussi, Thorn, Hoover and Husquovana. Together these brands give Electrolux the largest market share. But its rival, Hotpoint, with only one brand, outspends each of Electrolux's individual brands and consequently the Hotpoint brand is growing considerably faster.

Umbrella branding, however, is no panacea and failures of brand extensions are common. A product will fail, even if backed by a strong umbrella brand, if it offers no differential advantage over existing brands. Again it will fail if it does not get sufficient marketing support during its launch phase to generate awareness and trial. Many extensions fail because they are launched into a different target market from the original brand. In the new market, the brand's associations may not be valued. For example, Levi, which had built a brilliant brand in jeans, attempted to market a range of high-quality formal suits to middle-class males under the Levi name. The brand extension failed because the new target market did not see the informal, denim associations of the Levi name as adding value in this sector. Levi subsequently introduced the Docker brand to target successfully a different sector of the clothing market. Brand extensions often fail where the competitive advantage is different. For example, Procter & Gamble uses the Vidal Sassoon name for its cosmetic range of shampoos and Head and Shoulders for its anti-dandruff range.

In some cases, extensions can damage the core brand. A traditional beer brand might be damaged by the associations brought by a low-alcohol brand extension. A sharp brand positioning can be weakened by new category brands. This is a particular danger for names which have become almost generic product descriptions – Kleenex, Perrier, Tampax. Cadbury's association with high-quality chocolate was certainly weakened by its extension into mashed potato and dried milk. Excessive extension can lower the brand's quality image. The use of the Lacoste alligator on a wide range of clothing of varying quality eroded its image in the 1980s. Pharmaceutical companies have generally been wary of umbrella branding because of the danger of any bad publicity arising from one brand area, spilling over into other fields.

The principles for deciding between brand extensions and individual brand names are illustrated in Figure 6.7. The right approach depends upon the similarity of the positioning strategies of the brands. Four brand extension options are identified:

■ If the brands appeal to the same target market segment and have the same differential advantage, then they can safely share the same company or range name. Here,

	Differential advantage	
	Similar	Different
Similar	Company or range name (IBM, Timotei)	Company plus brands (Kellogg's Cornflakes, Kellogg's Rice Krispies)
Different	Company plus grade ID (Mercedes 200, Mercedes 500)	Unique brand names (Procter & Gamble: Tide, Bold, Dreft, Ariel, etc.)

Target market segment (row labels Similar / Different on left axis)

Figure 6.7 ■ Brand extension strategies

there is consistency in the positioning strategies and the same name is applied to different products. Examples of this type of extension are IBM, Timotei (from Unilever), Dunhill and Sony.

■ If the differential advantage is the same but the target market differs, then the company name can be extended because the benefit is similar. However, it is important to identify the 'grade'. For example, both the Mercedes 200 and 500 series offer differential advantages based upon quality, but the more expensive 500 marque appeals to a much more prestige segment of the market. The supplementary grade identification acts to preserve the prestige positioning of the latter marque.

■ If a company has different differential advantages, then it should use separate brand names. It can find some synergy if the brands are appealing to the same target market, by using the company name with separate brand names. For example, different brands of Kellogg's may well be selected within the same family unit.

■ But if both the target customers and the differential advantages are different, then using unique brand names is logically the most appropriate strategy. So Procter & Gamble believes that it is worth losing out on the advantages of a common corporate name in order to position the brands separately in the market – to give each brand a distinct positioning appeal to a separate benefit segment. Similarly, Toyota has recently separately positioned its Lexus brand because it wishes to position it uniquely, away from its existing models.

Revitalization, repositioning and rationalization

Over time it will be necessary to revitalize and reposition the brand. Many factors may erode a brand's franchise and profitability: market decline, new technology, changing tastes, rising costs and new competition. To improve brand performance, management have two broad alternatives: raising volume or increasing the brand's productivity (Figure 6.8). The former should be explored first. Sales volume can be increased by either expanding the market for the brand (revitalization) or enhancing its competitive position in the market (repositioning).

Brand revitalization

Brand revitalization can be explored in four directions:

■ *Finding new markets*. Brands such as McDonald's, Reuters and the *Financial Times* have compensated for the saturation of their domestic market by a strategy of geographical expansion. Expansion into new countries has been the major engine for the growth of these brands in the last decade. Pharmaceutical companies seek new markets for maturing brands by searching for applications in new therapeutic areas. For example, Merck's Enalapril was first approved for the treatment of hypertension and later it was allowed for use in cases of congestive heart failure.

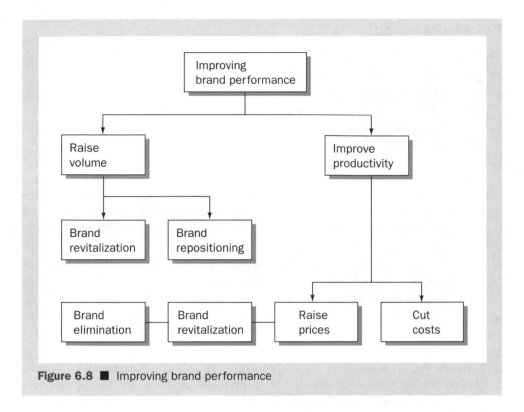

Figure 6.8 ■ Improving brand performance

- *Entering new segments.* Identifying new segments is one of the most common ways of expanding the market for a brand. Falling prices and increasing customer awareness facilitate such strategies. For example, Texas Instruments' growth in the electronic calculator market was achieved by successively pioneering technical users, then the office segment, then the general public and finally the schools' segment. Johnson & Johnson's baby shampoo was languishing until the company looked towards adults who wash their hair frequently and needed a mild shampoo.

- *Finding new applications.* The potential market for the brand can be expanded by suggested new customer needs. The classic example of this is Arm & Hammer Baking Soda, which increased its sales from $15 million in 1970 to $400 million in 1990 by finding new uses for baking soda – primarily as a deodorizer for refrigerators, sinks, animals, etc.

- *Increasing brand usage rate.* This may be done by increasing the frequency with which the brand is consumed: making it easier to use (instant tea), providing incentives for use (frequent flyer discounts), reducing the disincentives for use (decaffeinated coffee), or finding new ways to increase the quantity used (large bottles).

Brand repositioning

Brand repositioning focuses on increasing volume, not by expanding the market, but by winning share from competitors. Each of the following avenues can be reviewed:

■ *Real repositioning*. Management may need to update the brand by incorporating the latest technology, functions or design. Honda, for example, has continuously re-positioned its best-selling Accord model to maintain its position at the forefront of value and fashion.

■ *Psychological repositioning*. The company can seek to change the buyer's beliefs about the competitiveness of the brand. For example, the highly regarded Sainsbury supermarket group used its advertising in the early 1990s to emphasize that it had competitive prices as well as high-quality merchandise. Psychological repositioning will work only if the buyers truly underestimate the value of the brand.

■ *Competitive depositioning*. Comparative advertising is frequently used to seek to alter customers' beliefs about competitors' brands and to suggest that they represent poor value. Volkswagen used this strategy against Ford in its advertising.

■ *Reweighting values*. Sometimes buyers can be persuaded to attach greater importance to certain values in which the brand excels. For example, Volvo emphasized safety as a criterion for selecting cars.

■ *Neglected values*. Sometimes new choice criteria can be introduced to buyers. Unilever's new Radion detergent was positioned on the claim that it removes odours as well as dirt – a value not previously thought salient in this market. The Body Shop brand was founded on the then unique value that its products were not tested on animals.

■ *Changing preferences*. It may be possible to switch the preferences of buyers. Buyers may be convinced to switch from low-price products to brands offering higher quality and economic value, for example.

■ *Augmenting the brand*. A brand's competitive position may be enhanced by offering additional products and services alongside the core product. Guarantees, after-sales service and advice can all add value.

Brand productivity improvement

Brand productivity improvement focuses on profit rather than volume as the brand objective. Such a focus is appropriate when management have decided that the brand has limited market potential. There are three ways of squeezing more profit from a static or declining brand. First, *costs* – fixed and variable – can be cut. Inevitably, if this means disinvesting in the brand, it will have long-term consequences for the brand's market share. Second, *prices* can be increased. In the short term this will almost always boost profitability, even if volume declines. For example, if a typical brand has a gross contribution of 50 per cent and a net margin of 8 per cent, then pushing up prices by 10 per cent will boost net profit by half even if volume drops by 10 per cent. Finally, profits will be boosted normally by range *rationalization*. By eliminating marginal lines, costs and investments are likely to be cut by more than the volume lost.

Brand elimination

Finally, brand elimination may be the required decision. This may be because the brand is no longer profitable, but there are often other reasons. If a company has grown by acquisition, for example, it often ends up with too many brands. Its brand name portfolio may be too big because the brands overlap and cannibalize one another, some brands may be too small to be worth supporting, or the company may need to focus its resources around one or two brands to avoid being outgunned by competitors. Globalization is another motive for brand rationalization. Companies such as Mars, Nissan and Unilever which have previously supported national brands increasingly want to standardize around regional or global brand names.

The problem with eliminating a brand is that it is difficult to prevent many customers switching to competitors' brands. It is also expensive to manage the switch. For example, in the US Black & Decker acquired GE's small appliance business and quickly dropped the GE brand name. Four years later, and after spending £100 million promoting the Black & Decker name, it was found that the old GE brand was still preferred by two out of three buyers.

If it is necessary to focus resources around fewer core brands, three options should be explored. First, the company should look for economies which might reduce the costs of the minor brand. For example, its manufacturing, distribution and overheads could be merged and its market identity limited to a badging operation. Another alternative to killing the brand might be harvesting it – allowing the brand franchise to erode gradually rather than dropping it. Finally, brands can be amalgamated under a shared brand name. For example, when Whirlpool acquired Philips' white goods business, the brands were marketed for several years under a dual identity.

Regional and global brands

In the past, markets were dominated by local brands. Even the biggest multinationals allowed local subsidiaries great autonomy in developing brands to fit the local environment. In recent years, three forces have led companies to look more at global or at least regional brands. The most powerful force has been the pressure to reduce costs. Many western companies were hard hit in the 1980s and 1990s by Japanese competitors ruthlessly exploiting economies of scale in research, development, manufacturing and marketing to build high-quality, low-price global brands. Second, many companies have needed to accelerate the speed with which they innovate internationally. Companies such as GEC in telecommunications and Unilever in groceries proved too slow in recent years in rolling out breakthrough brands, and were often leapfrogged by faster competitors. Finally, the growing internationalization of tastes and buying patterns has made the development of global and regional brands more feasible.

Global and regional brands have obvious advantages. They usually mean lower development, production and marketing costs. They should facilitate the professionalism of brand planning and decision making. They should result in faster innovation by reducing the delays caused by local adaptation and policy making. Finally, global brands offer spin-offs in international brand leverage: increasingly mobile customers see the same brands in different countries. One constraint is that global brands may fail to match local requirements. In addition, taking key decisions out of the hands of local managers can severely affect the motivation and commitment of personnel in the host countries.

Much of the debate on global brands, however, is oversimplistic. In reality, it is not a matter of whether or not brands can be global, but rather which functions and tasks should be centralized and which should be left to managers in the local market. A brand, it will be recalled, is a core product upon which basic marketing features and then augmented attributes are superimposed to differentiate and add value to it. Some of these features and attributes are more open to standardization across markets than others. The core product, and the research and development which generates new products, are usually centralized. Product functionality and use (e.g. how people listen to music or drive a bulldozer) tend to be universal characteristics. In addition, scale economies tend to be important here as these are high-investment areas. Basic brand features – design, packaging, logo and name – can also generally be standardized across countries if planned systematically.

At the next layer of branding – positioning and advertising – the difficulties begin to become greater as culture, attitudes, economics and language impinge on the brand's values and make standardization more difficult. The degree of standardization possible varies with the product and the market. National values and traditions are still very important in food, but much less so in electronics. Cultural values are less important in youth and more affluent markets than they are in mature and low-income ones. Moving further down the marketing chain to selling, promotion and distribution, these decisions are invariably specified locally because of the sharp differences which normally occur in market and institutional characteristics. To summarize, global branding is a matter of degree. Few, if any, brands are marketed in an identical way across the world, or even across a region. But more brands have characteristics which are standardized across regions – with the product formulation and the brand name being towards the fore.

Critics often confuse the move towards global branding as implying greater homogeneity and standardization. This is certainly incorrect. Markets will be more segmented in the future than today, but the basis of segmentation will change. While in the past geographical boundaries were a major way of distinguishing customer groups, today segments cross geographical boundaries (Figure 6.9). Consumers living in London's Knightsbridge or Kensington have more in common with those in Mid-town Manhattan or the seventh *arrondissement* of Paris than they do with those living in London's Hackney or Bethnal Green. Across both industrial and

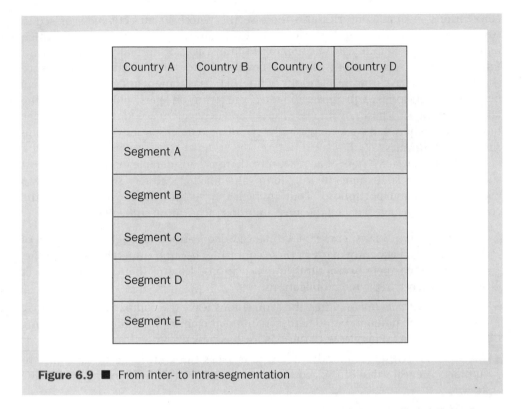

Figure 6.9 ■ From inter- to intra-segmentation

consumer markets the broad economic, social and cultural trends favouring first regional and then global brands are clear. Yet there will be no simple answers. For the foreseeable future, management will need to achieve a balance between the opportunities to be had from global brands and the need to recognize and adapt to local market differences.

Buying versus building brands

There are two routes a company can follow to obtain brands – it can build and develop them, or it can acquire them, or rather acquire the companies which possess them. The former is a high-risk, slow and expensive route. Studies show clearly the extraordinarily high failure rate which occurs in new brand development. Fewer than one in a hundred new product ideas makes a satisfactory profit in the market. Further, even with high-potential products it takes a long time and a heavy investment to build them into brands and position them successfully in the minds of consumers.

In contrast, acquisitions are a deceptively quick route to obtaining a brand portfolio. For example, in acquiring Cheseborough Pond and Fabergé, Unilever went from nowhere to become a leading player in the global cosmetics market. Accounting conventions in most countries also increase the perceived attractiveness of acquisitions. While internal brand development expenditures are treated as costs which reduce current profitability, acquisition expenditures are not normally immediately or fully written off against profits. Instead they are written off directly on the balance sheet. While the cash flow implications of internal development and acquisitions may be identical, the former will appear to reduce the return on shareholder funds and the latter to increase it. These advantages of speed and benevolent accounting conventions have made acquisitions an increasingly popular route, especially for British and American companies.

Despite the attractiveness of acquisitions, there is considerable evidence that most such acquisitions fail to generate long-term value for the acquirer's shareholders or to build lasting brand portfolios.[13] Four problems have brought down many of the companies which have pursued the most ambitious acquisition strategies.

■ *Excessive gearing*. Many companies financed acquisitions through high levels of borrowing. Subsequently many of these companies became vulnerable when profits failed to reach their overoptimistic expectations, leaving them unable to meet interest and debt repayment obligations.

■ *Incoherent brand portfolios*. Often the acquisitions leave the company with a rag-bag of brands, with different brand names in different countries, conflicting positioning strategies and no synergies with the existing business.

■ *Inadequate expertise*. Frequently the acquirer lacks the knowledge or capability to appraise the real value of the acquisition in advance or subsequently to add value to it.

■ *Pay too much*. Acquirers often pay too much to obtain a business. The stock market can be expected to value most companies fairly. However, to purchase a company, the acquirer usually ends up paying a premium of 30–50 per cent above the pre-bid valuation to win the acceptance of the target company shareholders. Such premiums can be justified only by quite exceptional synergies between the two businesses.

Of course, acquiring brands rather than building them sometimes makes sense. Table 6.4 provides a checklist for managers, highlighting those conditions under which acquisitions are likely to pay off. If it is a low-growth unattractive market, building a new brand may cost too much. It is generally cheaper to buy competition and competitors' distributive space than to beat out well-entrenched brands. This is why companies like Hansen and BTR have focused their acquisition strategies on these dull mature markets. The other advantage of these types of market is that the relative cost of acquisitions may be low. Often the stock market undervalues these apparently boring companies and there is substantial restructuring potential in selling off parts after the acquisition.

Acquisitions work when there is real potential synergy – when the acquirer can reduce joint costs or improve marketing competence by making acquisitions. Finally, the strategic opportunities offered by the acquirer's existing brand portfolio and its corporate cash situation play a major role. If the company's current products are 'me-too', and if it has limited skills but abundant cash spun off from its portfolio of mature products, then acquisitions appear attractive. By contrast, it is generally better to develop and build on the company's own brands if these are operating in growth markets, if the company possesses potentially strong brands and if inside the company there are strong marketing and development skills. These five sets of factors are the key criteria in making judgements about the balance between building and purchasing brands.

Valuing brands

Companies with strong brands are increasingly exploring how to quantify their value. Some companies want to place these brand values on their balance sheet to emphasize the company's asset strength. If prices are not put on brands, then a company can easily be undervalued by the stock market and become a takeover target. Brands too are sold or licensed so that buyers and sellers need to place a value on them. Finally, if companies are to invest in brands, it is important to see how their values change over time to judge whether the investment pays off.

There are five main methods of valuing brands:

■ *Price premium valuation.* Where successful brands obtain price premiums over unbranded products, the discounted value of these future premiums can be the basis for brand valuation.

■ *Incremental sales valuation.* If the value of the brand appears in higher market shares rather than premium prices, incremental sales over an unbranded product can be used to estimate the value of the brand.

■ *Replacement cost value.* The estimated cost of developing a brand with comparable stature to the current brand can be used for valuation.

■ *Stock market valuation.* For some companies it is possible to decompose the stock market valuation into its components: physical assets, industry factors and other intangible assets. The value of the brand can then be estimated as the residual.

■ *Future earnings valuation.* The most satisfactory approach is to estimate the discounted present value of future earnings attributable to the brand. Essentially this amounts to determining the multiple to be applied to current brand earnings – stronger brands achieving higher multiples. RHM, one of the first companies to value brands on the balance sheet, estimated brand strength from an analysis of the brands' rankings in terms of leadership, brand support, market attractiveness, international appeal and brand protection.

Brand valuation methods are always highly approximate. Future market conditions and hence long-term brand earnings are difficult to predict. In addition, brands are often not stand-alone. Where brands are marketed under corporate names (e.g. Philips) or both corporate and individual brand names (e.g. Kellogg's), it is virtually impossible

Table 6.4 ■ Buying versus building brands

	Build	Buy
Market attractiveness		
Market growth	High	Low
Strength of competitors	Weak	Strong
Retailer power	Weak	Strong
Relative cost of acquisitions		
Industry attractiveness	High	Low
Valuation of company	Full	Undervalued
Restructuring potential	Low	High
Brand's potential	Realized	Unrealized
Acquisition's potential synergy		
Cost reduction potential	Low	High
Marketing competence	Unchanged	Increased
Complementarity	Low	High
Relevant management expertise	Low	Transfers
Brand's strategic opportunity		
Product performance	Breakthrough	Me-too
Positioning concept	New	Mature
Market opportunity	High	Low
Corporate situation		
Growth potential	High	Low
Cash situation	Average	Abundant
Marketing/R & D capability	Strong	Weak

to separate the specific earnings attributable to a single brand. Finally, brand values are entangled with other intangible assets (e.g. staff, patents, market entry barriers). For example, the value of an advertising agency 'brand' could be substantially changed by a walk-out of senior personnel. These and other factors make all such estimates of value hazardous.

The branding dilemma

Brand management is at the centre of the conflict between short-term profits and long-term investment. For most successful companies, their brands are their most valuable assets. Brands generate customer loyalty and through this they build profit, growth and shareholder value. Yet in many western companies the task of building and sustaining the company's brands has not attained priority on their board's agenda.

The major reason for neglecting brands has been the short-term pressures that many management teams feel they face. The City's priority is seen as short-term company profits, and companies have built their management incentives and bonus schemes around achieving short-term profit targets. The ethos in many companies is for quick results: managers are expected to show results fast and high-flyers anticipate rapid career progression. All these pressures act to detract from the long-term consistent investments that brands require.

Investing in brands fits badly in a short-term profit-oriented business. Building and sustaining brands requires a long-term focus. It takes years to develop a brand image and augment it with support services and product enhancements. Such investments do not have a pay-off in increased short-term sales and profits. Not only is the pay-off long term, but it is uncertain and rarely quantifiable. Faced with such elusive, long-term and intangible benefits, it is not surprising that hard-nosed managers heavily discount the case for brands.

In contrast, brand managers find it easier to make the case for consumer and trade promotions. While above-the-line expenditures (brand image advertising) are long term, below-the-line spending generates short-term results. Because it provides a direct monetary incentive to consumers or the trade to purchase now, promotional spending is quick and measurable. Another advantage of promotions is that they are variable costs, incurred as sales are increased, and in this sense they are self-funding and less risky than up-front advertising investments. Unfortunately, promotions do not build brands and their short-term advantage is often at the expense of the brand's long-term positioning. Promotions can, in the long run, erode a brand's values by cheapening its image and focusing customers on price.

Another disincentive for investing in brands is that the resulting assets do not appear on the balance sheet. If a company fails to invest in its physical assets, this will show up as a diminution of the company's net asset base. But brand investments are treated as costs, which like other overhead expenses reduce the company's profitability and accrual of assets. Few companies have management accounting systems which effectively distinguish between brand-building investments and overhead costs, and so both are often treated as low value-added activities which can be cut back as necessary to boost profitability.

For management under pressure to boost short-term profits, brand investments are tempting targets. Cutting them is less painful than firing staff, and the positive impact on profits is fast. In fact, brand disinvestment has the opposite effects to brand investment. While, with the latter, the beneficial effects (on sales) come slowly and the apparent negative effects (on profits) are immediate, with brand disinvestments, the beneficial effects on profits are quick and the negative impact on the brand's market position occurs slowly. For example, taking £1 million out of the advertising budget of a strong established brand such as Kit Kat or Nescafé would, in the short term, have a negligible effect on market share and would consequently boost current profits by the £1 million. Managers are often tempted to believe that cutting back on brand support is less risky because the costs are not immediately apparent. Later they discover that market share, once given up, is almost impossible to regain.

Several companies have recently tried to develop safeguards to short-termism affecting their brand equity. Colgate Palmolive and Canada Dry, for example, have introduced 'brand equity managers'. Their task is to protect brand equity by measuring it periodically and being on guard for short-term policies which threaten to erode it. Heinz has changed bonus arrangements, to shift managers from an excessive preoccupation with short-term profits which were seen as damaging their brands' long-term positions. Procter & Gamble has long had management accounting systems which separate 'investments in the future' from operating and overhead costs. This differentiation means that managers seek to increase rather than cut back on brand investments. Perhaps the best support for brand investment is for top management to be articulate supporters of the value of their brands: stressing to shareholders their brand strengths and the long-term value of the brands for the business.

Summary

Building successful brands is at the heart of marketing management and strategy. When a company creates strong brands it attracts customer preference and builds a defensive wall against competition. Successful brands are founded on a high-quality core product. But since products are easily copied, brand building also requires skilful differentiations and the combination of added values which augment the core and offer customers enhanced benefits. A brand achieves its potential when target customers have complete confidence in its quality and image.

Strong brands obtain good prices and high market shares, and offer the company avenues for further growth through line extensions and the penetration of new markets. While products can come to the end of their life cycles, brands need not do so if they are continually updated and repositioned. Companies with portfolios of strong brands, not surprisingly, achieve premium valuations from stock market investors.

The creation of strong brands requires a long-term focus. It means investments in brand-building activities which do not have an immediate pay-off. Many of today's companies have become too short-term oriented. They are unwilling to invest in building brands. Worse, they often destroy long-term brand equity by reducing brand support. While such activities can boost short-term earnings, they permanently erode the company's long-term market competitiveness.

Questions

1. What is a brand? Are brands limited to consumer markets?

2. A company intending to roll out a new chain of fast-food restaurants aims to build them into a strong brand. What advice can you give?

3. How could you determine what the brand identity and image is of your company or product?

4. Why is it worth investing possibly millions of pounds to build a strong brand image?

5. Discuss the advantages and disadvantages of umbrella branding.

6. Why do some companies fail to appreciate the value of brands and neglect to invest in their brands?

Notes

1. 'Price to book ratio of brand name stocks', *Financial Times*, 23 November 1991, p. III.

2. Theodore Levitt, *Industrial Purchasing Behavior: A study of communications effects* (Boston, MA: Division of Research, Graduate School of Business Administration, Harvard University, 1965).

3. John Philip Jones, *What's in a Name? Advertising and the concept of brands* (Lexington, MA: Lexington Books, 1986).

4. Theodore Levitt, 'The morality of advertising', *Harvard Business Review*, July–August 1970, pp. 89–95.

5. David A. Aaker, *Managing Brand Equity* (New York: Free Press, 1991), pp. 130–52.

6. Jean-Noel Kapfferer, *Strategic Brand Management* (New York: Free Press, 1994).

7. Adapted from Theodore Levitt, 'Marketing success through differentiation – of anything', *Harvard Business Review*, January–February 1980, pp. 83–91.

8. Christopher W. L. Hart, 'The power of unconditional service guarantees', *Harvard Business Review*, July–August 1988, pp. 54–62.

9. Robert A. Buzzell and Barney T. Gale, *The PIMS Principles: Linking strategy to performance* (New York: Free Press, 1987).

10. 'The year of the brand', *The Economist*, 24 December 1988, p. 93.

11. Simon Broadbent, 'Diversity in categories, brands and strategies', *Journal of Brand Management*, August 1994, pp. 9–18. Also Donald K. Clifton, Jr and Richard E. Cavenagh, *The Winning Performance: How America's high growth midsize companies succeed* (London: Sidgwick & Jackson, 1985), p. 72.

12. Frederick F. Reichheld and W. Earl Sasser, Jr, 'Zero defections: quality comes to services', *Harvard Business Review*, September–October 1989, pp. 105–11.

13. Philippe Haspeslagh and David Jemison, 'Creating value in acquisitions', in Michael Gould and Kathleen Luchs (eds.), *Managing the Multibusiness Company* (London: Routledge, 1996).

Chapter 7

Innovation and new product development

Innovation and new product development have become the key strategic focus for today's most successful companies. Continuous innovation is perceived as the only way of sustaining above average growth and profitability. Today, companies know that aggressive, low-cost competitors make it increasingly difficult to maintain profit margins on current products. Only by continually updating these products, adding new ones and broadening the range can companies hope to maintain profit performance and market leadership. However, becoming one of these new fast-track innovators is not easy, since it requires fundamental changes in an organization's structure and philosophy. Top managers are realizing that unless they accept these challenges the competitive positions of their companies will be rapidly eroded.

This chapter explores the central questions of innovation and new product development. First, how should managers view innovation and how can opportunities for innovation be identified? Second, why are top companies now making innovation their number one priority? Third, what are the barriers to building organizations which can achieve fast innovation and how can they best be overcome?

 Meaning of innovation

For a manager, innovation should be defined as: *developing and delivering products or services that offer benefits which customers perceive as new and superior*. Opportunities for innovation are created by environmental changes which generate new customer needs or make possible better solutions to current needs.

Changes in the environment continually create opportunities for innovation in two ways. First, changes in demographics, living standards, political forces, technology culture, lifestyles and fashion create *new needs*. For example, the current concerns with pollution and protection of the environment create opportunities for electric cars, pollution control equipment and packaging which is more environmentally friendly. The ageing of the population creates opportunities for new retail concepts, health care and housing. The break-up of the Soviet Union has created new market opportunities in eastern Europe. The list of such changes and consequently the new needs generated can be extended indefinitely. Companies such as Mercedes Benz, Marks & Spencer, Siemens, Honda, Coca-Cola and Philip Morris owe their continued success to seizing these opportunities.

Second, environmental changes make possible *new solutions* to both current and new customer needs. In particular, advances in science, technology and the ability to handle information allow companies to apply this new knowledge to enhance the satisfaction they can offer customers. They have opportunities to develop and deliver new products or services which are more efficient than current ones. Not only does new knowledge make possible better products and services, but it can also provide the means for lowering costs and improving quality. For example, new management tools such as corporate re-engineering and total quality management enable cost, time and defects to be taken out of the firm's operational processes. Through such innovations companies boost their growth and earnings potential by offering superior customer value and making competitive offerings obsolete.

In summary, to identify opportunities for innovation managers need to analyze and assess the implications of the environmental changes taking place around them. They need to ask what are the key changes occurring in the economy, in society and in technology, and what threats and opportunities they present for customers, competitors and their own business.

Invention is different from innovation. Many inventions fail to build markets. An invention is a new product; an innovation is a new benefit. Customers do not want new products, they want solutions which offer new and superior benefits. To be a successful innovation, a new product must meet four benefit criteria:

- *Important*. The new product or service must offer benefits which will be perceived as important by customers. For example, a new watch, accurate to one second in a hundred years, would be a technical feat but would probably not be regarded as a substantial benefit by most consumers.

- *Unique*. The benefits offered by the new product must be perceived as unique. If customers believe that current offers provide the same advantages, the new idea will not be valued.

- *Sustainable*. A new product may offer benefits which are unique and important, but if it can be quickly copied by competitors, it will not offer much of a market opportunity. Sometimes patents provide a barrier to competition. But in most industries, speed to market and brand building provide the most effective means of sustaining the value of the innovation.

- *Marketable*. The company must have the capability to market the product. This includes designing a reliable and effective version of the product, producing it at a price customers can afford, and establishing an effective distribution system to deliver and support it.

Many companies introduce new products that fail on one or more of these criteria. Inventors, fixated by technical novelty, are particularly prone to undervalue these customer benefits. For example, Bell Labs invented the revolutionary transistor but failed to find a market for it. It was Sony which saw the opportunity to use transistors to build cheap, reliable radios. EMI invented the scanner but failed to develop an effective marketing programme or build barriers to entry. In fact, most of the really profitable and successful innovations have little in the way of radically new technology, but instead utilize current technology more effectively in solving customer problems.

Innovations can be classified by degree. A survey by Booz, Allen & Hamilton showed that 90 per cent of new products are not new to the world (Table 7.1).[1] Most are adaptations of products that a company is currently selling: product improvements, line extensions, penetration of new markets or the addition of new product lines. Only 10 per cent are products which are fundamentally new to the market. It is these latter types of innovation which make the newspaper headlines. But product improvements and line extensions should not be despised as forms of innovation. They are crucial ways to maintain the 'freshness' of established brands and consequently their sales and profit performance. Product improvements, cost reductions and repositionings keep brands profitable and up to date. Line extensions, new product lines and penetrating new markets capitalize on and develop established brand strengths.

Table 7.1 emphasizes another point. Even for those 10 per cent of innovations that were fundamentally new, only 2 per cent were new products. Most successful innovations – even the major ones – are new marketing concepts rather than new products. Such concepts include the following:

■ *New old products* are new uses or applications for familiar products. These can be extremely important. Examples are Arm & Hammer finding new uses for baking soda, from baking to deodorizing household equipment, toothpaste, etc.; and Merck extending the application of Enalapril from hypertension to heart failure.

■ *New markets* are new types of customer groups for an existing product or service. For example, Lucozade was positioned for decades as a medicinal supplement for the old and infirm. In the 1990s it was repositioned extremely successfully as a sports drink for athletes.

■ *New ways of doing business* are innovative approaches to delivering current products and services to customers. These are one of the most successful sources of innovation today. In particular, finding new ways to distribute and support customers is an area of great opportunity. For example, Direct Line transformed the car insurance market in Europe by cutting out the brokers that absorbed 40 per cent of the insurance cost. Dell did the same in personal computers, by selling direct to consumers rather than through high-cost retail chains. The Internet and other developments in IT offer major opportunities for innovating in how business is done.

Why innovate?

Today the pressures to innovate are greater than ever. Firms have always needed to innovate in order to survive. Just as environmental change creates opportunities for

Table 7.1 ■ Types of new product

	%
New to company	
1 Product improvement	25
2 Cost reduction	10
3 Repositioning	5
4 Product line extension	25
5 New product line	15
6 Penetration of new market	10
New to world	
1 New product	2
2 New old product	2
3 New market	2
4 New way of doing business	4

Source: New Product Management for the 1980s (Hamilton, NY: Booz, Allen & Hamilton, 1982), p. 9

innovation, so it creates threats by making existing products obsolete. Change creates new needs and provides the knowledge and means for better answers to them. The accelerating pace of environmental change – new technologies, changing consumer tastes and more competition – have all acted to shorten product life cycles. Businesses that fail to update their products are sooner or later squeezed out of the market by more innovative organizations.

Innovation is also necessary to achieve growth. Even if the firm maintains up-to-date products, the markets they are in may mature or decline. A firm may eventually need to push into new markets to find opportunities for growth. Innovation is also crucial in most markets to maintain or enhance profit margins. The profits of established products soon come under pressure as competitors emulate and more price-sensitive markets are tapped. Product improvements and line extensions can hold up margins, while truly innovative products can earn really substantial returns.

In recent years, innovation has been brought into sharp focus by the way some of the world's outstanding companies have turned to using an accelerated rate of new product development as their major competitive weapon. In strategic terms, these can be described as 'third-generation competitors'. The first generation of postwar competition was based upon cost advantages. In particular, Japanese companies such as Toyota, Casio and Honda built market shares by using initially low labour costs and subsequently high productivity and scale economies to undercut their western competitors. As companies sought to lower their cost structures, the best of these first-generation competitors added a second layer of competitor advantage – high quality. This powerful combination of low cost and high quality pushed many traditional western competitors out of the mass markets into a retreat to small specialized niche markets not targeted by their ambitious rivals.

It became conventional wisdom that companies had to *choose* between competing on cost and competing on product differentiation. These were what Porter called the 'generic strategies' open to the business.[2] But in the last decade, a new breed of competitors have shown that it was possible – indeed, increasingly essential – to be both low cost and highly differentiated. These third-generation competitors, in addition to low cost and high quality, offered customers the benefits of a stream of innovative products and a wide variety to choose from. These new competitors such as Sony, Swatch, Toyota and Honda had both cost structures that could match their low-cost rivals and speciality products which could compete in innovation, design and performance with the best of the niche players, such as Bang & Olufsen, Rolex, BMW and Porsche. Figure 7.1 illustrates the dominance of these new high-productivity, highly differentiated competitors and the vulnerability of the niche players and those relying only on cost. While the first generation of low-cost competitors dominated the traditional commodity marketers, the new third-generation competitors threatened to dominate both the low-cost and the niche players.

Honda is a good illustration of one of these new fast-track innovators.[3] In the early 1980s its motorcycle business was being attacked by Yamaha. Honda launched its counterattack with the war cry 'Yamaha wo tsubusu' (this roughly translates as 'We will crush, squash, butcher and slaughter Yamaha'). Rather than cut prices – a weak weapon in an affluent style-oriented market, Honda chose innovation. Over the next eighteen months it launched 113 new models. This wave of new product launches devastated

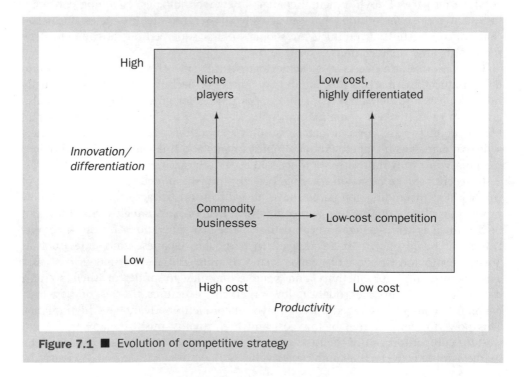

Figure 7.1 ■ Evolution of competitive strategy

Yamaha. First, Honda succeeded in making motorcycles a fashion buy, where newness and freshness became key attributes to customers. Second, Honda was able to incorporate the latest technology into its products, introducing four-valve engines, composites, direct drive and other sophisticated features. Next to Honda motorcycles, Yamaha's looked old, out of date and unattractive. Demand for Yamaha motorcycles collapsed.

Such third-generation competitors have achieved their breakthroughs by focusing on speed. They have reorganized to cut dramatically the time taken to develop new products, to manufacture and to distribute them. Managers in these companies have discovered that being the fastest in developing new products and responding to customer needs leads to the following important competitive advantages.

Leverage of fast-track innovators

Lower costs

If, for example, a car company can cut its model development time from six years to three years, it will normally cut its development costs massively. It will absorb only half the engineering time and tie up half the R & D facilities. Equally important, it will also slash the overhead costs sucked into administering and controlling the project. Consequently, it normally costs today's rapid innovators only a fraction of the amount of their slower-paced competitors to develop a new product.

More innovation

By freeing up R & D people and facilities and cutting costs, a company can increase the productivity of its R & D spend to pursue more projects and get out more new products for the same budget. This allows it continually to develop and fine tune its offerings.

Faster growth

With newer products and more choice to offer the market, fast-track innovators can grow more rapidly.

Higher profits

Innovators are invariably more profitable because it costs them less to develop their new products and because their products are fresher, more up to date and designed to incorporate the latest technology, so they can obtain higher prices. The shorter product life cycles become, the greater the profit premium on innovative products.

Brand strength

It is normally much easier to build a strong brand when it is the first into the market. An innovative product finds it easier to establish a differential advantage because it is a novel competitor. Late entrants have to prove that they are better than the innovator, which is normally much harder because differences are smaller. Customers tend to stay loyal when they are comfortable with the innovator, and it takes major advantages in performance or price to shift them. A strong brand can also spin off early line extensions to attract new market segments by using its existing brand name to build confidence.

Reduced forecasting errors

If a company can halve the time it takes to develop a new product, it does not need to guess about market requirements so far in advance. The shorter the gestation period, the more reliable the prediction of market potential.

Flexibility and synergies

Innovators can position products across more segments of the market and through more channels. This gives them greater market coverage and less vulnerability to the fortunes of any one niche. They will normally also obtain economies of scope, sharing components, technology and marketing facilities across the range. Finally, they can use cash flows generated from strong markets to support aggressive moves into new niches. For instance, Toyota's technological and financial strength built upon its position in the mass car market allows it to invest, transfer technology and cross-subsidize its move into the sports car market – an opportunity not open to a defender such as Porsche because it is a narrow single-niche competitor.

Strategic opportunities for fast innovators

Non-innovative businesses are vulnerable to more dynamic competitors, to shorter product life cycles and to the maturation of their markets. Western companies often try to meet these problems through the hazardous route of seeking acquisitions in growth markets. Fast-track innovators can, however, pursue other strategic options which more effectively exploit their core capabilities.

Creating new markets

By seeking to exploit fully their technical and marketing capabilities, innovators can create completely new and often unexpected markets. Sony, pushing forward its skills in electronics and miniaturization, created a whole new industry of portable entertainment with its Walkman, Watchman and Bookman products. Nintendo in electronic games and 3M with its Post-it notes also created new markets from existing strengths.

Expanding current markets

Innovation can expand mature markets by attracting new users and new uses. Mars expanded the whole ice-cream market in Europe when it introduced a new bar which incorporated top-quality ice cream into its Mars bar brand of chocolate. In Japan, Toto both dominates and expands the once mature bathroom fixtures market with a stream of new products. In recent years these have included a special women's shampoo sink, now accounting for 10 per cent of all sinks sold, and the Washlet – a toilet with a warm water rinsing nozzle, a dryer and a heated seat. Recently, it has introduced with great success an intelligent toilet which measures protein and sugar levels in the user's urine, together with blood pressure, temperature, pulse and weight!

Penetrating markets

Swatch became an outstanding success in the watch market through an innovative concept. Before Swatch the market was divided into two broad segments: the low-cost reliable Japanese products dominated by Seiko and Casio, and the prestigious and very expensive Swiss watches. Rather than seeking to compete directly with either of these competitor groups, Swatch aced both with a concept which was low cost, high quality and elegant (Figure 7.2). It transformed the market by making the watch a fashion item. Like a fashion house, Swatch introduces, with a wave of publicity, a stream of new watch designs each 'season'. For many customers, Swatch made the Japanese competitors look boring and the prestigious Swiss watches look old fashioned.

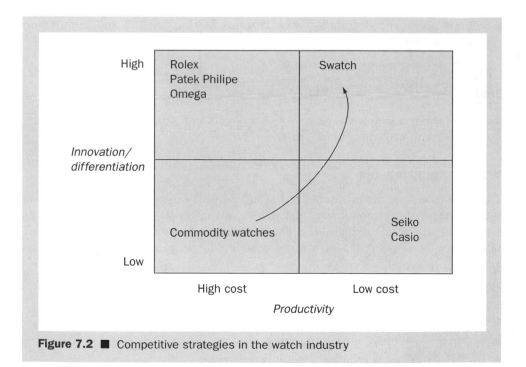

Figure 7.2 ■ Competitive strategies in the watch industry

Defending market share

A company that continually updates its line with a stream of small improvements will generally maintain its edge better than one which seeks the major breakthrough. General Motors' Saturn project contrasts with the power of incremental innovation. Concern about its lack of innovation and market share erosion led General Motors to launch its radical Saturn plan. This aimed to revolutionize car design and manufacture, enabling it to leapfrog its Japanese competitors. Unfortunately, Saturn took over ten years to complete. During that period Toyota introduced 24 new models, each building on its predecessor and incorporating the latest features. As a result, by the time Saturn was launched, rather than being a breakthrough, it was already obsolete.

Repositioning the business

Rapid innovators can push the application of their core competences into new markets, which eventually shifts the weight of the business into a new industry. Here are some examples:

■ Brother, changing from a sewing machine manufacturer to a maker of typewriters, printers and small computers.

■ Canon, changing from a camera company to an office systems business.

■ Honda, changing from a manufacturer of small motors to motorcycles and cars.

■ Nippon Steel, emerging from a steel business into a computer and information systems company.

 Barriers to innovation

Successful innovators introduce many new products and achieve higher success rates. Both tasks are related and neither is easy.

Why new products fail

There have been numerous studies of the success rates of new products. All of them suggest that *most* new products fail to achieve a reasonable return for the business. The failure rate is particularly high for consumer products. Typical studies suggest failure rates of around 80 per cent for consumer products, 30 per cent for industrial products and 20 per cent for new services.

Most researchers believe that failure rates are likely to continue to increase. Factors causing this include the following:

■ Shortening product life cycles.

■ Rising costs of developing new products.

■ Increasing environmental and consumer legislation.

■ Global competition.

■ More new products.

■ Increasingly segmented markets.

■ Declining profitability of brand followers.

This high and rising failure rate has three implications for management. First, new product development needs to be carefully planned. Second, since many, or most, new product ideas will be weeded out before the commercialization stage, management need to stimulate a large pool of potential new products from which a few winners may emerge. Finally, as risk taking, and consequently the acceptance of new product failures, is fundamental to the innovation process, management must look for ways to reduce the cost of these failures. Fast response, minimizing overhead and controlling investment are the means of limiting these downside risks.

Considerable evidence exists on the causes of new product failure. None of the reasons is surprising and most of the problems can be avoided, or at least substantially reduced.

Development too slow

Managers greatly underestimate the penalty for slow development. Today, with core technologies widely available and short product life cycles, speed to market is crucial. Companies that are slow to innovate usually end up with a high product development cost and achieve lower prices. Late entrants rarely obtain a significant market share or achieve scale economies in manufacture or marketing.

Speed to market is generally more important than fine tuning cost and quality. A study by McKinsey suggests launching a product six months behind schedule will reduce lifetime profits by one-third. In contrast, spending 30 per cent over budget on development will trim profits by only 2 per cent (Table 7.2)

Lack of differential advantage

Products fail when customers do not perceive them as better value than those they are currently using. This may be due to inadequate functional performance. Alternatively,

Table 7.2 ■ Impact of development problems on profitability

	Decrease in lifetime profit (%)
Introduced 6 months late	31.5
Quality problems reducing prices by 10%	14.9
Product costs exceeded by 10%	3.8
Development programme cost overrun by 10%	2.3

Source: Don G. Reinertsen, 'The search for new product killers', *Electronic Business*, July 1983, pp. 62–6

it may be due to poor competitive positioning – customers do not perceive the real values possessed by the product. The first problem is usually identifiable in blind product-use tests; the second through consumer research.

Poor planning

New product development is so complex, fast moving and competitive that mistakes will inevitably occur if management do not put in appropriate systems. Poor planning results in markets not being researched and segmented, targets and budgets not being set and monitored, positioning strategies not being tested, and product launches being inadequately implemented. Without proper planning, the result is invariably failure.

No management enthusiasm

Lack of management enthusiasm is another product killer. Management are often oriented to past winners and see new projects as taking resources away from the core business. IBM's historical strength in mainframe computers constrained management's commitment to the new fast-moving, lower-margin mini- and microcomputer markets. Many of today's established retailers are reluctant to adopt the Internet because they know its development as a shopping medium will cannibalize their existing branches. Short-termism is another factor handicapping many western companies. Where management incentives and focus are on current profit performance, new product development efforts are often sacrificed to boost short-term profits.

 ## Organizing for innovation

An innovative organization is one which continually seeks new ways to better what it offers customers, rapidly processes these ideas and effectively implements the best of them. In a very small firm, all employees naturally feel close to customers and know that their livelihoods depend upon satisfying them. As the firm grows, this clarity is lost. Senior managers give up day-to-day contact with customers and front-line employees. Increasing organizational complexity means that issues of internal administration and control take precedence over the problems of the customer.

Innovation is curtailed because inputs take over from outputs. Larger organizations are split into functions and often operate at different sites. Knowledge about customers' needs and how they might be resolved is no longer unified. Sales, manufacturing and R & D staff report to separate departmental heads. Functions develop their own goals, often jealously guard their own territories and expand their own cultures. Communicating information, priorities and direction then becomes a major problem. Not surprisingly, in many large organizations innovation languishes.

How this occurs is illustrated in Table 7.3. The company shown is a large engineering business which supplies the aerospace and motor vehicles industries.[4] It is organized on conventional matrix lines. It had become concerned about its slowness

Table 7.3 ■ Time and resources to complete a typical new product project

Total days inside the company	273
Total value-added days	19
Number of staff adding value	36
Departments involved	10
Back-pedalling among departments	9
Approvals:	31
Functional 21	
Management 10	
Committee approvals	15
Transfers between sites	8

in developing new products. For example, it took nine months to respond to a simple customer request for a new product proposal. On investigation, it was discovered that only for 7 per cent of the time had work on the proposal actually been taking place. For 254 of the 273 days it was in the company, the project had been stalled, waiting for information to be moved across departments and sites, and waiting for busy executives and committees to study, appraise and approve the steps that had been taken. Many companies are now seeking to cut development time by more effective teamwork among departments, or 'simultaneous product development'. For example, Ford took fourteen weeks from its development cycle by simply getting engineering and finance departments to review designs simultaneously rather than sequentially.

Other companies have found similar figures – generally under 10 per cent of the time developing a new product is adding value. Clearly, ways of organizing to run a complex ongoing business generally work badly when it comes to innovation. A key for management today is to develop different and special organizational arrangements for innovation.

Vision and objectives

Initially, top management must provide the vision and priority for innovation. Innovation needs to be placed alongside profits as an essential organizational goal. An 'innovation audit' is a good place to start. This is a critical assessment of the firm's innovation record, the internal obstacles to innovation and how performance can be enhanced. The first step should be a *benchmarking* exercise comparing the firm's innovation record with those of other leading businesses.

A leading European pharmaceutical company benchmarked its NPD performance against Merck, the industry leader. While it took twelve years to move a new drug through the research, development and registration process, it discovered that Merck did it in seven. As a result, Merck had over 50 per cent of its revenues generated by products launched in the last five years (versus 13 per cent); Merck had faster growth, higher profit margins (42 per cent versus 17 per cent) and four times the market share.

The second stage of the audit is to identify the obstacles to innovation. For the pharmaceutical company, the problems were identified as a lack of urgency among managers in looking for new products and in progressing them rapidly. Second, the NPD process was badly structured, with value-adding work being continuously held up for months at a time waiting for departmental and executive inputs and reviews. Finally, communications were inadequate. Many people were stalling projects simply because they lacked the information to understand the issues.

The final stage of the audit is to recommend what should be done. Quantitative innovation objectives need to be set on both the number of new products to be pursued and the time to get them to the market. The necessary organization and cultural changes need to be pursued with vigour and urgency.

People and skills

Innovation is based upon *knowledge*. Organizations that win in innovating have people who know more than their competitors about what customers want and about the technological solutions available. An innovative organization is a learning organization. Unless the business is investing in its people to keep them at the forefront of understanding environmental change and the potential of new technologies, it will lack the core capabilities to innovate.

Making the company's *information* easily accessible to all personnel is also crucial. If people are to contribute fully, information cannot be kept locked behind functional or hierarchical doors. Technical people need to know about customer needs and the market and financial performance and prospects of their products. Sales people require information about technical developments, manufacturing problems and new areas the company is exploring.

Staff also need *incentives* to innovate. If managers are evaluated on today's sales and profits, they are not going to put effort into tomorrow's businesses. This is why companies such as Hewlett-Packard, 3M and Rubbermaid link the pay of key executives to the number of new products they introduce. Contribution to innovation, the future of the business, needs to be explicitly built into the firm's incentive and evaluation systems.

Customer-focused innovation

Managers must stress that the objective of innovation is to produce a delighted customer. Customer involvement and feedback should be continual priorities throughout the project. For radical innovation an eye for customers is even more essential. Paradoxically, the really big successes often succeed with quite different customers from those they were intended to serve. Often they create markets that nobody before even imagined. For example, no one knew they needed an office copier before the first Xerox in 1960; five years later no business could imagine being without one. No one could see a use for the Walkman when Sony first researched it; now few homes are without one. Similarly, 3M developed both an adhesive tape and later a low-retention glue for the industrial market. They were never taken up by industry, but instead developed huge markets as Scotch tape and Post-it notes in households and offices. Upjohn's research into heart drugs produced Regain – a product that made millions when it was launched in 1990 as a hair restorer!

Even when the market focus is broadly correct, forecasts for genuinely new products can be hopelessly wrong. In 1950 Univac predicted that by the year 2000 a total of 1,000 computers would have been sold. The actual figure reached well over 1 million a year. When the first jets started to fly, the market research suggested that there were not enough passengers for the transatlantic liners. Five years later jets were carrying a hundred times more passengers each year than had ever sailed the Atlantic.

If the innovator has tunnel vision – wanting to stick to areas with which it is familiar – then it may succeed in only creating an opportunity for a competitor. Innovators need to expect a new product to have potential outside its original target market. They need to anticipate this by spending time outside: in the market, with different customers, with sales people, looking and listening. Interest from unexpected customers needs to be followed up and, if possible, exploited.

Autonomous teams, parallel processing

Innovation must take place outside the conventional organization. The task and objectives of running an existing business are quite different from those of starting a new one. The former focuses on efficiency and control; the latter on risk taking and creativity. The organization that is right for efficiently producing the millionth product or serving the millionth customer has to be different from that doing something for the first time. Ongoing organizations are too slow and unfocused for innovation.

These defects occur because conventional organizations work in series rather than in parallel. Traditionally, new products start with either the R & D marketing department getting a bright idea. After some months or years in research, the concept is then handed over to the engineering function, where a product is designed. After they have finished, it is passed to production for manufacture, before finally it goes over to sales to sell. At each stage there is likely to be delay, disagreement and cyclebacks among departments (see again Table 7.3). The production people send the design back to engineering because they say it cannot be produced at a reasonable cost; the engineers then spend more time redesigning the product. When the sales people eventually get the product, they are disillusioned because they find it is too late and because it does not offer customers any new benefits. Each of the functional departments blames the others for incompetence.

Such critical problems can be resolved only by taking responsibility for innovation out of the mainstream organization and placing it in the hands of a *special team* dedicated to the project. Most top companies now see project teams as the essential way to make innovation work. The team should consist of experienced people from R & D, marketing, engineering, production and sales. Each should share total responsibility for the success of the project. Their first task is to map out the value-adding tasks and seek to timetable the reviews, paperwork and approval processes so that they do not block the real work. At each stage from research, through design to marketing, the team's multifunctional skills are used. The key stages of the development process are then pursued in parallel rather than sequentially, collapsing time and eliminating much of the organizational conflict.

Systems

The planning and control systems of the firm need to be changed if innovation and an entrepreneurial climate are to be fostered. First, conventional return on investment criteria will choke off innovation if they are applied to new products. Even the best new products rarely show an adequate ROI until they have been on the market for several years. Second, systems can be used to influence attitudes. For example, some innovative companies have an annual high-level product review meeting. This reviews the firm's portfolio and aims to slough off weak and obsolete products to make room for new products.

Budget meetings can also be refocused. Currently such meetings concentrate on negative variances and so orientate managers to problems rather than opportunities. Instead, agendas should allocate time to identify activities which have exceeded budget and encourage managers to explore how such opportunities could be exploited. Finally, the annual strategic planning cycle should incorporate a thorough review of innovation performance. It should ask whether objectives are being met and whether the business is at the competitive forefront.

Integration

Innovation requires to be separate, but when it is complete a project must be integrated into the mainstream organization to ensure that it receives adequate resources. Organizational researchers have shown that this fine balance between the needs for differentiation and eventual integration is facilitated by three types of role within the business.[5]

First, an organization needs *product champions* who fight for the innovation and push it forward through the many obstacles which invariably arise. The product champions will normally belong to the project team. But an innovation also needs a *sponsor* in the mainstream organization who will lend authority, encouragement and resources to enable the product champions to carry the project closer to commercialization. These are normally middle to senior managers with a respected track record. Finally, an innovation needs an *orchestrator* who can handle the politics of change and obtain the backing of the organization. The orchestrator will be a member of top management – often the chief executive.

Ultimately, innovation requires commitment throughout the organization. Horizontal or functional support is integrated through the new product team. Vertical or hierarchical commitment is achieved through the different roles of product champions, sponsors and orchestrators.

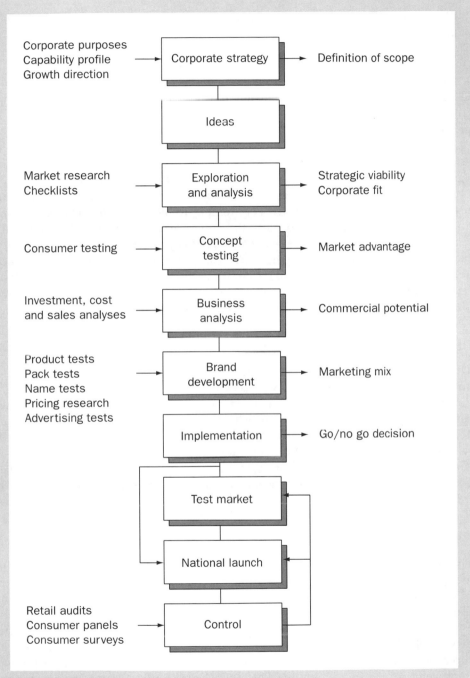

Figure 7.3 ■ The new product development process

New product development process

The cross-functional new product team has the task of successfully channelling ideas through the NPD process as shown in Figure 7.3. As many as possible of these stages will be undertaken in parallel to speed up the process. The exact process varies somewhat between industries. For example, test marketing is not usually required for industrial products. In other industries, additional stages are involved. For instance, in pharmaceuticals, clinical trials and registration requirements are critical steps.

More companies are now structuring their new product development process to accelerate results and control costs. 3M, one of the most consistently successful companies at innovating, uses the *stage-gate system*. At each of the main stages in the new product development process, the project team has to present specific evidence and results to move on to the next stage. For example, to move from the 'exploration and analysis' stage to 'brand development', the project leader has to provide convincing research results covering consumer attitudes, competitive analysis and technical performance. The gatekeepers are the senior managers who critically review the project at each stage and decide whether to go, hold, recycle or kill it. Such disciplined systems have a number of advantages: the project teams have clear goals and clear responsibilities, work is performance oriented and bureaucracy is minimized.

Corporate strategy and innovation

The firm should have a corporate strategy setting out its mission, core capabilities and the product and market areas it seeks to operate in. This should indicate the direction for researching and developing new ideas. The team will be oriented towards projects which are consistent with the overall strategy of the organization. The intensity of the innovation effort will be influenced by the ambitions of top management. For example, 3M expects each of its divisions to have a minimum of 25 per cent of its profits from products introduced in the last five years. Such a goal dictates that substantial managerial and financial resources will be devoted to innovation.

New product ideas

The process starts with generating ideas for new products. Two principles influence the idea generation phase. First, the business needs to have lots of ideas. A study by Booz, Allen & Hamilton found that it took 58 new product ideas to turn out one winner. In some industries the odds are even bigger. In the pharmaceutical industry it is currently estimated that around 10,000 substances have to be investigated for every successful new product introduction. Second, management have to recognize that not all successful new products are 'breakthroughs'. Instead many are the small product improvements and line extensions which, while apparently unremarkable, over time are crucial to keeping the business moving forward.

Employees

All new ideas originate from employees. Even new products licensed or acquired have to be identified and championed internally. Ideas can come from anywhere in the organization, but those of front-line employees – people who make the products and sell them to customers – are particularly valuable, since they are most knowledgeable about the technology and the needs of the market. In principle, large organizations employing thousands of people should have a major asset in this idea base. Some large companies such as 3M, Marks & Spencer and Toyota have tapped this potential to great effect. Toyota, for example, receives over 2 million ideas a year from employees, about 35 per head, and claims to implement about 85 per cent of them. But most large companies have not seriously tried to incentivize and reward such a massive drive to capitalize on the knowledge and creativity of their employees.

Senior managers should design systems to boost permanently the flow of ideas from employees. They should set targets for each department – say, five ideas per employee – and provide substantial rewards for implementable proposals.

Customers

Customers are invariably the best source of ideas. Innovations have commercial value only if they meet the needs of customers better than current products. Innovative customers – those individuals or organizations which are at the forefront in buying new products or applying new ideas – are the most valuable sources. Such customers see problems and opportunities well ahead of typical buyers and are generally willing to talk with potential suppliers about their requirements and how they might be met.

Research and development

Scientists play a pivotal role in high-tech businesses. Asking customers is not enough. Customers tend to be myopic – they cannot express needs for products and benefits they have never envisaged. It is important to allow scientists to pursue promising research directions. The skill is paralleling this technical thrust with constant probing and testing with potential customers to get feedback about possible uses and improvements. Without a close and early integration of technical research with market soundings, investments in R & D can be thrown away. All too often it is the imitator, rather than the inventor, who sees the real market opportunities in technical advances.

Competitors

Competitors can be a source of new ideas. Companies such as Canon, Xerox, Hewlett-Packard and Ford use competitor benchmarking – systematically comparing their products with the best competitor to look for potential advances.

Distributors

Dealers are particularly useful sources of ideas. They know both the ultimate customer and the competitors. Managers can turn a distributor into a valuable ally and powerful source of new ideas by listening to its problems and suggestions.

Creativity techniques

A variety of techniques have been developed by psychologists and market researchers to help individuals and groups generate creative ideas. These include brainstorming, synectics and morphological analysis.[6] Such methods can play an important role in inspiring people to release their latent capabilities for innovation.

Outside sources

Given the speed with which markets and technologies change, successful companies have had to break out of their 'not invented here' syndrome. To accelerate the rate of innovation, even companies with great track records – Merck, IBM, Apple, 3M and GE – carry a rising proportion of products invented by others. These product ideas are brought in or licensed from other companies, research agencies, universities and consultants. Top companies are dramatically extending their networks of relationships and strategic alliances to pull in new ideas and capabilities.

Screening ideas

The objective of the idea-generating process is to maximize the number of suggestions. The purpose of the screening stage is to select those few that have the potential to be winners. This is a fundamental strategic decision – with limited resources, the business must focus its efforts. Potential success depends upon three factors: the idea's compatibility with the firm's corporate strategy, the potential demand for the product, and the firm's capability to exploit the product opportunity.

Table 7.4 shows a screening technique which can be used to assess the attractiveness of ideas at an early stage. The first column lists three categories of factors determining potential success. The next column identifies the relative weights that management attaches to each of these components. Finally, each idea is rated on a ten-point scale (1 = bad to 10 = excellent) by managers and the total weighted score for each idea is obtained. The highest potential score is 100 per cent, and projects scoring below a cut-off of, say, 75 are candidates for elimination. Such techniques are used not to make decisions, but rather to assist a selection process.

Screening is a tricky problem because it involves balancing between two types of error. Type I errors result from not eliminating a product idea which subsequently fails. Type II errors result from eliminating ideas which would have been successful. The tougher the screening process, the fewer type I errors will occur but with the increasing probability of type II errors. Both IBM and Kodak committed type II errors when they

Table 7.4 ■ New product idea screening form

Factors	Importance weight	Ideas		
		A	B	C
1 *Corporate strategy fit*	(30)			
Consistency with objectives	20	10	7	7
Fit to product/market goals	10	10	6	7
2 *Demand potential*	(40)			
Customer need	10	8	8	4
Market size	6	8	7	3
Market growth	6	6	5	3
Potential share	6	6	5	3
Profitability	6	5	6	4
Sociopolitical risk	6	8	6	4
3 *Fit to capabilities*	(30)			
Technical	5	9	6	4
Marketing	5	9	6	5
Distribution	5	8	5	6
Production	5	8	7	5
Finance	5	7	7	7
People	5	8	6	7
Weighted total score	**100**	**82.4**	**63.9**	**52.2**

Note: Over 85: excellent ideas; 70–84: of substantial interest; 55–69: worth exploring; below 54: of low priority

rejected Chester Carlson's offer of the patents for his new copying machine. Millions were made instead by Rank which took up the offer. The costs of type II errors are underestimated, largely because most companies never discover the value of the ideas they throw away.

Concept development

An idea that gets through the initial screening process must be developed as a consumer proposition and tested against potential customers. Customers do not buy products; they buy solutions to their problems. Consequently, it is important to distinguish between a product idea and its positioning concept. The product idea is the new physical good or functional service that is being considered by the company. The positioning concept refers to the choice of target market segment and benefit proposition. This distinction is crucial because most new products can have very different positioning strategies.

Even a simple product idea such as a new brand of aspirin could have multiple positioning concepts. The target markets chosen could be adults or children, people with mild or severe illnesses, or cold or headache sufferers. The reason to buy might be that compared to competitors it is more efficient, faster, longer acting or easier to swallow, or has fewer side effects.

The dilemmas are equally great in industrial markets. IBM initially saw the computer as having a narrow scientific appeal. Its president, Thomas Watson, believed that a single computer could solve all the big scientific problems in the world. It was only when conceived as a business machine that its true potential was realized. The initial concept of the laser was for military use. The real opportunity, however, was positioning it as a key component in technologies as diverse as compact disc players, communications and medical surgery.

Not surprisingly, many of the biggest winners are not innovative products at all; rather they are innovative concepts. Here, managers take an existing product and find a new or better positioning concept for it. Acetaminophen was sold by a number of companies as a substitute painkiller for people who could not take aspirin. It was not particularly successful until Johnson & Johnson launched the Tylenol brand and positioned Acetaminophen as a general replacement for aspirin: a safer, better painkiller.

Testing alternative positioning concepts for the product is therefore essential in the NPD process. It involves presenting alternative benefit propositions to different potential target customers. Managers then research the following:

■ *Communicability*. Do customers understand the benefit being offered?

■ *Believability*. Do they believe that the product has the benefits claimed?

■ *Need*. Do they have a strong perceived need for the benefit offered?

■ *Need gap*. If there is a need, is it perceived as already being satisfied by existing providers?

■ *Perceived value*. Do customers see it as offering value at the price being considered?

■ *Usage*. How would they use it and how often?

Business analysis

So far in the NPD process, the firm's investments and costs have been limited, but if the project is to go ahead substantial investments will now have to be made in developing the product and the infrastructure to manufacture and market it. The costs of failure now threaten to become important to the firm. At the business analysis stage, the product champions need to present a business case to the project's sponsors. Management will want to base their go-ahead decision on four factors:

■ Their faith in the profit projections put to them.

■ The assessments of the commercial risks involved.

■ The investment required.

■ Other strategic issues involved in the decision.

The business case will draw in all the functional skills of the team. The sales forecast will be built up from the proposed marketing strategy and a detailed understanding of the market. The costs and investment estimates will be developed from an understanding of the manufacturing, marketing and distribution tasks required. These projections will then be built up into a cash flow statement covering perhaps the first ten years in the product's life. Since these projections are highly uncertain, it is valuable to produce optimistic and pessimistic as well as a median forecast of cash flows.

The expected net present cash flow of the project is:

$$ENPV_i = \sum_{i=1}^{n} \frac{C_i P_i}{(1+r)^i}$$

where $ENPV_i$ = expected net present value of project in year i
C_i = net cash flow generated in year i
r = firm's cost of capital
P_i = probability estimate attached to the cash flow in year i.

A product with a positive expected net present value should generate wealth for shareholders and be in their interests.

However, it is a mistake to base the decision on purely a financial criterion. The problems with this decision rule are that it ignores the interests of stakeholders other than shareholders and that it fails to capture some broader strategic issues facing the firm. For example, a company may find that the final financial return on a prospective product does not reach its target rate of return. Despite its unprofitability, such a product may be the key to maintaining a presence in the market. Failure to develop a new product may permanently close the option of being a major player in the industry. A new product may not be in the narrow interests of shareholders, but it may preserve the jobs of long-term valuable employees and demonstrate the firm's commitment to the community.

Decisions whether to proceed with the new product therefore require judgement based on both quantitative and qualitative information.[7]

Brand development

If a product concept satisfactorily passes through the business analysis gate, it will move into the product and brand development phase. The first objective here is to design and develop a product prototype which matches the positioning concept and which can be mass-produced and delivered in an efficient way. The second task is to develop the elements of the marketing mix – name, pack, price, distribution and promotion – which will augment the physical product and communicate its value to the target market.

The brand development stage depends upon close and sympathetic co-operation between the different functional areas of the business. It is the project team's task to facilitate this partnership. The development experts will be leading the design of the product; manufacturing will be seeking to achieve low-cost production; marketing and distribution will be aiming at optimizing the marketing mix, sales and logistics plans. The brand development stage should be characterized by a series of design decisions rapidly tested to achieve feedback from the market. Product tests with potential customers should carefully evaluate functional performance, efficiency, safety and apparent benefit to the customers. For consumer goods, pack tests should check ease of use, performance and the image presented of the product. Name tests should measure memorability and perception of the brand that is evoked. Where advertising is employed, research should pre-test the presentation for its communications effectiveness. Finally, pricing research is necessary to determine what customers would be willing to pay for the product with the values it is designed to offer. Product development and testing agencies have developed a variety of scientifically based techniques for pre-testing the elements of the product and the marketing mix.[8]

Implementation

If the pre-tests are encouraging, the team will push for implementation and launch of the project. The exact alternatives depend on whether it is a consumer or industrial product. However, broadly the management at this stage has three alternatives – test market, regional roll-out or national launch.

Test marketing

Pre-tests during the brand development stage should isolate major problems. However, pre-tests can be blunt and even biased measures because they do not take place in a realistic market place. Pre-tests ask customers if they would buy the product. In practice, with aggressive competition, the perceived risks of changing suppliers and other constraints, the decision might be different from that suggested in the pre-test. Test marketing involves launching the product in one or more parts of the country and determining how the product would fare in realistic conditions.

The objectives of the test market are three. First, the test market aims to develop a more reliable forecast of sales. If in tests a new brand does not achieve a specified target market share, it can be dropped before the major investment in a national launch is undertaken. Second, the test market can be used to evaluate alternative marketing plans. For example, in one area a high promotional budget can be put behind the launch, while in another a more modest investment might be made. This allows an estimate of the promotional elasticity of the product. Third, the test may identify unsuspected problems. These may be problems of obtaining distribution or unexpected reactions from customers. By identifying such problems early, the company can fix them before the real national launch.

Test marketing is a help, but it is no panacea. One increasingly important drawback is that it can delay the launch for a year or more. During this time, competitors can learn about the project, develop defensive strategies and occasionally even be first into the market place. Further, no single area will exactly mirror the country as a whole. Specific factors in the area, such as local competition or the weather, can produce misleading results and forecasts. Finally, markets change over time. While the product might be launched effectively in the test this year, next year circumstances might have changed: new competitive products might have been launched or customer fashion and tastes may have moved on. Test marketing reduces the uncertainties, but does not eliminate them.

Regional roll-outs

Many products are launched on a sequential regional roll-out basis. This has the advantage that the initial regions are effectively test markets which can be used to fine tune the marketing programme. In addition, it allows production capacity to be built up steadily. For industrial goods and prescription pharmaceuticals, the nature of the market makes conventional test markets or regional roll-outs more difficult to apply. Instead products are launched first at innovative customers. The reactions of these opinion leaders will strongly influence whether the product is adopted by the rest of the market.

National launch

If the company aims to pre-empt competition, then, providing it has the resources, it may move swiftly to a national or even international launch. There are many advantages in being first into the market. Getting in first makes it easier to gain a differential advantage. Followers have the more difficult job of showing that they are better. On average, the pioneer maintains a market share two-thirds higher than the next follower and more than double a later entrant.[9] These figures apply in both consumer and industrial markets.

Customer adoption process

When a new product is launched on to the market it should not generally use a mass-market approach – distributing it everywhere and assuming anyone might be a buyer. Again careful customer targeting is essential if resources are not to be wasted. This section looks at four questions:

■ How do new products build acceptance among consumers?

■ How does the market develop?

■ What are the characteristics of innovative customers?

■ What determines whether an innovation will succeed quickly and easily?

Product adoption process

Before customers can buy a new product, they must learn about it. This learning is called the *adoption process* and is commonly viewed as consisting of five stages (Figure 7.4).

■ *Awareness*. First, the innovator has to create awareness of the product. Advertising and PR are common tools for achieving awareness.

■ *Interest*. Next, customers need to be stimulated to seek information about the product's uses, features and advantages.

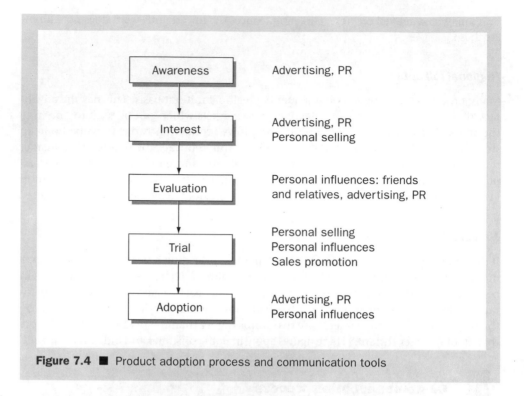

Figure 7.4 ■ Product adoption process and communication tools

- *Evaluation*. Customers consider whether the product will meet their particular needs. Personal sources – friends, colleagues, opinion leaders – become important influences at this stage.

- *Trial*. The customer tries the product for the first time and decides whether to adopt it.

- *Adoption*. The customer decides to make regular use of the product.

In targeting a market segment, the innovator needs to consider at what stage of the adoption process it is. Each stage requires a different media and message emphasis. Public relations and advertising can be effective at generating awareness and interest. Personal selling, sales promotion and sampling can be better for creating evaluation in trial. The launch plan needs a careful sequencing of promotional tools to accelerate the adoption process.

Market diffusion process

The adoption process describes the way an individual customer learns about an innovation. The diffusion process describes how an innovation spreads through a market. Knowledge of this process can assist management in identifying target customers. The major point is that a market develops not uniformly, but by drawing distinctive new segments into it. It is common to identify five segments distinguished by the time they take to adopt the product (Figure 7.5).

■ *Innovators*. These are the first to adopt the new product. Technically, innovators are defined as the first 2.5 per cent of customers. Innovators are venturesome – they are willing to take risks in trying new ideas. They are important first as the initial target segment for an innovative product. Second, they personally influence later adopters. A new product which fails to win the esteem of these innovators will find it difficult subsequently to penetrate the mass market.

■ *Early adopters*. These are the next segment to adopt the product, technically 13.5 per cent of the market. Early adopters tend to be opinion leaders and, since personal influence plays a large role in adoption of new products, they are particularly important.

■ *Early majority*. The next group, 34 per cent, completes the first half of the potential market for the innovation. The early majority are deliberate – they adopt new ideas before the average person, although they are rarely leaders.

■ *Late majority*. These are more sceptical about new products and harder to persuade. Eventually they adopt because of economic necessity or social pressure.

■ *Laggards*. The last 16 per cent of the market are the most reluctant, and the most economically incapable of adopting the innovation. These are described as tradition bound – they are suspicious of changes, mix with other tradition-bound people, and adopt the innovation only when it takes on a measure of tradition itself.

For the innovating company, this diffusion process has several implications. First, it has to target the appropriate segment. Promoting to the 'average' consumer will be ineffective unless the innovators and early adopters have first experienced the product and are willing to recommend it. Second, the marketing mix will need to change radically as the product moves through the segments. Innovators, for example, normally

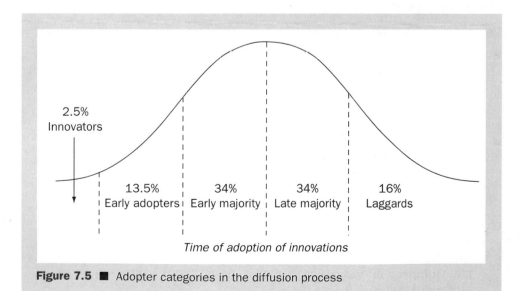

Figure 7.5 ■ Adopter categories in the diffusion process

use different media, have lower price sensitivity and buy through different distribution channels than later adopters. Consequently, the company will need to employ different communication strategies, charge lower prices, modify the product line and change distribution channels as the market evolves and as it targets different groups.

Innovator characteristics

It would be ideal if managers could have general descriptions of the demographic, socioeconomic and media characteristics of these different innovator segments. Unfortunately, although perhaps not surprisingly, such generalizations are hazardous. A person or firm which is an innovator in one product area may easily be a laggard in another. An individual may want the latest hi-fi, but be indifferent and conservative concerning clothes or cars. The marketing manager therefore has to try and identify the innovators in his or her particular market. The essential question is: which customers will perceive the greatest value from the new product? In industrial markets this value will predominantly be economic. For example, a new labour-saving machine will have the highest value to customers in areas with high labour cost, so that they will be more likely to be innovators here. For a new cardiovascular drug, the value will be perceived first by hospital specialists dealing continually with patients with acute heart problems. Family doctors will be later adopters and will rely on the advice of the specialists. For individual customers, image plays an important role and innovators may be those with higher disposable incomes.

Studies of innovations suggest some tentative hypotheses about innovators and early adopters.

Consumer markets

Innovators and early adopters tend towards the following characteristics:

■ Demographics
  - Somewhat younger
  - Higher education
  - Higher income
  - Higher occupational status

■ Social factors
  - Greater social participation
  - Higher social mobility
  - Greater geographical mobility
  - Greater opinion leadership

■ Personality factors
  - More risk taking
  - Oriented towards new things
  - More information sources
  - More print media readership

Industrial markets

The characteristics of organizational buyers most likely to be fast adopters are the following. First, they will be organizations which obtain the highest *economic value* from the product. This may be from either superior performance (higher output, quality, uptime) or lower costs (installation, operating costs). Second, they will be organizations which can utilize *low state of art* innovations. Generally, the initial innovation is a basic version and does not have the sophistication or features of later models. Third, the *cost of failure* must be manageable to the customer. Innovators are often those who can try a product out on a sample of their operations rather than take the entire risk. Fourth, low *switching cost* encourages innovation. If a company has recently trained its workers to use one operating system, it will be reluctant to switch to a completely different one. Finally, some organizations have a higher *perception of technical change* than others, perhaps because they are high-tech business themselves or because they need to utilize the most up-to-date technology to stay competitive.

Characteristics of the new product or service also influence the speed of adoption. Six factors can be identified:

- *Relative advantage.* The greater the perceived added value possessed by the new product, the quicker it is likely to be adopted.

- *Compatibility.* Adoption is quicker if the new product is consistent with current use and practice. For example, the video achieved rapid market penetration because it was compatible with current TV viewing habits.

- *Complexity.* Speedy adoption is hindered by products which are difficult to understand and use.

- *Divisibility.* Adoption is stimulated if a customer can sample the product in a part of its operation or sample it for a limited period.

- *Risk.* The greater the economic or social risk attached to new product failure, the more reluctant buyers will be to try it.

- *Communicability.* Where product performance can be seen or easily demonstrated, adoption is facilitated.

Summary

Peter Drucker wrote that management have only two key tasks: marketing and innovation. Marketing aims at satisfying customers today; innovation focuses on satisfying tomorrow's customers. Without a capacity to innovate continually, a company will fade away as needs change, technology advances and competitors progress.

In the 1990s the pace of innovation is accelerating. Innovation is used by the top companies as a central strategic weapon. They beat their competitors not by price, but by making competitors' offers obsolete, by providing customers with new products which offer superior value. Creating a strategy for innovation requires far-reaching changes in the organization. It requires vision, a focus on speed of development, constant testing against customers' expectations and careful planning.

Questions

1. What are the differences between the way scientists see innovation and the way marketing people tend to see it?

2. What advantages do companies which focus on innovation obtain?

3. Why do many companies fail to innovate?

4. What advice would you give to a company which wishes to accelerate its pace of innovation?

5. Some new products get adopted much more quickly than others. What accounts for such differences?

6. In developing a marketing plan for the launch of a radically new industrial product, what factors would influence the choice of target market segments?

Notes

1. *New Product Management for the 1980s*, (New York: Booz, Allen & Hamilton, 1982).

2. Michael E. Porter, *Competitive Strategy* (New York: Free Press, 1980), pp. 34–46.

3. This and the following section draw heavily from George Stalk and Thomas M. Hout, *Competing Against Time* (New York: Free Press, 1990).

4. Adapted from Stalk and Hout, *op. cit.*, pp. 169–95.

5. For example, Paul Laurence and J. Lorsch, *Organisation and Environment* (Boston, MA: Harvard Business School, 1967); Jennifer George and Gareth Jones, *Understanding and Managing Organisational Behaviour* (New York: Addison Wesley, 1996).

6. Simon Majaro, *The Creative Process* (London: Allen & Unwin, 1991).

7. Patrick Barwise, Paul R. Marsh and Robin Wensley, 'Must finance and strategy clash?', *Harvard Business Review*, September–October 1989, pp. 91–8.

8. Robert Worcester and John Downham (eds.), *Consumer Market Research Handbook*, 3rd edn (London: McGraw-Hill, 1986).

9. Peter N. Golder and Gerard J. Tellis, 'Pioneer advantage: marketing logic or marketing legend?', *Journal of Marketing Research*, May 1993, pp. 158–70.

Chapter 8

Pricing policy: delivering value

Pricing is key to the firm's profitability in both the short and long run. In the short run, pricing decisions invariably have the biggest impact on the profit and loss statement. For example, for a typical company with a contribution margin of 40 per cent and a net profit of 10 per cent, the achievement of 10 per cent higher prices would potentially double profits (Table 8.1). Analogously, if prices are cut by 10 per cent, profits could disappear altogether. By contrast, a 10 per cent volume increase in this business would generate only 40 per cent more profit, and a 10 per cent cut in overheads only 30 per cent more. Even if a 10 per cent price hike cut demand by 10 per cent, total profits would still rise by 50 per cent. Pricing therefore has the greatest impact on the immediate performance of the business. Many senior managers do not sufficiently understand this. More effective pricing is normally the single most important thing new management can do to enhance profits quickly.

In the long run, pricing is even more crucial. The fundamental objective of business strategy is to offer customers enhanced value so that prices can be raised substantially above costs. In other words, the long-run aim of business is to charge customers higher prices! At a minimum, the aim is to achieve volume or market share gains without eroding profitability. Customers select suppliers that offer superior value. Value is a combination of price and the relative functional and psychological advantages that the supplier's brand offers. Companies seek to provide superior offers through innovation, quality, speed of delivery and service and other product enhancements, so that they can be preferred suppliers, rather than having to compete on low prices and margin erosion.

Low prices rarely provide a sustainable basis for competitive advantage in today's markets. Fierce international competition from countries with low labour costs and high productivity, together with changing exchange rates, makes substantial cost advantages increasingly fleeting. In addition, outside commodity markets, many customers are not highly price sensitive – price is only one dimension of value. Finally, in those commodity-like markets where demand is highly price sensitive, competitors will inevitably match price cuts to prevent substantial market share losses, even if this means taking losses in that produce line.

Table 8.1 ■ Income statement: Alpha Products

		£ million
Turnover		200
Discounts and allowances	30	
Materials	30	
Direct labour	40	
Other variable costs	20	–
Profit contribution		80
Marketing and advertising	10	
Research and development	10	
Fixed costs	40	–
Net profit		20

Sensitivity analysis: Effect of 10% changes in price and costs on varying assumptions about volume losses

	Change in profits £m (+%)		
		Volume loss	
Change in	**0%**	**–10%**	**–15%**
Price (+ 10%)	20 (100)	10 (50)[1]	5 (25)
Total overhead (– 10%)	6 (30)	–2 (–10)[2]	–6 (–30)
R & D (– 10%)	1 (5)	–7 (–35)	–11 (–55)
Marketing and advertising (– 10%)	1 (5)	–7 (–35)	–11 (–55)
Fixed costs (– 10%)	4 (20)	–7 (–35)	–11 (–55)
Volume (+ 10%)	8 (40)	–	–

[1]For example, if prices are increased by 10% and volume falls as a result by 10%, then profits rise by £10m (or +50%)

[2]If total overhead costs are cut by 10% (£6m) and volume falls as a result by 10%, then profits fall by £2m (–10%)

Many companies are poor at pricing. One common mistake is to base prices upon mechanical cost-plus formulas. Managers fail to appreciate how seriously such methods can erode profits and detract from exploiting market opportunities. The drive to lower costs is important. But the motivation for cost reduction should be not to lower prices, but rather to permit more resources to be made available for investment in new products and product enhancements. Another common mistake is to overestimate the price elasticity of the market. In particular, sales people and marketers often blame poor sales on the company charging too high prices. Of course, it is easier for them to sell at low prices, but the real challenge is to train those at the customer interface to demonstrate value, not opt for the easy solution of selling on price.

In the following sections the major pricing issues faced by senior managers are discussed. First, how can they assess whether their current pricing strategy is appropriate? Second, how should prices be set initially when a product is about to be launched? Third, how can the company manage reseller mark-ups to prevent profit

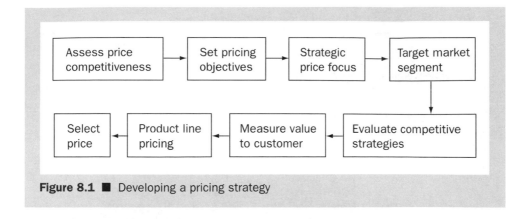

Figure 8.1 ■ Developing a pricing strategy

being eroded by strong trade buyers? Finally, how should managers change prices, particularly when they need to raise prices to preserve margins?

Assessing price competitiveness

Developing a pricing strategy starts with the assessment of price competitiveness and the formulation of pricing objectives (Figure 8.1). The first task is to determine which competitors in the market are seen by customers as offering the best value. Value is a combination of price and perceived quality. Assessing value therefore requires research into how consumers perceive the quality of alternative offers. There are several methods of varying technical sophistication for researching such perceptions. The most useful of these techniques focus around the following steps:

1. *Identify the dimensions of quality.* Find out what product and service attributes customers are looking for when they choose suppliers.

2. *Weight quality dimensions.* Determine which of the attributes are regarded as the most important by customers.

3. *Measure competitors along dimensions.* Customers are then asked to rate competitors' offers along the dimensions of quality that have been identified.

4. *Discover price/quality preferences.* What are the combinations of price and quality most preferred by customers?

For example, a manufacturer of industrial cutting equipment was concerned about its poor market share and wondered whether its prices were the problem. It undertook a market research study which identified the product and service attributes most desired by customers and evaluated how its product (X) and its key competitors were rated (Table 8.2). The resulting perceived quality ratings together with the company's prices were then displayed on a value map (Figure 8.2). This showed that there were three segments in the market: a premium segment dominated by company A; an economy

Table 8.2 ■ Assessing price and value competitiveness

Importance weight (%)	Quality dimensions	Competitors			
		A	B	C	X
35	Precision	6	5	4	6
25	Reliability	6	6	3	4
15	Durability	5	3	2	5
20	Service	5	3	5	1
5	Delivery	2	5	5	5
	Weighted score	5.5	4.6	3.7	4.3
	Actual prices (£000)	29	21	15	22
	Market share (%)	27	45	20	8

segment led by company C, where prices were half those of A; and the largest segment in the middle, dominated by company B with a 45 per cent market share. Product X's problem was clear: it was competing against B, but customers saw X's reliability and service as significantly inferior. It was positioned in the poor value area of the value chart – an unfavourable combination of quality and price. The obvious requirement for the company was to reposition X by either enhancing its quality or lowering its price, or some combination of the two, to improve its relative value.

In using these techniques, two caveats are needed. First, it is important to remember that all markets are segmented; not all customers have the same needs. Some are exceptionally price sensitive; others rate service or product reliability and presentation much higher. Therefore it is important to look at differences between customers and to shape strategy accordingly. Second, the buying criteria generally vary among members of the buyer's decision-making unit (DMU). For example, in industrial markets, purchasing executives tend to be the most price sensitive, technical staff are more quality oriented and senior executives look more at lifetime costs and whether the seller can offer a potential competitive advantage to the company. Consequently, by tailoring communications to specific members of the DMU, the manufacturer can partly shape the purchasing criteria that become most important.

Establishing initial prices

How should a company establish the price? Economic theory focuses on this question. Every first-year student of economics can prove that the profit-maximizing price is determined by estimating the quantity that would be demanded at different prices and then projecting total costs for these volumes. The optimal price is that which maximizes the difference between these estimated revenues and costs. Unfortunately, like many things economists tell us, while this formula is true in theory, it is not very helpful in practice.

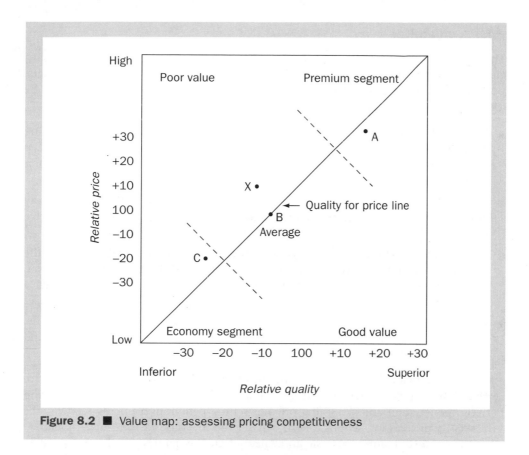

Figure 8.2 ■ Value map: assessing pricing competitiveness

There are several problems which intrude on the elegant simplicity of the economist's pricing theory. One is that demand depends upon many other factors besides the price. The customer is also influenced by the supplier's reputation for service, quality and reliability. It is also influenced by the effectiveness with which the sales people, publicity and advertising convey any differential advantages the brand or the company possesses. Sometimes higher prices increase demand. The classic story is Chevas Regal Scotch whisky, which was a dying brand until its price was raised to be dramatically higher than competitors. Its sales then took off. Since the product remained identical, it was clear that price had become a quality cue. A second problem is that pricing decisions have impacts on competitors. A price cut can fail to improve market share because competitors match it. Third, markets are not homogeneous but highly segmented, and consequently are made up of not one, but rather a series of demand functions. Finally, pricing is substantially influenced by the firm's strategy. For example, the price which maximizes profits in the short run will be very different from that which maximizes them in the long run. These varying influences on the pricing decision are described next.

Pricing objectives

The initial pricing decision will be influenced by the underlying marketing and financial objectives of the business. Since virtually all companies have multiple products, portfolio considerations will be important. Four strategic pricing objectives can be distinguished:

- *Harvest*. If the product is mature with a core of loyal users but facing increasing competition from low-price or superior-value products, it may well pay to keep prices high and allow market share to erode gradually. The cash generated can then be funnelled into new products.

- *Maintain market share*. If the product has long-run strategic value, the company may aim at holding share. It will adjust prices defensively to prevent competitive erosion.

- *Growth*. If the product is in an attractive market and has a differential advantage, the company may use price as an aggressive weapon to build share or enter the market. The Japanese zip manufacturer YKK built its global dominance on just such a pricing strategy.

- *Quality leadership*. A company may seek to be leader in a premium price niche. Companies like Rolex, Bang & Olufsen and Rolls-Royce ignore the mass market and cultivate customers who can pay substantially more for superior products.

Even if a company is aiming to expand the business, it does not mean that low price is the right approach. These strategic choices are highlighted in the distinction between penetration and skimming pricing. With a penetration pricing strategy, the firm sets its price as low as possible to expand the market and maximize its market share. Texas Instruments, YKK, Bic and Amstrad are companies which have pursued this strategy. With skimming pricing, the firm sets its prices high to achieve high unit margins, recognizing that it will attract only a small layer of price-insensitive purchasers. Du Pont, Bang & Olufsen and Gucci are examples of companies pursuing this strategy.

Table 8.3 highlights the factors influencing the choice between penetration and skimming pricing. In general, penetration pricing is more ambitious in terms of market share and industry leadership. The downside is the higher risk that competitive retaliation will destroy the margin, or that changes in demand or technology will make the product obsolete before the investments are recouped. Skimming pricing is less risky financially and is particularly appealing for really new, unfamiliar products or where markets are highly segmented. Here the downside is the opportunity cost of competitors quickly pre-empting the market potential by offering lower prices and better value to the customer.

Figure 8.3 illustrates the dilemmas in these pricing strategies.[1] Positions along the diagonal or to the right of it offer combinations of quality and price which represent value to customers. High-price strategies are viable only when associated with high quality. Even then they may be vulnerable to competitors entering the market with

Table 8.3 ■ Choosing between penetration and skimming pricing

Determinant	Penetration	Skimming
Objective	Long-run market share	Short-run profit
	Risk taking	Risk aversion
Demand	Price elastic	Price inelastic
	Few market segments	Multiple market segments
Competition	Deter new compctitors	Accept new compelitors
	Few barriers to entry	High barriers to entry
Product	Image seen as unimportant	Seeks prestige image
	Long product life cycle	Short product life cycle
Price	Pressure for prices to fall	Prices can be sustained
	Need to move fast	Fewer pressures in market
Promotion	Customers understand product	Unfamiliar product
Distribution	Existing system	Unfamiliar channels
Production	High scale economies	Few scale economies
	Experience curve effects	Few experience effects
Finance	High investment	Low investment
	Slow payback	Fast payback

similar-quality products at lower prices, so offering higher value. Toyota's Lexus entry into the executive car market, for example, threatens Mercedes Benz's premium pricing strategy. Similarly, low-price, low-quality, economy strategies are sustainable only so long as competitors cannot offer better quality at parallel prices. Any position to the left of the diagonal represents a clearly unsustainable strategy.

Strategic focus

The second determinant of the price will be the stage of evolution of the market. If the market is still at the innovatory stage, so that the firm is focusing on first-time buyers or market segments which have not yet been penetrated, demand will usually be less price sensitive. Buyers at the start of the product life cycle are drawn by the benefits of the innovation and are normally able and willing to pay higher prices. Low prices are usually a bad idea because initially the market is constrained by lack of awareness and risk aversion. Investment in selling, advertising or promotion is a better way than lower prices to expand the market.

As the market develops, however, more price-sensitive customers are brought in. This phenomenon, together with declining unit costs and new competitors, usually requires the firm to lower its average price to maintain momentum. Because different segments of the market generally retain different price sensitivities, it will normally pay a firm to price discriminate. Rather than having a single product and reducing its price steadily, it will often be better to introduce new brands or brand extensions. Premium brands will be targeted towards the more sophisticated, less price-sensitive

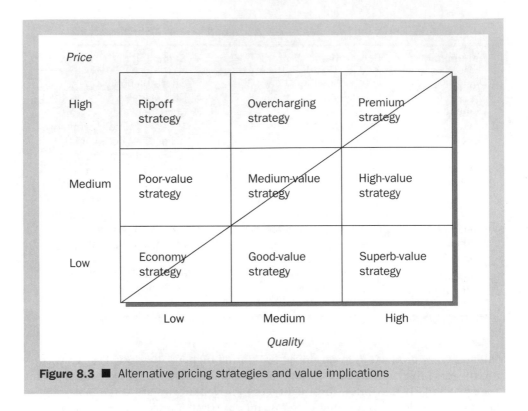

Price

	Low	Medium	High
High	Rip-off strategy	Overcharging strategy	Premium strategy
Medium	Poor-value strategy	Medium-value strategy	High-value strategy
Low	Economy strategy	Good-value strategy	Superb-value strategy

Quality

Figure 8.3 ■ Alternative pricing strategies and value implications

segments, and discount brands to the new more price-conscious buyers. This way the firm can curtail the erosion of its gross profit margin as the market evolves.

Target market segments

Most markets today are made up of a large and increasing number of market segments. These segments are dynamic, often ill-defined and continually evolving. They are triggered by the strategies of competing firms as well as by exogenous changes in tastes, technology and economic forces. In any market, these segments differ enormously in the prices that are obtained. In cars, computers, watches, clothes, hotels, airline tickets and numerous other fields, prices between the 'economy' and 'premium' segments differ by a factor of at least 10. The spread in the profit margins on these products is even greater.

Clearly, therefore, how a brand is positioned in the market – the choice of which target market segment it chooses to appeal to – is crucial for its pricing and profit performance. This choice of segment will depend upon an evaluation of the size, growth, profitability and competitiveness of the alternatives, as well as an analysis of the brand's ability to compete in them.

Normally, however, an aggressive competitor will not limit itself to one segment, but seek to operate in several or all of them. This strategy provides, first, economies of scope – operating and development costs which can be shared across customer groups. Second, it provides a barrier against competitors entering undefended segments. Third, it allows the company to take advantage of the differing price and quality requirements across the segments. Finally, multibranding will allow the company to obtain more intense distribution by getting more floorspace or additional distribution channels. So, for example, in the 1990s Canon was offering a range of fax machines from basic models at £250 for small businesses or private usage, up to sophisticated combination models for £2,500. A British Airways return ticket to New York ranges from £179 standby to £3,200 on Concorde. Tyre companies like Michelin and Goodyear produce a range of tyres: expensive innovative ones for drivers of BMWs and Porsches, plus second- and third-tier brands under different names aimed at mid-price and budget customers. Such strategies enable them to cover the whole market without sacrificing the profit obtainable on upper-niche brands.

Equally importantly, a firm can create new market segments through imaginative pricing and innovatory marketing. For example, Ciba-Geigy gained both a substantial share and high brand loyalty in the highly competitive market for hypertension drugs by offering patients a 'lifetime guarantee' on the prices they paid. Shell created a new premium segment in the car lubricant market with its Gemini brand. Swatch created a new fashion segment in the watch market with the combination of low prices and high design content.

Competitor targets

Unfortunately, the firm does not set prices in isolation. Even if customers are price sensitive, it does not make sense to enter the market with a low price if this triggers competitors into price-matching strategies. In setting prices, the firm has to estimate the likely reaction of current competitors.

Several factors affect the likelihood of competitor response. If competitors see the firm as a potentially major player in the industry, they cannot afford to ignore its moves. If the market is not growing, a low-price entrant will be seen as highly aggressive and threatening. Retaliation is more likely when the customers see few differences between competitors. Here the industry approaches a commodity-like market in which significant price differences between suppliers cannot be sustained. Finally, if the industry is characterized by high fixed costs, competitors will be loath to lose volume, and prices may drop to very low levels.

Competitive retaliation is less likely if the firm signals that its market share objectives are modest. In this case, current competitors may see it as less costly to live with the newcomer than to slash their own margins. If the industry is growing and there are substantial differences in the positioning strategies of competitors, retaliation is again less likely.

Measuring value to the customer

A differential advantage is obtained when a firm offers customers value they cannot get elsewhere. By creating such a differential advantage, the firm can obtain higher prices and earn higher profit margins. This advantage can be economic or psychological, or both. The first is particularly important in business markets where buyers are motivated by the aim of increasing the profitability of their own enterprises.

Economic value to the customer (EVC) is a central concept in pricing industrial products. By developing an offer with high EVC, a company can charge significantly higher prices and still offer its customers superior value. The higher-priced product may offer value because it generates more output than its competitor or because the operating costs associated with it (e.g. maintenance, labour, depreciation) are lower over its economic life.

The concept of EVC is illustrated in Figure 8.4.[2] Suppose the market leader is selling a machine tool (product X) at a price of £30,000. In purchasing this product, the customer will also have to cover start-up costs of £20,000 (installation, initial training, etc.) and post-purchase costs over the life of the machine with a present value of £50,000 (labour, maintenance, power and other operating costs). Thus the total life cycle cost of the machine is £100,000. In other words, the price is under one-third of the total cost of employing the equipment.

If a competitor wants to dislodge the market leader, it must offer superior EVC. One way is simply to price cut. But this is not likely to be a decisive strategy here because, even if the machine price is cut by 20 per cent, the saving to the customer of £6,000 is only 6 per cent of the total cost. A better way may be to focus on building a more effective machine which cuts start-up and operating costs. For example, a new product, Y, is shown as reducing these costs by £30,000. Here the EVC that product Y offers the customer is £60,000 (£100,000 less £40,000). That is, the customer should be willing to pay up to £60,000 for Y. At this price both machines would have the same total cost. Below the £60,000 price, it would be rational for the buyer to switch to Y, providing, of course, all other things were equal between the two suppliers. To give the customer the incentive to switch from product X, the price of Y might be set at, say, £45,000. Here the manufacturer would be selling at 50 per cent price premium and the customer would have a saving of £15,000 in total life cycle costs.

Besides lowering a customer's costs, a new product may also enhance its revenues. For example, the new machine might turn out more finished products for the customer, or products with superior quality. Product Z in Figure 8.4 illustrates this. This product offers the customer a cost saving of £10,000 over the market leader and £30,000 extra contribution margin arising from enhanced output. Here the EVC and the maximum price the customer should be willing to pay are £70,000 – more than double the price of the market leader.

Using this concept, the firm will target those market segments where the EVC is highest. In such segments the product is most attractive and so it is here that the firm can obtain the highest prices. In the above example, it may pay the firm to launch two new brands: a higher-priced brand Z to the quality-oriented customers and a lower-priced Y brand to the cost-oriented segment of the market. EVC is one of the most crucial concepts in marketing and an essential tool in business-to-business pricing decisions. But effective employment of it requires highly sophisticated and well-trained sales people who are adept at segmenting customers, analyzing their value chains and demonstrating economic value to them.

The concept of EVC is important because it can be shown that often the initial purchase price is only a small proportion of the total user cost. For example, the initial purchase price of a corporate personal computer accounts for only 10 per cent of the average lifetime cost. The rest is troubleshooting, administration, software and training. If the company pays £2,000 for the PC, the total cost amounts to £20,000. EVC goes to the heart of marketing – customers do not want products; they want to meet their needs. In business the crucial needs are to cut costs, increase profits and raise sales. When a salesperson tries to sell a product, the customer focuses on the cost of acquiring it and quickly moves to comparing it with the cost of competitors' products. This comparison invariably pushes down the price. With EVC, however, the supplier focuses on what it can do to improve the customer's performance. Here the supplier focuses on the costs that the customer can save, rather than the costs it has to incur.

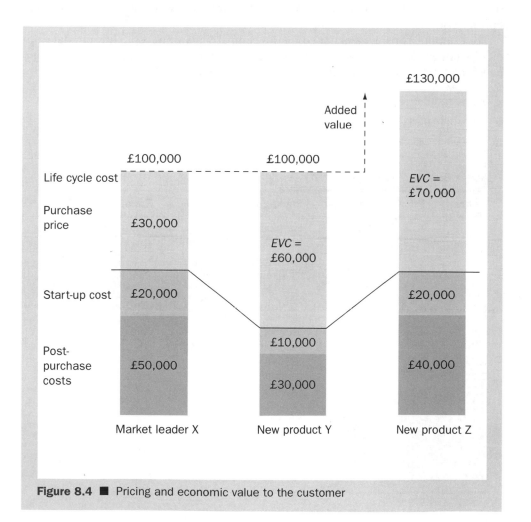

Figure 8.4 ■ Pricing and economic value to the customer

Perceived value

The concept of EVC is most useful when a new brand has demonstrable economic advantage for the buyer. At other times the advantages of the brand are perceived or psychological rather than economic. This is generally the situation in consumer markets. There are a number of research methods to determine the perceived value of a brand. One of the most popular in recent years has been conjoint or trade-off analysis. This has been applied successfully across a wide range of consumer and industrial products and services.[3]

Trade-off analysis recognizes that in developing a new product the manager has to decide among a range of potential features. These features add costs, but they may also substantially enhance the perceived value of the product to the buyer. Trade-off analysis helps the manager choose the combination of product features and price which will optimize profits.

For example, consider a major cosmetics company planning a pricing and development strategy for a new men's aftershave. In developing a positioning strategy for the new brand, the product manager has to decide between the following:

- Three retail price levels (£13, £16, £19 per 50 ml bottle).
- Two dispensers (regular, spray).
- Two pack designs (normal, premium).

Table 8.4 ■ Customer preference rankings of eighteen product concepts

Concept	Price	Dispenser	Package	Perfume	Brand name	Rank
1	£16	Regular	Premium	Menthol	Solo	6
2	£19	Spray	Normal	Menthol	Zolex	5
3	£16	Regular	Normal	Musk	GTI	10
4	£19	Regular	Normal	Musk	Solo	16
5	£13	Spray	Normal	Musk	Zolex	1*
6	£13	Regular	Normal	Floral	GTI	13
7	£16	Spray	Normal	Floral	Solo	11
8	£19	Regular	Premium	Floral	Zolex	17
9	£16	Spray	Premium	Menthol	GTI	2
10	£19	Regular	Normal	Menthol	Solo	14
11	£13	Regular	Normal	Menthol	Zolex	3
12	£19	Spray	Normal	Musk	GTI	12
13	£13	Regular	Premium	Musk	Solo	7
14	£16	Regular	Normal	Musk	Zolex	9
15	£19	Regular	Premium	Floral	GTI	18
16	£13	Spray	Normal	Floral	Solo	8
17	£16	Regular	Normal	Floral	Zolex	15
18	£13	Regular	Normal	Menthol	GTI	4

*Highest preference ranking

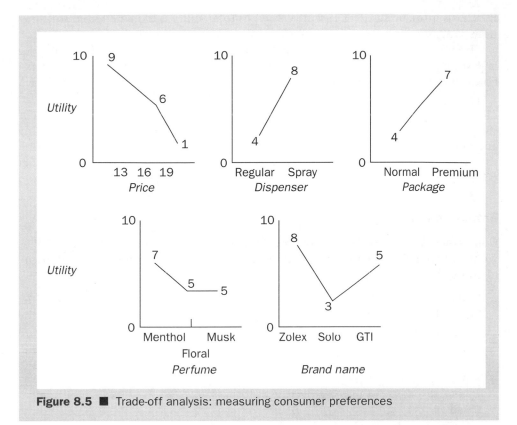

Figure 8.5 ■ Trade-off analysis: measuring consumer preferences

- Three perfumes (menthol, floral, musk).
- Three brand names (GT1, Solo, Zolex).

With these combinations there are 108 (3 × 2 × 2 × 3 × 3) possible product concepts – far too many for any consumer choice test. However, it can be shown that through a specific sampling procedure the crucial information can be obtained from a set of only 18 of these concepts (Table 8.4). Customers are asked to rank these 18 concepts, and from these preferences the values (or utilities) of the various features are derived from a computer analysis. These are shown in Figure 8.5. From these utility functions it can be seen that customers prefer the £13 price, the spray dispenser, the premium pack design, menthol and the Zolex brand name. Of course, this most preferred option is not necessarily the most profitable one for the company – low price and premium features, for example, imply very low profit margins.

The next step is to estimate the long-term potential market shares that alternative versions of the new product could achieve. For example, suppose the market is currently dominated by three brands, A, B and C, with the features shown in Table 8.5.

If Zolex is introduced with a low price, then its total utility is estimated from the functions as 39, significantly higher than the existing brands in the market.

The final stage is to estimate the profitability of the new brand at different price levels. Suppose that the size of the market is 10 million units, the variable cost is £5 per bottle and the distribution channels absorb 100 per cent mark-up. As Table 8.6 shows, while the low price maximizes utility and expected market share, because of the low margin it is the least profitable alternative. Even though the premium pricing strategy is estimated to cost substantially more in marketing overhead (additional advertising and brand support), the higher margin makes it the best choice. At a retail price of £19, the potential market share is only 5 points lower and revenue, contribution and net profit are substantially higher than under the two alternative pricing policies.

Product mix pricing

Companies normally sell a range of products and develop a product line pricing policy within which individual product prices are determined. Several common situations are identified:

■ *Product line pricing.* A marketing-oriented company will normally develop a product line rather than a single brand. By developing a graduated line of brands, the company can market and pursue a differential pricing strategy. For example, Castrol

Table 8.5 ■ Trade-off analysis: utilities of competitive brands

Brand	A	B	C	D
Price (£)	19 (1)	19 (1)	13 (9)	13 (9)
Dispenser	Spray (8)	Regular (4)	Regular (4)	Spray (8)
Package	Premium (7)	Normal (4)	Normal (4)	Premium (7)
Perfume	Menthol (7)	Floral (5)	Musk (5)	Menthol (7)
Name	A (5)	B (5)	C (5)	Zolex (8)
Total utility	**28**	**19**	**27**	**39**

Table 8.6 ■ Predicted profit performance of Zolex at different prices

Price	Utility	Market share (%)	Revenue (£m) Retail	Net	Costs (£m) Variable	Fixed	Profit (£m)
£13	39	35 (39/113)	45.5	22.8	17.5	2	3.3
£16	36	33 (36/110)	52.8	26.4	16.5	3	6.9
£19	31	30 (31/105)	57	28.5	15.0	5	8.5

Note: Assumptions: market size 10 million units; 100% trade mark-up; variable cost £5/unit

sells a range of car lubricants from a low-price GTX, to more expensive GTX2 and GTX3, and up to GTX7 in Japan. By such price positioning the company can exploit different price elasticities among consumers and distributors, and encourage customers to trade up to higher-margin brands. In these situations, price points are selected to signal clear quality differences between the brands in the line.

■ *Follow-on products*. Some products require subsequent purchases. For example, purchasers of a specialized computer or telephone switch will need subsequently to buy software products. Buyers of a camera will need to buy film. Suppliers of the initial product may price low to stimulate demand, with the objective of making higher margins on subsequent products. To be effective, however, the manufacturer needs to be sufficiently dominant or specialized, to prevent competitors taking advantage of this strategy by attacking the ancillary market with lower-priced substitutes.

■ *Blocking products*. Sometimes it will pay a company to sell at uneconomic prices to block competitive entry. It may cross-subsidize sales in one segment or geographical area to dissuade competitors from expanding into this market.

■ *Bundled and option pricing*. To reduce the perceived price, a product may be advertised at a low, stripped-down price. At the point of purchase, the salesperson will then seek to encourage the buyer to add high-margin features. A typical buyer of a £40,000 Mercedes will be persuaded to spend another £10,000 on options and features which will add £3,000 to the company's margin. In contrast, Japanese competitors normally bundle a comprehensive range of features into the sticker price to offer customers a superior value proposition.

■ *Parallel imports*. Increasingly, pricing is an international problem. With differences in living standards and distribution systems, countries normally differ in price responsiveness. It would therefore be more profitable to set different prices in each country. Unfortunately, legal restrictions and parallel imports increasingly make such strategies difficult. Companies may then have to price too high in some markets to protect their margin in other, less price-sensitive ones.

Initiating price changes

Normally the pressure on firms is to reduce prices. The experience curve, increasing competition and rising customer price sensitivity as markets evolve all stimulate falling real price levels. On the other hand, inflation, the stock market's expectation of growing profits and the difficulty of finding enough new products to replace established brands all encourage entrepreneurial managers to consider ways of increasing margins. Of course, cost reduction is the most obvious way to improve margins, but price increases can have a major impact.

In periods of high inflation, obtaining price increases is easier. With an inflation rate of 20 per cent a year, buyers do not see a 23 per cent price increase as remarkable, but at low rates of inflation real price increases are much harder to achieve. Strategies to

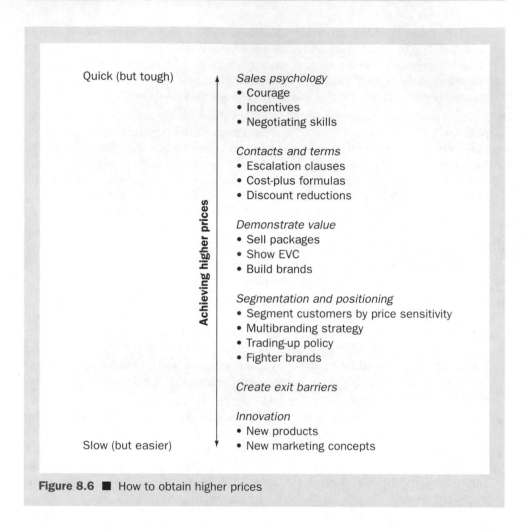

Quick (but tough)

Sales psychology
- Courage
- Incentives
- Negotiating skills

Contacts and terms
- Escalation clauses
- Cost-plus formulas
- Discount reductions

Demonstrate value
- Sell packages
- Show EVC
- Build brands

Segmentation and positioning
- Segment customers by price sensitivity
- Multibranding strategy
- Trading-up policy
- Fighter brands

Create exit barriers

Innovation
- New products
- New marketing concepts

Slow (but easier)

Achieving higher prices

Figure 8.6 ■ How to obtain higher prices

obtain higher prices can be seen as a spectrum (Figure 8.6). On the one hand, there are some techniques which management can try immediately, but their success is uncertain. On the other hand, there are straightforward ways to obtain better prices, but they often cannot be implemented for several years. The best example of the latter is the introduction of a superior product – customers normally expect to pay more for products with superior benefits or higher EVC.

Influencing the psychology of the sales team

These tactics relate to sales training and motivation. Sales people are often order focused rather than profit focused. They are often so worried about losing the order that they cave in too easily to price pressure. Management need to instil the virtue of *courage* in the salesforce – a willingness to take more risks in pushing for justified price increases. Next *salesforce incentives* should be reviewed to encourage a focus on prices. Some sales teams are still bonused on volume, which invariably undermines efforts to improve gross margins. Tying rewards to gross margins obtained or even realized prices can often have a significant impact on results. Third, professional *negotiating skills* are essential in today's markets. Management should not permit individuals to engage in price discussions with buyers without a thorough training in negotiation.

Contracts and terms

With long-term contracts or agreements where there is a significant gestation period between order and delivery, skilled managers can often negotiate *escalation clauses*. Such clauses allow the supplier to protect its margins by having prices rise automatically with inflation. With the increasing shift to favouring long-run relationships between buyers and sellers, such clauses can have an enormous impact on profitability and avoid the necessity of destabilizing annual price negotiations. *Cost-plus formulas* are another contractual approach to margin protection. Suppliers can agree to meet new customer needs on the basis of protected margins. Enhanced products can then be introduced without downside risk. Finally, *reductions in discounts* act in the same way as price increases. Most companies erode their high prices with cash discounts for early payment, quantity discounts, trade discounts, seasonal discounts and other allowances for promotion or trade-in.

Demonstrating values rather than products

Where sales people focus on selling their product or its features, they fail to take advantage of many opportunities to differentiate their company's offer. When differentiation is weak, price competition becomes paramount. To avoid this, one essential approach is to sell *packages not products*. Packages include the services, technical support, terms and guarantees offered alongside the product. A further step is to *show economic value to the customer* (EVC), rather than price. This means showing the life cycle savings resulting from accepting the firm's offer. Here the supplier demonstrates economic benefits rather than purchase costs. A more general move is to *build brands* and emphasize the confidence and reduced risk involved in purchasing a well-known brand. When a bluechip company signs up with McKinsey or a youth buys a pair of Levi 501s, they willingly pay the price premium because they perceive the brand as unique, conveying an image, reputation and confidence not possessed by competitors.

Segmentation and positioning

Basic to any marketing strategy, and particularly fundamental to pricing, is the recognition that customers differ enormously in price sensitivity. For some customers, price is the dominant criterion, but for others quality, service and image are much more significant. An average 5 per cent price increase is almost invariably best achieved by recognizing that some customers will not accept any increase at all, while others will accept a 10 or even 20 per cent increase. *Segmenting customers by price sensitivity* is therefore a crucial step. It requires building up an understanding of what factors most influence the buying decisions of individual customers. What is the relative importance of price, service dimensions and the supplier's commitment to the customer? Such an analysis should lead to different types of package and levels of price being offered to each segment.

A further step to provide even greater scope for price and offer discrimination is the development of a *multibranding strategy*. Here differentially priced brands are targeted to different segments of the market. So Distillers sells Johnnie Walker Red Label Scotch whisky at £9, Black Label at £16 and Blue at £90. Such a strategy often permits a *trading-up* policy to be employed, where customers who start with entry-level brands (e.g. American Express green card) can be encouraged to move up to the more expensive versions (e.g. the Amex gold card). It also permits *fighter brands* to be employed against aggressive competitors in low-price market segments. A fighter brand allows a company to defend its market share without having to cut prices across the entire market.

Exit barriers

Skilful companies create exit barriers which make it difficult for the customer to switch to lower-price competition. Such barriers include outstanding levels of service, loyalty schemes, electronic data interchange (EDI) links between supplier and customer, provision of specialized equipment, and research and development partnerships. Exit barriers act to fuse the customer to the buyer, making it unattractive to throw away the investment embodied in the relationship.

Innovation

In the long run, innovations which offer customers superior value are the only way to achieve better prices. All the other routes are one-off or limited opportunities which eventually erode market share. New product development is the most obvious source of innovation. But marketing innovations in the form of new varieties (e.g. Diet Coke), new presentational formats (e.g. patch-based delivery systems for pharmaceutical products in place of tablets) and new services (e.g. telephone banking) are equally important. Without bringing new value to the market, a company's products and prices are invariably commoditized by competitors and new formats.

Controlling reseller mark-ups

In discussing prices, it is important to be clear about what price is being considered. There is a big difference between the price the consumer pays and the price the manufacturer receives. A supplier designs an offer and conceives a price that will make it

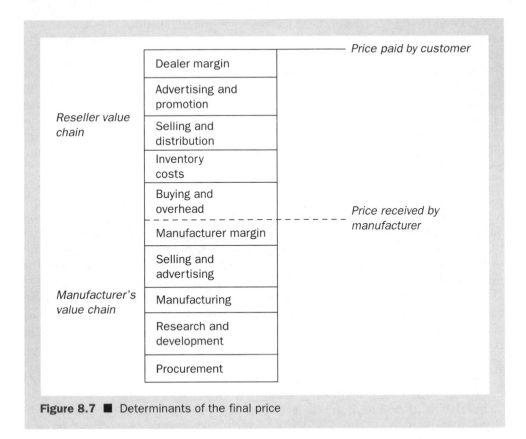

Figure 8.7 ■ Determinants of the final price

attractive to end customers. Unfortunately, in practice it does not normally set this price. Usually, suppliers sell through resellers – distributors, wholesalers, retailers or some combination of these – and it is these organizations which establish the final price to consumers. These resellers can easily acquire a mark-up of 100 per cent of the supplier's price. This mark-up covers the value-added activities met by the distributor – carrying stock, selling, distribution, customer support, its corresponding overhead costs and profit (Figure 8.7).

A business is likely to be concerned to influence the mark-up taken by its resellers. After all, a business has four ways it can increase its total profit:

■ Increasing its sales volume.

■ Cutting its costs.

■ Raising the price that its products or services can command in the market.

■ Raising its price to its resellers without them in turn raising the price to customers.

This last option – reducing the trade mark-up, is the most neglected strategy, but it can be the most powerful method of improving profits. For example, if the reseller's mark-ups amount to 100 per cent of the ex-factory price and the manufacturer is operating on a 10 per cent net profit margin, a cut of one-tenth in the reseller mark-up would double the manufacturer's profits.

There are three ways in which the manufacturer can reduce these reseller mark-ups. The first option is coercive power, where the manufacturer threatens unilaterally to change or terminate the relationship if the distributor does not accept higher prices and lower mark-ups. If the distributor is highly dependent upon the manufacturer, this may work in the short term. But since this strategy cuts the reseller's profits, it invariably produces resentment and curtails its support for the business. In the long run, coercive power is rarely effective.

A better alternative is to seek a reduction in mark-up without a corresponding reduction in the reseller's profitability. One way is to create strong customer pull. Strong brands invariably offer dealers smaller margins than weak ones. While end customers may pay the same prices for a brand leader and a brand follower, the latter will invariably have had to offer the trade substantially higher discounts to obtain distribution and compensate for the lower stock turn. Strong products compensate the dealers for lower mark-ups by offering higher turnover.

Another alternative is to explore the dealer's value chain (Figure 8.7). The margin that the dealer takes is to cover its costs and make its profit. It may pay the manufacturer to take over some of these tasks and negotiate a lower margin with the reseller. In this case, both can be better off. The manufacturer can undertake some distribution and wholesaling tasks for distributors and retailers; it can support their selling and promotional activities; or it can provide information and knowledge about its markets to enhance their competitive performance.

In retailing, the new concept of *category management* reflects this type of approach. Some major retailers are choosing partners to manage an entire category of merchandise in the store. For example, Safeway might choose Coca-Cola to manage its entire soft drinks category. The supplier guarantees the retailer specific profit and sales volume results, and in return takes over the management of the category, including the purchase of competitor products, layout and stock control. Similar trends are apparent in other areas. In business-to-business markets, car companies such as Ford and GM are selecting *first-tier suppliers* which take over entire areas. For example, Delco might be given responsibility for sourcing and managing all Ford's vehicle electronics, while Shell might be given all the lubricants areas (see Box 8.1). In health care, *disease management* is a similar concept. Here pharmaceutical companies such as Glaxo and Merck, instead of selling just drugs, offer to take over responsibility for managing and treating all aspects of a particular disease category (e.g. cancer or asthma). The health care service obtains the benefit of guaranteed cost, while the pharmaceutical company moves away from an adversarial relationship focusing on price.

One increasingly powerful method of offering economic value to the distributor is through a time-based advantage.[4] Retailers, for example, can substantially increase their return on investment by carrying less inventory. Particularly for fashion-based retailers, large stocks involve not only high inventory carrying costs, but also high risks of the stock being obsoleted by changes in demand and forecasting errors. If a manu-

Table 8.7 ■ Retailer's economics: regular versus rapid response

Manufacturer's response		Regular	Rapid
Price paid by retailer (£)	25	25	30
Price paid by customer (£)	50	50	50
Gross margin (£)	25	25	20
Inventory turn	3×	12×	12×
Gross margin return on investment (%)	300	1,200	800

BOX 8.1

Suppliers in the factory of the future

In the past a vehicle assembly plant has relied upon purchasing inputs from thousands of suppliers. All this is now changing, with Volkswagen's new factory in Brazil being the pioneer. Here vehicle assembly is divided into just seven modules. Each module is the responsibility of one first-tier supplier. For example, Bridgestone is responsible for all wheels and tyres; Cummins for engine and transmissions; Eisenmann for all painting. Of the 1,400 workers in the factory, only 200 are VW employees; the rest are employees of suppliers who are responsible for assembling their modules, installing their own machine tools and fixtures, and controlling their own JIT inventories.

The seven first-tier suppliers are responsible for negotiating terms with the second- and third-tier suppliers which provide the thousands of individual parts making up the modules.

First-tier suppliers no longer negotiate on individual product prices, but share in the risks and rewards of the new venture as partners with VW.

Source: Business Week, 7 October 1996

facturer can increase its flexibility by focusing its factories around small lot sizes, shorter lead times and fast order processing, it will find retailers willing to pay higher prices.

The retailer's economics are illustrated in Table 8.7. A retailer pays £25 for an item and resells it for £50. The retailer's inventories typically turn three times a year, giving the gross margin return on investment of 300 per cent. However, if the retailer can receive orders from the supplier a day or two after placing the order, the GMROI increases dramatically. If the manufacturer retained the original price, the GMROI would increase fourfold. In practice, retailers would normally be willing to pay more for a fast response supplier which is providing both fresher merchandise and higher asset utilization. The final column of Table 8.7 shows that the retailer could pay 20 per cent more to the manufacturer and still increase its GMROI from 300 to 800 per cent. For a typical retailer this might mean doubling its overall return on capital employed.

Summary

Pricing is the only element of the market mix which directly generates revenue; all the others add costs. Pricing decisions almost invariably have the biggest impact on both short- and long-run profits. In the short run, inertia among buyers invariably means that price increases will substantially boost profits. But such a strategy is extremely dangerous in the long run. Over the longer term, higher prices depend upon offering superior perceived quality and value to both consumers and resellers.

Questions

1. A company has variable costs of 50 per cent and a 5 per cent net profit margin. What is the effect of a 5 per cent price increase, first under an assumption that no volume is lost, and second under an assumption that 10 per cent volume is lost?

   What effect will a 5 per cent price cut have, first if volume is unchanged, and second if volume increases by 10 per cent?

2. Poorly trained sales people often allow buyers to squeeze them down too easily on price. Why is this?

3. What factors should be taken into account in deciding between a penetration and skimming pricing strategy?

4. An industrial goods company has seen prices being gradually eroded by competition for several years. Suggest some approaches it could consider to avoid having to cut prices further.

5. Under what circumstances is EVC likely to be a useful pricing technique?

6. Show how value chain analysis may be used in developing a pricing strategy.

Notes

1. Derived from Philip Kotler, *Marketing Management: Analysis, planning, implementation and control*, 9th edn (Englewood Cliffs, NJ: Prentice Hall, 1997), p. 496.

2. Based on John L. Forbis and Nitin T. Mehta, 'Economic value to the customer', McKinsey Staff Paper (Chicago, IL: McKinsey & Co., Inc., February 1979), p. 3.

3. Philippe Cattin and Dick R. Wittink, 'Commercial use of conjoint analysis: an update', *Journal of Marketing*, July 1989, pp. 91–6.

4. George Stalk and Thomas M. Hout, *Competing Against Time: How time based competition is reshaping global markets* (New York: Macmillan, 1990).

Chapter 9

Communications strategy

This chapter looks at what managers need to know to guide the development of a successful communications strategy. Since much of the work is highly specialized or technical, most companies use outside agencies to help implement their advertising, promotion and public relations policies. But managers cannot abdicate their responsibilities for communications. The decisions are too important and the costs (typically 15 per cent or more of turnover) are too significant for top management not to get involved. Management must accept responsibility for setting the communications objectives, determining the budget, allocating expenditures among alternative communications vehicles, agreeing strategy with their agencies, and evaluating the results of the campaign. To undertake these tasks, managers need to understand how communications work and what the alternatives are.

Introduction

It is not enough to have good products and services. To generate sales and profits, their benefits have to be communicated to customers. Marketing communications is the process of transmitting messages with the objective of making the organization's products or services attractive to target audiences. The two most important audiences for marketing communications are customers and the trade, but the audiences communicated to can also be employees, shareholders, government bodies and community groups which the organization may wish to influence favourably towards its activities.

There are several reasons why managers want to communicate to these markets or audiences:

- *Inform.* Management may need to make the audience aware that their product or service exists, and to explain exactly what it does. Such tasks are obviously important for new products and services.

- *Persuade.* A further stage is creating favourable attitudes to the company or its brands. Management will seek to persuade customers and the trade that their brand has benefits which are superior to those of competitors.

- *Image creation.* In some markets, the image created by the firm's communications will be the sole or main differentiator among brands. The lager market is one example of the importance of image creation. All mainstream lagers are similar products, and the low temperature at which they are served today masks any differences that may exist. In blind product tests, drinkers cannot discriminate between them. Instead they talk about their preferred brands – Carlsberg, Heineken or Carling Black Label – in terms of the slogans, symbols and actors used in the advertising. The communications – the images, confidence and attitudes created – become the brand. In such markets, where the products are so simple and similar, communications-created images provide consumers with the only means to differentiate.[1] Effective communications becomes the key to market share.

- *Reinforcement.* Much communication is aimed not at winning new customers, but at reassuring existing ones that they have made the correct choice. For most established businesses, retaining existing customers is more important to future sales than winning new ones. Effective communications reinforces current customers by reminding them that their brand is still reliable, relevant and good value. Without them, customers would be seduced by other brands offering new benefits and values.

Marketing communications normally covers personal selling, media advertising, direct response marketing, sales promotion and public relations. The relative importance of these items varies from country to country depending upon media availability and local regulations. The pattern for the UK is shown in Figure 9.1. Personal selling costs are the largest element, followed by sales promotion and media advertising. The most rapidly growing medium is direct response, with the Internet and on-line marketing likely to be particularly important in the future.

Two other forms of communication need to be noted in addition to these specific communication tools. First, the product's appearance, its price and how it is displayed all communicate to customers. Thus, the whole marketing mix, not just the communications mix, needs to be co-ordinated. Second, communications do not have to be paid-for promotional activities. Word of mouth is a very powerful communications vehicle. Marks & Spencer created Europe's most successful retail business without advertising, relying largely on customer experience and word of mouth. If you have a brilliant product or service, people will learn about it anyhow, and they will not need persuading to buy it.

However, there are two reasons why personal experience and word of mouth need to be supplemented by a professional communications programme. First, personal experience and word of mouth are too *slow* for building a market. Without a professional communications programme, it may take generations before the product becomes well known. By then competitors will almost certainly have copied it, or its features will have become obsolete. Second, many companies have products or services which are *non-unique.* Effective communications can be a means of creating this difference. Successful communications can add value for customers, the trade and other stakeholder groups.

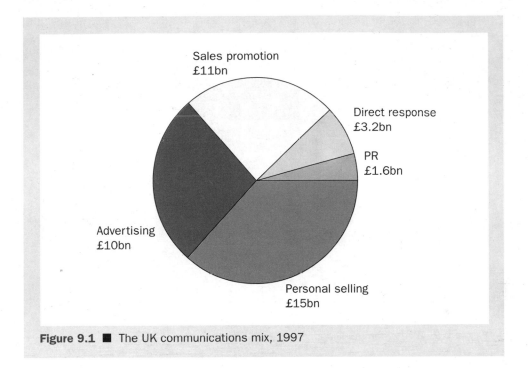

Figure 9.1 ■ The UK communications mix, 1997

In the next section, the ways in which organizations send and people receive messages are shown, along with their implications for marketing. The chapter then explores how plans are developed for advertising, direct response, sales promotion and public relations. The next chapter discusses the complementary activities of personal selling.

 Communications and buyer behaviour

The communications process

Communication is defined as the transmission and receipt of a message. For communication to take place, two parties have to be involved: the sender and the audience. If the audience does not pick up the message sent out, no communication takes place. The effort and expense have been wasted. Unfortunately, wasted communication is a major problem in marketing. The nature of the communications process and the problems that occur are illustrated in Figure 9.2.

The communications process starts with a *sender* that wants to communicate a message to an *audience*. The sender could be a salesperson calling on a potential customer or a firm sending a message to millions of consumers through an advertisement. The sender has to put the *intended message* into words, pictures or symbols that can be transmitted. This is technically called *encoding*. The encoded message is then

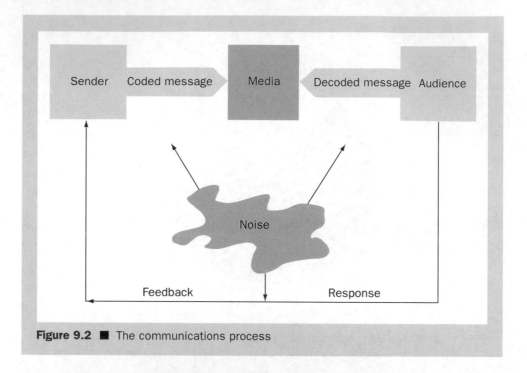

Figure 9.2 ■ The communications process

transmitted through a medium such as a television advertisement or a letter mailed to a client. If the audience receives the message, it is then *interpreted* (or *decoded*). The audience may then *respond* in some way. Finally, there is *feedback*, which is the information that the sender obtains about the audience's response.

The construction and transmission of the message form the communications plan. Whether the message is received and how it is interpreted by a member of the audience form the perceptual process. In framing the communications plan, two major problems have to be anticipated in the perceptual process: obtaining attention and achieving a correct interpretation of the message.

Attention

For an advertisement or other communications message to be effective, it must achieve first exposure and then attention. Selecting the right media is crucial because of the exposure problem. Many messages are simply not seen by large sections of the target audience. People see only a fraction of the newspapers and magazines published, they miss all or large parts of most television programmes, and never drive past some billboards. Then, even if the person is exposed to an advertisement or message, no attention may be paid to it as it is viewed as boring or irrelevant. An average person is estimated to see over 500 advertisements a day, but pays attention to only around 10 per cent of them.[2]

What determines whether a message receives this *selective attention*? Research shows that it depends first upon the characteristics of the audience and second upon the impact of the message. The main factors are as follows:

■ *Messages of practical value.* If customers are in the market for the product, they are more likely to pay attention to the information conveyed in the message.

■ *Messages that are consistent.* People look for information that justifies recent buying decisions. New car buyers, for example, are the most avid readers of advertisements for the car they have bought. Psychologists call this phenomenon cognitive dissonance reduction.

■ *Messages that interest.* If the communicator knows what interests the target audience, it can capture attention by reflecting these interests in the message.

■ *Messages that are new.* People pay more attention to messages which announce new news about the brand or the company.

■ *Messages with impact.* Besides gearing the message to the interests of the target audience, attention can be increased by spending more to convey the message and enhancing the creativity with which it is expressed. For example, impact is increased with the size of the message, the use of colour and movement, the creativity with which it is expressed, and the purchase of prime positions in newspapers and TV programmes.

Interpretation

Even if the message gets through the attention filter, it may be misinterpreted by the receiver. People have their own set attitudes which lead to expectations about what a message should say about an object. They see what fits into their belief system, ignore things which are discordant, and add things which are consistent to the beliefs. Many well-known and trusted brands use advertising with messages that are purposely incomplete. They leave the customer to 'fill in' the advertising message, believing that this will create more interest and involvement.

How people interpret a message is influenced by three factors:

■ *Needs.* The greater the need, the more value is placed on a product which may satisfy it. A message about a food product is likely to be more carefully interpreted if seen immediately before dinner than just after.

■ *Values.* Words and expressions which are familiar are more likely to be interpreted correctly than those which are unfamiliar.

■ *Group pressure.* People tend to interpret messages in the same ways as other members of their group. People generally seek to conform to their peer groups.

The communications tasks, then, are to choose media which achieve high exposure of the target market segment and to develop messages that are noticed, remembered and interpreted in an unambiguous fashion.

The response process

The objective of the communicator is to get a response from the audience. In marketing, the ultimate response the firm normally wants is to get customers to try and then repurchase the brand. However, measuring the effectiveness of communications in terms of sales results is usually fraught with difficulty. There are two main problems. The first is that sales depend upon many other factors besides the communications efforts of the firm. It depends upon external factors such as the buoyancy of the market and the activities of competitors. It also depends upon other components of the marketing mix, such as the quality of the product, the efforts of the people selling it, its price and the firm's ability to obtain distribution. Second, communications activities usually have lagged effects. Successful communications affects not only immediate purchase decisions, but decisions far into the future. This is because some customers will remain loyal and repeat buy. In addition, satisfied customers will tell others. Consequently, immediate sales effects will generally substantially underestimate the effects of a successful communications campaign.

As a result, communications effects have tended to be judged on intermediate variables. These are variables such as brand awareness or attitudes to the company, which are more directly associated with the communications message and which ultimately should lead to sales increases. In rationalizing the use of these intermediate variables, several researchers have postulated what are usually termed *hierarchy of effects* models.[3] These models make the intuitively appealing argument that communication works by moving the customer through three phases: first, a 'learning' phase (awareness, comprehension); then a 'feeling' phase (attitudes, preferences); and finally an 'action' phase (trial, repurchase). The advantage of setting communications objectives in terms of these intervening variables is that they are more clearly a consequence of communications than ultimate sales. Managers responsible for communications can therefore be held more responsible for achieving results on these measures. In addition, they are normally easy to measure both before and after a campaign.

Figure 9.3 presents a model for judging the effectiveness of a communications campaign. The hierarchical variables are presented vertically along with some common measures. The elements of the communication plan are presented horizontally. The first task of management is to define the communications *objective*. For a new product this might be achieving defined levels of awareness and interest. Later the objectives may well shift to creating positive attitudes and trial. Then, management will need to develop a communications plan to achieve the given objective.

Each element of the communications mix has a particular role. The choice of *media* has the key role in achieving the awareness objective. Management will choose the media mix which maximizes the number and frequency of exposures for a given budget. The *message* is crucial for generating interest among the exposed audience. The creative use of copy, colour, novelty, humour and movement can all enhance the interest in the message. The quality of the message is also crucial to get the audience to comprehend the information about the product. Attitudes are influenced particularly by the credibility of the *source*. A product endorsement by a leading authority of

Hierarchy	Measures	Source	Message	Media	Market
Awareness	Recall				
Interest	Attention				
Comprehension	Knowledge				
Attitude	Preference				
Action	Purchase				

Figure 9.3 ■ Hierarchy of effects and the communications plan

known independence will have a positive effect. *Action* is likely to result when the audience is correctly targeted. For example, with a really new product, it is necessary initially to target opinion leaders rather than the ultimate mass market. The former provide the product endorsement and word-of-mouth influence necessary to encourage adoption among others in the market.

The last point highlights the importance of seeing the communications process as a whole. A message may be successful in achieving high awareness, but ineffective in producing results because it is not understood, not credible or hits the wrong target market segment. Analogously, a message may achieve low general awareness but be highly effective on the few prospective customers who are in the market at the time it is presented.

The matrix of Figure 9.3 can be used to evaluate a company's communications campaign. A simple 0 to 5 score can be given for each variable to indicate how well it contributes to each step in the hierarchy of effects. The resulting profile will indicate the strengths and weaknesses of the campaign and suggest areas for improvement. For example, a humorous advertisement message might score well on creating interest in the product, but score badly in generating comprehension and positive attitudes to it. Similarly, a particular media mix may do well on the awareness variable, but poorly on action because it is oriented to the wrong target market.

Buyer behaviour

Marketing communications seeks to influence buyer behaviour. To see the scope of this influence and how it is best directed, the nature of buyer behaviour needs to be understood. There are three key questions that management need to study. First, *what* influences buyer behaviour in their market; second, *who* influences buying decisions; and third, *how* do buyers make decisions?

Buyer motivations

Buyers – either consumers or industrial buyers – are influenced by two types of factor: social and commercial.[4] Social influences are the most important and are largely outside the control of the firm. The commercial influences are those marketing tactics that the firm and its competitors employ to influence buyer behaviour.

There are four broad social factors which play a key role in influencing what people buy. These are as follows:

■ *Cultural factors*. The products people buy and how they respond to communications are heavily influenced by their culture, nationality, religion, race, location and social class. Asians still have different aspirations from Europeans. Upper-class people, not surprisingly, have innate values, preferences and behaviour which are significantly different from those of the rural working class.

■ *Social factors*. Attitudes and behaviour are also influenced by reference groups, family, role and status in society. Reference groups are people with whom one inter-acts. These may be co-workers, friends or professional groups. Most people want to 'fit in', so reference groups create pressures for conformity. A group of teenagers will aspire to the same brand of running shoes. Doctors in a practice will tend to prescribe the same medicines. A person's place in a social group is defined in terms of role and status. A job involves a role in the organization together with a status level. People tend to choose products to communicate their status. Such *status symbols* include cars, clothes and electric gadgetry. For example, a manager will seek to look different from a front-line employee.

■ *Personal factors*. Buying decisions are also influenced by individual factors. The most important of these are the person's age, occupation, income, personality and lifestyle. People buy different types of product as they get older. Richer people tend to buy different goods and brands than poorer. Extrovert types often buy different products than introverts.

■ *Psychological factors*. Psychological factors have a major influence on the perceptual process. Psychologists such as Freud, Herzberg, Maslow and Dichter have developed various theories of motivation. The most widely quoted one in marketing has been *Maslow's hierarchy of needs*. Maslow postulated that an individual's needs are satisfied in order of importance. The most basic needs are physiological – for example, the need to satisfy hunger and thirst. Once these are satisfied, an individual tries to meet the other needs. These are in turn safety, social needs, esteem and finally self-actualization (see Figure 9.4). In affluent western societies, marketers would assume that esteem and self-actualization are common needs affecting product and brand choices.

These four social forces are major influences on the perceptions, preferences and behaviour of buyers. The second set of forces motivating buyers are *commercial*. These are the marketing activities that firms engage in to attract buyers. They are incorporated in the firm's marketing mix – the design of the product, its price, the services that augment the product, how it is distributed, and finally how its values are communi-

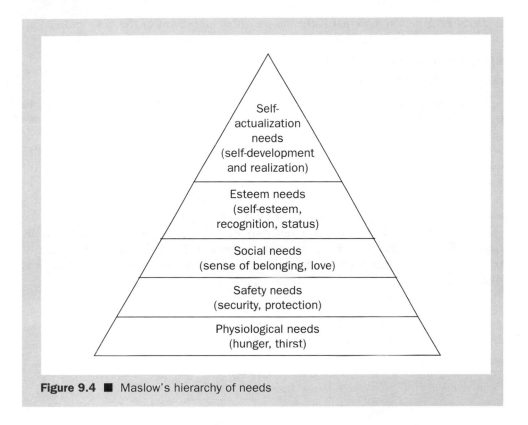

Figure 9.4 ■ Maslow's hierarchy of needs

cated to the audience. The key is to develop a marketing mix and a communications campaign which are consistent with the social, cultural, psychological and individual forces shaping the expectations of the target audience. Messages which offer benefits and information discordant with people's fundamental beliefs and aspirations are not going to be effective. Managers therefore need to study the social environment of their target markets.

Buying roles

In simple, routine buying situations it is usually easy to identify the buyer. But in more complex buying there is often no single customer, rather there is a *decision-making unit*. When a firm buys computers or a household purchases a car, many people may be involved.

Five buying roles can be distinguished (Figure 9.5):

■ *Initiator* – the person who first suggests buying the product or service.

■ *Influencer* – a person who advises on the buying decision.

- *Decider* – a person who makes the choice on a component of the buying decision: whether to buy, what to buy, how to buy it, or where to buy it from.
- *Buyer* – the person who makes the actual purchase.
- *User* – the person who uses the product (the consumer).

Marketing management need to understand the decision-making unit, since it will be a key determinant of the communications plan. How shall the communications message be structured? Who should it be targeted to? For example, 70 per cent of women's perfume is bought by men! Should perfume advertising then be targeted to men and positioned in media read mainly by men? The answer is probably not! Research suggests that the male buyer usually finds out what his partner normally uses or would like. If in doubt, he asks advice from shop assistants or colleagues (influencers). In large industrial buying decisions, the decision-making unit can be extremely complex with many different functions being involved and interactions taking place between them over an extended period. Understanding the nature of these networks and interactions is crucial for effective marketing and communications planning.

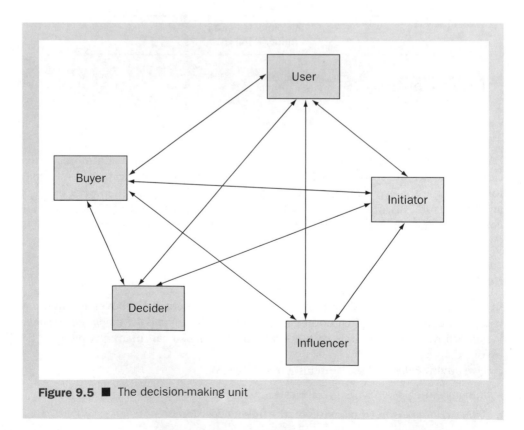

Figure 9.5 ■ The decision-making unit

Types of buying behaviour

There are different types of buying decision. Buying a house is very different from buying a newspaper. For a business, buying a factory is quite different from buying stationery. Complex, infrequent and expensive purchases are likely to involve more detailed analysis of information and more participants in the decision-making unit. Different types of decision imply different types of communications strategy.

A characteristic of most business and household customers is *repertoire buying*. Particularly for items that are purchased frequently, most customers are not brand loyal; they buy within a repertoire of four, five or six brands. A consumer might buy a Mars bar one day, a Kit Kat the next and Snickers the day after; he or she might even buy them all together. Brand preference is therefore a relative phenomenon and creating it is more about getting the brand included in the customer's repertoire and then nudging them to choose it slightly more often. But generally, the brand chosen on any particular occasion may be driven by habit, availability, the desire for a change, a price promotion or a particular need. The company's communications can very rarely create a truly loyal customer.

Buying decisions can be classified on two criteria:[5]

■ *Degree of customer involvement.* Customers are likely to be highly involved in the purchasing decision where purchases are infrequent or involve large amounts of money, or where a mistake poses a significant economic or social risk. High-involvement products are industrial capital equipment and consumer durables. But highly visible, status-oriented products such as sportswear or whisky, and new products tried for the first time, also attract high involvement. Conversely, low-involvement decisions – where little thought goes into the purchasing process – are mainly items which are frequently purchased, which are low cost and where there is little risk. Most grocery products fall into this group.

■ *Degree of customer rationality.* A decision is 'rational' if choice is based primarily on the perceived functionality of the product. Most industrial buying is rational. So are most purchases of consumer items such as washing powder, petrol and life insurance. Subjective or 'irrational' decisions are those made on the basis of taste, feelings or image. Perfumes, lagers, confectionery and sports cars normally fall into this category.

Using these two dimensions, purchases can be put into a six-element matrix (Figure 9.6). Most industrial decisions fall into the high rationality or 'thinking' column. Many, though certainly not all, consumer decisions fall into the low rationality or 'feeling' column. Each type of decision implies a different style of perceptual process and consumer learning. Correspondingly, each suggests a different approach to developing a communications strategy.

■ *Extensive problem solving.* For infrequent, expensive and risky decisions, customers search for information and seek to make rational choices. The hierarchy-of-effects model is an apt description of the perceptual process for this type of buying. Customers need first to learn about the product, and then to develop positive preferences before a

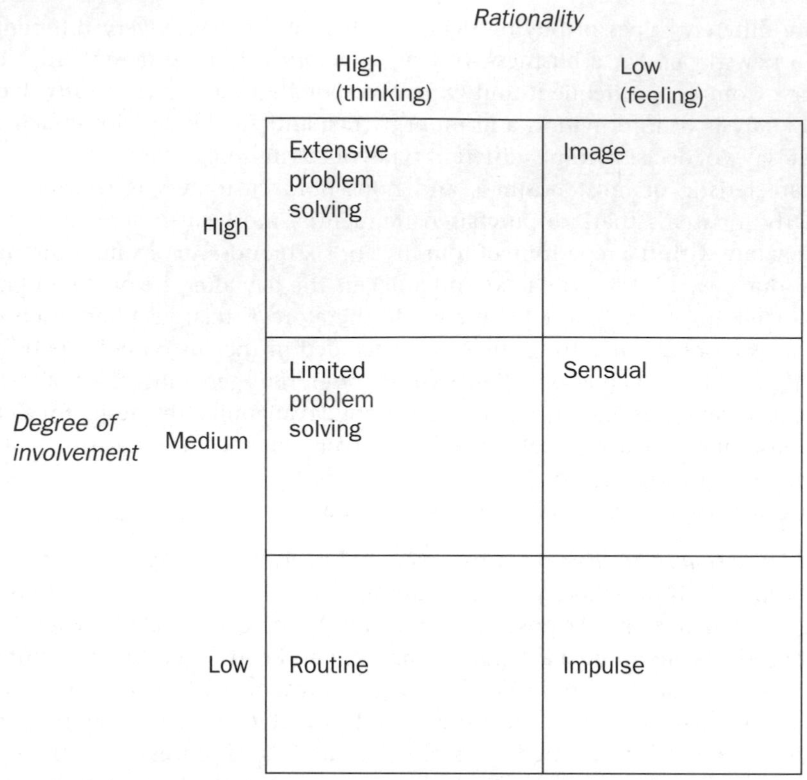

Rationality

		High (thinking)	Low (feeling)
	High	Extensive problem solving	Image
Degree of involvement	Medium	Limited problem solving	Sensual
	Low	Routine	Impulse

Figure 9.6 ■ Six types of buying behaviour

Source: adapted from Richard Vaughn, 'How advertising works: a planning model', *Journal of Advertising Research*, October 1980, p. 30

considered choice is made. Here effective communication requires researching the performance needs of target customers. Since buying is rational, the message should feature product performance and economic benefits. Given the high involvement of customers, they are more likely to expect fuller and more detailed information in the communications message. For these difficult decisions, the message is also important in the post-purchase stage to reassure customers that they have made a wise choice.

■ *Limited problem solving*. Here the buyer is familiar with the product category and is not inclined to do much more information seeking. However, the buyer's rational attitude predisposes him or her to notice dramatic claims or promises. The key here is to develop a simple, powerful message (often called a USP or unique selling proposition). If the message is too complicated, it is unlikely to be decoded or remembered. If the message is persuasive, the customer is likely to act rationally and try the brand.

■ *Routine problem solving.* When a product is bought very frequently, it requires little consideration. Habit, based on successful experience, is the main determinant of choice. Breaking this routine to introduce a new product is a tough marketing task. For example, of the 23 leading grocery brands in 1923, 19 had survived as number one into the 1980s. The other four were still in the top five!

For these products, the hierarchy-of-effects model does not apply. Customers do not want to learn about new products. They screen out information which is inconsistent with the current routine. For the brand challenger, research suggests that the best way to *change* habit is to *force* new behaviour. Free offers, samples, price cuts and other promotions are better than advertising for such a task. Once people have successfully tried the brand, cognitive dissonance theory suggests that customers may change their attitudes to make them consistent with the new behaviour. In contrast with the hierarchy-of-effects model, in routine buying decisions, attitude change follows behavioural change. For the market leader, the task is to bolster habitual buying against the promotions of competitors seeking to stimulate new behaviour patterns.

■ *Impulse decisions.* On the low rationality or 'emotional' side of the matrix, the lowest consumer involvement category is impulse buying. Here the consumer sees a brand in a store and tries it on the spur of the moment. But even if the product is satisfactory, it does not guarantee repurchase. Brand switching occurs for the sake of variety rather than any through dissatisfaction with the previous product. For these items (e.g. soft drinks, confectionery), distribution is often the key marketing variable. Market leaders try to switch impulse buyers to routine buying by dominating the shelf space and investing in frequent reminder advertising. Since buying is not based on rational factors, communications rely on using a strong creative idea, rather than on factual information. Challengers, on the other hand, seek to encourage impulse buying by offering lower prices, deals, samples and advertising that promotes reasons to try something new.

■ *Sensual decisions.* Here buying decisions are based on the desire for pleasure rather than on any rational assessment of the product's features. Many advertised brands fall into this category: biscuits, desserts, drinks, complete meals, ice cream, etc. The task of the communications message is to convey this pleasure through sensual images and fantasies.

■ *Image decisions.* Image decisions are high on involvement and low on rationality. These occur where the consumer sees the product as reflecting his or her status or personality. Perfume, whisky, cars and branded sportswear are examples. The communications tasks are to discover an image that appeals to the target segment and to find a subtle way of presenting the appropriate associations.

General implications

What implications do these theories of communications and buyer behaviour have for managers who are charged with developing communications policies?

■ *Most marketing communication is ineffective.* Customers are bombarded with so many messages and promotional stimuli that most communications are wasted. As Lord Leverhulme, once head of Unilever, is alleged to have said, 'Half my advertising is wasted – but I do not know which half.' Most communications are not seen by customers, or, if seen, are not noticed. Of the small percentage that are noticed, many are misunderstood or perceived by customers in a distorted fashion.

■ *High investments or highly creative communications are necessary to achieve an impact.* To overcome the noise in the communications system, the message needs to be exceptional in either weight or creativity. Communications impact is normally a function of the size of the presentation, its frequency, novelty and creativity.

■ *Communications must be matched to the interests of the target audience.* Customers notice messages which provide information in which they are interested. Messages which do not fit their social circumstances or individual needs are filtered out.

■ *Communications work in different ways for different types of buying decision.* For rational decisions, where the customer is highly involved, the classic hierarchical learning process occurs: awareness has to be created for a new product, comprehension built and preference stimulated before action is taken. For other decisions, where the functional differences between products are imperceptible or subjective, the buyer chooses on the basis of 'feelings'. Here the task of communications is often to provide the images which are the only differentiator among products. For low-involvement decisions, behaviour often has to be triggered before attitude change occurs.

■ *The type of communications mix will vary with the type of buying behaviour.* Promotions (e.g. free samples) which can trigger direct behaviour change have an important role in low-involvement decisions. For highly rational, high-involvement decisions (extensive problem solving), personal selling is more likely to be effective in dealing with the buyer's information requirements. Advertising has an obviously important role in decisions based upon emotional responses.

■ *Marketing communications are more powerful in creating brand switching than in generating category sales.* Sales of a product category (e.g. cigarettes, computers) are usually determined by social factors such as the cultural, income or psychological background of the customer. The role of marketing communications is highly constrained. Instruments of communications such as advertising and sales promotion tend to affect brand decisions within the product category.

 ## Advertising planning

Advertising is the most visible, although no longer the largest, component of the communications mix. In per capita terms, the Swiss and the Scandinavians spend the most on advertising, the Italians, Greeks and Portuguese the least (Table 9.1). Advertising is defined as the paid presentation and promotion of products or services through mass media such as television, radio and newspapers.

Table 9.1 ■ Advertising expenditure per capita, 1996

Country	Index	Distribution by media (%)			
		Press	**TV**	**Radio**	**Other**
Austria	109	62	22	10	6
Belgium	81	52	31	8	9
Denmark	135	78	17	2	3
Finland	97	74	19	4	3
France	90	48	32	8	12
Germany	133	70	21	4	5
Greece	55	28	66	4	2
Ireland	77	62	25	8	5
Italy	54	39	57	1	3
Netherlands	115	72	20	4	4
Norway	116	74	18	6	2
Portugal	42	34	55	5	6
Spain	64	48	37	9	6
Sweden	107	75	19	1	5
Switzerland	205	76	9	3	12
UK	119	61	33	3	3

Source: NTC Publications, 1996

The steps in developing an advertising programme are outlined in Figure 9.7.

Identifying the target audience

As with all marketing decisions, advertising starts with the segmentation of the potential market to identify the key target segments. Most advertisements aim to persuade customers that the product or service featured will meet their needs and offer them value. The characteristics of the target segment should determine what the advertising will say, how it is presented, when it is shown and the media chosen to display it.

Advertising planning therefore starts with an analysis of the market. There are three central steps:

1. *Segmentation of the market.* The heterogeneous market has to be broken down into customer groups that are similar in needs. Different customer groups have different expectations and so require different types of communication. Business people have different travel needs to tourists; hospital specialists want different information from pharmaceutical companies to GPs; speciality businesses want different types of product support to commodity businesses.

2. *Assessing the potential of the different segments.* Companies then have to choose which segment or segments to focus on. This depends first on the attractiveness of the

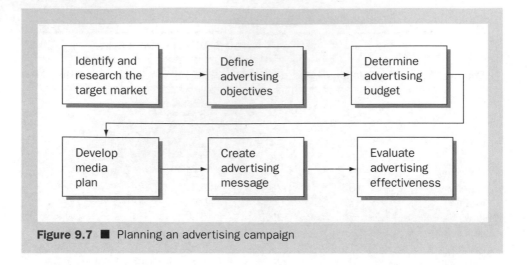

Figure 9.7 ■ Planning an advertising campaign

segments: their size, growth, profitability and competitiveness. Second, it depends upon where the company is in the best position to develop a competitive advantage. Which segments would most value the firm's products and expertise?

3. *Analyzing needs and behaviour.* An advertising message will work when it is in tune with the culture of the target audience, is interesting to them, and presents a solution to their needs in a persuasive way. To develop a message and a media plan, the advertising agency will need research on the needs of the target audience, the nature of the decision-making units, and when and where they buy.

Determining advertising objectives

Next it is necessary to define objectives. This is particularly important for advertising because, given the technical nature of much of the planning, most of the campaign is usually developed by an outside professional advertising agency. The agency will usually be delegated to organize the research, create the message and propose the media. In these circumstances, it is important for the agency and the client to agree objectives. Objectives serve several purposes. First, they provide for effective communication and co-ordination between the client and the agency. Second, they provide a criterion for decision making: for choosing between alternative advertising plans. Third, they provide the norms with which to evaluate the campaign when it has been completed.

To serve these purposes, objectives must be specific, measurable and operational. Specific means that the sales or communications objectives should be clearly defined. Measurable means that numerical goals, achievable in a specific time period, can be established, so permitting subsequent evaluation of the campaign. Operational means that the agreed objectives and results can be clearly related to the advertising employed.

Ultimately, the objective of advertising, as with all marketing investments, is to increase the firm's profits. It can do this by either raising sales or increasing prices. Usually the objective of advertising is seen as increasing sales. Unfortunately, targeting sales as an objective normally fails the operationality test. It is difficult to disentangle the effects of advertising from the many other factors influencing sales. Second, for many types of buying behaviour, purchase is the end result of a long process of consumer decision making. Current advertising, therefore, may not produce sales results until well into the future. Similarly, current sales may be the result of awareness and positive attitudes to the brand built up by expensive and consistent investment long ago.

Exceptionally, short-term sales may be a good measure of advertising effectiveness. This occurs when advertising is the overwhelming determinant of sales and where long-term carry-over effects are small. Perhaps the best example is direct response advertising. Here a newspaper advertisement is expected to get people sending in orders immediately. After a week the advertiser knows whether the promotion is a success or failure. Some retailer advertising – especially price-oriented promotions – also aims at immediate sales.

Much advertising is defensive in nature. Its aim is often less to increase sales than to maintain them by encouraging customers to continue buying the brand. The advertising acts to reinforce customers' existing beliefs and patterns of behaviour. If a customer has bought a product and found it satisfactory, subsequently seeing an advertisement confirms his or her judgement and increases the probability that it will be bought again.

Advertising's role in achieving higher prices can also be important to a firm's profit performance. Leading advertised brands normally sell at prices substantially above own-label and minor brands. Advertising supports this premium by reinforcing the values of the brand to the consumer. But as with sales objectives, it is difficult to disentangle the effects of the advertising on the premium from the other factors that play a role, such as its market share and positioning. Lagged effects also complicate evaluation: changes in advertising are not likely to have much of an impact in the short run.

For these reasons, advertising objectives are normally framed in terms of intermediate communications goals which meet the criteria of specificity, measurability and operationality better than sales and prices. The first task is to benchmark where the company or the brand is now along these communications measures. Figure 9.8 illustrates the situation for one brand of lager. Here the problem is obviously one of attitudes. Most people knew about the brand, but only 35 per cent had positive attitudes towards it.

Strategically, the brand can be compared to brand D in the awareness–attitude matrix of Figure 9.9. Each brand in the matrix presents a different advertising problem. Brand A has the best position. Customers know it and like it. The advertising task is to reinforce this position. Brand B's position can be greatly improved by advertising, since it is a well-liked brand but more people need to be made aware of it. Brand C is in the most difficult position, since it is not well known and those who know it do not like it much. Brand D's problem is the unfavourable attitudes towards it. It means changing the product or changing the attitudes to it.

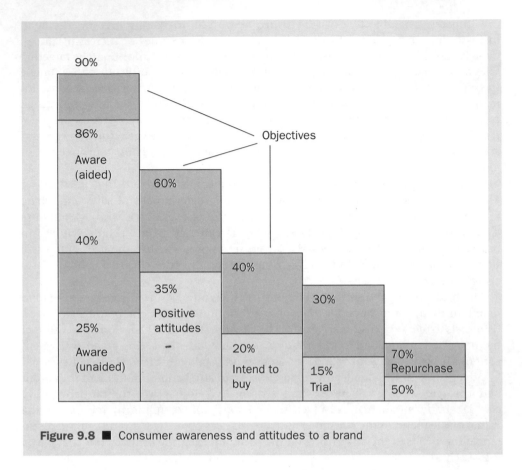

Figure 9.8 ■ Consumer awareness and attitudes to a brand

In this example, product research proved that there was nothing wrong with the brand. In blind product tests it scored equal to the brand leaders – its real problem was image. Its poor image led to a weak brand profile along the choice dimensions mentioned by the customers.

The primary advertising objective was to achieve a measurable change in customers' attitudes by creating a new image for it. The brand would be repositioned as a 'cool' and fashionable drink, so creating an aura of popularity and success which would build confidence of consumers in their choice. Objectives agreed for the campaign are summarized in Table 9.2.

Developing the message

Once decisions have been made about *who* the advertiser is targeting and *what* objectives it wants to achieve, the next task is *how* to produce a message to achieve the objective. The message has to meet two criteria. First, it must be presented in a way that

Table 9.2 ■ Setting advertising objectives

	Now	1 year on
Market share (%)	7	10
Brand awareness		
Unaided	25	40
Aided	86	90
Attitude rating	35	60
Intent to buy	20	40
Trial	15	30
Repurchase	50	70

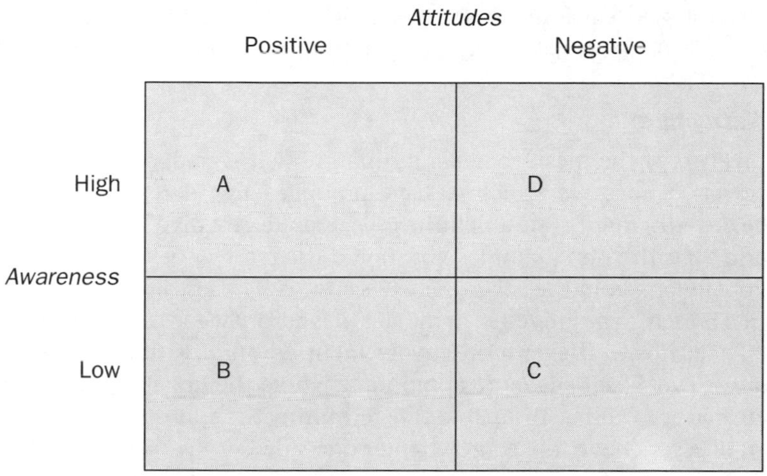

Figure 9.9 ■ Awareness–attitude matrix

will attract attention. Given the low level of interest that consumers normally have in advertisements and the hundreds of others competing for their attention, this is a difficult task. Second, it must produce the desired type of perceptual or behavioural response and not be misinterpreted or rejected. The audience should find the message clear, believable and motivating. Again this is a tough job, given the brief attention scan that the message is likely to receive.

The creative department of the advertising agency, which will normally be responsible for developing the message, will work on four aspects – content, structure, format and source.

Message content

Content refers to the appeal the advertisement will employ to motivate the customer. Figure 9.6 suggests that there are two broad types of appeal: rational and emotional. *Rational appeals* focus on the functional benefits of the product. They seek to persuade customers of its superior performance, lower cost or better value. Where buying decisions are predominantly rational – industrial buying, expensive consumer durables and functional items – this is the obvious type of appeal to motivate consumers. *Emotional appeals* seek to evoke positive feelings about the brand to motivate purchase. These appeals work where there are no real differences between products and when brands are bought for personal indulgence or image purposes. Watches, cigarettes, beer and cosmetics are obvious examples where emotional appeals are relevant.

Emotional appeals can be split into positive and negative. Positive emotional appeals include humour and the promise of success, beauty or happiness. Negative appeals include fear, guilt and shame. The latter are often used in anti-smoking, drink-driving and insurance advertising. Research suggests that excessive use of negative appeals, particularly the use of fear, can discourage people from looking at the message and so be counterproductive.

Message structure

The effectiveness of the message depends upon how it is said, as well as what is said. Several aspects of message structure have produced useful research findings. First, should the advertisement state a definite *conclusion* (e.g. 'Volvo is the safest car in the market for dads with young families') or should the receiver be allowed to draw his or her own conclusions from the advertisement's appeal? The research suggests that, where the customer is likely to be interested in the area, it is advantageous to leave the conclusions unstated. This tends to trigger more involvement and motivation to think about the brand. Stating conclusions is more appropriate where the target segment is less likely to be motivated or would be incapable of determining the appropriate conclusion.

Other researchers have looked at whether one-sided or *two-sided* arguments should be used. That is, should some of the negatives of the product be set alongside the positives? (e.g. 'Using Sensodyne dental floss does take extra time but …'). The research suggests that two-sided arguments work better for educated audiences and where people are not initially positive about the product.

Comparative advertising – where the brand is compared against another specific brand in the product class – has been a growing phenomenon. There are no simple answers about the relative effectiveness of comparative advertising. In general it works best for unknown brands or brands with a small market share which are seeking to challenge the leaders. It is less attractive for brand leaders, which will not in general wish to encourage comparisons or publicize smaller rivals.

Message format

The format of the presentation depends upon the media used: TV, press, radio, billboards, etc. Format includes *copy* – the verbal portion of the advertisement; *artwork* – the illustrations used; and *layout* – the physical arrangement of headlines, sub-headlines, copy, illustration and brand identification. The creativity with which the elements are put together has a major impact on the effectiveness of the advertisement.

One clear research finding is that 'a picture is worth a thousand words'. People's attention is almost invariably engaged more by the picture in an advertisement than by the headline or copy. Furthermore, people have an enormously greater ability to recall pictures than words. Pictures too are more flexible. A picture can say things which stated verbally would sound pretentious, absurd or impossible. An important area of research at the moment is just why people can remember pictures with such extraordinary facility.[6]

Message source

All advertisements feature a source which is perceived to be the spokesperson of the brand. The source in the advertisement may be the company itself, the brand name or the actor who endorses the product. Research shows that the effectiveness of a source depends upon its credibility and attractiveness. *Credibility* means the degree to which the source is perceived as being an expert with respect to the product and is unbiased in the claims being made for it. An expert loses credibility if the audience believes that he or she is being paid to make the claims about the product. A credible source will greatly enhance the effectiveness of the advertisement.

The second factor affecting the source's effectiveness is its *attractiveness*. Attractiveness is the receiver's perception of the prestige of the source, the degree to which the source is similar to the receiver, and his or her physical or personal attractiveness. Top sportsmen and film stars are not surprisingly often seen as attractive sources. A reputed brand name is also an attractive source.

Ten commandments

Dr Dieter Steinbrecher, a German authority on advertising, after reviewing hundreds of advertisement tests, offered ten commandments which successful advertising messages usually obey. He suggested that these can be used as a checklist by managers to evaluate their company's advertising messages:[7]

1. *Attract attention.* The advertisement must be sufficiently impactful to attract the attention of the target market. This is indispensable: without being perceived there can be no response. But attracting attention is only a necessary condition and not a sufficient one for advertising effectiveness. An advertisement can attract attention but irritate the customer and actually deter purchase.

2. *Visual clarity.* The advertising, its copy and illustrations must present a clear 'gestalt' or visual whole. Its central meaning must be clear and understandable even after a quick viewing. Muddled and complex advertisements do not get through the perceptual barriers.

3. *Concentration.* An advertisement should not claim more than one or two central benefits. Advertisements which are overloaded with information cannot be

retained and stored by customers. The search for a unique selling proposition (USP) is often a powerful advertising discipline.

4. *Comprehension and credibility*. It is important that the message is understood. The advertisement should speak in the language of the customer and the images should be within the horizons of the customer's experiences. For example, studies have been shown that business people do not understand the highly scientific language used in advertisements for electronics and telecommunications companies. Credibility here means that the claims look reasonable to the client.

5. *Positive emotions*. An advertisement should be tested to confirm that it evokes positive feelings towards the product or company. If it generates negative or neutral feelings, customers are likely to avoid looking at it.

6. *Unity of style*. The style of the advertisement should match the style of the brand. A brand with solid functional benefits should have these reflected in the advertisement's presentation. Similarly the emotional images of the brand and the advertisement should be in concert.

7. *Constancy of style*. The style of the advertising should be maintained over a long period to retain and enhance the message. Brand managers are often too quick to change advertising or the advertising agency radically. They believe that because they are bored with the advertisement, customers are too. They forget that customers are a lot less interested in the advertising than they are. Frequent and abrupt changes in advertising erode the brand's image and confuse the market.

8. *Match the client's world*. Communications start with the receiver not the sender. To be effective, the message must match the reality of the receiver's world. Does the message reflect the environment and ideals of the customers? Customers in different international environments may require different messages. A message which is extraneous to the client is likely to be misunderstood and rejected.

9. *Differential advantage*. The advertisement should convey a clear competitive advantage. It should give the customers a reason why the product or service should be preferred to others in the market. If it looks the same or no better than other products, then the money promoting it will be wasted.

10. *Images rather than words*. Research has clearly shown the superior impact of images over words for conveying complex messages. This is especially true for advertising, where the receiver normally reserves only a few seconds for looking at the message. Pictures need less time to be transmitted and they are better understood.

Advertising messages should always be *pre-tested* before they are transmitted. Research agencies have developed a variety of techniques for measuring the ability of an advertisement to attract attention, build understanding of the product, change attitudes and create an intention to buy. These involve customers viewing alternative advertisements and having their reaction to them tested. While pre-tests are not perfect, they do allow the advertiser to obtain rough indications of effectiveness.

Determining the budget

Determining how much to spend on advertising is a very difficult problem. The amount that should be spent depends upon two factors: the profit contribution margin and the shape of the advertising–sales response curve. Unfortunately, while the former can generally be estimated, the latter is virtually impossible to measure. Consequently, decisions rely heavily upon judgement.

Advertising decisions in practice appear to rely on rules of thumb which have very little justification. Managers tend to follow one of three methods:

■ *Percentage of sales method.* The most common method is to set advertising at some percentage (e.g. 2 per cent) of current or anticipated sales. This provides management with a stable measure, but very little else. There is no rationale for the percentage chosen (except tradition) and there is no effort to consider whether a higher or lower amount would be more profitable.

■ *Competitive parity.* Another approach is to spend the same percentage as competitors in the industry. This gives managers the illusion of safety in numbers: that the collective wisdom cannot be far wrong. Again, however, there is little rationale for this approach. Firms differ in their market opportunities and profit margins, so that significant divergences should exist in a market. Those with better products and higher margins should spend more.

■ *Affordable method.* Another common method is to base spending on what the company thinks it can afford. If it is exceeding its budgeted profit, then marketing management are allowed to spend more on advertising and promotion. Again there is no logic in this approach. Changes are not related to the profit opportunities that can be exploited by advertising.

A more rational approach is to consider how sales might respond to different levels of advertising. For example, if a product has a profit contribution (price – unit variable cost) margin of 0.5 (i.e. margin/price or total contribution/sales revenue), then to justify an advertising budget of say £10 million, incremental sales of £20 million are required, i.e.

$$\text{Break-even} = \frac{£10\text{m advertising budget}}{0.5 \text{ profit contribution margin}}$$

Judging whether such a budget would generate £20 million extra sales requires estimating the sales response curve (Figure 9.10). There are two problems in practice. One is that sales are affected by a myriad of other factors besides advertising. Second, advertising has lagged effects. Today's expenditure may affect purchases long into the future. There have been three types of more-or-less scientific approach to overcoming these problems:[8]

■ *Econometric methods.* These are computer-based statistical techniques which attempt to parcel out the effects of advertising from the variety of other factors affecting sales. In principle, it is also possible for these techniques to measure the lagged

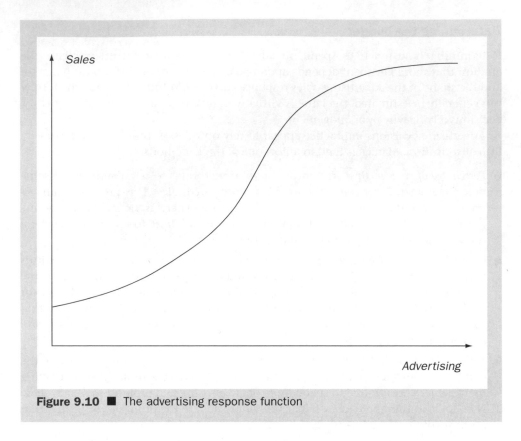

Figure 9.10 ■ The advertising response function

effects of advertising. Such methods normally rely on the analysis of past sales data. In practice, there are several limitations with econometric analysis. First, it is often difficult to get all the data needed to take into account other variables. Second, there is often insufficient variation in advertising to get good estimates of the response curve. Finally, there is a more general question about how valuable estimates are of what happened in the past to predicting what will happen in the future.

■ *Experiments and tests*. Another method of isolating the effects of advertising is to run an experiment whereby one region of the country gets a higher level of spending than others. Company sales then give an estimate of the incremental effect of advertising. While such approaches may give insights, they again run into a host of practical problems. How representative is the test and the test area? Is everything else similar across the regions? Has the experiment lasted long enough to judge any long-term effects?

■ *Judgemental methods*. More recently, techniques have been developed to elicit formally the judgements of the managers most directly involved about the shape of the response curve. Managers are asked to judge what sales level will be attained with no advertising support, advertising at half the current level and advertising at 50 per cent more than the present level. Putting together the consensus estimate allows a projection of the optimal level of expenditure. This is a promising approach in that managers are forced to use their judgement and experience in a rational manner. The downside is that the method is only as good as the collected wisdom of those participating in the exercise.

Thinking about advertising in a rational manner does permit some useful *generalizations* about when and where advertising is likely to pay off:

■ The bigger the profit contribution margin, other things being equal, the more it pays to advertise. If the margin is 67 per cent, only £1.5 million extra sales are needed to justify a £1 million expenditure on advertising. If the margin is 33 per cent, over £3 million sales are needed.

The other generalizations relate to the expected shape of the sales response curve:

■ New products are more likely to respond to advertising. Advertising can solve the problem of the market's initial lack of awareness and knowledge.

■ Fast-moving consumer goods are likely to respond more because the time-gap between seeing the advertisement and being in a purchase situation is short.

■ Products with a differential advantage should be advertised. Customers have a reason to switch to the product.

■ Advertising is more effective in larger markets. It is usually easier to meet an incremental sales target of £3 million if the market is worth £300 million than if it is worth £10 million.

Objective-and-task method: a compromise approach

Management have to find a way of budgeting which steers a path between the impracticalities of the theoretical approaches and the irrationality of the common rules of thumb. The objective-and-task method represents such a compromise. It involves first setting sales and profit targets, then working backwards to the specific communication objectives (awareness, intentions, etc.) necessary to achieve the desired sales level. Once these objectives are set, the advertising reach and frequency needed to achieve them have to be estimated. Finally the cost of the campaign needed to achieve these levels of reach and frequency has to be calculated. By comparing the cost with the expected increased gross profit, the financial viability of the campaign can be judged.

The advantage of this method is that it encourages managers to define their goals, to articulate the assumptions about the relationships between awareness, trial and regular use, and to link these intermediate objectives to the profitability of the advertising investment.[9]

Media selection

The next step is to select the vehicles which will carry the advertising message. Should the company use television, radio, press, magazines, outdoor billboards or the Internet?

If it uses magazines, which magazines should be chosen and where should the advertisements be placed inside them? The media planner will seek to answer this problem by selecting those media which will maximize the number of exposures to the target market for the given budget.

Implicit in this model is the assumption that product trial or repurchase is a function of the number of people who are exposed to the advertisement (*cover*) together with the number of times they are exposed to it (*frequency*). The idea is to choose a media schedule which has high cover and high frequency. A third factor in the selection is *impact*. Impact is the qualitative value of an exposure through a given medium (e.g. a corporate advertisement may have a higher impact in *The Economist* than in *The Grocer*).

The advertising agency will look at a media schedule's *gross rating points*. This is the total number of exposures it receives. If a schedule reaches 90 per cent of households with an average exposure frequency of 3, it achieves 270 gross rating points. It is also likely to produce a *weighted number of exposures* which weights the gross weighting points that a vehicle achieves with its relative impact score. It should be added that exposures and frequency refer to the number of people seeing the vehicle carrying the advertisement, rather than the advertisement itself. The number of people actually noting the advertisement in the magazine will normally be substantially less than the reported number of exposures.

A problem for the planner is that there is a direct trade-off between cover, frequency and impact. For example, the planner can spend the budget on increasing the number of people likely to see the message, or increasing the frequency with which a smaller number of target customers see it. If the planner pays a premium for a high-impact vehicle then he or she trades off in terms of lower frequency or exposures. The art of scheduling is to choose the combination of cover, frequency and impact which will be the most effective. Most experts, for example, argue for a minimum frequency of 3 or 4. The first exposure creates awareness and the second builds comprehension. It is only when a third or fourth exposure takes place, so the argument goes, that a predisposition to action occurs. If such a target frequency is set, then the reach is determined automatically by the budget.

Each of the different broad types of media – press, TV, radio, etc. – has characteristics which influence its cover, frequency and impact. Four criteria affecting the choice of media vehicles are as follows:

- *Target market*. If the product is aimed at a narrow segment, such as architects, broadbeam media like television and national newspapers are very wasteful.

- *Budget*. If the firm can afford only a small expenditure on advertising, costly media such as television will be ruled out.

- *Product*. If a product is bought largely on rational grounds, the advertisement is often more effectively placed in a newspaper or magazine. Television is good for products bought on emotive grounds, where images of pleasure, status and style can be exploited.

- *Message*. Television is outstanding both for impact and for the presentation of emotional messages. It offers greater creative scope than other media.

Once the planner has made the broad strategic choice across the media (the inter-media choice), specific choices have to be made within each medium (intra-media choices). If the planner is to use newspapers, then the matter of which ones has to be determined. Each vehicle has a *cost per thousand* people reached. For example, the *Daily Mirror* has an estimated readership of 8 million. If a one-page spread costs £30,000, the cost per thousand is £3.75. The *Daily Telegraph* cost per thousand is over £13 and the *Financial Times* over £40.

The planner inclines towards the lowest cost per thousand. But these figures have to be adjusted for *audience quality*. If the target audience is senior executives, few read the *Daily Mirror* while most read the *Financial Times*. Some agencies have computer-based media selection models which also adjust for *audience-attention probability*. Readers of *Country Life*, for example, pay more attention to advertisements than do readers of the *Sunday Times*. Another adjustment factor is *editorial quality*. The prestige of a magazine may also affect the exposure value. Finally, *placement* of the advertisement in the vehicle is an important factor. A back page in a magazine is worth more than the right-hand page in the middle.

Once the schedule is determined, next comes the *timing* of the expenditure. Should the money be spent to maintain a continuous level of advertising, or should it be spent on short, sharp bursts? The answer depends upon the nature of the market. In particular, it depends upon whether the product is seasonal or bought throughout the year, whether it is a frequent or infrequent purchase, whether it is a growing or static market, and whether people usually forget about the product because it is a low-involvement purchase. Planners distinguish four timing patterns:

- *Continuous.* A continuous schedule aims at an even spread of exposures over a period. It is appropriate for expanding markets where new buyers can be attracted and for frequently purchased products.

- *Concentrated.* A concentrated schedule focuses the expenditure in a single period. It is appropriate for seasonal items like ski gear and Christmas gifts.

- *Flighting.* This involves alternating advertising with gaps without support. It is used when the budget is small and for infrequently purchased items.

- *Pulsing.* This involves periods of low advertising spend reinforced with occasional bursts of heavy spending. This is often used with strong, mature brands. Strong brands have been found capable of maintaining market share for up to a couple of years with little advertising, but then they need to be boosted before people begin to forget and shift towards newer ones.

Evaluating advertising effectiveness

During the campaign and after it is completed, the results need to be evaluated. Has it produced the results expected? Has the advertising been effective? To answer these questions, it is necessary to have had clearly defined objectives at the start and to have collected the appropriate information. If managers have done this well, then they can compare the results, identify the variances and explore the reasons for the successes and failures.

Table 9.3 ■ Monitoring advertising effectiveness

Measure	Objective	Result	Variance (%)	Source
Market share	10	9	–10	Retail audit
Awareness				Survey
Unaided	40	45	+13	
Aided	90	88	–2	
Brand attitude	60	68	+13	Survey
Intent to buy	40	47	+18	Survey
Trial	30	22	–27	Consumer panel
Repurchase rate	70	75	+7	Consumer panel

Table 9.3 compares the results of an advertising campaign with the objectives originally established for it. It appears that the campaign did well in creating positive attitudes to the brand and intention to buy, but the brand failed to achieve the targeted trial rate. This in turn led to a failure to achieve the market share objective. Anticipating variances, the company had also asked questions in its post-campaign telephone survey about the reasons for non-trial, when the respondents had not purchased the brand. The main reasons were found to be failure of the salesforce to achieve distribution targets – many customers were not able to try the product because it was unavailable in the shops. This reinforces the point that advertising always depends upon other factors in the marketing mix. Here the advertising can be judged as achieving its communications goals, but the campaign needs to be reinforced by boosting existing distribution levels. This last objective depends on the effectiveness of the salesforce.

Direct response marketing

Direct mail and telesales are examples of direct response marketing. These have been growing very rapidly in the last decade in most countries. Direct response marketing differs from advertising in three important ways. First, it usually targets named individual customers rather than operating indirectly through a mass medium like newspapers or television. Second, it normally aims at an immediate response rather than an increase in awareness or positive feeling about the brand. Finally, purchases are made directly from the manufacturer rather than through an intermediary like a shop or a salesperson.

Direct mail (including mail order catalogues) is the largest component of direct marketing. The average European received over 70 direct mail pieces in 1996, with Switzerland top at 120 pieces per capita and Portugal bottom with 15. Telemarketing has been growing at around 30 per cent per annum. In recent years we have also seen the growth of fax, the use of radio and television, and the beginning of the Internet to generate direct sales, whereby the customer responds by phoning in his or her credit card order, or orders by mail or computer.

Several factors explain the rapid growth of direct response marketing. For the customer, it is often more convenient and time saving to buy from a catalogue or over the phone than to go visiting suppliers or meeting their representatives. For the supplier, direct marketing is often more effective. It allows a finer targeting of customers than relying on mass media. As today's markets get more and more segmented, this is a considerable advantage. It is also much cheaper than direct selling, where a call by a representative may cost an average of £100. Finally, direct response is now increasingly used in forging continuing relationships with high-value customers. Companies like British Airways and American Express use their customer databases to maintain continual contact and provide a stream of tailored offers to carefully targeted customers.

Planning direct marketing

Developing the database

To make effective use of direct marketing, a company needs a good database of those customers that should be targeted. Many companies buy or build databases that are insufficiently targeted. They mail to the top 10,000 companies rather than to those prospects likely to respond to an offer. The results of such poorly targeted databases are junk mail, low response rate and irritated customers.

In recent years, sophisticated companies have become more alert to the value of targeted databases. Market research agencies have been developing new lifestyle and geodemographic databases which allow consumer goods companies to identify more precisely those households most likely to be in their particular target segments. The client receives a list of addresses of customers whose consumption behaviour, age, income and other profilers closely match its desired market. Retailers and industrial companies, too, are now getting more skilful at developing their own databases from records of the activities of their existing customers, and are using these to create additional sales. With the enormous power and flexibility of modern computers, databases are certain to become more sophisticated, tailored and widely used in the future to market goods and services.

Objectives

If investments in direct marketing are to be evaluated, then the objectives need to be clarified. Traditionally, the objective has been to generate immediate sales. But with the growing appreciation of the power of direct marketing, other tasks are being assigned to it. Some companies use it to generate leads for targeting the salesforce. More companies are now using it to build individual relationships with customers which reinforce attitudes and loyalty to the company. Direct mail can provide information about new services, the benefits of brand loyalty and offers which will be available in the future.

Strategy

Direct marketing strategy focuses on maximizing the response rate. Each medium such as direct mail, telesales and catalogue mail order has its own rules. Response rates can be a major problem. But recent research shows that in the UK 61 per cent of mail shots are opened and read. In the USA the comparable figure is 42 per cent.

Various studies have been made to determine the factors which will enhance response rates. Starting on the outside, characteristics of the envelope which increase attention and response are the use of illustration, colour and a strong reason for opening the envelope (e.g. a free gift or contest). The sales letter or brochure should be simple, easy to read and with a clear and interesting offer. A letter and an envelope which are personalized rather than addressed to a firm or a department do significantly better. Reply-paid cards and free-phone telephone numbers also greatly improve response rates. Timing also has to be considered. It is best to avoid periods when letter boxes are crowded, such as Christmas. Similarly, Mondays are best avoided, with Tuesdays and Wednesdays the preferred days.[10]

An advantage of direct response marketing techniques is that different methods and elements can easily be tested. It is straightforward to experiment with different mailing lists and offers and to compare responses. This way major users like banks, airlines and book clubs build up a detailed understanding of what types of direct response work in their markets.

Evaluating direct response

While it is fairly easy to test and choose between two direct response options, it is less straightforward to calculate the economic pay-off of a campaign. It is natural to start with a break-even calculation. If the cost of a direct response campaign is £50,000 and the profit contribution rate on the products being sold is 50 per cent, then the campaign needs to generate over £100,000 of incremental sales to be profitable. There are two reasons why this type of marginal analysis tends to undervalue the campaign.

First, there are likely to be carry-over effects. Some of the customers who respond to the campaign will also buy in subsequent periods. The campaign creates assets: customers who generate revenue over a period longer than that measured by the campaign. Second, while only 2 or 3 per cent may buy the item promoted in the direct marketing campaign, the communications effects may enhance sales in future periods. A much larger proportion than those buying the product are made aware of it, and some will intend to buy in the future.

The precision of direct marketing, its relatively low cost and the acquisition of more information about customers mean that it will play an increasingly central role in marketing in the future.

Interactive marketing

The most recent and by far the fastest-growing channel for direct marketing is interactive marketing. Interactive marketing can be defined as providing and responding to information by the computer or television. Currently, the most significant forms of interactive media are the Internet, CD-ROM and interactive television.

Interactive marketing looks certain to change fundamentally the way in which organizations market and communicate in the years ahead. For the consumer, interactive marketing offers convenience, a source of objective and comprehensive information about alternative products, and a relatively hassle-free shopping environment. People can shop from their homes 24 hours a day. For companies, the power of interactive marketing lies in its ability to generate a direct and immediate response from consumers. Unlike advertising or other forms of direct marketing, there is no built-in delay (such as having to write a letter, telephone a response or visit a shop). Interactive marketing has several advantages.[11]

First, it requires the audience to be proactive by asking for a response to the message. Research shows that people who respond to messages (rather than merely receiving them) tend to retain information far longer and more accurately. Second, interactive messages are more flexible. The recipients can search for the details they want, study them at their own pace, and ignore information they do not want. Third, interactive messages can be relationship building. For example, the grocery chain Tesco has a Web site where users can input data about their requirements (e.g. for wine) and receive in return customized quotations and suggestions for purchases from an intelligent catalogue. Interactive marketing can also be very low cost. For small firms, it can break down industry entry barriers. They do not need to invest in stores or heavy TV advertising, and the cost of digital catalogues is a fraction of the cost of printing and distributing mail catalogues.

There are two types of interactive medium: on-line and off-line. Off-line media are discrete packets of information (e.g. a floppy disk or CD-ROM); on-line media are communications systems that link two computers together (e.g. the Internet). At the moment, off-line media have the advantage of access: only 10 per cent of homes with a PC are equipped with a modem. In the next few years this will change dramatically, making on-line communications more attractive. On-line systems have several advantages, including continuously updated information, the ability to create a two-way dialogue, and the opportunity to develop 'club-like' sites which encourage customer loyalty.

■ *Internet.* The growth of the Internet has been the most astonishing technological phenomenon of the last decade of the twentieth century. It is a global web of up to 100,000 computer networks that have made instantaneous personal global communications possible. In 1990 only a few academics had heard of the Internet; now up to 100 million people use it. It is estimated that the number of users is doubling every twelve months. Currently the most popular uses of the Internet include E-mail, controlling bank accounts, shopping for products, exchanging views and accessing news and information across an infinite variety of subjects. The Internet itself is free, though most users pay a one-off monthly fee to the firm that offers them a Net connection (e.g. Compuserve, America-on-Line); and then home users typically have the additional cost of the local call every time that they log on.

- *CD-ROM*. This is a rapidly growing off-line medium. Currently about 10 per cent of PCs have CD-ROM drives, but the proportion is growing rapidly. Sales of CD-ROMs were estimated at $3 billion in 1997 and are growing by around 200 per cent annually. Early CD-ROMs were mainly directories and educational titles. Now more magazine formats are appearing, focusing on entertainment. Advertising is an increasing feature of these CD magazines.

- *Interactive television*. This will probably be the future of domestic communication. Cable television is likely to offer in the future a wide range of interactive services, including video-on-demand, shopping and home banking. This will represent a major new opportunity for marketing.

Businesses are increasingly exploring the potential of interactive media for marketing purposes. Both off-line and on-line media are now often used to promote organizations. Off-line media such as CD-ROM and floppy disks are increasingly used to supplement company annual reports and advertisements. Thousands of organizations are now placing a home page on the Internet to advertise and promote their products and services. Newspapers and magazines use their Web sites to allow customers to sample their products. Businesses can also use E-mail and participate in forums and news groups to increase their visibility and credibility. As with all media, interactive marketing requires careful planning: setting clear objectives, defining the target audience, developing effective messages and following up with careful implementation and evaluation.

Sales promotion

The amount spent by companies on sales promotion now exceeds that spent on advertising and it is growing faster. Whereas advertising and direct response marketing give customers a rational or emotional argument for purchase, sales promotion gives an economic incentive in the form of price reductions, free goods or the chance to win prizes. Sales promotions are of three main types: consumer promotions, trade promotions and salesforce promotions (Table 9.4). Each is geared to trigger actions from one target group.

Why have sales promotions generally taken over from advertising as the primary method of persuasion? The first reason is the short-term pressures that managers are under to maintain or increase performance. Generally, sales promotions produce results quickly. Brand advertising can take months or even years for its full effects to appear. Second, there is a feeling in some circles that advertising effectiveness is declining, in part due to the sheer number of messages that customers receive daily. In addition, unlike advertising, sales promotions are normally a variable rather than a fixed cost. If the incentives do not trigger extra purchases, the costs of the promotion are not incurred. In many mature markets, customers also know that most brands will be satisfactory. In these cases, they become deal-prone: looking to buy brands which offer special incentives. Finally, the increasing power of the retailer has pressured

Table 9.4 ■ Types of sales promotion

Consumer promotions	Trade promotions	Salesforce promotions
Price reductions	Dealer loaders	Bonuses
Coupons	Loyalty bonuses	Commissions
Vouchers	Sale or return	Coupons
Competitions	Range bonuses	Free gifts
Free goods	Credit	Competitions
Premium offers	Delayed invoicing	Vouchers
Trade-in offers	New product offers	Free services
Stamps	Competitions	Points
Guarantees	Trade-in offers	Money equivalents
Events	Free services	
Displays	Training	
	Reciprocal buying	

manufacturers to offer more and more inducements to obtain distribution and trade push. In the UK, for example, ten retailers now account for 50 per cent of the £70 billion total grocery market, and four account for over one-third of it. Similar concentration ratios occur in many western European markets.

Trade promotions

Promotions undertaken by manufacturers to incentivize retailers and wholesalers exceed the amount spent on consumer promotions. Manufacturers provide the trade with special deals to achieve one or more of the following objectives:

■ *To persuade outlets to stock the brand.* Especially for new products, but increasingly for existing brands, retailers and wholesalers use their negotiating power to demand extra rebates, allowances, free goods and extended credit terms.

■ *To persuade outlets to push the product.* Manufacturers often want the outlet to give their brands more shelf space, to participate in consumer promotions and generally to put additional effort behind the brands. Professional trade buyers invariably expect to be paid extra for pushing the product.

■ *To compensate for price increases.* Manufacturers will often give special allowances to compensate the trade for temporary sales reductions which occur when the price of a brand is raised.

The characteristics of trade promotion are contrasted in Table 9.5. Marketing and brand management are generally hostile to trade promotions, seeing them as 'wasted' money. This fear is often a source of considerable friction with the company's salesforce, who have to deal with the trade. The salesforce believe that trade promotions are essential to gain retail support and that without imaginative deals they will lose share to competitors.

Table 9.5 ■ Comparing three promotional tools

Advertising	Consumer promotion	Trade promotion
Franchise building	←——————————→	Non-franchise building
Brand benefit emphasis	←——————————→	Price emphasis
Higher marketer control	←——————————→	Low marketer control
End consumer is primary target	←——————————→	Trade is primary target
Pull strategy	←——————————→	Push strategy
Long-term impact	←——————————→	Short-term impact
Fixed cost	←——————————→	Variable cost

Source: adapted from John A. Quelch, Teaching Note for 'Chesebrough-Pond's: Vaseline Petroleum Jelly', Boston, MA: Harvard Business School

In contrast, the marketers see the growth of expenditure on trade promotion as reflecting the naked use of buying power by dominant retail chains. They see trade promotions sucking cash out of advertising and consumer promotions to the long-term detriment of the brand franchise. This they see as producing a vicious circle of weakening brands, leading to greater retail power over the distribution chain, resulting in turn in lower manufacturer margins. It is estimated already that the cost of trade promotions to grocery manufacturers is double what they currently report in profits.

Second, marketing managers believe that price-based trade promotions do not create any loyalty. Once the promotion is finished, retailers will regress back to their previous purchasing patterns. Worse, retailers often time their buying to take advantage of manufacturers' promotions – stocking up when a deal is on, and cutting back when there is no deal being offered. This results in a greater than anticipated cut in the suppliers' margins. A short-term boost in sales is more than offset by a subsequent drop when the product is back at full margin. A final problem is the lack of manufacturer control over the results of the trade promotion. Retailers often fail to push the product in the way the manufacturer expected when the promotion deal was agreed. Generally the manufacturer cannot monitor the retailer's behaviour or enforce its wishes.

But while these criticisms are often justified, marketers have to recognize the realities of today's marketing environment. Competitive conditions have changed. The large, modern retailing group adds value for customers and the manufacturer has to meet the economic expectations of such businesses. Increasingly, customers are more loyal to their retailer than they are to the brands of manufacturers. The manufacturer has to meet the needs of both the customer and the retailer. Trade promotions will remain an essential part of the negotiating process.

Consumer promotions

Manufacturers use consumer promotions such as samples, coupons, stamps and price-off deals to incentivize consumers. Consumer promotions can increase sales in one or more of the following ways:

■ *Attracting new customers to try the brand*. There are three types of new trier: those previously not buying the product class, those buying other brands exclusively, and those switching among a variety of brands. Promotions can be targeted to each type of new trier.

■ *Increasing the loyalty of existing customers*. Promotions are often used to try to increase the loyalty of current customers. For example, a promotion might offer a gift in return for ten proofs of purchase of a brand.

■ *Inducing customers to use more of the product*. This might be done by promoting new uses of the product or encouraging customers to use it more frequently.

Again, traditional marketers are sceptical about the value of consumer promotions. First, they point out, frequent promotions can cheapen the image of the brand. Second, promotions normally attract frequent brand switchers who only look for low prices or good deals. Such customers are unlikely to stick to the brand once the promotion finishes. In general the evidence supports this view: promotions do bring immediate sales gains, but unlike advertising they do not build long-term consumer loyalty. Promotions usually produce only temporary blips from the underlying trend of sales.

However, the case against consumer promotions can be too one-sided. First, there is a defensive argument: if all the competitors are using promotions, it is difficult to stand aside without losing market share. Second, consumer promotions can be an important tool for a market challenger seeking to shake habitual buying patterns in low-involvement markets. Free samples and special offers can force buyers to break from their routine buying patterns, giving the challenger the chance to demonstrate the advantage of its brand.

Promotional planning

As with all elements of the marketing mix, sales promotions have to be carefully planned and co-ordinated. The manufacturer has to be clear about the objectives. Is the aim to obtain trial or enhance loyalty? The size of the incentive has to be decided. Some promotions cost much more than others. For example, a consumer promotion offering 20 per cent off the regular retail price can easily involve selling the product at a net loss. On the other hand, a 'self-liquidating offer', where the customer sends money and a coupon for a promotional item, can cost the manufacturer nothing at all. Other decisions concern the duration of the promotion, its timing and implementation. Again, it is a good idea to pre-test the sales promotions to assess their effectiveness.

Public relations

Public relations can be defined as those activities that the organization undertakes to communicate to its publics which are not paid for directly. Most medium and larger organizations will have a public relations department in their head office. The biggest companies also typically retain a specialist independent public relations firm to handle the most difficult and important assignments.

The publics that the firm may seek to communicate to can include customers, the trade, shareholders, government bodies, local communities and employees. The major activities undertaken in public relations are as follows:

■ *Achieving positive coverage in the media.* A major task is proactively getting newspapers, journals and television to carry positive and persuasive stories about the company, its people or its products.

■ *Creating and reinforcing the corporate image.* The company's publications, including annual reports, brochures, stationery, business forms and uniforms, should be designed to communicate a visual identity that the public immediately recognizes and feels good about.

■ *Sponsoring special events.* Organizations can draw attention to their products and activities by presenting events which attract target publics. These include news conferences for journalists, exhibitions, competitions and the sponsorship of sports events or activities in the arts.

■ *Lobbying politicians and officials.* Major organizations seek to inform and influence those responsible for framing legislation which may affect the success of the company and its products. Companies and their trade associations make sure that key people are fully informed about the advantages of their products or activities, and are aware of the implications of unfavourable legislation.

■ *Advising management about key public issues.* Operating managers are often not sufficiently sensitive to the opportunities presented by effective PR. The PR office needs to encourage managers to publicize their most valuable activities. They also need to be made aware of the consequences of negative public reaction to their work.

While much PR is aimed at the City and the government, it should be seen as potentially a highly effective marketing tool. Companies such as Marks & Spencer, Virgin and Body Shop have used PR as a cheaper and more effective option than advertising. PR can contribute to the following marketing tasks:

■ *Creating product awareness and interest.* New stories fed to the press and television are highly effective in communicating the firm's activities.

■ *Launching new products.* The media are always looking for new stories that might be of interest to their audience.

■ *Influencing specific target market segments.* PR can be highly effective for demonstrating the value of the firm to the local community or to minority groups, for example, as a source of employment or prestige.

■ *Coping with crises.* Well-planned PR can be crucial for dealing with the occasional potential disasters which occur. Perrier used PR to reassure customers after the product had to be withdrawn on a world scale in 1991 following a contamination scare.

■ *Enhancing corporate image.* Anita Roddick created a unique international image for her Body Shop chain through her speeches, autobiography and interviews with the media.

The main advantage of PR is its effectiveness as a communications vehicle. Positive stories about the company or products which appear in the media are seen as independent and consequently a more reliable source than advertisements. If it is a prestigious medium such as the *Financial Times* or the BBC, additional credibility is attached to the information. Achieving the same type of impact through advertising would be enormously expensive, if indeed it were possible at all. Yet PR achieves this exposure for a minimal investment.

Developing a PR strategy is analogous to other communications vehicles. First, management have to decide what the PR objectives are. Second, the target market has to be clear. Is it trying to communicate to shareholders or customers for example? Third, what is the message that the company is trying to put over? For example, is it trying to position itself as a caring, environmentally friendly company, or one at the front end of a dynamic technology? Fourth, what are the best media to seek to utilize? It is easy to get information into the local press, but is this worthwhile? Will leading decision-makers read the *Wigan Weekly News*? In contrast, a report in the *Financial Times* can have an enormous impact on top management in the City. Fifth, how is the programme going to be implemented? Who is going to get the stories placed and the events organized? How and when will it be done? Finally, the activities of the PR department and the investment in agencies and events have to be evaluated.

There are three ways to evaluate the effects of PR. The easiest and the crudest is to count the amount of coverage achieved in the media. How many stories appeared in the media, and how many column inches were achieved? Such a count is better than nothing. The problems are that it does not allow for the varying quality of the media and the value of the message communicated. A second approach is to research the communications effects. What were the changes in awareness or attitudes that occurred as a result of the campaign? How many of these changes can reasonably be attributed to the PR? Finally, sales and profits are the most useful indices of effectiveness. But, as with advertising, it is very difficult to disentangle the effects of PR from the variety of other factors affecting business performance.

Companies that are really effective at PR know that it is a long-term process. To get the ear of the top journalists and political influencers, a relationship has to be developed based on mutual interest. The company's PR representatives should be known as credible and attractive sources of information. Such a relationship takes time to be built. Without this investment, press releases or invitations to media events tend to fall on deaf ears. Also the media, as a whole, prefer to talk to operating managers rather than PR agencies. In general, they want to talk to the people responsible for the news, not just those people paid to convey it. Consequently, it is a good investment to train executives in the techniques of handling media briefings and interviews.

Determining the communications mix

The manager has to allocate his or her budget among direct selling, advertising, direct marketing, sales promotion and PR. What factors should determine the mix? In principle, the answer is to switch expenditure between the categories to equalize the marginal returns on the investments. In practice, measuring such marginal returns is a pretty impossible task, so commonsense rules-of-thumb have to be applied.

The promotional mix varies even between firms in the same industry. Unilever, for example, has spent relatively more on promotions; Procter & Gamble more on advertising. The mix has changed over time, with movements in the costs and effectiveness of different media. In many industries, for example, the size of salesforces has declined due to their relative cost, whereas promotion and PR have increased. But these alternative vehicles are normally complements rather than substitutes. Today, companies operate in complex environments. They have to appeal to more than one target market (e.g. both customers and the trade), with multiple messages and multiple media. Each of the communications elements has a different but complementary role to play.

The weight that any vehicle receives depends upon a number of factors, including the following:

■ *The company's objectives and resources*. If the company's objective is to increase awareness in the mass market, then advertising is the obvious medium. On the other hand, if it wants an immediate boost to sales, promotion is relatively attractive. Resources available also influence the choice. Television is very expensive; PR can be quite cheap.

■ *Characteristics of the target market*. If the target market consists of hundreds of customers, direct selling will be an attractive vehicle. If the market consists of millions, then mass media will be more efficient.

■ *Type of product and market*. In general, personal selling is the most effective vehicle for products which are expensive, complex and high risk, and for markets with few, large buyers. For products which are cheaper and routine and where emotions play an important role in the choice process, and for large markets, advertising and sales promotion are more important.

■ *Push versus pull strategy*. A major factor affecting the choice is whether the manufacturer is pursuing a push or a pull strategy (Figure 9.11). A pull strategy focuses promotional activities (mainly advertising and consumer promotion) at the end customers with the aim of getting them to induce the retailer or other intermediary to stock the product. Advertising and promotion encourage customers to pull the product through the distribution chain by creating the demand. A push strategy directs promotion (mainly salesforce and trade promotions) at retailers and the trade with the aim of incentivizing them to carry the product and in turn promote it to consumers.

■ *Stage of market evolution*. At the early stage of the market, advertising and public relations are usually the most appropriate tools to build awareness of the new product. In the mature phase, sales promotion and personal selling become relatively more important. In the decline stage, advertising, PR and direct selling are cut back as there is little to say about the product. Then sales promotion becomes more important for stimulating the trade and customers.

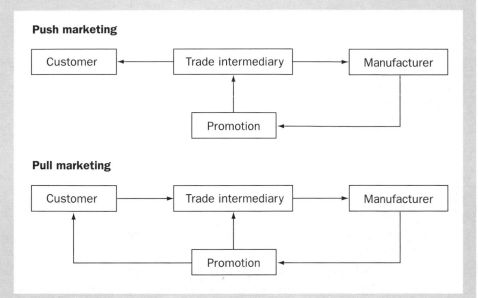

Figure 9.11 ■ Push versus pull marketing

Summary

The choices that buyers make are a function of three stimuli. First, their broad social environment – their culture, personalities and social and economic situation – has the most important influence on what they buy. Second are the offers made by competing organizations: the relative quality of the products, the prices charged, the services which augment the offers, and the style and efficiency of their distribution support. Third are the messages that the organization transmits to its target markets.

The role of this communication is to inform the market about the company's offer, to persuade customers about its advantages and to reinforce the decisions of existing customers. Lastly, in certain situations, the communications can be the point of difference between the offers. How effective communications are depends upon how well they conform to the social milieu of customers and how well they are supported by an attractive marketing mix.

There is a large and growing number of communications vehicles that organizations can employ. The primary instruments – advertising, direct response, sales promotion, public relations and direct selling – are not competitive but complementary. Each has different strengths, can be oriented to different audiences and presents different messages. With the changes in the market environment, the importance of these vehicles has changed. For example, trade promotions have become much more important, mass media advertising less. With the dramatic evolution of technology and media, further significant changes can be expected in the communications mix.

Planning is essential for the communications mix as a whole and for each of the major components. Planning means setting clear objectives, defining the target audiences, developing effective messages and following through by careful implementation and evaluation.

Questions

1. If you have a good product, why do you need to spend money on advertising and promotion?

2. Why is it difficult to predict the effects of advertising on sales and profits?

3. Referring to Figure 9.6, find advertisements in newspapers and magazines which match each of the six types of buying decision described there.

4. A university is proposing to set up a major fund-raising campaign to raise £10 million. Outline a communications plan to achieve this objective.

5. A book club is proposing a direct mail campaign to recruit members. The price of membership is £40 a year, which entitles the member to five free books. The club estimates that a membership generates an annual contribution of 25 per cent. The cost of direct mail is estimated to be £100,000. What would you set as objectives for the campaign? What response would you regard as sufficient to evaluate it as a success?

6. What PR does your organization undertake? What are its objectives? How effectively is it planned and evaluated?

Notes

1. For many examples of how advertising agencies develop such images, see the annual papers published for the Institute of Practitioners in Advertising Effectiveness Awards: for example, Gary Duckworth (ed.), *Advertising Works* (London: NTC Publications, 1997).

2. Stuart Henderson Britt, Stephen C. Adams and Alan S. Miller, 'How many advertising exposures per day?', *Journal of Advertising Research*, December 1972, pp. 3–10.

3. For example, Russel H. Colley, *Defining Advertising Goals for Measured Advertising Results* (New York: Association of National Advertisers, 1961).

4. A comprehensive presentation of buyer behaviour is Leon Schiffman and Leslie L. Kanuk, *Consumer Behaviour* (Englewood Cliffs, NJ: Prentice Hall, 1997).

5. This section draws on an excellent advertising text: Judith Corstjens, *Strategic Advertising: A practitioner's handbook* (Oxford: Heinemann, 1990), pp. 57–107.

6. For an interesting review of this topic, see Fleming Hansen, 'Towards an alternative theory of the advertising communication process', *International Journal of Research in Marketing*, January 1984, pp. 69–80.

7. Dieter Steinbrecher, 'The ten commandments of good advertising' (Basle, Switzerland: Ciba-Geigy Marketing Development), mimeo.

8. For comprehensive accounts of these techniques, see Gary L. Lilien, Philip Kotler and K. S. Moorthy, *Marketing Models* (Englewood Cliffs, NJ: Prentice Hall, 1992); Philippe Naert and Peter Leeflang, *Building Implementable Marketing Models* (Leiden: Martinus Nijhoff, 1978).

9. For an example, see Naaras V. Eechambadi, 'Does advertising work?', *McKinsey Quarterly*, Autumn 1994, pp. 117–29.

10. Louis K. Geller, *Response: The complete guide to direct marketing* (New York: Free Press, 1996); John Wilmshurst, *Below-the-Line Promotion* (London: Butterworth-Heinemann, 1993).

11. Jeremy Swinfen-Green, 'Why interactive marketing is here to stay', *Admap*, January 1996, pp. 28–31; John Hagel and Arthur G. Armstrong, *Netgain: Expanding markets through virtual communities* (Boston, MA: Harvard Business School, 1997).

Chapter 10

Managing personal selling

Personal selling is the marketing function dealing with customers on a direct or face-to-face basis. It is similar to advertising, promotion and other forms of publicity, in that it serves as a communication bridge between the organization and the target audience. However, personal selling is particularly effective because it permits a direct two-way communication between buyer and seller. This gives the organization a much greater opportunity to investigate the needs of the buyer and a greater flexibility in adjusting its offer and presentation to meet these needs.

While personal selling is highly effective, employing sales people is expensive. The average cost of maintaining (including relevant overheads) a salesperson in the field was £45,000 in the UK in 1997. In the USA, the average cost of a direct sales representative was estimated at $330 per hour.[1] Direct selling is the largest element of the communications mix. All the figures underestimate the resources going into face-to-face selling. In the modern organization, many managers in technical, marketing and general management functions spend a high proportion of their time selling. The top salesperson is the chief executive, who should be allocating a high proportion of his or her time to maintaining key customer relationships. As Robert Louis Stevenson accurately observed, 'Everybody lives by selling something.'

This chapter explores the management of sales. It begins with an analysis of sales objectives and strategy. It then reviews how to determine the size and organization of the salesforce, and how to recruit, motivate and evaluate performance.

The review focuses on the changing role of the salesforce today. Three forces are shifting the nature of selling and sales management. First, many companies have been steadily reducing the size of their full-time salesforces. One reason is the increasing concentration of buyers. For example, major food manufacturers are predicting that by the year 2000, there will be only ten major multiple grocery outlets controlling most of the retail supermarkets in Europe. It has been predicted that eventually there will be only five car manufacturers in the world. The second reason is the sheer expense of employing full-time sales people. Huge salesforces now remain in only a couple of industries where the profit margins are exceptionally high (e.g. ethical pharmaceuticals). Finally, more companies are buying in specialist sales companies.

This allows them to reduce fixed costs and to access specialist skills and industry knowledge.

A second change is the move towards relationship management. Traditionally, selling has been about identifying prospects, making persuasive presentations and closing the deal. It has been transaction oriented. Today, however, both buyers and sellers are increasingly wanting to build long-term relationships and to move away from the series of one-off sales transactions. For buyers the move towards total quality management (TQM) leads to a desire to reduce the number of suppliers and to build a team-like relationship with specific companies who become fully involved in development and operations. For the seller, creating a long-term relationship offers the opportunity to bind in the buyer, to erect barriers to competitive entry, and to reduce the pressure on prices and margins.

A third shift is in the salesperson's skill requirement. In the past, his or her dominant task was to deliver volume. But today companies find that such a volume focus can erode profitability and detract from the development of long-term relationships. Sales people now need broader marketing and business skills to understand customer needs and build long-term value-added partnerships with the client. This has important implications for the selection, training, motivation and compensation of sales people.

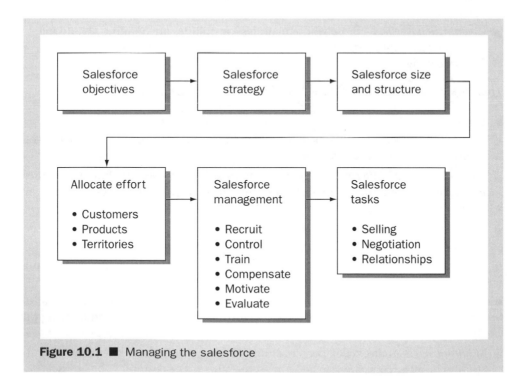

Figure 10.1 ■ Managing the salesforce

Salesforce objectives

The major issues in salesforce management are shown in Figure 10.1. Planning starts with determining objectives – what do management want the sales people to achieve? There is no single answer to this question, since there are many different types of salesperson depending upon the industry and the strategy of the company. Montcrief, after analyzing the jobs of nearly 1,400 sales people in 51 organizations, devised a five-category classification of sales people.[2] In order of increasing creativity these were as follows:

- *Order takers* – those whose primary responsibility is responding to customer orders, resupplying them and handling their problems (e.g. shop assistants).
- *Customer servicers* – those whose main tasks are increasing business from present customers by providing them with personal assistance (e.g. stocking shelves and maintaining inventory).
- *Missionaries* – those whose primary tasks are increasing business by providing customers with new information and advice (e.g. medical representatives).
- *New business sales people* – those whose primary responsibilities are winning new business by identifying prospects, preparing bids and assessing the creditworthiness of clients.
- *Organizational sellers* – those whose main responsibilities are building up and maintaining relationships with major customers. This is the most complex and creative form of selling.

There are seven potential tasks which a salesperson has to be trained to undertake:

- *Find new customers*. Sales people have to find and gain new business.
- *Provide information*. Sales people need to communicate information about what the company can provide to customers.
- *Sell and negotiate*. They need to know how to sell and negotiate: how to identify prospects, make persuasive presentations, handle objections, close deals and follow up on sales.
- *Service*. Sales people are responsible for seeing that customers are properly serviced in terms of delivery, financial support, technical assistance and problem solving.
- *Market research*. Sales people are important sources of information about changing customer requirements and competitive activities.
- *Management*. The professional salesperson is responsible for managing and allocating his or her time efficiently between customers and products, and drawing on the resources and personnel of the company to achieve the sales objectives.
- *Maintain relationships*. Sales people should aim to bond in the client by demonstrating how the company can add long-term value to the customer's business.

The job of sales management is to determine what priority and time should be given to each of these various tasks. Management then have to devise strategies and sales organizations which are capable of achieving these objectives. They are also responsible for recruiting and training sales people able to undertake these tasks and for devising compensation, motivation and control procedures to follow through on their achievement.

Salesforce strategy

The ultimate objective of sales management is to contribute to achieving the company's objectives of growth and profitability through meeting the needs of customers. Today's top managers see this as best accomplished by creating a *strategic partnership* with the client. Where such partnerships are created, the business escapes from the continual series of competitive bids against other suppliers which erode margins and increase uncertainty. Creating a stable partnership has other advantages for the supplier. Customers are a major source of ideas. Von Hippel, for example, studying industrial innovations, found that 67 per cent of 'minor improvements', 85 per cent of 'major improvements' and nearly all significant innovations were generated by ideas from customers.[3] The pattern is similar in consumer goods, where the major retailers increasingly provide the innovatory ideas for manufacturers. Clearly, suppliers that work closest with the customer are most likely to be the recipient of these benefits.

To see the opportunities for strategic partnerships, the supplier has to understand the viewpoint of the customer. A good example of a modern purchasing operation is that of the German industrial giant, Siemens. Siemens has sales of $50 billion and 120,000 suppliers worldwide, of which 20,000 are designated 'first-choice suppliers'. To determine the relationship it seeks, Siemens classifies all suppliers on two criteria: degree of differentiation and impact on profitability. Differentiation is measured by the technical complexity of the product or service and the difficulty Siemens would have in finding a replacement supplier. In marketing technology, this is the degree to which a supplier has a sustainable differential advantage. The profitability impact is measured by the relative amount the Siemen's business unit spends with the supplier. The larger the amount spent, the greater is the value of negotiating a 1 per cent price cut. This leads to a purchasing matrix which classifies supplier relationships into four types (Figure 10.2):

■ *Strategic partnership*. This is the ideal position for a supplier. Here the customer desires an intense, long-term co-operative relationship and a joint effort to build the business. Outside suppliers are effectively excluded from competing.

■ *Preferred supplier*. Here the customer again wants a long-term relationship with the supplier. While the amount spent is not great, the product or service is critical to the buyer. Specialist tools or software are examples.

■ *Regular supplier*. These are small-volume, routine purchases. Generally a customer will want to reduce the number of suppliers, and streamline and simplify the ordering process. Price will be important to customers, but because they are small items, they will not be prioritized by buyers.

■ *Commodity suppliers*. Suppliers of these high-volume standard products are the most vulnerable. A small price cut would have a big impact on the customer's profitability. Purchasing staff will have a major incentive to push down prices and encourage alternative suppliers.

Note that a supplier may be in different positions with different customers. For example, a printing ink manufacturer was a 'commodity supplier' to customers in the packaging industry and a 'regular supplier' to companies producing compact discs. The same product sold at £7 per kilo to the packaging industry, where the ink was a significant cost and where margins were tight. For customers producing compact discs, where the ink was a small cost component and where gross margins were high, the supplier was able to charge £40 per kilo.

What are the implications of the purchasing relationship matrix to the supplier? Clearly the task of the sales team is to strengthen its position, were possible, on these two dimensions, thus making itself more important to the customer.

Profit impact dimension

A supplier's position on the profitability impact factor can be increased by seeking to meet more of the needs of the customer. This may mean broadening its product range or forging alliances with companies producing complementary products or services. It should be noted, however, that this strategy can be dangerous if a company is not able

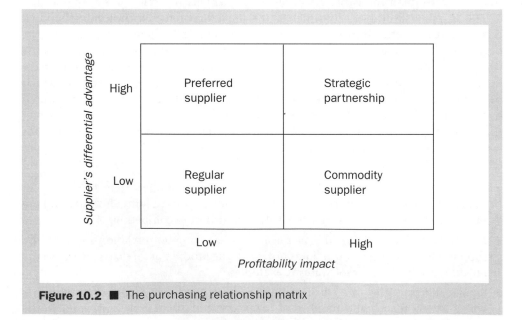

Figure 10.2 ■ The purchasing relationship matrix

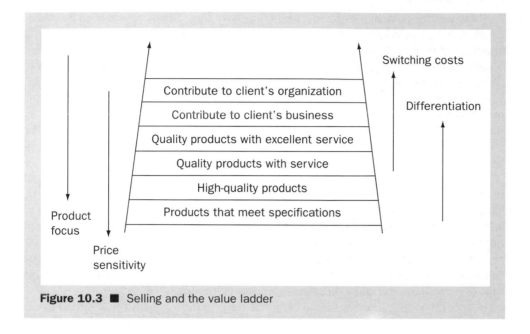

Figure 10.3 ■ Selling and the value ladder

to create a differential advantage. A major commodity supplier is a tempting target for an aggressive purchasing staff.

Differential advantage dimension

Seeking to create a differential advantage is always a good strategy. Today, however, it is getting increasingly challenging to do this. This is illustrated by the concept of the value ladder in Figure 10.3. The first step on the value ladder is to offer a product that meets the customer's specifications. The problem today is that many companies can do this or, if it is an innovation, they can soon copy it. With this type of product focus, competition is fierce, price sensitivity is high and it is easy for the customer to switch to alternative suppliers. A supplier has therefore to seek to move up the value ladder. Normally this means adding superior quality and then higher-quality service and support. Again, however, today's competitors are fast to follow these product and service enhancements. A company can *establish* a differential advantage with good products and good services, but it is hard to maintain it.

To *maintain* a differential advantage, the seller has to make a quantum leap to the fifth and sixth steps on the value ladder, which establish a strategic partnership with the client. The fifth level is reached when the supplier is regarded as someone who can contribute to the client's business by helping it identify new market opportunities, to lower its costs or to improve its productivity. The final step is where the supplier becomes a partner which the client can call on for advice and consultancy on its broad organizational problems, such as its strategic direction, organizational culture, structure or systems.

For example, the design company Wolf Olins is usually initially approached by clients (such as British Airways, Shell and ICI) wanting an update of their corporate logo and visual identity. But Olins' sales people avoid offering such simple 'products', which are usually easily emulated by competitors. Instead they persuade clients to employ them to do a comprehensive review of how the company communicates to its publics. Subsequently, they advise the company on its corporate mission, organizational structure, marketing and employee relations, as well as its visual communications. By moving up the value ladder, Olins makes a quantum leap in the potential contribution it makes to the effectiveness of the client's business and organization. This differentiates it from competition and shifts the relationship away from comparisons of price and product features.

There is a fundamental distinction between the bottom four rungs of the ladder and the top two. To be good at the former, the salesperson or account executive has to be expert in *his or her business* – he or she needs to have a first-class product and service to sell. The salesperson's company needs to be expert in producing and supporting top-quality products. But with the top rungs the supplier needs to be expert in *their business*. The company needs to understand the client's business and its value chain. The supplier is a consultant rather than a salesperson. Clearly the skill requirements for this type of consultancy are quite different from normal product and sales training.

In general, selling strategy should be about shifting from a focus on closing transactions involving price and product comparisons, to one of bonding a relationship based upon mutual advantage. Box 10.1 suggests some ways of creating such bonding relationships. Achieving these partnerships depends upon customers perceiving the supplier's sales people as experts in the customer's business and the technologies relevant to it. They will listen to sales people who have expert knowledge about the marketing, organizational and technological problems they face. If the customer perceives that it has more expertise than the supplier, the customer will set the product and service specifications and transform buying into a transaction based upon the lowest price.

 Structure and size

Determining the structure of the salesforce

The objectives and strategy of the business will influence the structure and size of the salesforce. If the company is selling a single product line to one end-user industry with customers spread throughout the country, a geographically structured salesforce may be appropriate. If it is selling many products to different types of end-user markets, a product or market salesforce structure may be better. If it depends upon a handful of major buyers, an account management structure is likely to be superior.

Geographically structured salesforce

The simplest structure is to assign each salesperson an exclusive territory where he or she sells the company's entire product line. This has three advantages. First, the sales

BOX 10.1

Bonding and the buy–sell relationship

Joint venture projects
- assigning staff to the customer
- creating joint project teams
- involving the customer in joint business ventures
- pooling research and development facilities
- working with the customer in market research
- a shared customer database

Building exit barriers
- making the customer dependent on technical support
- loaning equipment
- signing long-term contracts
- giving financial support
- creating inter-company trading
- incorporating unique component design and tooling
- moving into shared premises

Creating entry barriers
- electronic links
- joint innovation teams
- superior products and applications
- network of relationships
- joint long-term planning
- pricing based on overall business

Developing trust
- high frequency of contact
- giving warning of future problems
- open communication
- involving top management
- ensuring promises are kept
- social activities and entertainment
- sharing of mutual problems

Source: Adapted from Ken Burnett, *Strategic Customer Alliances* (London: Pitman, 1992), pp. 54–5

representative has clear responsibility and accountability. Second, the salesperson's performance can be judged by comparing his or her results with those of other sales people in other territories. Third, travelling costs are minimized as the salesperson has a relatively small geographical area.

In designing territories, management will normally want to make them of equal size so that equity exists among sales people. Unfortunately, there is generally a conflict between equalizing size in terms of workload and equalizing it in terms of sales potential. Generally, some areas of the country have little potential while others, where industry or population are concentrated, have enormous opportunities.

If the territories are structured to *equalize workload*, sales people in sparsely populated areas will have fewer opportunities than those in the better areas. If sales people are paid a commission, such a structure would be particularly unfair. If, on the other hand, the territories are structured to *equalize potential*, then the problem becomes that sales people in territories where many customers are concentrated in a small area can achieve sales much more easily and quickly than those in large, thinly populated territories. In general, companies often seek a rough balance between the two criteria. Alternatively, they may pay somewhat lower commissions in areas of high potential, or decide to place the better or more senior sales people in the more attractive territories.

Product-structured salesforce

A geographically structured salesforce runs into problems when the products are diverse and highly technical. Sales people may then lack the knowledge to sell to sophisticated buyers. One solution often adopted is divisionalizing the company along product lines, with each having separate specialist salesforces. While this makes for a more technically equipped team, it can have the disadvantage of a customer being called on two or more times by different sales people from the same company. It also involves extra costs, with several representatives travelling over the same routes and spending time waiting for the same buyers.

Market-structured salesforce

The trend in many advanced companies today is to structure sales teams around market segments. For example, a construction materials company, rather than focusing its salesforce around concrete, aggregates, sealant products, etc., will organize them into teams focusing on different types of customer, such as residential construction companies, roads, water and utilities. The logic of this approach is that developing a partnership with a customer and selling value requires that sales people are able to be problem solvers. To do this, sales people need to be experts on the marketing and technical problems that customers face.

Even in low-technology businesses, detailed customer knowledge is crucial. As noted earlier, customers in different segments normally pay quite different prices even for a commodity product. This is due to differences in price sensitivity and buying power. However, unless selling and information are oriented around customer segments, these differences are often missed. This is illustrated in Table 10.1. An industrial chemicals company sells grouts and anchors (used to control shrinkage and stability in cement) to the construction industry at an average price per ton of almost £56. However, as shown, there are substantial price differences between segments. If the sales team can utilize their specialist knowledge to negotiate even marginally higher prices, the results are enormous in these typically low-margin businesses. For

Table 10.1 ■ Capitalizing on differences in price sensitivity across market segments

Segment	Tons (000)	Price (£/ton)	Sales (£000)	Contribution £/ton	Contribution Total	Additional contribution (£000) from price increases of: 1%	2%	5%
Construction	300	45	13,500	7	2,100	135	270	675
Residential	450	50	22,500	12	5,400	225	450	1,125
Industrial	75	84	6,300	42	3,150	63	126	315
Water	43	96	4,128	52	2,236	41	82	206
Transport	127	60	7,380	20	2,460	74	148	369
Power	27	105	2,835	60	1,620	28	56	142
Total	1,022	55.4	56,643		16,966	566	1,132	2,830
			Overheads		14,702			
			Profit		2,264	2,830	3,396	5,094
			Profit improvement (%)			+25	+50	+125
	Profit improvement if 50% sold at premium (%)					+12.5	+25	+62.5

example, a 1 per cent price increase could raise total profits by 25 per cent. A 5 per cent increase would more than double profits. Even if only half the customers could be upgraded, the results would still be very high. Achieving such value enhancements, however, requires a salesforce with detailed knowledge of which customers are the least price sensitive, which are likely to remain loyal, who the key buying influences are and which companies could benefit from more marketing and technical support.

Of course, market- or customer-structured salesforces necessarily involve trade-offs in product expertise and additional costs. But many companies believe that accepting such disadvantages is worthwhile in the light of the increased sales and revenues that can be generated.

Account management structure

One step further than a market-structured salesforce is organizing sales people around individual customers. This further enhances a salesperson's capacity to sell higher up the value ladder. Again such structures have become common for several reasons. One is the increasing concentration in many industries. Today many companies – perhaps most – have 50 per cent of their business coming from just 5 per cent of their customers. This is true for all sectors – industrial, consumer and service companies. A second reason is the increased centralization of buying decisions. Many organizations have shifted from decentralized buying by SBU to centralized buying which utilizes more effectively the company's buying power. A third factor is the increasing complexity of buying–selling relationships. The more functions and people are involved, the greater the co-ordination that becomes necessary. As a result, many organizations have created account managers who lead the sales relationship with a specific customer and make sure these key relationships are maintained and enhanced.[4]

This structure is discussed further later.

Hybrid structure

In practice, many companies find it effective to adopt a combination of two or more structures. A company like Unilever will have one salesforce for its household and detergent products, another for food and drinks, and another for personal care products. Representatives within each product group have individual sales territories. Alongside the geographically based representatives are national account managers who sell to the big central buying groups such as Sainsbury and Carrefour. In these complex structures, managers seek to achieve the required combination of product expertise, geographical cover and customer specialization.

Determining the size of the salesforce

How many sales people does an organization need? The answer depends upon two factors. First, it depends upon the strategic judgement of management about the relative effectiveness of direct sales as against other ways of communicating and selling, such as advertising, telesales and direct mail. Sales people are very expensive and it may be more efficient to replace direct selling by telesales for small, low-value accounts. Second, it depends upon estimating how sales and profits will respond to additional sales people.

In practice, companies approaching this problem use one of three approaches.

Workload approach

The most common method is to decide the number of sales people from an estimate of the total selling time needed to do the job. It involves the following steps:

1. Group customers by type of account (e.g. size, type of end user, potential).
2. Determine call frequencies for each type of account, i.e. how many calls a year each type of customer should receive.
3. Calculate the total workload by multiplying the number of accounts by the target call frequencies.
4. Estimate the average number of calls a year that a salesperson can make.
5. The size of the salesforce is then the total workload divided by the average call rate.

For example, if a company has 200 type A (high potential) accounts, 300 type B and 500 type C (low potential), and the target call rates are 26, 12 and 6 calls per year, then the total workload is 11,800 calls. If an average salesperson can make 600 calls a year, then the company needs 20 sales people.

While the workload approach is simple to operate, it does not necessarily lead to a particularly good solution. The call frequency rates are often chosen quite arbitrarily. Management need to evaluate what would be the effect on sales and profits of higher or lower call rates. Similarly, they need to explore other methods such as direct mail or telesales for dealing with small accounts.

Sales potential method

A more scientific approach is to seek to forecast how sales would respond to an increasing number of sales people. One method was suggested by Semlow, who noticed the obvious point that the bigger the territory a sales person has, the more difficult it is to achieve intensive coverage. In the company he analyzed, a salesperson with a territory consisting of 1 per cent of national potential achieved $160,000 sales; one in a territory with 5 per cent of the total potential obtained sales of $200,000, or the equivalent of only $40,000 for every 1 per cent of potential.[5]

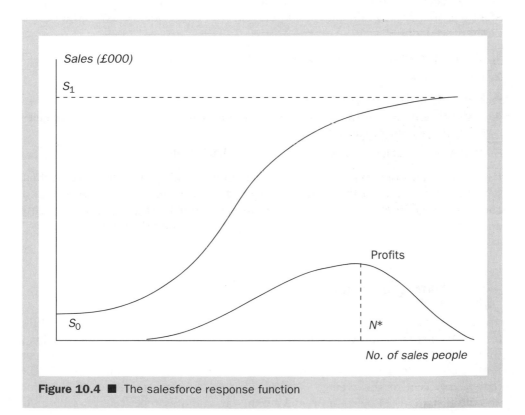

Figure 10.4 ■ The salesforce response function

Using the above results, if a company employed 100 sales people and gave them territories of equal sales potential (1 per cent each), then total sales should be $16 million (i.e. 100 × $160,000 sales per 1 per cent of potential). If it employed only 20 sales people, each would have to have 5 per cent of the potential, and sales should be $4 million (i.e. 100 × $40,000). By such reasoning a sales response curve like Figure 10.4 can be estimated. Semlow then used information on profit contribution margins and the costs of employing sales people to estimate the salesforce size which maximized profitability.

This is an interesting approach, but its application is fairly limited. First, it requires a sufficiently large number of sales territories to estimate the response curve statistically. Second, it assumes that it is desirable to create territories of equal sales potential. Finally, it assumes that sales productivity is a function only of territory potential and is unaffected by the mix of accounts in an area, local competition and other factors.

Expert estimation

In recent years, another approach to estimating the response curve illustrated in Figure 10.4 has been developed. This involves using the expert judgements of managers. Managers are asked to estimate sales levels that would be obtained as a result of five different scenarios:

1. No sales people employed (this gives an estimate of S_O in Figure 10.4).

2. Half the current salesforce.

3. Maintaining the current salesforce.

4. A 50 per cent increase in the size of the salesforce (this together with 2 above gives an estimate of the shape of the curve).

5. A salesforce sufficient to saturate the area completely (this gives S_1).

Usually a number of managers who are closely involved with the market put in their separate estimates. Then the answers are compared, differences are discussed and a concensus projection is developed. Once the sales function is estimated, profit margins and cost figures can be applied to the revenue projections and the optimal number of sales people (N^* in Figure 10.4) estimated.[6]

 Allocation of resources

A salesforce is a very expensive resource and there are usually enormous opportunities for management to improve its efficiency and effectiveness. These opportunities lie in three areas. First, the proportion of selling time can be increased. Typically, only 30 per cent of a salesperson's time is spent with customers. McDonald estimated in the UK that 50 per cent of the average salesperson's time is spent travelling, 20 per cent on administration, 24 per cent on making the call and only 6 per cent on selling.[7] It is easy to see how better route planning and more efficient administration could increase selling time substantially. Yet few companies undertake systematic studies of how their representatives use their time. Second, the allocation of sales time can be greatly improved in most companies. Typically, a company's products and customers differ greatly in potential. Yet most do not systematically direct sales people towards the high-potential products and customers. Finally, the profit generated from a sales call can usually be significantly increased by better training. Most sales people are volume rather than profit driven, and are not trained or motivated sufficiently to present the real value of what they offer to customers. As a result, prices and margins suffer.

Allocation to customers

The 80:20 rule invariably applies in selling – 20 per cent of customers will account for at least 80 per cent of sales. The first task is to split current customers into those of high potential (or key accounts) and low potential. This task is fairly easy; the more difficult one is to identify prospects or potential new customers and to segment these by potential. The 80:20 rule is even more striking when it comes to prospects, the vast majority of whom will represent a wasted effort. It is important therefore to develop a system which partitions prospects into A, B and C categories and allocates efforts proportionately. Type A prospects are those 10 per cent of buyers who are likely to represent 50–60 per cent of the new business generated in the next year or two. Type B prospects are the next group of customers, who might bring in 20–30 per cent of the new business. Type C customers are small buyers or those where the chances of developing a relationship do not look bright.

After defining the customer and prospect sets, call rates should be defined for each group. The key principles are first to make sure that sufficient time is allocated to existing customers. Most companies spend too much time chasing new accounts and insufficient time maintaining existing relationships. Almost invariably, current customers represent higher potential than new ones. The probability of them buying more is exceptionally high, so that they represent particularly valuable assets. In contrast, the chances of a 'cold call' generating substantial new business is minuscule. Companies should therefore build in a high call rate for current customers and, in particular, the key accounts. Next adequate call rates should be assigned to category A prospects and lower ones to B prospects. For type C prospects, management should look at more cost-effective solutions such as telemarketing or direct mail. These are much cheaper. For example, a telesales person can contact up to 50 prospects a day as against around 4 for a salesperson.

In recent years, management scientists have developed a number of computerized models to assist in these allocation decisions. One of the best known is CALLPLAN, which uses management judgements to optimize the allocation of sales people's time among the different types of account and between current customers and new prospects.[8] As with many other models, it is more applicable where companies have large salesforces selling a limited number of products.

Allocation to products

Most sales people sell a range of products. Typically, products vary greatly in their profitability and responsiveness to selling effort. The task of management is to group products by profit contribution rate and sales responsiveness, as illustrated in Figure 10.5. This groups products into four types:

■ *Top priority*. These high-margin, high-response products should receive the highest call rates and be the primary focus for selling. These are often new products which require market development.

■ *Second priority*. These respond well to additional selling efforts, but they generate less profit on account of their low margin. A product with a 20 per cent profit contribution has to achieve twice the sales response to justify a representative's time than a product with a 40 per cent margin.

■ *Low priority*. These high-margin, low-response products are the next priority. These generally mature products are well known to customers and sales people cannot add much.

■ *Minimum effort*. These low-margin, low-response products should receive the least resources.

Again there are various models including CALLPLAN which utilize these profiles to help management allocate the time of sales people to the various products.

Allocation to territories

From time to time, firms have to design or redesign sales territories. In defining areas, management will want to meet several objectives. First, they will want to minimize travelling time and costs. This leads to a preference for circular territories of densely spaced accounts. Second, territories should be roughly equal in either workload or potential. This results in a feeling of equity and enhances motivation among the salesforce. Finally, territories should be clearly defined and permit a rational evaluation of sales people's performance. Management scientists have developed computer-based programming models to help design territories along these lines. The best known is the GEOLINE model, which uses linear programming to create territories to match the chosen criteria.[9]

Sales management

The tasks of sales management normally cover recruitment, training, supervision, motivation, compensation, planning and evaluation. In developing these activities, management should have the following priorities in mind:

■ *Building sustainable customer relationships*. Long-run growth and profitability are more likely to be achieved by having sales people forge partnerships with clients based upon shared benefits. Focusing on closing one-off deals, however profitable

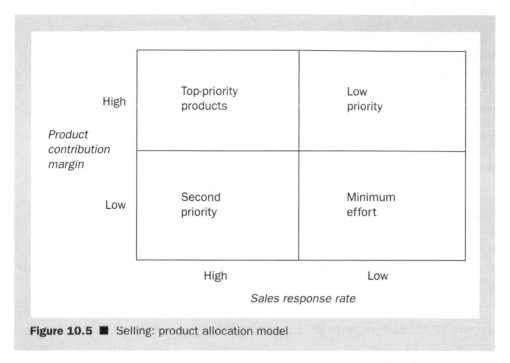

Figure 10.5 ■ Selling: product allocation model

they may be in the short run, is unlikely to create sustainable profits. Always remember that an existing customer is invariably more valuable than a new one, and make sure that good current customers receive the top priority.

■ *Selling on value rather than price.* Buyers will naturally seek to push down the price. The salesperson's job is to prevent this by adding value to the offer and demonstrating this. Value selling requires exceptionally high levels of motivation and training.

■ *Customer segmentation and positioning.* Effective selling requires representatives to segment markets because different customers have different needs and price sensitivities. Sales people have to be trained to position these offers to the different segments, to build value-enhancing relationships and to negotiate good terms.

■ *Augmenting the offer.* Few sales people today are selling products which are substantially better than, or even different from, those of competitors. Marketing and sales management have to build supplementary values to augment the core offer. These include guarantees, services, financial support and consulting on technical, business and organizational issues which allow the company to be differentiated and move up the value ladder.

Recruitment

The firm's success at selling depends upon the quality of the people it hires. For larger salesforces, hiring is an almost continuous activity because of the high turnover of sales people, which can easily reach 25 per cent a year. Mistakes are costly. Few companies avoid a long tail of poorly performing sales people. Typically, half the salesforce will generate over 80 per cent of the sales achieved. The cost of recruiting, training and financing a salesperson in the first year can be around £75,000. If the profit contribution margin on the sales is 30 per cent, then the salesperson needs to generate £250,000 sales to recover the cost. A poor salesperson's inability to achieve adequate sales, however, may be only the tip of the iceberg. If they lose current customers, the losses may be appalling. A customer currently buying £100,000 a year may represent an expected discounted sales value of up to £1 million over the next decade. Worse, disaffected customers tell others, so that before long the company's reputation in the industry can be destroyed.

Much empirical research has gone into seeking to identify the characteristics of high-performing sales people.[10] Most studies show that successful performers have three broad traits:

- *A high achievement motivation*. They have an urgent personal need to be a winner.
- *Empathy*. They can understand the feelings of buyers and build warm personal relationships.
- *Self-confidence*. They believe they have the expertise to meet the needs of the customer.

But these generalizations provide at best very broad guidelines for selection. Successful sales people appear to come in many guises: some are extrovert while others are introvert; some are well turned out, others dress rather shabbily; some are exceptionally energetic, others are laid back. In addition, the required characteristics vary greatly with the job. The salesperson from Rolls-Royce negotiating multi-million pound deals for jet engines, requires very different skills from a Unilever representative selling detergents to cash-and-carry operators.

The identification of selection criteria should therefore start with an analysis of the selling job to specify the responsibilities and tasks required. This will suggest the education, training, experience and personal characteristics needed. These will provide the data for a first-line screening procedure. Management will then want to supplement this with interview impressions, recommendations and, perhaps, attitude and personality testing. Finally, one needs to add that selling has not been seen as an attractive job. Many people dislike the pressures and travel involved, and perceive it as a low-status occupation. These views are perhaps changing for the better, but outstanding candidates are usually in scarce supply. Companies have to market themselves to attract the best people. They need to demonstrate the potential of the job, the rewards and the career progression that can be offered.

Training

Many companies recruit sales people and put them in the field without adequate training. As a result they enter a selling situation with inadequate knowledge of the customers' business, the technologies involved and the strategies of competitors. What happens then is that the salesperson lacks the expertise and confidence to exploit any differential advantages that his or her business possesses and ends up giving away margin.

Companies like Ericsson, Nestlé and Glaxo will spend 5–10 per cent of the salesforce costs on training. Proper training can easily boost a salesperson's productivity by 20 per cent and boost profit margins by much more.[11] The core components of a sales training programme should include the following:

■ *Understanding customers*. Sales people need to be trained to segment markets, to understand the customers' business and to analyze how decisions are taken. They also need to know about the strategies of competitors.

■ *Understanding the company, its products and technologies*. Sales people should be trained to be seen by buyers as experts and authorities on the products, services and technologies they represent. The buyer should see the representative as a source of advice and wisdom.

■ *Analyzing the decision-making unit*. A buying organization can contain many decision-makers and influencers. Each may have different technical priorities and price sensitivities. It is important that the salesperson influences the right people in order to optimize the relationship.

■ *Planning and resource allocation*. Sales people need to be trained to plan their time effectively, to identify the balance between current and new accounts and to prioritize prospects.

■ *Creating value for customers*. Most importantly, they need to be trained to show how customers can obtain superior performance or lower costs from building a close relationship between the two businesses. They need to know how to focus on profit and value rather than on volume and price.

Motivating sales people

A few sales people are inherently highly motivated to succeed. But most can have their motivation levels enhanced by the right type of stimulus. Certainly in today's competitive markets, if a company's sales people do not possess an urgent drive to succeed, they will not be able to create and maintain strong customer relations.

It is particularly easy for sales people to lose their drive and slip into a vicious circle of depression, dissatisfaction and failure. Selling is a highly pressured job: failures are usually very visible, the representative works alone for much of the time and frequently lacks authority, and he or she is perceived to have a lower status than buyers. Not surprisingly, the best sales managers view motivational skills as crucial.

The principles of motivating a sales team are illustrated in Figure 10.6. This shows the potential of creating a virtuous circle of highly motivated sales people leading to greater effort, which in turn results in higher performance, higher rewards and greater job satisfaction. The model shows that sales management can intervene by stimulating motivation and providing effective rewards. The ways in which management can *motivate* people are as follows:

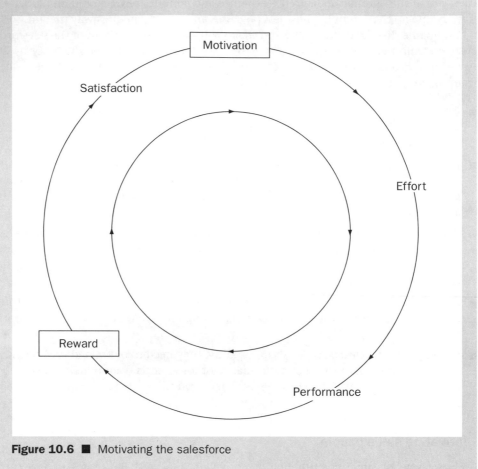

Figure 10.6 ■ Motivating the salesforce

- *Inspirational leadership.* Some managers have charismatic personalities which inspire their teams to work at high levels of performance.

- *Positive effect.* Sales people usually respond positively to praise, positive feedback, warmth and understanding from their managers.

- *Persuasion.* Teaching sales people new techniques which will help them sell and perform better are also motivational.

- *Performance goals.* Sales quotas encourage people to aim high if the quotas are agreed and perceived as reasonable.

- *Supplementary motivators.* These include sales meetings, which encourage individuals to identify with a larger peer group, and competitions, which offer them the chance to win prizes or recognition for special effort.

If management can motivate extra effort, they also need to reward the performance improvements which result. Research suggests that the *rewards* which are most wanted by sales people are, in descending order of importance:

■ *Financial rewards*. First, they expect to receive salary raises, commission or bonuses for achieving good results.

■ *Promotion*. The best sales people expect to be promoted to higher-status positions and to get enhanced career opportunities.

■ *Personal growth*. They want to feel that they are moving forward. Further training and new experiences provide positive rewards.

■ *Sense of accomplishment*. Visible successes satisfy the intrinsic need for achievement felt by most sales people.

In contrast, research suggests that liking and respect, security and recognition are less valued by high performers.

Compensation

What and how sales people are paid has a major impact on a company's ability to recruit good people and to stimulate high performance from them. Many different compensation methods are employed by companies. The most common alternatives are straight salary, commission only, salary plus bonus, salary plus commission, and salary plus bonus plus commission.

There are two aspects of compensation that have to be decided: the level and the composition. The *level* of pay is important in determining the company's ability to attract and retain good people. If a company pays under the market rate, then it is hard to get able sales people. If it pays more, it should pull in potential high performers. However, it is not easy for candidates to judge fine differences in levels of compensation. Differences in the way bonuses or commissions are calculated often make simple comparisons misleading.

Deciding the *composition* of compensation and, in particular, the split between fixed and variable pay is more complex. Sales people want pay which is regular, but they also believe that above average performance should be rewarded, and that pay should generally increase with age and experience. The company, on the other hand, wants a pay system which motivates a certain behaviour, which is economical and which is simple to operate. The specific scheme that a company employs reflects its own balance between these different goals. There are three main alternatives.

Straight salary

Around one-third of sales people are paid a straight salary. The advantages are that it gives sales people a predictable income, and for the company it is easy and simple to administer. It also makes it easier for management to change duties without the sales people feeling that they are going to be worse off.

It does have some major disadvantages. First, it does not reward high performance. This can be a real problem in today's highly competitive environment. Second, it makes all selling costs fixed: if the company's sales decline, salaries remain the same. Third, it does not incentivize sales people to focus on the products and customers offering highest potential.

Straight salary can only really be justified where it is difficult to disentangle a sales-person's contribution to sales, when other factors such as advertising or promotion are the major determinants of demand, or when the salesperson plays predominantly a supportive role. Straight salaries are also often used when selling is performed by a team, or when negotiations cover a long period of time. However, even in these circumstances, management should consider whether some sort of bonus scheme would give the representative a more direct financial interest in results.

Straight commission

This is the opposite of a straight salary. Here the salesperson is paid a percentage of either sales or gross margin, usually 3–20 per cent depending upon the product. Straight commission is used in only a few areas, such as door-to-door selling, insurance and office equipment.

A commission-only system has three advantages. First, it provides a powerful incentive to achieve results. Second, by varying the commission rates, companies can motivate sales people to allocate their time to strategic products or customers. Finally, selling costs become variable: when sales are low so are costs. There are, however, often major problems with this type of plan. Sales people may be demotivated by the highly unpredictable pattern of their incomes. Also they will resent undertaking activities which do not generate immediate income, such as collecting market research information, providing customer service or following up long-term opportunities. They may encourage high-pressure selling tactics or price discounting, which may not be in a company's interests.

Mixed plans

Not surprisingly, most companies compensate sales people using a combination of salary, commissions and bonus. This way they try to get the best balance of a salary element which sales people can rely on, plus a variable element to motivate higher performance. Typically, 70–80 per cent will be salary and the rest commission or bonus payments.

In fixing bonuses or commissions, management can base them upon sales or gross margin performance. The latter is generally much better. Sales-based incentives invariably encourage sales people to give way on price and exaggerate the price sensitivity of customers. It is tough to get sales people to undertake difficult, but essential, value selling if they are paid for shifting volume rather than generating profitable sales.

Evaluating performance

Effective control of the sales effort requires establishing standards and measuring performance against them. The objective of such a measurement system is to distinguish between high- and low-performing sales people, and to identify how differences in effort, ability and efficiency have contributed to such variations. Unfortunately, there are two reasons why this task is not straightforward. One is that there are many different measures of performance which may not be correlated, particularly over the short run. Such measures include sales, market share, gross profits, new accounts, customer satisfaction ratings, number of calls made, selling costs and supervisors' ratings. Second, performance may be affected by factors other than the efforts of sales people. Such factors include competition, other forms of promotion, economic variables and special market conditions.

If the company has a reasonably sized salesforce, the performance of representatives can be compared against each other. Performance can also be compared over time. Such comparisons can be used to screen out the effects of some of the exogenous variables which affect performance.

Performance variables can be divided into input and output measures. *Input* measures reflect the efforts and costs that a salesperson incurs. Effort variables include the number of calls made and the time spent in selling activities. Expense variables include travel and entertainment costs.

Output measures are generally more useful. They can be divided into three types. First are sales measures. The most important of these are total sales and percentage of quota achieved. The latter is generally more relevant in that, if a quota is carefully set, it allows for the differences in opportunities among territories. Thus it reflects more accurately the salesperson's ability to generate revenue. New business generated is another important sales measure.

A second type of output measure is the profit generated by a salesperson. If sales people are evaluated on sales measures alone, they can erode margins by making insufficient effort to sell at adequate prices. It is usually crucial to incentivize sales people to push the right products at the right prices.

A final type of output measure is qualitative ratings of the sales people by customers and supervisors. Regular surveys of customers are being increasingly used for evaluating sales people. Top companies like British Airways, Xerox, SKF and others are realizing that the best way of creating satisfied customers is systematically to collect information on customer satisfaction and incentivize customer contact personnel to achieve high levels of satisfaction. Companies are realizing that strong customer evaluations today represent sales gains tomorrow.

The selling process

Some people appear to be natural sales people: they have an instinct for understanding the aspirations of customers and for motivating them to want what they can offer. But today selling has become more professional. A large amount of research and a vast collection of experiences have allowed experts to put together a convincing, and generally accepted, sequence of good selling practice. While flair and instinct will still allow some individuals to be outstanding, we know enough to train most people to be effective at selling.

It is useful to distinguish between the old-fashioned sales-oriented and the modern customer-oriented approach to selling. The *sales-oriented approach* involves the use of high-pressure techniques of persuasion to manipulate the customer into buying what the salesperson has. It may involve intruding into the buyer's office or home, exaggerating the features or benefits of the product, fast-talking presentations and inflated concessions to obtain quick agreement. In the past, such an approach has often been associated with people selling cars or encyclopaedias. Today, however, such approaches are either illegal or generally ineffective. Certainly, they can never be the foundation for building long-term customer relationships.

Modern selling is based upon a *customer-oriented approach*. It focuses on finding out what customers want and coming up with solutions that match these wants in a way which is profitable to both parties. This approach is highly professional and requires both skill and integrity. The first skill is in helping customers to articulate their real wants. The salesperson may be able to bring a breadth of business, marketing and technical skills to illuminate and bring further insights into the buyer's underlying problems and needs. A highly trained salesperson should have information and knowledge not possessed by the buyer. The second skill is getting the buyer to understand what value a solution would bring. This value may be economic – higher profit for a business buyer – or psychological – pleasure, confidence and self-esteem for a household consumer. The third skill is coming up with a solution that matches the wants of the buyer. The salesperson generates real value if he or she can offer the customer enhanced satisfaction, greater output or higher productivity. The fourth skill is in building the foundations for a long-term business relationship by demonstrating a commitment to the customer's performance.

The key steps in the selling process are summarized in Figure 10.7.

Prospects

The first step in the selling process is to identify prospects – people who are likely to buy. A *prospect* is someone who can benefit from buying from the company, can afford to, and has the authority to make a purchasing decision. A *lead* is someone who might possibly be a prospect. A lead must be 'qualified' before it can be considered a prospect.

Leads may come from many sources. Current or past customers are normally the best source of additional business. Classified lists and directories, advertising, exhibitions and references from service personnel, dealers, bankers, trade associations and suppliers are all used to generate leads. To avoid wasted calls it is important to 'qualify' serious leads. *Qualifying* means investigating whether a lead possesses the three qualities of the prospect:

- Could it benefit from what the salesperson can offer?
- Is there the money to buy it?
- Has the person identified the authority to buy?

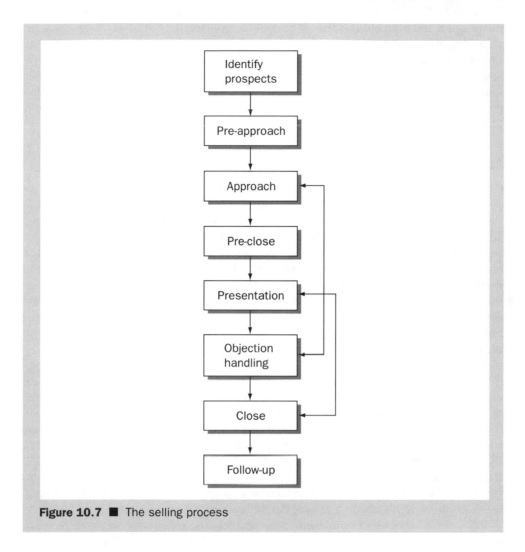

Figure 10.7 ■ The selling process

Pre-approach

Once a prospect is identified, the salesperson will need to draw up a sales plan covering selling objectives and strategy. Such a plan depends upon information about the customer. During this planning stage, the salesperson should seek to research four main issues. First, he or she needs additional qualifying information. Is the prospect really in the market? When is it likely to buy? What is the value of the prospect? Second, the salesperson will want information about the decision-making unit. Who will influence the choice process? Who are the key decision-makers? How are decisions arrived at? Third, the salesperson will want information for the presentation he or she plans to make. In particular, the salesperson will want to learn about the likely needs of the prospect and what benefits should be emphasized. Finally, he or she will want to learn about the nature of the competition. How satisfied is the prospect with the existing supplier? What are the comparative strengths and weaknesses of the prospect's company? Sources of this information will include other sales representatives, annual reports, trade journals and directories. Generally, the best source will be the prospect itself. If the salesperson looks genuinely helpful, the prospect is likely to be willing to talk on the telephone or in person about his or her business and its needs.

Approach

Once the salesperson is sufficiently prepared, he or she will seek a meeting with the prospect. This begins the sales process proper. The approach stage should consist of three sections: the first probes the buyer's wants; the second confirms that the want list is complete; and the third section seeks to value fully the benefits which arise from a solution.

The probing stage can be separated into several steps. The first is asking what the buyer is looking for – what benefits are sought. It means listening to the prospect and noting down essential requirements. The next step is to explore whether these requirements should be modified. The reason for questioning the buyer's list is that the customer may not be aware of new technologies or solutions that may be available now. The sales representative may be able to advise on better approaches which will benefit both of their companies.

During this process, the salesperson should anticipate that, sooner or later, the buyer is likely to come up with objections which may prevent an agreement being signed. These objections may be excuses because the buyer does not want to deal with the company, or they may be real problems from a perceived mismatch between what the salesperson is offering and what the buyer wants. During the approach stage it is best to anticipate such objections and prehandle them to prevent them later becoming obstacles. For example, common objections at the end of the sales presentation are the buyer saying that he or she does not have the authority to make a deal, or that the budget is insufficient. At an early stage the salesperson can seek to anticipate such problems by asking, for example, 'Are you able to make the decision yourself, or does it have to go higher?'

Once the buyer's list of requirements is complete the salesperson can seek to introduce any differential advantages that his or her company can offer. This might mean highlighting certain of the buying criteria where the offer is particularly strong, or introducing new benefits such as guarantees, fast delivery or back-up service. Stage two of the approach requires the salesperson to confirm with the buyer that the list of requirements is complete. The representative will not want the buyer to start adding criteria later, which will in effect act as objections to closing the deal. The final stage of the approach seeks to put a value on the benefits being sought by the buyer. If the buyer obtains a solution to the list of requirements, what will it be worth to him or her? If it is an industrial firm, the salesperson and the buyer should calculate the economic value of a solution in terms of the lower costs that would be achieved, the higher output or the enhanced quality. It is crucial that the buyer appreciates the value of any solution that the salesperson may subsequently offer. This way the salesperson focuses the negotiations on value rather than price. This ability to create and demonstrate value to the customer is the single most important skill possessed by a top salesperson.

Pre-close

At the end of the approach phase, the salesperson should move on to the pre-close. The buyer is asked, 'If we can develop a solution which will match your requirements, have we a deal?' The purpose of the pre-close is to expose any final doubts in the buyer's mind and to ensure that the development and presentation of the solution by the seller will not represent a fruitless waste of resources.

Presentation

Sometimes the salesperson can immediately begin the presentation of his or her solution. But for complex products or buying situations, it might be many months before the seller can develop the required product. Once the company produces an effective solution, the presentation stage should be straightforward if the salesperson's approach work has been thorough. The presentation should not be a showy extravaganza or high-pressure set piece. Instead the simple objectives should be to show how the company meets the criteria agreed with the buyer and confirmed by him or her at the pre-close. In general, the presentation should begin with a review of the criteria as agreed with the buyer and a detailed re-elaboration of the economic value placed on a solution. The salesperson should then proceed to present the company's solution, checking off point by point against the buyer's criteria. If the buyer then confirms that the solution matches his or her requirements, the salesperson can go straight to the closing stage of the selling process. If, on the other hand, the buyer raises problems, the salesperson has to move to the objection-handling phase.

Handling objections

During the presentation, or when asked for the order, many customers will bring up objections. These may be either real problems or simply psychological resistance to signing the order. Common objections are as follows:

- It is not the right specification.
- It's too expensive or I have not got enough in my budget.
- I cannot do anything until my boss has agreed it.
- I am happy with my present supplier.

The best approach to objections is to have anticipated them and pre-handled them at an earlier stage. Difficulties on the specification, for example, should have been resolved during the approach phase. Similarly, a problem over price should have been identified earlier and been outweighed by building up an appreciation of the additional value incorporated in the company's offer. The salesperson should have shown how the offer generates real cost savings or increased profits for the buyer which significantly offset the price premium.

If objections do occur, they have to be dealt with in a very positive way by the salesperson, who should first ask the buyer to clarify the problem. For example, an objection that the price is 'too high' could mask several different meanings such as: the buyer wants a discount; it is outside his or her budget; it is more expensive than anticipated; or the buyer is not the decision-maker. Each of these meanings requires a different type of response if the problem is to be handled. Once the objection is clear, the salesperson can seek to 'outweigh' it by showing compensating benefits, 'remove' it by demonstrating that it is not important in the buyer's situation, or 'weaken' it by showing that it is not a serious problem in practice.

Closing

Finally, the salesperson needs to close the sale by asking the buyer for the order. Many sales people are poor at closing deals: they often lack confidence or fear embarrassment if their move is rejected. However, if the selling process has been done properly, the salesperson has little to fear and the buyer should want to wrap up the deal. General principles which apply to closing are that the salesperson should make clear that he or she now wants the buyer's decision, not by hinting or making vague statements, but rather by asking a straightforward question which requires a direct answer from the buyer. However, the seller should not seek to close too early. He or she should only ask for the order when the matching is complete and a real understanding of the value of the offer has been created. Sales people use a variety of techniques to close. These include the following:

■ *The direct method*. The simplest and often the best approach is just to ask, 'Can I get your signature now for my order form?'

■ *The assumptive close*. The salesperson assumes that the sale is agreed and asks, for example, 'To whom shall I send the invoice?'

■ *The alternative close*. 'Would you like it sent this week or will you have it at the beginning of the month?'

■ *Standing-room-only close*. The salesperson suggests that the buyer might lose the opportunity to buy if he or she does not agree now, e.g. 'It is the last one we have' or 'The price goes up by 20 per cent after this week'.

■ *Special inducement*. 'If you buy now, you get a free ...' will often prod prospects into prompt action.

Maintaining relationships

The salesperson will not just want a one-off deal, but will want rather to build a long-term business relationship with the client which can be the source of business for years to come. For this reason he or she should follow up to make sure that the product works as promised and that the customer is happy with the service, and to express that the company has a continuing interest in helping the customer resolve its problems and capitalize on its opportunities.

Negotiations

Negotiations and selling are closely related. In some simple selling situations, the seller independently defines the product and the price and seeks to persuade the buyer to purchase on his or her terms. However, the situation is frequently more complex and the contract, including the product, price and terms of payment, is negotiated between the buyer and the seller. Negotiation can be defined as the process of coming to a mutually agreed exchange. Negotiation, like selling, has become a highly professionalized discipline which can be learned by managers.

The two fundamental characteristics of negotiation are the existence of at least two parties, each of which has something of value to offer, and the voluntary decision to make an exchange. The aim of a negotiation is to reach an agreement. A good agreement should conclude with all parties satisfied, it should be reached efficiently and it should be concluded amicably. Such conditions facilitate future exchanges between the parties.

Types of negotiation

Negotiations differ in their complexity and in the problems of reaching an agreement.

■ *Number of parties.* The most straightforward type of negotiation is between two parties: a buyer and a seller. But some negotiations have multiple parties: for example, the General Agreement on Tariffs and Trade (GATT) negotiations have 140 parties to satisfy. Also sometimes a negotiator may be representing a coalition of interests, not all of whom may be willing to agree to the terms that he or she is offering or willing to accept on their behalf.

■ *Number of issues.* Some negotiations focus on a single issue such as price, while others may have a whole range of items to agree. The negotiator will have to decide which of the issues are most crucial and in which order to take them.

■ *Continuity.* Negotiating attitudes will be affected by whether it is a one-off deal (e.g. selling a house), or one of a continuous series (e.g. between a retail chain and a grocery manufacturer). For the latter, it is particularly important that both parties feel that the deal struck is a fair one.

■ *Strategies employed.* The negotiator's attitudes and strategies affect the process. If a negotiator is hostile and disagreeable, the chances of an efficient settlement will diminish.

Negotiations can be divided into three phases: pre-negotiations, the negotiating phase and post-negotiations.

Pre-negotiating phase

This is the planning phase, during which negotiators gather information and plan their negotiating strategy. Top negotiators regard this as the most important phase of the negotiating process, and they often rehearse and role play with colleagues to simulate the forthcoming meetings. In this planning period, the negotiator should consider the following issues:

■ What are his or her own key objectives?

■ What are the objectives of the other party?

■ What information is needed? The negotiator needs information to legitimize his or her demands. He or she needs to judge the reliability of the other party, and to know whether the other party has the ability to make agreements.

■ What are the negotiating conventions? For example, how long will the negotiations be allowed to proceed? If there are multiple issues, in which order would they be best negotiated?

■ How can good relationships be built up with the other party? How can the other party be encouraged to be reasonable, reliable and constructive? How can our positive approach be communicated to them?

■ What is the settlement range that the negotiator will consider? Negotiators should plan an upper and a lower limit. The *maximum supportable position* (MSP) is what the negotiator would really like to achieve. This should be ambitious, but at the same time it has to be sufficiently reasonable that it can be justified and legitimized during the negotiation. The *best alternative to a negotiated agreement* (BATNA) is the minimum amount the negotiator will accept. Below this floor the negotiator will be prepared to do without a settlement. By keeping his or her BATNA in mind, the negotiator can avoid being pressured into an unsatisfactory agreement.[13]

Negotiating phase

In commencing the negotiations proper, the negotiator has to choose a style, strategy and tactics.

Negotiating style

The key to good negotiating is to view the negotiations as a joint problem-solving exercise. Both parties want a solution and each can prevent a solution unless it is satisfied with the outcome. Good negotiators seek to encourage their opposite numbers to look on the process as a shared problem of finding a solution which can meet the constraints of each and provide benefits for all. Effective negotiators seek to create an environment where they view each other as participants in problem solving rather than as enemies. They seek to be constructive rather than destructive and to use persuasion rather than coercion. Even if the other party refuses to play the game in this positive fashion and resorts to shouting, irrational behaviour and bullying, it still pays to respond coolly, reasonably and politely, so that communications are maintained as long as possible.

Negotiating strategy

The strategy is to seek to gain acceptance of your position and to demonstrate that it is justifiable and compatible with the interest of the other party. For example, in negotiating a construction contract, the representative will seek to build credibility for his or her MSP. He or she will emphasize the value and benefits of the company's expertise and seek to raise doubts about the buyer obtaining another deal which could offer comparable value. At the same time, the representative will mask his or her BATNA, thus discouraging the buyer from discovering the bottom line on price or terms. The representative should also have inducements and persuasive arguments to increase the buyer's desire to settle.

Position versus interest bargaining

The most influential new approach to negotiations has developed from the work of Fisher and Ury and their Harvard Negotiation Research Programme.[14] Their 'principled negotiations' approach is built upon four foundations:

■ *Separate the people from the problem*. Negotiations should specifically focus on issues and avoid allowing personalities to become involved. If the personalities and egos of the negotiators become involved, the process can deteriorate into an emotional and destructive test of wills. Negotiators should therefore be careful to avoid personal criticisms or accusations.

■ *Focus on interests not positions*. Interests are the fundamental requirements of the parties. Positions are specific demands which a negotiator uses in seeking to achieve his or her interests. For example, a buyer's interest may be in cutting his or her company's operating costs, but 'my maximum price is £10,000' is the position taken. Focusing on interests works better because there may be several alternative positions which could meet the buyer's underlying need. These could include free delivery, more product, greater productivity or financial support.

■ *Invent options for mutual gain*. If both parties see themselves as problem-solvers, they can look for solutions which provide gains for both. Brainstorming sessions can be employed to generate options which offer shared benefits.

■ *Insist on objective criteria*. To avoid the risk of negotiations getting bogged down into opposing positions, the negotiator can propose fair, objective criteria to be used to arbitrate a settlement. For example, in negotiations over the price of a property, an independent valuation can be sought from a third party.

Table 10.2 contrasts this type of 'principled negotiations' with the more common positional bargaining employed by untrained negotiators. Some of these positional bargainers adopt a 'hard' stance, while others adopt a 'soft' or conciliatory approach.

Table 10.2 ■ Positional versus principled negotiations

Problem Positional bargaining: which game should you play?		Solution Change the game: negotiate on the merits
Soft	**Hard**	**Principled**
Participants are friends.	Participants are adversaries.	Participants are problem-solvers.
The goal is agreement.	The goal is victory.	The goal is a wise outcome reached efficiently and amicably.
Make concessions to cultivate the relationship.	Demand concessions as a condition of the relationship.	**Separate the people from the problem**.
Be soft on the people and the problem.	Be hard on the problem and the people.	Be soft on the people, hard on the problem.
Trust others.	Distrust others.	Proceed independent of trust.
Change your position easily.	Dig in to your position.	**Focus on interests, not positions**.
Make offers.	Make threats.	Explore interests.
Disclose your bottom line.	Mislead as to your bottom line.	Avoid having a bottom line.
Accept one-sided losses to reach agreement.	Demand one-sided gains as the price of agreement.	**Invent options for mutual gain**.
Search for the single answer: the one *they* will accept.	Search for the single answer: the one *you* will accept.	Develop multiple options to choose from; decide later.
Insist on agreement.	Insist on your position.	**Insist on objective criteria**.
Try to avoid a contest of will.	Try to win a contest of will.	Try to reach a result based on standards independent of will.
Yield to pressure.	Apply pressure.	Reason and be open to reasons; yield to principle, not pressure.

Source: Roger Fisher and William Ury, *Getting to Yes: Negotiating agreement without giving in* (Boston, MA: Houghton Mifflin, 1981), p. 13

Neither is particularly successful in practice. Soft approaches often result in 'giving in' to a tougher opponent. A hard negotiating stance will often generate a similar response from the opponent, in which case a settlement often fails to be reached and both parties are left worse off.

Post-negotiations

After an agreement is reached, effective negotiators turn to the next phase. First, it is important to make sure that the agreement reached is clear to both sides and that there is no possibility of misunderstandings souring subsequent relations. All the essential clauses of the agreement should be written down and signed by both parties. Second, the representative will want to create the basis for a positive long-term relationship with the party. For this reason, negotiating 'too sweet a deal' may be a short-run victory to be overturned with a vengeance once the loser has the power to retaliate. Both parties should leave the negotiations with a feeling that the process has been fair and constructive.

Managing account relationships

Underlying all selling and negotiations should be the aim of building long-term relationships with customers. But for major customers this aim needs to be translated into specific organizational arrangements and resource commitments. For many, perhaps most, organizations today a handful of key customers will account for 80 per cent of sales and profits. Not surprisingly, more companies are shifting to the appointment of key account managers whose job is to manage and enhance these relationships.

The shift to key account management is driven by the following factors:

- *Vulnerability*. The loss of one or two key accounts can destroy the profitability of the company.
- *Commoditization*. Competitors now offer not only products, but also services of comparable quality. Consequently, companies need to get closer to the customer's business to identify new sources of value.
- *Innovation*. Customers usually provide the major source of profitable new ideas.
- *Potential business*. Current customers invariably represent better prospects for further sales than new customers.

Developing an account management programme begins with the identification of these key accounts. The handful of customers who account for the bulk of the firm's revenues and profits should be singled out. Management should put together a list in descending order of sales of all its customers. At this stage they should consider pruning some of the small, low-potential accounts to free up resources for the key accounts. Next, account managers should be assigned to the major customers. Managing key accounts requires different skills from traditional selling and negotiating. The focus is on building personal relationships and creating long-run strategic partnerships rather than on immediate results. Management must ensure that the account manager has, or is trained in, the skills of relationship management. Finally, account managers have to develop detailed plans to develop a profitable relationship. Miller and Heinman identify the following components of a successful account plan:[15]

- *Charter statement*. The charter is like a mission statement with respect to the particular customer. It states *who* the customer is (company, subsidiary or division), *what* product or services you are seeking to sell and *why* the customer should buy from you. The last item is crucial. A sustainable business relationship with a customer depends upon being able to help the customer create additional profits. This means helping it to sell more to *its* customers, reducing its costs or raising the level of its productivity. For example, a charter statement for a particular account might say: 'We supply construction chemicals to the building division of Alpha Company that enable it to provide buildings which are superior to its competitors in quality and finish.'

■ *Situation appraisal.* The situation appraisal establishes where you stand now in relation to the client. It looks at your competitive strengths and weaknesses, the profit opportunity that the client's business presents, the trends facing the client and the characteristics of the decision-making unit.

■ *Account strategy.* Strategy starts with the statement of the long-term goal of the relationship. This should be stated in terms of the value to be perceived by the customer as resulting from working with the supplier: for example, 'Our goal is to be seen as the company that guarantees that Alpha has the best externally finished buildings in the industry.' Second, the strategy statement should define what types of resource (technical, support, research, budget) will be needed to achieve the goal.

■ *Implementation.* This requires first that the long-term goals are translated into specific, quantifiable objectives for the next twelve months: for example, what products will be sold and what revenues will be expected. Second, sales and support plans should be scheduled. Third, milestones should be set for periodically reviewing progress and revising the plan where necessary.

Summary

Selling is about communicating value to customers. While most companies employ specialized sales people, most managers, and top managers in particular, need to be heavily involved in selling.

Two factors have changed the nature of selling. One is the increasing concentration in many industries which makes satisfying certain key accounts essential for the future of the business. Second is the increasing commoditization of the products and services that companies offer. In these circumstances, the traditional focus on selling volume simply leads to price erosion. Selling today requires finding new sources of value by helping the customer to increase its total profit or level of satisfaction. Here the salesperson needs the skills of a consultant, able to analyze the customer's markets and its manufacturing operations to identify new sources of business or productivity improvement for the client.

This requires new ways of organizing, training, motivating and compensating sales people. Companies that manage these processes effectively achieve increased competitiveness, new sources of innovation and the creation of long-term profitable relations with customers.

Questions

1. An industrial chemicals company sells the same commodity-like product at rather different prices to different customers. What is likely to explain such differences and what are the implications for selling strategy?

2. A company wishes to forge 'strategic partnerships' with its key customers. Outline how such a strategy might be developed.

3. The head of a building supplies company complains that his customers buy solely on price. He sees no way of raising prices. Suggest some avenues for exploring value-adding strategies.

4. Compare and contrast structuring salesforces by (a) geographically defined territories, (b) product specialization, and (c) market or segment specialization.

5. A new industrial sales manager is determined to raise significantly the margins achieved on orders. However, her sales people are insistent that customers are highly price sensitive and that if they raise prices by 10 per cent, they will lose 70 per cent of their business. Why might the sales people be overcautious? How should the sales manager proceed if she is confident that her strategy should work?

6. Compare and contrast the principles of effective selling with the techniques of good negotiating.

Notes

1. Based on estimates for the Chartered Institute of Marketing, 'Money the motivator', *Marketing Business*, December 1989, pp. 19–24; 'What salespeople are paid', *Sales and Marketing Management*, February 1995, p. 30.

2. William C. Montcrief, 'Selling activity and sales position taxonomies for industrial sales-forces', *Journal of Marketing Research*, August 1986, pp. 261–70.

3. Eric von Hippel, 'Users and innovators', *Technology Review*, October 1978, pp. 98–106.

4. Robert B. Miller and Stephen E. Heinman, *Successful Large Account Management* (New York: Henry Holt, 1991).

5. Walter J. Semlow, 'How many salesmen do you need?', *Harvard Business Review*, May–June 1954, pp. 126–32.

6. John D. C. Little, 'Models and managers: the concept of a decision calculus', *Management Science*, April 1970, pp. 66–85.

7. Malcolm H. B. McDonald, *Strategic Market Planning*, (London: Kogan Page, 1992).

8. Leonard M. Lodish, 'The vaguely right approach to sales force allocation', *Harvard Business Review*, January–February 1975, pp. 30–6.

9. Stephen W. Hess and S. A. Samuels, 'Experiences with a sales districting model', *Management Science*, April 1971, pp. 41–54.

10. See, for example, Olville C. Walker, G. A. Churchill and N. M. Ford, 'Motivation and performance in industrial selling: present knowledge and needed research', *Journal of Marketing Research*, May 1977, pp. 156–68.

11. See, for example, Peter Doyle and David Cook, 'Evaluating the pay-off of retail training programmes', *European Journal of Marketing*, Spring 1985, pp. 72–83.

12. D. J. Dalrymple and L. J. Parsons, *Sales Management* (New York: Wiley, 1995).

13. Adapted from Roger Fisher and William Ury, *Getting to Yes: Negotiating agreement without giving in*, 2nd edn (Boston, MA: Houghton Mifflin, 1992).

14. *Ibid.*

15. Miller and Heinman, *op. cit.*

Chapter 11

Managing marketing channels

After product, promotion and price, the fourth 'P' of the marketing mix is place. More often this element of marketing management is called distribution. Distribution management is the set of decisions and processes concerned with the flow of products or services from producer to consumer.

The term 'distribution', however, hides the scope of the issues of concern to management. Today most companies do not sell and distribute their goods directly to the final user. Instead many of the tasks, which include distribution activities such as transportation and storage, but also marketing activities such as selling, pricing and promotion, are undertaken by a variety of external intermediaries. The choice and control of these intermediaries we call marketing channel management. Marketing channels are those interdependent organizations involved in the process of making a product or service available to end users.

The choice and management of marketing channels are crucial management decisions (see Box 11.1). Marketing channel costs and margins can easily account for up to 50 per cent of the price paid by the final customer. Channel efficiency is therefore a key determinant of the firm's profitability and cost competitiveness. But channels are also crucial to the firm's effectiveness. The capabilities and motivation of the organizations within the channel determine the business's ability to create a competitive advantage in satisfying and servicing the customer. Channel management is one of the most important ways in which firms add value and enhance their competitiveness.

The choice and design of the marketing channel is also strategically important because it is a long-term decision and not easily changed. For example, a computer company such as Hewlett-Packard can choose to sell and distribute through its own salesforce, through direct marketing media or through an independent reseller. If it chooses the last, it will need to make a long-term commitment if it is to motivate the intermediary to invest in and develop its business. If conditions change, or things go wrong, it is not easy to shift to an alternative channel without a major disruption of the business. Marketing channel strategy is therefore a major determinant of the firm's long-run effectiveness and efficiency. Management guru Peter Drucker predicted that

BOX 11.1

Channel power in ice cream

The importance of channel management is exhibited in the European ice-cream market. The market is dominated by Unilever-owned Walls. Until recently, Walls was (and some would say, still is) a very ordinary product. At least two outstanding new products have entered the market backed by large, well-resourced corporations: Mars Ice Cream and Häagens-Dazs. Both offered great quality advances and were brilliantly promoted. Yet neither got to a break-even market share level and both have lost millions.

Unilever's dominance lies not in superior products, lower prices or better communications, but simply in control of the distribution channels. Years ago it gave freezers to the hundreds of thousands of small shops which sold ice cream – with the stipulation that only Unilever's products could be stocked in them. The competitors have great offers, but unfortunately they are locked out of the channels necessary to access the mass market.

in the twenty-first-century business, the biggest change will not be in new methods of production or consumption, but in distribution channels.

This chapter first explores the tasks of the marketing channel and why managers will often find it better to use third parties to undertake many of these activities. Second, it presents the criteria that managers should use in designing a channel strategy. Third, it looks at how marketing channels should be managed: how channel members should be selected, motivated, evaluated and controlled. Fourth, it reviews how marketing channels are changing and at the growth of integrated vertical, horizontal and multichannel networks. Finally, it explores the key logistics decisions that determine distribution costs and service levels.

The role of channels

Figure 11.1 shows the generic value chain describing the activities involved in the manufacture, marketing, delivery and support of the product or service produced by the firm.[1] Inbound logistics are those activities associated with receiving, storing and disseminating inputs to the production process. Operations covers the tasks involved in transforming inputs into the final product form. The activities which can be undertaken by the firm's marketing channels are the three remaining areas of the value chain. These are as follows:

- *Outbound logistics* – activities concerned with collecting, storing and physically distributing the product to customers, such as order processing, storage, transportation and delivery scheduling.

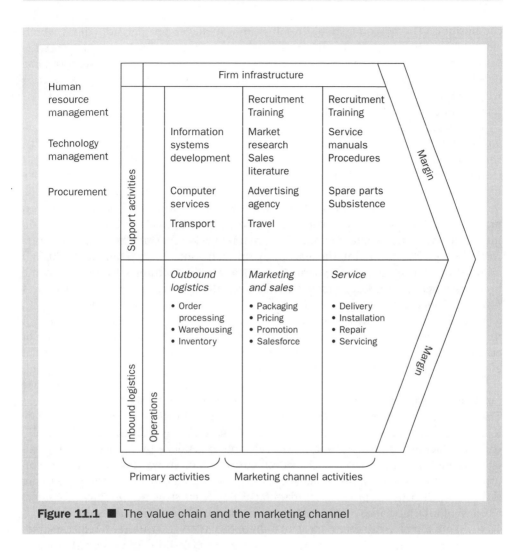

Figure 11.1 ■ The value chain and the marketing channel

■ *Marketing and sales* – activities concerned with obtaining information about the needs of customers and persuading them to buy, such as market research, personal selling, advertising and promotion, pricing and negotiation.

■ *Service* – activities associated with providing services to enhance or maintain the value of the product, such as installation, repair, training, parts supply and product adjustment.

These three vital sources of both cost and competitive advantage can be undertaken by the producer, independent intermediaries (such as wholesalers, agents or retailers) or, more usually, a combination of the two. How management decide to configure these activities is a fundamental strategic decision having a major impact on the future of the business. The outcome should result from a management decision about which activities should be regarded as the firm's core competences. Which activities does the firm need to do better than anyone else? Those activities not regarded as core should be delegated to third parties that have specialized skills. There are a number of reasons why intermediaries are often more efficient or effective than the producer in undertaking some of these logistics, marketing and service tasks.

The superior efficiency of intermediaries arises from what theorists term the *discrepancy of assortment*.[2] Most producers make only one or a limited number of products. Customers, on the other hand, desire a vast number of varied products and services. It would be hopelessly inefficient for each producer to go to individual customers or vice versa. Intermediaries sharply reduce the communications and transport resources required.

This is illustrated in Figure 11.2, which shows three producers – a farmer, a food processor and a beverage manufacturer – marketing to ten customers. If there is no intermediary, thirty separate contacts are required. However, if the three producers work through a common intermediary, only thirteen contacts are required. A *zero-level channel* (or a direct-marketing channel) is where a manufacturer sells directly to the final customer.[3] Figure 11.2, which contains one intermediary, is a *one-level channel*. A *two-level channel* contains two intermediaries. For example, a manufacturer first sells to a wholesaler, which in turn sells to retailers, which in turn sell to the final customer. A *three-level channel* contains three intermediaries, and so on. The greater the number of customers and the more specialized the manufacturers, then the greater the potential efficiencies from introducing multiple channel levels.

Intermediaries may not only be able to do some logistics, marketing and service tasks more cheaply than the manufacturer, but they may also be able to do them better. The superior effectiveness of intermediaries arises from the *discrepancy of quantity*. The logic of manufacturing differs from the logic of marketing and distribution. Normally the manufacturer obtains economies of scale and experience by producing standardized products in large quantities. However, customers often want to buy tailored solutions in small, often highly variable quantities. Companies which define their core skills as product development and manufacturing often struggle to match the effectiveness of intermediaries organized to serve the needs of specific markets.

A manufacturer will often have to sell to a variety of different target market segments to achieve scale economies in production. Generally, intermediaries which are dedicated to serving specific markets will have superior knowledge of these customers. They can add value to the manufacturer's products by tailoring solutions to the specific needs of clients. In addition, the wholesaler, retailer or other intermediary will often put together complementary products or services from other manufacturers to obtain scale economies in distribution and marketing.

In summary, there are comparative advantages in specialization. While manufacturers may be able to afford to set up their own channels, they can often earn a higher return by investing in their core business. Intermediaries are often more efficient and effective in making products available and attractive to target markets.

However, while it may be rational to delegate certain *activities* to intermediaries, it does not make sense to delegate logistics, marketing and service *strategy* to these

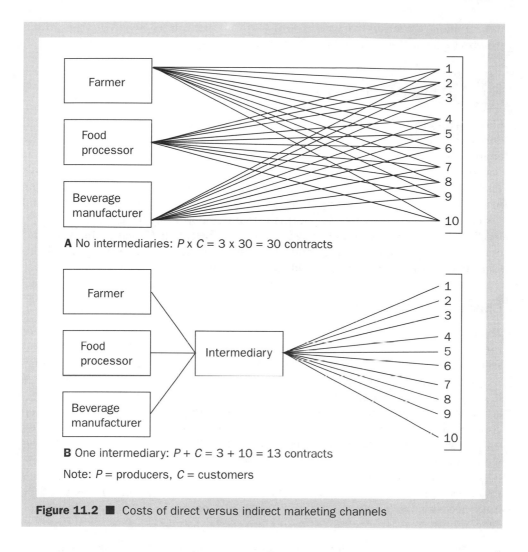

A No intermediaries: $P \times C = 3 \times 30 = 30$ contracts

B One intermediary: $P + C = 3 + 10 = 13$ contracts

Note: P = producers, C = customers

Figure 11.2 ■ Costs of direct versus indirect marketing channels

outside organizations. The supplier is ultimately dependent and responsible for the success of its distribution and marketing activities. Management therefore have to make the right decisions on the selection of channel members and they are responsible for motivating and evaluating them to perform well. Consequently, distribution decisions should never be totally delegated to intermediaries, rather they should be shared. For example, while a retailer or dealer may be responsible for selling the product once a customer enters his or her premises, the manufacturer may well have the lead responsibility in 'pulling' customers into the showroom through advertising and promotion. While an intermediary may undertake the servicing of the product, the manufacturer has to ensure that the intermediary's personnel are trained and motivated to do the job well. If management do not seek to control the strategic decisions, then profit in the supply chain will flow disproportionately to those channel members which do.

Designing distribution channels

Many managers lack the luxury of being able to design an optimal channel strategy. Often they have inherited a salesforce or set of intermediaries which cannot be changed easily or quickly. Some firms lack the resources to create the distribution system that would optimize the potential of their product and have to make do with established distributors. Sometimes there are no suitable channels available for the particular product that the firm wishes to market. Consequently, the firm's channel system usually evolves over time as its markets and opportunities change.

Choosing the right channel design requires management to define the business's objectives, its marketing strategy and the activities to be trusted to the channels, to identify the basic channel options and to evaluate the alternatives.

Channel objectives

The choice of marketing channel will be affected by the sales and profit objectives of the firm, the resources it has available and its positioning strategy. A business willing to sacrifice short-term profit for the sake of ambitious long-term market share goals may well find setting up its own salesforce more attractive than using a distributor. This is illustrated in Figure 11.3. Selling direct involves establishing a high fixed-cost operation. By contrast, selling through a distributor's salesforce involves a minimal fixed cost but a high variable cost element because of the discounts paid. For a company satisfied with a small market share (below M), using a distributor is cheaper. Companies aiming at a high share will find that the company salesforce is more efficient.

Selling direct normally requires a higher resource commitment. Thus the firm's resources will constrain the channel choice. Finally, the choice of channels will be influenced by the firm's positioning strategy. In particular, how intensive is the geographical coverage required? Three options can be distinguished:

■ *Intensive distribution.* For low-priced, convenience or impulse products, companies will generally want to maximize the number of outlets carrying them. The more places carrying the product, the more likely it is to be bought. The more intensive the distribution required, the greater the efficiencies offered by intermediaries.

■ *Exclusive distribution.* For high-priced, luxury products, the manufacturer will often limit distribution to a very small number of intermediaries. The intermediary normally gains better margins and the exclusive right to sell the product in a specific area. The manufacturer hopes to achieve in return a greater sales effort, greater control of pricing and selling practices, and a superior brand image.

■ *Selective distribution.* Manufacturers of speciality goods will often look for a compromise between intensive and selective distribution. Here the manufacturer aims to

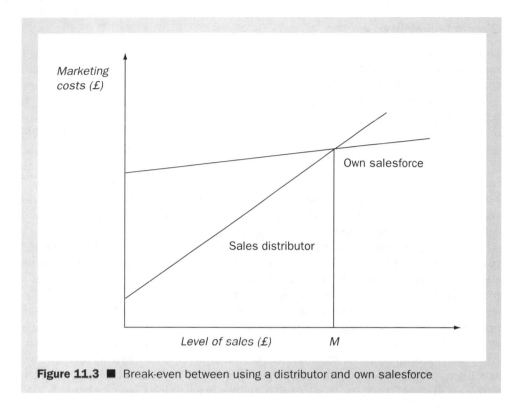

Figure 11.3 ■ Break-even between using a distributor and own salesforce

have sufficient cover, but to restrict it sufficiently to be able to select motivated, knowledgeable dealers.

Channel strategy

Two aspects of strategy should be central in selecting channels: the market segments targeted by the supplier and the differential advantage it seeks to exploit. First, it is crucial to choose a channel which has experience and credibility in dealing with the target markets that the supplier seeks to serve. The channel selected should have the capability to understand the needs of target customers, and the sales personnel and distribution facilities to match their requirements properly.

Second, the channel must be capable of effectively presenting and supporting the supplier's differential advantage. For example, if the channel is handling a technical product which offers the customer operational cost savings, the intermediary sales people must be sufficiently expert to analyze the buyer's value chain and to demonstrate the product's economic value to the customer. The more innovative the product and the more complex the customer value chain, the greater the competence required from the channel.

Channel reliability

Besides capabilities, an assessment needs to be made of the motivation of the channel's management and personnel, the extent to which the channel can be controlled and the risk attached to the relationship. The motivation of a channel member will be influenced by the impact of the supplier's product on its overall business. How much does the intermediary expect its own bottom line to be enhanced by the effort it puts behind the supplier? But motivation can also be increased by fostering a long-term relationship and the appropriate mix of incentives and rewards for performance.

The supplier will prefer a channel over which it can exert control. It will want to influence the way in which the intermediary develops a strategy for the business and how it promotes and presents the product to customers. The ability to exert control will depend upon the relative power of the supplier and its ability to impose sanctions for unsatisfactory performance.

Finally, commitment to a channel may involve risk. One risk is that the channel may subsequently become a competitor on the basis of the knowledge it acquires from the supplier. For example, major retailers often develop 'own label' versions after a manufacturer's brand creates a sizeable market. Second is the risk of dominance. A supplier can become so dependent upon a single channel that the latter is able to appropriate the value added and erode the supplier's margin. Last, the manufacturer may become locked into a channel and unable to adapt to opportunities or threats from newly emerging marketing channels. For example, IBM's commitment to its own salesforce and selected dealers allowed it to be leapfrogged by other PC companies which exploited discount stores, mail order and other newly emerging low-cost channels.

Channel alternatives

Management can choose from among three generic marketing channels. Figure 11.4 summarizes these alternatives.

- *Direct marketing.* This involves selling to customers primarily through mass communications media. It includes advertisements in newspapers and magazines, and on radio and TV, telephone selling, mail and catalogues. If the buyer places an order (usually by phone or letter), the seller sends the goods by mail or delivery service.

- *Salesforce.* This is selling through sales people. A company might build its own salesforce, utilize the services of another firm or hire an independent contract sales team.

- *Intermediary marketing channel.* This is a network of independent organizations involved in the process of making a product or service available to the final customer. A myriad of organizations undertake such activities. These can be classified according to whether they buy and take title to the goods. *Merchants* are those intermediaries that buy, take title to and resell the merchandise. Dealers, jobbers, distributors, wholesalers and retailers are the main types of merchant. *Agents* prospect for customers and may negotiate prices, terms and other conditions of sale on behalf of the supplier, but they do not take title to the goods. Examples are brokers,

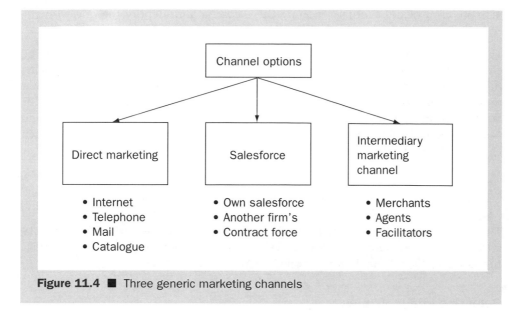

Figure 11.4 ■ Three generic marketing channels

commission merchants, manufacturers' agents and sales agencies. Finally, *facilitators* are agencies which perform or assist in performing certain marketing and distribution functions, but which neither take title to the goods nor negotiate purchases or sales. These include transport companies, independent warehouses, insurance companies, advertising agencies, market research companies and banks.

Intermediary marketing channels can also be classified according to their degree of integration and control. *Conventional channels* are loose networks of independent merchants, agents or facilitators, each of which is competing to maximize its own profits rather than the channel profits overall. *Vertical marketing systems* are integrated networks of producers and channel intermediaries which are professionally managed and controlled to maximize overall channel performance. These include co-operatives, franchised operations and channel networks dominated by large producers, wholesalers or major retail chains. The advantages and growth of vertical marketing systems are discussed further below.

Evaluating channel options

Selecting the best channel alternative logically involves the following steps:

1. List the objectives, strategy and channel reliability attributes which form the criteria for evaluating the alternatives.
2. Rate the importance which should be attached to each of these criteria.
3. List the channel alternatives being considered.

4. Score each of the alternatives along these criteria and identify the one with the highest score.

This method is illustrated in Table 11.1. Here a particular form of vertical marketing channel scores best. The benefits of such a methodology are not in the specific numbers, which are inevitably subject to the vagaries of managerial judgements about weighting and scoring. Rather its use is, first, to encourage managers to specify the attributes they need from an effective channel. Second, it identifies the strengths and weaknesses of the alternative chosen and highlights which problems in the chosen channel still need to be addressed.

Managing distribution channels

The major issues in the management of channels are how to select individual organizations, how to motivate them, how to evaluate and control them, and how to manage the conflicts that inevitably arise among independent businesses.

Selecting intermediaries

After management have chosen a type of channel system, individual firms have to be selected. Major suppliers with a record of success normally have little difficulty in attracting intermediaries wanting to market and distribute their products. But small companies will often have to market themselves professionally to attract interest from the best dealers and retailers.

Table 11.1 ■ Evaluating alternative channel options

	Importance weight	Channel options			
		Direct	Franchise	Conventional	Vertical
Channel objectives					
1 Goals	0.1	5	2	3	4
2 Resources	0.1	1	2	5	3
3 Positioning	0.1	1	4	2	5
Channel strategy					
4 Target market	0.15	3	3	4	4
5 Differential advantage	0.2	4	4	1	5
Channel reliability					
6 Motivation	0.24	5	4	2	4
7 Control	0.1	5	3	1	4
8 Risk	0.1	2	2	2	3
Weighted scores	**1.0**	**39**	**35**	**26**	**45**

In targeting intermediaries, the criteria will be similar to choosing channels and the selection scheme of Table 11.1 should be applicable. Management will need to assess whether a specific intermediary would be able to further the supplier's business objectives, whether it has access to the right target markets, whether it can exploit the supplier's differential advantage, and whether it can be motivated, controlled and relied upon.

Motivating intermediaries

If channel members are to market the supplier's products efficiently and effectively, they need to be motivated. It is useful to distinguish between promotional and partnership motivators. *Promotional* channel motivators are essentially short-term, economic inducements to push the supplier's products or services. The most obvious of these is the margin that the manufacturer gives to the intermediary for its services. Normal trade discounts can be supplemented by quantity discounts, promotional discounts and cash discounts to further incentivize dealer effort. Negative sanctions can also be used to induce behaviour that the manufacturer considers appropriate. Such sanctions can include threats to terminate supply or to reduce margins. The limitations of promotional motivators are that they are very expensive, they do not build loyalty and they can be exploited by short-term-oriented dealers.

Partnership motivators seek to build a long-term community of interest between the supplier and other channel members. Such a scheme may start with a joint task force to analyze what is needed to create a competitive advantage in the market. Activities are then assigned and integrated among channel members in a way which maximizes their effectiveness. Incentives and rewards are then developed which meet the criteria of fairness and instrumentality. Such a system will include not only financial terms, but also agreement on channel goals, strategy, training requirements and targeted investments to develop the business partnership.

Controlling intermediaries

The producer should be able to control or at least significantly influence channel members to act in a way that is instrumental to its interests. Control depends upon defining agreed performance targets. These should include sales quotas and levels of service for such items as inventory, customer delivery time, support, promotion and training programmes. Performance has then to be periodically compared against these targets, deviations highlighted and action taken.

To exert effective control, the producer must build up *channel power* – defined as the ability to influence the activities of other channel members. Social scientists suggest that the ability to control or lead a channel derives from both economic and non-economic sources of power.

Figure 11.5 shows that the two economic sources of power rest upon the producer creating resources (e.g. products, financing) desired by other members and also upon the relative size of the firm. The non-economic sources of power are rewards, expertise,

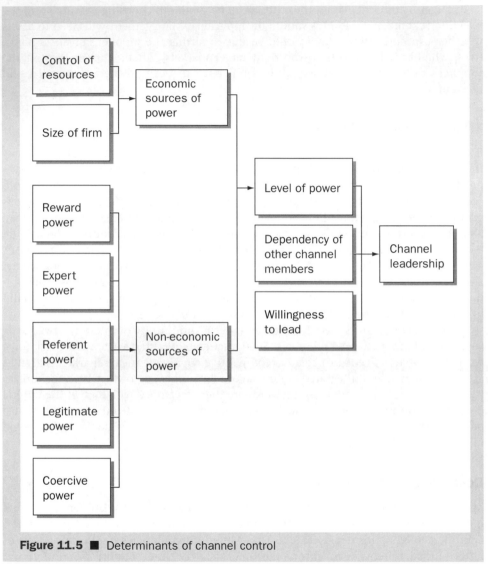

Figure 11.5 ■ Determinants of channel control

Source: adapted from Ronald D. Michman and Stanley D. Sibley, *Marketing Channels and Strategy*, 2nd edn, Columbus, OH: Publishing Horizons, 1980, p. 143

reference, legitimate and coercive power. A company gains reward power by offering attractive financial benefits. Expert power occurs when other channel members see the producer as having special knowledge to enhance channel performance. Reference power exists when other members admire or identify with the producer. Legitimate power emerges when other channels recognize that they are subordinate to the producer. Coercive power is a function of the producer's ability to discipline other members of the channel. Besides the level of power, control is influenced by the dependency of or alternatives open to other channel members, and the desire of the producer to control the channel.

Managing channel conflict

Channels should be designed and managed to elicit a partnership between members. In practice, however, conflicts and disagreements are bound to occur among independently owned businesses. To a certain extent conflict is positive in that it encourages management to question the status quo and to consider changes in the system. But conflict that gets out of hand can quickly erode the support of channel members and affect the competitiveness of the business.

Three types of channel conflict can be distinguished. The most common is *vertical* channel conflict between different levels within the same channel. Manufacturers of grocery brands, for example, are often disgruntled about the terms and conditions demanded by the powerful supermarket chains which purchase their brands. *Horizontal* channel conflict occurs between firms at the same level of a channel. For example, some smaller Toyota car dealers in Europe complained that larger dealers were getting better terms and access to superior models. *Multichannel* conflict occurs where a supplier has created two or more separate channels to serve a market. For example, IBM's independent dealers resented the company selling directly to some customers.

How channel conflict starts is easy to understand. There are five common sources. The first is an inevitable conflict of interest. For example, a manufacturer wants a dealer to devote primary attention to its brand, but the dealer may have a portfolio of products, some from other manufacturers which may offer it higher profit or growth potential. Second, conflict arises over the allocation of resources: for instance, over how the profit margin should be split between manufacturer and retailer. Third, conflicts are created by the use of coercive power. If one party attempts to threaten the other, resentment and distrust often cause lasting problems. Fourth, poor performance causes difficulties. Failure to meet promises or obligations fuels dissatisfaction. Finally, personality conflicts between managers in the different channels can disrupt the effectiveness of channel relationships.

When conflict arises, various mechanisms can be used to recreate effective relationships.[4] One is for the members of the channel to work together to develop a set of *superordinate goals* which all agree would be mutually beneficial. The hope is that an agreement on these ultimate ends would diminish the damage caused by narrow self-seeking on the part of members. A second mechanism is the use of *channel diplomacy* – personnel are appointed to act as diplomats, mediators or arbitrators, to bring together the warring parties and settle disputes.

A third approach is the exchange of personnel between channel members to build up an understanding of each other's point of view. For example, McDonald's has all its suppliers send managers to work for one week in one of its restaurants. Another device is co-optation, where the producer seeks to win support by including managers from other channels on advisory councils, boards of directors and the like. The objective is to create greater understanding, and shared goals and interests. *Joint membership* of trade associations is yet another conflict resolution mechanism with obvious co-operative goals.

Given the probability of at least some conflict arising in any channel arrangements, management would be wise to establish in advance an agreed forum and set of procedures for resolving such problems.

Channel evolution

Any channel design will become obsolete if it does not change. Two sets of factors erode the effectiveness of existing channels. One are changes in the market place. Evolving customer needs, market growth, the increasing reliability of products and new competition all change channel requirements. Second, increasing knowledge, technical progress and innovation create new and better ways of delivering value to customers. Such companies as Benetton in clothing, Dell in personal computers, Direct Line in insurance and Federal Express in overnight delivery owed their rapid growth to innovations that they made which introduced faster, lower-cost marketing channels.

If management do not anticipate or react to change, they will get locked into high-cost, ineffective channels. Changing channels, however, is not easy and invariably creates conflict with current intermediaries. To prepare themselves for these challenges, management need to keep under continual review the strategic fit of their channel system and have in place plans and timetables to get closer to the changing ideal.

Four changes in channels are particularly apparent today – the development of low-cost channels, and the growth of vertical, horizontal and multichannel systems.

Growth of low-cost channels

As a market evolves, the value added by a channel tends to decline, creating opportunities for new, low-cost distribution. This is illustrated in Figure 11.6. When an innovatory product or concept (e.g. the PC, designer-label clothes) is first introduced, management need high-value-adding channels. Intermediaries provide high-level support in helping manufacturers find customers, educating buyers and supporting them with advice and service. Later, as the market grows, customers become more familiar with the product, prices decline and product reliability improves. This leads to a shift from specialist to higher-volume, lower-value-adding channels. As the market moves to maturity, growth slows and competitive pressures erode margins further, encouraging companies to look for lower-cost, mass-merchandising channels. Finally, the product becomes a commodity and even lower-cost channels emerge (e.g. mail order, discount shops).

An analogous pattern of development in retailing is termed the *wheel-of-retailing hypothesis*.[5] Looking at the historical evolution of retailing, it was observed that estab-

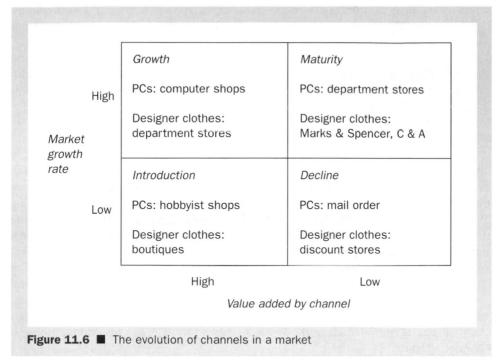

	Growth	Maturity
High	PCs: computer shops	PCs: department stores
	Designer clothes: department stores	Designer clothes: Marks & Spencer, C & A
	Introduction	*Decline*
Low	PCs: hobbyist shops	PCs: mail order
	Designer clothes: boutiques	Designer clothes: discount stores

Market growth rate

High   Low

Value added by channel

Figure 11.6 ■ The evolution of channels in a market

Source: adapted from Miland M. Lee, 'Change channels during your product's life cycle', *Business Marketing*, December 1986, p. 47

lished retailers tended to offer many services to customers (e.g. wide assortment, convenient location, pleasant atmosphere to shop in) and had to price high enough to cover these costs. This provided the opportunity for entrepreneurs to create new types of shop with fewer services, lower operating costs and hence lower prices. Over time the pattern repeated itself. As the discounters grow at the expense of the conventional stores, they in turn tend to upgrade their facilities, add services and move into more expensive sites, forcing them to raise prices. This then stimulates a new entrepreneurial phase as another round of low-cost innovators enter.

While the wheel-of-retailing hypothesis is too simple to explain the heterogeneous segmentation and positioning strategies employed by today's retailers, it does provide insights into the evolution and difficulties faced by today's department stores and major food retailers as they come under attack from new discount operators.

Growth of vertical marketing systems

In the past, marketing channels consisted of independent organizations, each pursuing its own individual goals. As illustrated in Figure 11.7, in this type of *conventional marketing channel* the member firms sought to optimize their own buying and selling policies, often at the expense of those above or below them in the channel. In recent years, such channels have been replaced by *vertical marketing systems* in which channel activities are managed and integrated by one member of the channel – either the manufacturer, an intermediary or a retailer.

Vertical marketing systems have three advantages over conventional marketing channels. First, they reduce channel costs by avoiding replication of functions. Second, they minimize conflict among channel members by laying out clear goals and programmes. Third, they maximize the experience and expertise of channel members. Not surprisingly, go-ahead managers are seeking to create such vertical systems. There are three types of vertical marketing system – corporate, administered and contractual.

A *corporate vertical marketing system* exists where successive stages of the channel are under a single ownership. For example, the Dutch multinational retailer C & A has its own manufacturing facilities and wholesaling organization serving its shops. Before the Second World War, such vertically integrated systems were common. But today most businesses cannot afford, or do not wish, to invest in fixed assets and skills where they lack clear competitive advantage. Instead they build *administered vertical marketing systems*. Here, channel participants maintain their financial independence and legal autonomy, but are effectively controlled and led by the most powerful member of the channel. Dominant retailers like Marks & Spencer in the UK and Ahold in Holland provide such leadership in co-ordinating and integrating the product development, manufacturing, purchasing and sales activities of the suppliers making up their channel. Strong manufacturers like Mercedes, Shell and BSN can also dominate their channel systems.

Contractual vertical marketing systems are inter-organizational relationships formalized through contracts. Channel members' rights and obligations are defined by legal agreements. The two most frequent types of contractual system are collaborative and franchise arrangements. Under *collaborative agreements*, separate organizations share resources and often agree to joint purchasing arrangements. The most common form are co-operatives. These can be led by producers (e.g. farmers), wholesalers or independent retailers banding together. All three types of co-operative are common in Europe.

Franchise arrangements are the other type of contractual system. Here a seller (the franchiser), gives an intermediary (the franchisee), specific services and rights to market the seller's product or service. In return, the intermediary agrees to follow certain procedures and not to buy from others or sell competing products or services. The strong integration has made franchising a rapidly growing form of channel in Europe. In the United States it now accounts for one-third of all retail sales. Also, the failure rate for franchisees is only a fraction of that for new businesses generally.

Growth of horizontal marketing systems

Another rapidly growing channel development has been the readiness of two or more autonomous organizations at the same level in a channel to co-operate in exploiting marketing opportunities. Even companies that are normally competitive increasingly explore such co-operation.

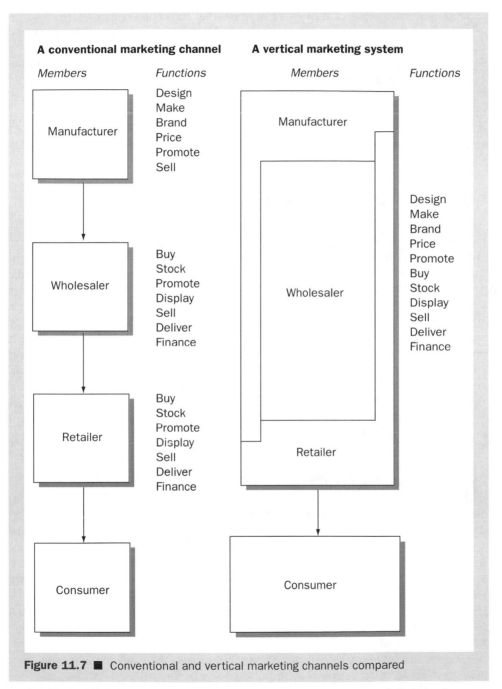

Figure 11.7 ■ Conventional and vertical marketing channels compared

Source: adapted from David J. Kollat, Royer D. Blackwell and James F. Robeson, *Strategic Marketing*, New York: Holt, Rinehart & Winston, 1972, p. 321

Four reasons account for the growth of horizontal marketing systems. First, co-operation reduces the resources at risk that an individual firm has to incur. Second, access to another company's marketing channel can accelerate the speed with which a company can penetrate a new market and pre-empt competition. Third, co-operation can give a company access to new technologies and knowledge.

Co-operation can exist at many levels. Philips and Du Pont co-operated in the development of compact discs; Toyota and General Motors collaborated in the assembly of cars; ICI Pharmaceuticals sells Merck anti-hypertensive drugs in Europe. Through horizontal collaboration a partner gains access to additional distribution channels, salesforces and outlets.

Growth of multichannel marketing systems

In the past, many firms sold to a single market through a single channel of distribution. Today, however, most markets have become highly fragmented. Different customers have different product and service needs and have different price sensitivities. As a result, different channels emerge to meet the expectations of these segments.

For example, a computer company such as Hewlett-Packard sells PCs through its own salesforce, but it also uses computer stores, direct marketing techniques and value-added resellers. ICI Paints sells directly as well as through supermarkets and merchants.

The advantage of a multichannel marketing system is that it enables the firm to serve a range of market segments effectively. However, such systems invariably create channel conflicts. These arise because an intermediary will usually face additional competitors and because different intermediaries normally obtain different terms from the supplier. As a result, the supplier developing a multichannel system needs to anticipate carefully the areas of strain and to communicate channel programmes which are perceived as fair among channel members.

 Organizing distribution

Once management have decided on their marketing channels, the next step is to design and operate a physical distribution system that will deliver products and services to customers efficiently and effectively. This is a complex problem because management have to reconcile two quite conflicting objectives. First, they want to keep distribution costs low. Typically, distribution costs (transportation, inventory, warehousing, order processing, etc.) account for up to 20 per cent of sales. Since trading profits often account for only 5 per cent, there is obviously a major incentive for managers to cut distribution costs. On the other hand, distribution is a major source of competitive advantage. Companies that can offer immediate availability and fast service can get better prices and win new customers. The task of management is to achieve effective customer service without excessive expenditure on distribution.

This trade-off is illustrated in Figure 11.8. Higher levels of customer service are associated with higher costs of transportation, order processing and inventories.

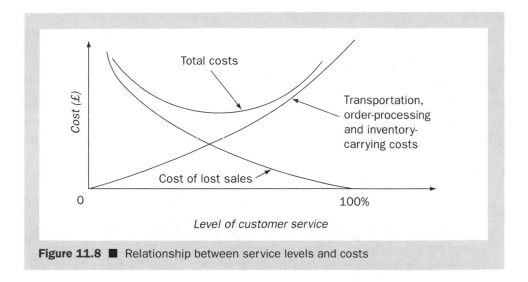

Figure 11.8 ■ Relationship between service levels and costs

Management have to estimate how much customer orders will increase with better service and how many out-of-stock conditions will be avoided.

In the past, management have focused on physical distribution primarily as a cost. A production-oriented viewpoint has dominated thinking. The objective has been finding low-cost solutions to get the product to the customer. Today, modern managers prefer the concept of *marketing logistics* to physical distribution thinking. Marketing logistics starts by asking how customers want to receive the product and then working backwards to the design of materials, final goods, inventory scheduling, transportation, warehousing and customer services to meet these wants.

Customer service

In developing a logistic strategy, management should start with identifying what customers want and then estimate the benefits and costs of meeting these wants.

The needs that an effective distribution system can meet are the following:

■ *Availability*. Ideally, a company should be able to meet all customer orders from its stock of finished goods. If it has run out of stock, the customers are likely to go elsewhere. However, guaranteeing a 100 per cent in-stock position would normally be prohibitively expensive in carrying costs.

■ *Speed of delivery*. Customers like rapid delivery and some will pay a substantial premium to obtain it. Delivery can be speeded up by fast order processing and rapid transportation.

■ *Reliability*. Customers want dependability – they want to know when they are going to receive the merchandise. They might not care whether it takes seven or eight days as long as they are guaranteed that it will be there in ten days.

- *Lot size.* The lot size is the number of units that customers are permitted to buy on a single purchasing occasion. The smaller the lot size, the greater the distribution cost that the channel incurs.

- *Product variety.* The greater the breadth of assortment carried, the more choice the consumer receives.

- *Convenience.* The more outlets the channel has, the more convenient it is for the customer to purchase.

- *Service and support.* The distribution system can increase customers' satisfaction by understanding their requirements, supplying financial support, installation, maintenance, etc.

In the past, management underestimated the value of good customer service and the costs of not providing it. Many orders were lost because of slow delivery, unreliability, lack of availability and poor service. Given the increasing lack of product differentiation between major manufacturers, service has become a key differentiator.

The steps in developing a distribution system which balances the benefits and costs are as follows:

1. *Identify the dimensions of service that customers value.* Market research is required to find out what aspects are important. The answers are likely to vary by segment. Some customers will prioritize speed, availability and service; others will rate price as more important.

2. *Weight the service dimensions by importance.* Again the weights need to be provided by samples of customers to obtain objective data.

3. *Obtain ratings of the business and its competitors along these dimensions.* This will allow management to compare the strengths and weaknesses of its customer service offer.

4. *Estimate the revenue effect of changes in service levels.* Management can provide judgements based upon the information obtained from customers and the performance of competitors with different service levels.

5. *Estimate the costs of providing different levels of service.* Management will need to judge the impact on transportation, inventory and warehousing costs of different service levels. Putting the revenue and cost projections together will identify the service level which maximizes profit contribution.

This method is illustrated in Figure 11.9. Here a manufacturer estimated that an in-stock level of service of 93 per cent was more profitable than the 99 per cent it was currently offering. In this case the costs of the extra safety stock to meet a 99 per cent service level exceeded the revenue gain from better service. The resulting savings in such situations can often be very substantial.

Several qualifications, however, need to be added to such analyses. First, the method should be applied on a segmented basis. Different types of customer have different expectations about service. Some market segments are willing to pay high prices to obtain premium service; others give priority to low prices and are willing to accept

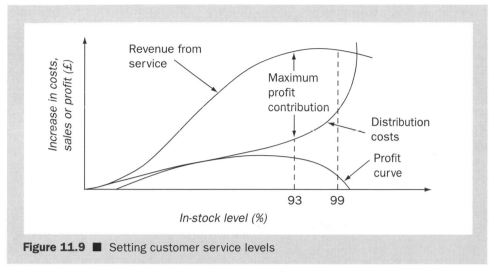

Figure 11.9 ■ Setting customer service levels

Source: adapted from Ronald H. Ballou, *Business Logistics Management: Planning and control*, 2nd edn, Englewood Cliffs, NJ: Prentice Hall, 1985, p. 66

minimum service levels. The company has to decide which market segment it is appealing to and develop the appropriate price–service balance. This is illustrated in Figure 11.10. Companies can offer either high or low service levels as long as they are offering price combinations which place them to the left of the diagonal. If they fall to the right, either the price is too high or the service-level combination is too low to offer value to any market segment.

A second qualification with all profit maximization models is distinguishing short-term from long-term profits. While cutting service levels (as in Figure 11.9) almost invariably increases short-term profits, its negative long-term impact on the company's image and competitive positioning should not be underestimated. Finally, price–service equilibriums are always temporary. Continual developments in flexible manufacturing, just-in-time management and innovations in logistics act to reduce the costs of high service levels. Companies which 'satisfice' on service tend to be gradually overtaken by more dynamic operators raising the competitive benchmarks.

Once the company has determined its target service levels, it then needs to design the physical distribution system which can deliver it at minimum cost. To achieve this, the major issues for management's attention should be as follows:

■ How can communications and order processing be speeded up?

■ Where should goods be produced and stocks held?

■ How much stock should be held?

■ How can transportation be handled more efficiently?

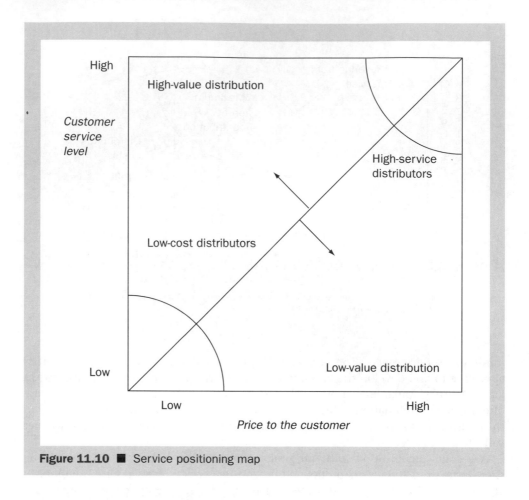

Figure 11.10 ■ Service positioning map

Communications and order processing

The physical distribution process starts with the company receiving an order. Copies of this order are then routed to the various departments responsible for inventories, purchasing, credit control, manufacturing, dispatch, warehousing, shipping and invoicing. If these activities are speeded up, the company can service customers better and take out costs from its own operation.

Modern computing systems offer major opportunities for companies to reduce overhead costs and delays. Sales people can send in orders to the relevant departments immediately with today's networking technology. In addition to booking orders, systems can give sales people instant status reports on the creditworthiness of customers, the status of past orders, inventory levels and recommended alternatives for out-of-stock items. Once the order is booked, modern systems can automatically generate orders to

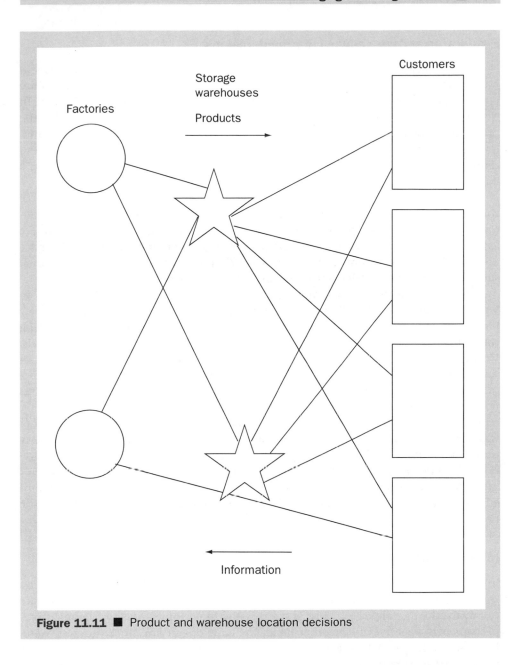

Figure 11.11 ■ Product and warehouse location decisions

ship, billing of customers, updating of stock records, the scheduling of purchasing and production for new stock and the issue of customer delivery confirmations.

The re-engineering of order processing and internal communications is offering companies major sources of competitive advantage and cost savings.

Production and warehouse location decisions

If the company is to meet orders speedily, it needs to have produced the goods and have stock available. As Figure 11.11 illustrates, a key determinant of such availability is the choice of the number and location of production facilities and warehouses. In making decisions about numbers, there is the usual dilemma. More locations offer the potential of increased customer service in terms of rapid delivery. On the other hand, more facilities increase costs and capital employed, acting to reduce profit margins and return on capital. Consequently, the number of warehouses and facilities must strike a balance between customer service levels and distribution costs.

Deciding on the right number of facilities and their location is complex because of the enormous number of possible facility combinations and sites, particularly when one is looking at the European or global market place. Increasingly, such decisions are assisted by computer-based mathematical models.[6] These programming models centre around choosing locations and numbers which minimize total distribution costs, subject to the supply and demand constraints facing the business.

While these models can help managers to optimize steady-state distribution problems, they cannot easily reflect the changing strategic opportunities created by new knowledge. For example, the new trend towards 'flexible' manufacturing is reducing the number of both factories and warehouses required to achieve given service levels. In the 1960s, companies built 'focused' factories geared to achieving economies of scale by producing large volumes of a narrow range of products. Today's 'flexible' factories work in the opposite way, by radically reducing the costs of variety. This means fewer factories and fewer warehouses to carry inventory.

The capital employed in factories and warehouses can also be reduced in other ways. Joint ventures can lead to co-production agreements whereby the company utilizes a partner's facilities. Co-marketing deals can also lead to the sharing of warehouse facilities. Finally, new swifter forms of transportation can reduce the number of production and storage facilities required. Overnight delivery services now permit customers to be serviced throughout Europe with minimum storage facilities in the field.

Inventory management and control

Inventory control is a key decision area in managing distribution. Ideally a company should have enough stock to meet customers' orders immediately. If merchandise are not available, the sale may be lost and a dissatisfied customer goes to a competitor – perhaps permanently. On the other hand, the costs of carrying stock (interest, warehousing, insurance, deterioration) can be exceptionally high and can seriously erode profits. For most companies, meeting the needs of all customers immediately from stock is financially non-viable. Thus the goal of inventory management is to find the right balance between customer service and the cost of carrying additional stock.

Inventory control centres around two related decisions: how much to order and when to reorder. Deciding *how much* to order requires balancing the cost of carrying

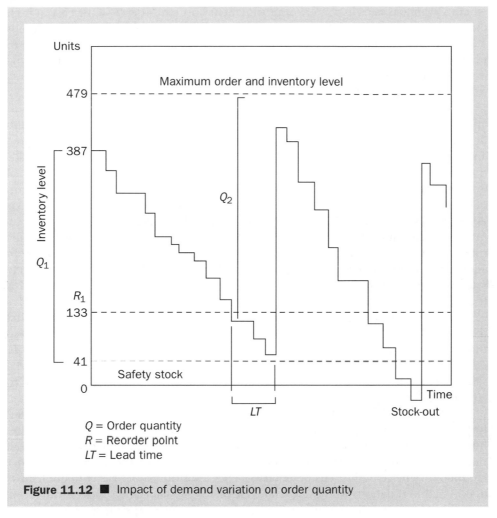

Figure 11.12 ■ Impact of demand variation on order quantity

Source: adapted from Douglas J. Dalrymple and Leonard J. Parsons, *Marketing Management*, 5th edn, New York: Wiley, 1990, p. 581

inventory against the cost of lost sales. Large orders reduce the chances of being out of stock, but increase the size of the inventory. For example, if annual demand is 1,000 units and 500 are reordered at a time, then the average inventory is 250 and there are two chances of becoming out of stock. However, if the item is reordered in lots of 100, average inventory is 50 but there are ten chances of running out each year.

One way to calculate the right balance is by using the economic order quantity (EOQ) formula.[7]

$$EOQ = \sqrt{\frac{2SY}{IC}}$$

where S = annual sales in units, Y = procurement cost per order, C = the cost of each unit and I = carrying costs as a percentage of cost. For example, suppose an item sells 1,200 per year and that procurement and the cost of lost sales due to stock-outs are £75 per order. If carrying costs are 25 per cent and the item costs £6, then the economic order quantity would be 346. It is easy to see from the formula that as carrying costs rise and profit margins fall, the EOQ comes down.

This formula works well when stocks can be replenished instantly. In most situations, however, this assumption does not hold and a different approach is required to decide *when to order* and how much. A more general method is to measure the lead time and forecast the demand that will occur during this period. Suppose management decide that they need to target a 98 per cent in-stock position to be competitive. Using the normal distribution, a 2 per cent out-of-stock probability represents a 2.05 standard deviation of demand. Assuming the standard deviation of demand during the lead time period is 20, an extra safety stock of 20 × 2.05 or 41 units is required (Figure 11.12).

The initial physical inventory of 387 in Figure 11.12 is made up of the economic order quantity (Q_1) of 346 plus a safety stock of 41. The reorder point is obtained from adding the safety stock to average demand during the lead time. In this case, weekly sales average 23 units (1,200/52) and the lead time is 4 weeks. Lead-time demand is therefore estimated as 92 units (4 × 23). Consequently, the reorder point is 133 (41 + 92), and new orders are placed when inventories fall below this level. During the first reorder cycle, additional demand takes stocks substantially below the reorder point so that the reorder quantity (Q_2) exceeds the EOQ to bring the safety stock back up to 41 units. In the second cycle, unexpectedly high demand leads to a stock-out despite the safety stock. If delivery time tends to vary widely, then extra safety stock is needed to control stock-outs.

In recent years there has been enormous interest in *just-in-time* approaches to inventory control. Just-in-time consists of arranging supplies to come into the factory, warehouse or retail store at the rate they are needed. If suppliers are dependable, the lead time for reordering is minimized, allowing dramatic cuts in the level of inventory required to achieve desired customer service levels. Just-in-time is easier to implement in production situations where usage rates are relatively stable and suppliers can locate near the factory. It is harder in distribution networks, where customer demand varies widely and buyers are often a long distance from the production centres. Nevertheless, many top distributors and retailers are already seeing major gains from exploiting just-in-time techniques.

Transportation management

Transportation is the largest cost element in physical distribution. The choice of transportation mode affects the level of inventories that need to be held, the cost of the product and the service provided for customers in terms of on-time delivery and the condition of the products when they arrive.

In choosing the method of transportation, management will need to identify the options available and to specify the criteria for choice. The options may be road, rail,

Table 11.2 ■ Comparison of transport modes

Criteria	Importance weight	Rail	Road	Air	Shipping	Pipeline
Speed	0.15	3	4	5	2	1
Service frequency	0.2	4	5	3	2	5
Reliability	0.15	3	4	3	2	4
Cost	0.15	2	2	1	3	5
Availability	0.25	3	5	2	2	1
Flexibility	0.1	3	5	2	2	1
Weighted scores	**1.0**	**31**	**43**	**26**	**22**	**28**

air, shipping and sometimes pipeline. The criteria will include speed, service, frequency, reliability, cost, availability and flexibility. Table 11.2 presents a simplified example of how decisions should be made.

In practice, companies are likely to combine two or more methods for transporting goods to their warehouses, dealers or customers. Also the solution is likely to change over time as transportation costs change. In recent years there has been an increasing trend towards companies subcontracting the whole transportation operation to outside operators. More manufacturers, wholesalers and retailers are recognizing that transportation is not an area of core competence and are electing to have it done by specialists who can achieve more efficiency and effectiveness.

Summary

The choice of marketing channel is a key strategic decision. It is a major determinant of cost, since marketing channels can easily absorb 50 per cent of the price that the final customer pays. It can also be a central determinant of the firm's marketing performance, since important marketing activities are normally delegated to intermediaries. The effectiveness of these intermediaries determines the customer service level and hence the ability of the firm to win and hold customers.

Intermediaries can often perform distribution and other marketing tasks more effectively and efficiently than suppliers that lack core competences in these areas. But suppliers can never delegate responsibility for strategy to these intermediaries. Management have to have a strategic plan of how to get the best out of their marketing channels. This means making the right initial channel selection, managing the channel members and assessing how the marketing channel needs to evolve with the changing environments in which the firm operates.

Questions

1. A new company is set up to manufacture men's shirts. What factors should govern its choice of channel strategy?

2. Marxist writers regard merchants as profiteers who exploit both producers and consumers. Why are they wrong?

3. What criteria should determine the choice of marketing channel?

4. Why does conflict often arise between the manufacturer and its distributors? How should conflict be handled and controlled?

5. A producer of a new industrial product wants to create a strong vertical marketing channel for its innovation. How can this be done and what advantages would it obtain?

6. Outline the goals and major aspects of an audit of a company's marketing logistics system.

Notes

1. Michael E. Porter, *Competitive Advantage* (New York: Free Press, 1985), pp. 33–61.

2. Wroe Alderson and Michael H. Halbert, *Men, Motives and Markets* (Englewood Cliffs, NJ: Prentice Hall, 1968).

3. Philip Kotler, *Marketing Management*, 9th edn (Englewood Cliffs, NJ: Prentice Hall, 1997), pp. 530–1.

4. The following section draws on Louis W. Stern and Adel I. El-Ansary, *Marketing Channels*, 3rd edn (Englewood Cliffs, NJ: Prentice Hall, 1996).

5. Stanley C. Hollander, 'The wheel of retailing', *Journal of Marketing*, July 1960, pp. 37–42.

6. See, for example, R. G. Dyson, *Strategic Planning Models and Analytical Techniques* (London: Wiley, 1992).

7. The following example is adapted from Douglas J. Dalrymple and Leonard J. Parsons, *Marketing Management*, 6th edn (New York: Wiley, 1996), pp. 579–80.

Chapter 12

Marketing in service businesses

This chapter looks at how to get the best out of service businesses. There are three reasons why services deserve a special chapter. The first is the sheer size and growth of the service sector in the modern economy. In the major European countries, the USA and Japan, more people are employed in the service sector than in all other sectors of the economy put together. In these countries, the public and private service sectors account for between 60 and over 70 per cent of national output. Services are also the fastest-growing part of international trade, accounting for 20 per cent of total world exports.

Even these figures underestimate the true importance of services to both output and jobs, since many activities in manufacturing firms are really services. On average, half the input costs of manufacturers are now bought-in services (e.g. advertising, transportation, health care, financial services). Also more people in manufacturing firms are employed in service jobs such as design, marketing, finance and after-sales services than are employed in making things. Managing such internal services shares many of the same problems as service businesses.

Second, managing services raises special issues. These arise from the specific characteristics of most services: the intangibility of the offering, the inseparability of production and consumption, the difficulty of achieving standardization and the perishable nature of the services. Such features prioritize three managerial concerns not normally centre-stage in 'marketing'. These are quality control problems, concern with the productivity of the operations and the management of human resources.

Finally, it is in some of today's service companies that one sees the new models of successful management practice. In the past, the computer industry provided the success models, and before that the car industry, but today it is the service firms that are providing most of the economic growth and new jobs.

The service sector covers a varied range of industries. The government provides a major array of services in most countries. These include education, health, legal, military, social, transportation and information services. Private sector services include profit-oriented businesses such as banks, insurance companies, airlines, management consulting organizations, solicitors, architects and advertising agencies. The private sector also includes non-profit organizations involved in providing charity, artistic, leisure, church and education services.

Some services are geared to individual consumers and households; others are oriented to satisfying the needs of businesses and other organizations. Both consumer and industrial services have been growing rapidly. In an affluent society, services tend to provide higher marginal utility for consumers than goods. The marginal utility of products tends to fall as incomes rise. The additional satisfaction provided by more food or more consumer durables tends to diminish. In contrast, services have no such ceiling. Greater affluence increases the desire of individuals to contract out mundane activities such as cleaning, gardening or preparing meals. Also, rising incomes both generate a demand for services that creatively consume leisure time (e.g. arts, sports, holidays) and provide the resources to pay for them. Services can provide self-fulfilling experiences; goods only provide ownership. Increasingly sophisticated technologies in the home also generate a need to buy in specialist services to install and maintain them. Finally, politics – electoral competition between parties seeking office – leads to promises of more and better services. Education, healthcare and policing are services that win votes.

Spending on business and industrial services has increased even faster than spending on consumer services. One reason is the increasing complexity of markets and technologies. Companies need to buy in the services of knowledge organizations like management consultants and market research agencies to advise them on the alternatives. Second, companies now want to focus on their distinctive competences and buy in activities which they consider non-core. This has led to the growth of specialist transportation, warehousing, sales, advertising and other business service organizations. Finally, the increasing turbulence and unpredictability of today's marketing environment has encouraged firms to cut fixed overheads dramatically. If services are bought in, they become variable costs and hence help dampen the impact of sales downturns.

This chapter first examines the nature and special characteristics of service businesses. It then looks at the implications of these characteristics for management generally and marketing in particular. In the final sections, the special features of non-business institutions are examined, and how managers can improve their efficiency and effectiveness.

 ## Nature of services

Services are not easy to define or classify. The essential characteristic of services is their intangibility. A service is an act or benefit that does not result in the customer owning anything. This definition expresses the central idea, but it is limited in that it does not sufficiently distinguish between the marketing of goods and services. Goods also supply intangible benefits. After all, the essence of the marketing concept is that customers do not want goods for their own sake, but for the benefits they provide. Recall Charles Revson's famous comment on the business of Revlon: 'In the factory we make cosmetics. In the store we sell hope.' Second, most manufacturers also supply bundles of services (e.g. delivery, repair and maintenance, insurance, advice, training) alongside their goods. Indeed, most service companies also supply goods alongside their core service. An airline, for example, alongside its core service of transportation, also provides food, drinks, newspapers and magazines.

Consequently, there is rarely such a thing as a pure good or pure service. Most offers are a combination of tangible and intangible elements. As Professor Theodore Levitt put it, 'There are no such things as service industries. There are only industries whose service components are greater or less than those of other industries. Everybody is in service.'

This is illustrated in Figure 12.1.[1] For some offers the tangible or intangible element is overwhelmingly dominant, but for others the customer is offered a combination of products that can be physically possessed, plus ephemeral experiences and benefits. In fact, by creatively changing this balance, managers can develop new offers or appeal to new market segments. For example, Castrol has traditionally sold a machine lubricant to industrial workshops. More recently it introduced a service where, rather than sell its lubricant, Castrol maintains customers' machines in top operating condition. Customers subscribe to a continuing service rather than purchase a product by the litre. The offer shifts from the tangible to the intangible-dominant area of the continuum. The benefits to the customer are in contracting out a non-core maintenance activity to specialists who guarantee performance. The advantages to Castrol are in a more sustainable differential advantage and a shift away from a customer focus on the price of the product.

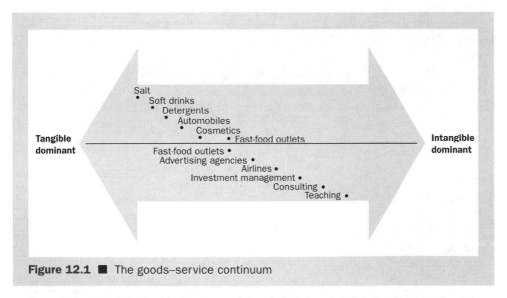

Figure 12.1 ■ The goods–service continuum

Source: G. Lynn Shostack, 'Breaking free from product marketing', *Journal of Marketing*, 41 (2), 1977, p. 77

Classifying services

Because the service sector covers such a heterogeneous collection of activities, it is useful to look for classification schemes which group organizations with common management concerns. This is illustrated in Table 12.1. One major distinction is between public sector and private sector services. In general, public or government service organizations do not depend upon customers for their incomes. Consequently, they often lack a customer orientation: satisfying customers is not essential for their survival.

Private sector service organizations are a varied assortment. Most are geared to making profits, but many, like charities or educational bodies, do not have shareholders. Another important distinction is in the competitiveness of the market. Some services such as electricity, water and, until recently, telecommunications are essen-

Table 12.1 ■ Classifying services

Category	Examples
Ownership	
Public	National Health Service, police
Private	Banks, transport firms
Goals	
Profit	Hairdressers, insurance
Non-profit	Education, charities
Degree of competition	
Monopoly	Water companies, electricity
Competitive	Consultants, financial services
Type of market	
Consumer	Retail, childcare
Industrial	Advertising agencies, consultants
Income source	
Customers	Airlines, dry-cleaners
Donations	Charities
Taxation	Police, National Health Service
Customer contact	
High	Healthcare, hairdresser
Low	Postal service, garage
Labour skill	
Professional	Legal, accounting
Non-professional	Domestic service, transport
Labour intensity	
Labour-bound	Education, healthcare
Equipment-bound	Telecommunications, public transport

tially monopolistic. Not surprisingly, such organizations often lack a culture of customer service and innovation. For this reason, and also because services are inherently risky to purchase, they tend to be more highly regulated than goods. Some are regulated by the government; others, like accountancy and law, are regulated by their professional bodies.

Another very important distinction for management is whether the service is high or low in customer contact. High-contact services are directed at people (e.g. airlines, hairdressing, healthcare); low-contact services are directed at things (e.g. car repair, postal service, dry-cleaning). The former typically involve the customer going to the supplier's premises. Here the appearance and ambience of the facility and those staffing it have a major impact on how the service is evaluated. The quality of the service process or experience is as important to consumers as the core service itself. For example, a good restaurant meal can easily be spoiled by the experience of dealing with a rude waiter. With low-contact services, on the other hand, the customer is not usually present for the service process, so that appearance and interpersonal skills are less critical.

Services differ according to whether they are predominantly people based (e.g. education, healthcare) or equipment based (e.g. automatic car washers, bank cash dispensers). People-based services can rely on highly professional workers (e.g. universities, law firms, management consultants) or non-professionals (post office, garden care, secretarial). As we shall see, each type of service raises specific problems in the areas of quality, productivity and marketing.

Service characteristics

Services have five important features that greatly affect how they need to be managed and marketed. These are summarized in Table 12.2.

Intangibility

Services are intangible. Unlike goods, they cannot be seen, touched, tasted or smelled. They are an experience or process. This has a number of implications for the consumer and the supplier. First, for the buyer, uncertainty is increased because services lack what psychologists call search qualities – tangible characteristics that the buyer can evaluate before purchase. For example, while buyers can examine in detail the shape, colour and features of the car they intend to buy before purchase, they cannot do the same for a haircut or visit to the dentist. For services, the quality of what buyers will receive, and how they will receive it, is substantially unknown until afterwards. At the same time, services are usually high in experience and credence qualities. Experience qualities are those characteristics that the buyer can assess after purchase (e.g. quality, efficiency, courtesy). Credence qualities are those features that are difficult to evaluate even after purchase. For example, most people would find it difficult to assess how well a car has been serviced even after the job is done.

Table 12.2 ■ Characteristics of services

Service characteristics	Management implications
Intangibility	No product; an act or experience
	Sampling difficult: consumer perceived risk
	Cannot be displayed: differentiation difficult
	No patents: low entry barriers
Inseparability	Consumers involved in production: intimate contact
	Other customers involved: control problems
	Employees personify business: personalized relationships
	Service environment: differentiates the business
	Mass production difficult: growth requires networks
Heterogeneity	Standardization difficult: depends upon people involved
	Quality difficult to control: heterogeneity of environment
Perishability	Cannot be stored: no inventories
	Peak load problems: low productivity
	Difficult to cost services: pricing problems
Lack of ownership	Customers cannot own the service: services are leased

Because services are low in search qualities and high in experience and credence qualities, consumers feel more risk in their purchases. Consequently, in making choices, buyers are more influenced by the credibility of the greater personal information sources such as word of mouth than by advertising messages paid for by suppliers. Second, they often seek tangible clues to judge the quality of the service. Such clues include the appearance of the facility and the staff and the prices being charged. Finally, if customers find a service which provides satisfaction, they tend to remain loyal to it.

Intangibility also causes problems for the supplier. The lack of physical characteristics makes it difficult to display and differentiate the offer. Intangibility also makes it impossible to patent service innovations. To deal with these problems, management can pursue strategies that include the following:

■ Stimulating personal influence sources such as word of mouth. For example, encourage satisfied customers to recommend the service to their friends. Opinion leaders can be targeted and incentivized to try the service.

■ Developing tangible cues which suggest high quality service. These can include the appearance of the place, staff, equipment, advertising and the symbols used to brand the service.

Inseparability

Related to intangibility is inseparability. Services are normally produced and consumed at the same time and in the same place. A medical examination is an example. The doctor cannot produce the service without the consumer being present. Further, the consumer is actually involved in the production process, answering the doctor's questions and describing his or her symptoms. Several consequences follow. First, particularly for high-contact services, since both provider and consumer are present, the interaction between the two is an important factor in determining the consumer's satisfaction with the service. Often the staff will personify the business to the client. If a consumer likes or admires the staff, he or she is likely to be pleased with the service.

Second, other consumers are also normally present. They may be waiting in the line at the bank, or present at the next table in the restaurant. Their behaviour can affect the satisfaction that the service provides. Third, growth is difficult. For a manufacturer of goods, a growing demand can be met by a bigger factory and using more distributors and resellers. But because of the simultaneous nature of production and consumption, this is not possible for services. The buyer and the seller have to meet. This means that service organizations have to put up many small factories (restaurants, aeroplane trips, hospitals) where the consumers are located. Production and marketing cannot be separated. If the service operation requires highly professional staff, this difficulty of achieving scale economies can be a major hindrance to growth. The challenge for management is to find ways of levering these scarce resources to achieve higher productivity. The implications of intangibility for management include the following:

■ Training staff to interact effectively with clients: teaching them to listen, empathize and act courteously.

■ Looking for ways to prevent customers from impeding each other's satisfaction (e.g. separating smokers and non-smokers in a restaurant).

■ Growth can be facilitated by the following:
   - Training: more high-quality staff permit faster growth.
   - Larger groups: scarce personnel can be leveraged by building facilities which permit larger numbers to be serviced simultaneously (e.g. bigger purpose-built lecture halls).
   - Faster working: tasks can be streamlined and non-essential work put off-line.
   - Multisite locations: standard service modules can be opened (e.g. by franchising).

Heterogeneity

Heterogeneity is the potential for high variability in the quality and consistency of a service. For example, two successive visits to a restaurant or two campaigns run by the same advertising agency will not be identical in performance. This arises because services involve people at the production and the consumption end. The quality of the result will depend upon the individual staff members in charge of it, the individual consumers receiving it and the time at which it is performed. All are extremely variable. Unlike machines, people are not normally predictable and consistent in their attitude and behaviour. This makes it difficult for the service organization to develop a consistent brand image.

Three ways of reducing the effects of heterogeneity are as follows:

■ *Investing in personnel selection, motivation and training.* Better-trained and motivated staff are more able to follow standard procedures and cope with unpredictable demands.

■ *Industrialize service.* Sometimes equipment can be substituted for staff (e.g. vending machines). Also the consistency of employee performance can be improved by detailed job procedures and closer supervision (e.g. McDonald's).

■ *Customizing service.* The heterogeneity can be converted to an advantage by emphasizing how staff tailor the service to the individual requirements of the customer (e.g. Ritz Hotel).

Perishability

Perishability means that services cannot be saved. Hotel rooms not occupied, airline seats not purchased and telephone line capacity not utilized cannot be stored and sold later. If demand is steady, this is not much of a problem since staff and capacity can be planned to match the requirements.

Unfortunately, for most services demand fluctuates, creating major peak-load problems. A city centre subway or restaurant may be working on average at 50 per cent of capacity. But this average can mask dramatic differences. At rush-hour a subway system may be running at 120 per cent of capacity; at off-peak times, it may be only 20 per cent occupied. Failure to meet peak demands creates great customer dissatisfaction. But putting in the capacity to meet this demand normally results in a very low average return on assets and low labour productivity.

To reconcile good service with satisfactory productivity, managers need to explore ways of achieving a better match between demand and supply. The problems of demand peaks can often be mitigated in the following ways:

■ *Differential pricing.* Peak users can be made to pay more than off-peak users. This has the double advantage that peak demand is reduced and those responsible for incurring the incremental capital costs pay more towards them.

■ *Making waiting times more acceptable.* If peak users have to wait, they can, for example, be given comfortable seats or complimentary refreshments.

■ *Increase off-peak demand.* This involves opening facilities for other uses (e.g. business hotels promote to tourists for weekend use).

■ *Use of reservation systems.* Demand can be managed to control the peaks and encourage acceptable substitution at other times.

As well as dampening peak demand, peak supply can often be increased in the following ways.

■ *Using part-time employees.* Staff can be hired just for the off-peak periods.

■ *Rescheduling work.* Staff only perform essential tasks at peak times and push administrative and routine maintenance to off-peak times.

■ *Increasing consumer participation*. Consumers can be encouraged to undertake certain straightforward tasks, such as clearing their table after they have finished their restaurant meal.

Ownership

Lack of ownership is a basic difference between a service and a good. With goods, buyers have full use of the product and the benefits it provides. They can consume it, store it or sell it. But with a service, a customer may only have personal access to it (e.g. a hotel room, an airline trip) for a limited time. Payment is usually for the use of, access to or hire of items.[2]

To overcome this problem, management can employ one or more of the following approaches:

■ Stress the advantages of non-ownership (e.g. easier payment terms, less risk of capital loss).

■ Create membership associations to provide the appearance of ownership (e.g. executive clubs for air travellers).

■ Provide incentives for frequent use (e.g. discounts, free flights).

Service tasks

These special characteristics lead to four central tasks facing managers of service organizations. These are the management of quality, productivity, human relations and differentiation.

Managing quality

Studies show that the perceived relative quality of a product or service is the single most important factor determining its long-run market share and profitability. The Strategic Planning Institute found that businesses that rate poorly on service quality lose market share at the rate of 2 per cent a year and earn on average only 1 per cent on sales. Companies that score high on service quality gain market share at 6 per cent a year and average a 12 per cent return on sales.[3] The pursuit of quality has probably been the most important competitive priority in the last decade as managers have sought to respond to the demands of consumers for ever-improving standards.

However, 'quality' in the service sector is a concept that customers find difficult to articulate and researchers find hard to quantify. Most of the research on quality has come from the goods sector. The Japanese define it as 'zero defects – doing it right the first time'. Philip Crosby, one of the quality 'gurus', defines it as 'conformance to requirements'.[4] Garvin measured quality by counting the number of 'internal' failures (those identified before a product leaves the factory) and 'external' failures (those occurring in the field after a product has been sold).[5]

But these concepts are harder to define and achieve in services. First, it is hard to measure quality because intangibility means that there are rarely physical quality standards (e.g. colour, fit, tolerance) that can be set and measured. Second, heterogeneity means that achieving consistency in standards is particularly difficult. Third, the inseparability of production and consumption mean that consumer participation makes it even more difficult for management to control the quality process.

This last point raises one other problem in the management of quality. The interaction of the consumer and producer, which is a particular feature of services, means that consumers evaluate quality not just in terms of the outcome, but also in terms of the process or the manner in which the service is delivered. For example, a hairdresser is judged not just in terms of the haircut received, but also by such things as the courtesy of the staff and the ambience of the shop. Managers of service organizations therefore have to focus on both the quality of outcomes and the quality of the processes.

Determinants of service quality

If managers are to improve quality, what should they focus on? One influential study found that there are up to ten criteria used by consumers to judge quality.[6] The first five are particularly related to the quality of the 'outcomes', while the remainder refer mainly to the quality of the 'process'.

- *Reliability*. How consistent and dependable is the service?
- *Access*. Is the service easily accessible and delivered with little waiting?
- *Credibility*. Can consumers trust the company?
- *Security*. Is the service free from risk and danger?
- *Knowledge*. Does the company make every effort to understand the needs of the consumers?
- *Responsiveness*. How willing are employees to provide service?
- *Competence*. Do staff have the knowledge and skills required to give good service?
- *Courtesy*. Are staff polite and considerate to consumers?
- *Communication*. Does the company clearly explain its service?
- *Tangibles*. Does the appearance of the personnel, the facility and other tangible evidence of the service project an image of high quality?

Expectations and performance

Customers judge quality by comparing the service they receive along these dimensions with what they expected. If perceived quality exceeds expectations then they are satisfied, even delighted. If performance falls below expectations, they will be dissatisfied and are likely to look for alternative suppliers. The expectations of consumers are created by past experience, word of mouth, advertising and other forms of communication. This is illustrated in Figure 12.2. The task of management is to seek to meet these expectations.

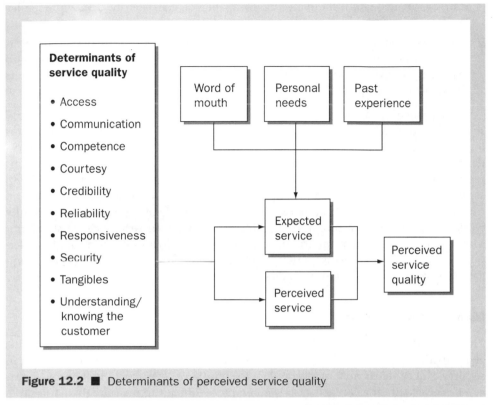

Figure 12.2 ■ Determinants of perceived service quality

Source: A. Parasuraman, V. A. Zeithaml and Leonard L. Berry, 'A conceptual model of service quality and the implications for further research', *Journal of Marketing*, Fall 1985, p. 48

Four problems can cause a gap between what consumers expect and what they perceive that they receive. To improve quality, these are the areas upon which management must focus.

■ *Management misperception.* A quality gap often occurs because managers do not research the important service attributes desired by customers. Managers often think they know what consumers want, but because they have never undertaken any objective research, these perceptions are wrong. Management are not focusing on the right areas.

■ *Misspecification of service quality.* Even if management know where the company is failing to meet expectations, they are often unwilling, unable or simply do not care enough to put the resources into solving the problem. For example, many banks are aware that customers have aggravating waits at lunchtimes, but they are unwilling to reschedule staff hours to resolve the issue.

■ *Service delivery gap.* Even when managers recognize problems and put in the resources, service quality may still be substandard because the customer contact staff are inadequately motivated or incapable of consistently achieving service targets.

■ *Communications that overpromise*. If the firm's advertising or selling overpromises, it will lower perception of quality when the performance fails to reach the hyped-up expectations. Even good service can be judged harshly if it exaggerates how high its service levels actually are.

These concepts identify where managers need to focus to achieve high-quality service. To summarize: first, managers need to develop the right strategy. This means identifying the business's target market and finding out what attributes are most desired by consumers. What does quality mean to them? Second, service organizations require an overriding top management commitment to high service standards. Third, service quality requires detailed implementation. This involves setting high and measurable performance standards, training and motivating staff, and carefully working out systems for monitoring performance and comparing against standards. Monitoring is particularly important. Successful service organizations regularly undertake consumer surveys to ensure that standards are being achieved. Finally, communications should be designed to avoid making promises that will not be kept.

Managing productivity

There is considerable concern about low productivity in the service sector. In part this is a statistical problem – it is extremely difficult to measure output improvements in services, since there is no tangible product to count. While productivity improvements can be measured for a car factory, it is much more difficult to measure them for, say, a management consultancy. However, there are real productivity issues in services. These stem from three main areas. First, the high consumer involvement makes it difficult to standardize and automate the service process. Second, services are usually labour intensive. Third, the perishable nature of services generally leads to excess capacity and a consequent downward pressure on return on investment.

In seeking to improve the productivity of the operation, management hit the familiar conflict between efficiency and effectiveness head-on. For example, efficiency could be increased by having teachers teach bigger classes, or getting doctors to handle more patients by giving less time to each one. But in both cases, a reduction in effectiveness or perceived quality for the consumer would be the probable trade-off. Management creativity is needed to handle this dilemma. There are four possible routes to improving productivity without sacrificing quality.

Separating high- and low-contact activities

The greater the amount of customer contact involved in providing the service, the more difficult it is to streamline and expedite it. The manufacturer of goods, for example, can be highly automated because consumers are not involved in the production process. Some services are extremely high contact (e.g. healthcare); others are less so (e.g. post office). More interestingly, most services are a mixture of high- and low-contact activities. For example, an airline has high-contact ticket counters and low-contact baggage handling. Banks have high-contact front desks and low-contact back offices which process information.

If management can sharply compartmentalize the two activities, they can seek to maximize the efficiency of the low-contact area and maximize the effectiveness of the high-contact area. The former is organized to maximize productivity, while the latter is geared towards maximizing the quality of the service.

Production-line approach to service

Theodore Levitt advocated the use of a production-line approach to both the 'front' and 'back' of the house activities by the application of hard and soft technologies.[7] Hard technologies mean substituting machinery for people. Examples are the automatic car wash, bank cash dispensers and automatic vending machines. Soft technologies are the use of systems to cut down on the number of service people. Examples are the self-service salad bar in a restaurant, the supermarket and the McDonald's type of fast-food outlet.

So far, such technological solutions have been largely limited to services where customers will accept standardized outputs. However, with continual technical progress, particularly in computing, and customers' increasing familiarity with technology and systems, the production-line approach looks likely to advance into even more customized service areas.

Increasing customer participation

Another way of taking costs out of the service operation is to get customers to do more of the work themselves. People are now used to filling their own car petrol tanks, direct dialling to overseas countries without the help of the operator, and clearing their table at McDonald's. But taking staff out should not be done lightly. Customers will often resent the loss of a familiar service.

Any such changes need to be based upon an understanding of how customers behave and what they want. Changes should be pre-tested and the benefits should be carefully explained. If the changes are introduced properly, consumers often like a more active role. Changes can also be positioned as benefits. For example, many budget hotels have put tea-makers in the bedrooms to economize on staff. The facilities are presented to guests as for their convenience and 'an extra'.

Balancing supply and demand

Matching fluctuating demand with a fixed capacity is a special problem with services because of the inability to hold inventories. Opportunities to increase productivity lie in smoothing demand or increasing the flexibility of supply.

As noted earlier, demand peaks can sometimes be influenced by differential pricing, reservation systems, attracting non-peak demand and extending courtesies to customers who have to wait at peak times. Supply flexibility can often be increased by greater use of part-time employees, sharing services with other organizations and more efficient use of peak-time facilities and employees.

Managing service staff

Human relations has to be a particular concern in managing services, especially in high-contact services. The inability to separate manufacturing from marketing means that the consumer normally meets a wider spread of employees. Each interaction between employee and consumer will differ. Each is a 'moment of truth' for the organization – where it is decisively judged by its customers. Normal methods of supervision and quality control do not work because, unlike a product, an unsatisfactory service transaction cannot be halted, examined and recycled before the consumer sees it.

In goods companies, marketing's primary focus is external – on customers – but in services it also has to be internal – on employees. Unless the needs of employees are understood and met by management, the organization will not have staff who buy into the service mission. Heskett describes the objective as producing a 'quality wheel' (see Figure 12.3). Highly motivated employees deliver high-quality service, which in turn leads to satisfied customers, more business and on to employee satisfaction and enhanced motivation. Here are some techniques used with good results to motivate employees and trigger this quality wheel:

■ *Employee-of-the-month awards*. These involve monetary and non-monetary incentives to emphasize quality.

■ *Increase employees' visibility and proximity to customers*. Employees become more conscious of quality when they can see and hear directly how the customer responds to their work.

■ *Training and indoctrination*. It is important to get new staff to feel pride in the company and a sense of its special tradition or mission.

■ *Peer group control*. Commitment and team building are reinforced when staff are chosen and reviewed by the colleagues with whom they work.

■ *Appropriate environment*. Motivation depends upon employees having the appropriate equipment, facilities and systems to be able to satisfy the customer.

Achieving differentiation

It should be clear that achieving a differential advantage for a service operation raises particular difficulties. These arise from the following problems:

■ *Integrated marketing and operations*. In manufacturing, marketing and production decisions are usually taken by separate functional managers. In services, unit managers (e.g. bank managers, hospital administrators) are normally responsible for both marketing and operational activities. Marketing thinking can often be 'crowded out' by the operational problems of keeping the bank or the hospital functioning efficiently.

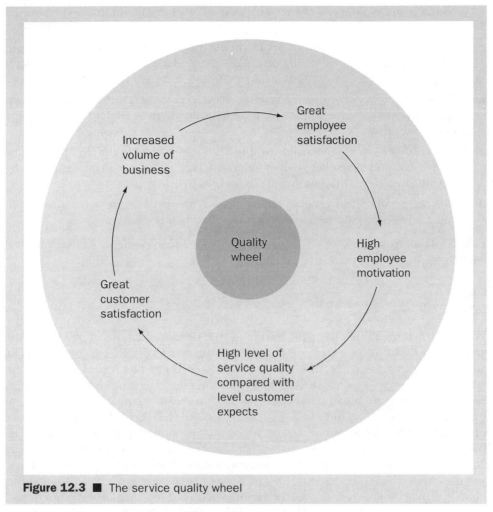

Figure 12.3 ■ The service quality wheel

Source: James L. Heskett, 'Lessons in the service sector', *Harvard Business Review*, March–April 1987, p. 23

- *No product differentiation.* Unlike goods marketing, there is no tangible product to compare. A prospective buyer of a car can compare the design, engineering and specifications of alternative models in advance; a prospective buyer of a management consultancy service cannot see which of the alternative suppliers looks most attractive.

- *No patent protection.* Service advantages generated by innovative systems or layouts are normally easily copied. As a result, it is often easy for new competitors to enter or to erode the differential.

- *Difficult to control customer interface.* Consistent performance in quality is hard to obtain because it depends upon the unpredictable behaviour of individual consumers and employees. The result is that a consistent brand image is not easily built.

■ *Problems of growth.* Scale economies in producing services can rarely be achieved. Growth normally requires setting up a network of small, autonomous 'factories'. It means that growing services must attract more and more 'general' managers.

■ *Difficult to improve productivity.* Services are hard to automate without driving down service quality. Consequently, unlike products, the prices of services do not usually decline over time.

■ *Problems in innovation.* Service innovations normally have the added problem of requiring consumers to change their behaviour. For example, consumers had to be motivated to use cash dispensers and taught how to use them.

■ *Restrictive regulations.* In general, service managements are more constrained than manufacturers in what they can do and say about their businesses.

In the following sections we will look at how service managements can seek to deal with these problems of marketing and differentiation.

 ## Services marketing strategy

Because of the high interface with consumers, the development of services marketing strategy must place much greater attention on integrating with an effective operating strategy. Marketing and operations have to be designed together if the company is to achieve high service quality with a viable cost structure. This is often misunderstood, particularly by managers who move into services from the manufacturing sector. For example, Bass, one of Europe's largest brewers, decided to diversify by building a chain of American-style restaurants aimed at younger professionals and their families. The company did thorough market research and came up with a first-rate marketing concept. Restaurants were internally and externally charismatic, and the food and service were excellent. Financially, however, the business was a disaster. The locations chosen were extremely expensive, the facilities required too high an investment and the service was very labour intensive. In addition, the menu was too broad, resulting in high wastage and high variable costs. The result was that the restaurant needed an 80 per cent occupancy rate just to break even.

There are four central components of a services marketing strategy. First, the target market segment has to be defined and analyzed. Second, a clear differential advantage and service positioning concept has to be developed. Third, an operating strategy has to be created which is internally consistent with the marketing strategy and which achieves high value–cost leverage. Finally, the marketing mix has to be specified and implemented.

Target market segmentation

As always, the initial task is to analyze the market. This entails first breaking the potential market down into segments according to how customers differ in needs and price sensitivities. Second, management should measure the attractiveness of the different segments and choose the segment or segments which look most appropriate. Attractiveness will be a function of the size of the market segment, its growth rate, the intensity of competition, average profit margins and the fit to the organization's own current or potential capabilities.

The next step is to research in detail the existing and latent wants of customers. What are the problems that customers face? What does good service quality mean to them? Who are the competitors serving this target market? How well are competitors meeting the expectations of consumers?

Differential advantage

After the target market is defined, a positioning concept has to be created which will give customers a strong reason for preference. Such a service concept needs to be based upon an understanding of what service attributes are most important to consumers, and where competitors are not meeting the actual or potential expectations of consumers. This service concept may be based upon superior reliability, faster response time, better work, greater convenience or some other attribute.

Once the service concept is formulated, management then need to plan how it is to be communicated to consumers in terms of design, delivery and promotion. What type of facilities will be required? What kind of people are needed to provide the service? How do standards need to be defined and communicated internally and externally? Finally, managers should think about the sustainability of the concept and the creation of barriers to entry. Any successful service concept will soon find that competitors seek to emulate and improve on it. Competition can sometimes be pre-empted by fast market entry and gaining a dominant market share. Alternatively, barriers can often be introduced by advertising and image development.

Operating strategy

Management have to develop an operating strategy which can transform a marketing opportunity into high performance for the company. There are four steps. The first step is to search for value–cost leverage. This means maximizing the difference between the value of the service, as perceived by the customer, and the costs to the company of providing it. A useful starting point is to separate those activities which directly provide customer value ('front desk') and those which are support activities, which the customer does not normally see ('back office'). The criterion for the former should be: how can the operation be designed to maximize customer service? The criteria for the back office should be: how can we minimize cost by standardization and automation? Methods of levering value include exploring the sources of any gaps between customer expectations and perceived performance, and finding new ways of motivating service personnel to work more effectively. Cost structures and break-even can be lowered by better management of capacity and demand, introducing hard and soft technologies into the operation and exploring whether the consumer can play a greater part in the production–delivery system.

The second step in developing the operating strategy is the design of the service delivery system. This consists of three main issues. How will quality and costs be controlled? This involves setting targets, incentives and rewards for achieving goals. It also means defining what results will be expected in terms of service quality, costs, productivity and staff loyalty and morale. Next, what are the key elements of the service delivery system? This involves designing the role of staff, technology, equipment and procedures. Then it is necessary to determine what capacity will be provided and to estimate what its utilization will be, both normally and at peak times.

The third component of operation strategy is strategy–systems integration. It is crucial to ensure that the service delivery system and the positioning strategy are consistent. Customer service quality should not be sacrificed in a vain effort to maintain smooth operations or keep costs down. If customers' expectations are not met, they will go elsewhere. At the same time, there is no point in management developing a wonderful consumer service concept if the organization cannot achieve a level of productivity to break even with it.

The final component of strategy is one that Heskett calls the inner-directed vision.[8] Services are such that performance quality will always depend upon the creation of a shared vision with employees. The service concept has to be designed from the beginning with the needs of employees in mind. The central questions that managers have to answer when building the service are: what needs do the employees have, how do they perceive the service concept, and how can employees share in the ownership and rewards of the operation?

Service marketing mix

Once a target market, differential advantage and operating strategy are defined, management will then need to decide on the marketing mix.

Product

Goods can be viewed in terms of their physical attributes, but services are intangible. This creates two problems for the customer. First, it is often difficult to understand the service that is being offered. Second, because the customers cannot check out a service in advance, they do not know in detail what they are going to receive and how they are going to receive it. The result is higher perceived risk.

Fortunately, most services do employ some tangibles – facilities, people, equipment and advertising materials – alongside their core service. The most effective approach to generating confidence is usually to emphasize tangibles that customers can understand. A private hospital should look clean, calm and efficient. A management consultant's office should look innovative and prosperous.

Second, since contact personnel are seen by the customers as embodying the service, it is crucial that they look right and reflect the image that the organization wishes to present.

Price

Price has a psychological and an economic role. The psychological role of the price is particularly important in the service sector. Because there is greater uncertainty attached to buying services, price is sometimes used as a cue to quality. In other words, low prices may indicate low quality and vice versa. However, such an effect should not be regarded as universal. It is only likely to apply when there is no other information available and when the consumer has limited experience of using the service.

Economically, price is a key determinant of the organization's revenue and profitability. As with goods, the price that can be charged depends upon the perceived quality of the service offer. Customers will pay a premium for services that they see as offering superior value. Most markets are highly segmented, so there are usually major opportunities for companies to price discriminate. Time is a particularly useful basis for segmentation in service markets. For example, business people want to travel at convenient hours, while leisure travellers may put up with the inconvenience of very early or late travel times in order to obtain discounts. Besides time of travel, time of booking is also often used as a basis for segmentation. Business people normally book late and want flexible tickets. The airlines, for example, charge very different prices depending both upon the time of day and the time of booking.

Price discrimination also enables the organization to utilize its fixed capacity better. At peak times, high prices ration capacity and low off-peak prices can stimulate demand.

Communications

Intangibles are more difficult to advertise, promote and communicate than products. It is not easy to depict in the media the performance of a service. The key is therefore to choose tangibles and symbols which the consumer can more easily grasp and associate with the characteristics of the service. Shostack contrasted the approach to advertising goods and services. She noted that, in product advertising, the advertiser seeks to enhance the physical product with abstract images. Coca-Cola, for example, is surrounded with associations of youth and glamour. By contrast, services are already abstract. To compound this abstraction would dilute the 'reality', so instead the advertiser relies on boosting the reality with tangible items.

Because of the experiential nature of services, word of mouth is generally more powerful than advertising. Consequently, service firms should seek to encourage customers to tell their friends about the good performance they receive. Some firms, such as American Express, provide rewards for customers who introduce friends or colleagues to the service. Direct selling can also be a powerful opportunity for service firms. Because consumer and contact staff meet, there is scope for personnel to promote the reputation of the organization and sell additional services.

Finally, one should note that service advertising and communications often have a dual audience – the external and internal customer. Many service organizations design their messages with an eye on having a positive effect on customer contact personnel. Television advertising, for example, can be an important tool for motivating employees.

Distribution

Almost by definition, high-contact services have to be distributed directly because the supplier and the consumer have to meet. However, economies can often be obtained by using indirect distribution for components of the service. There are two common forms of indirect distribution of services. The first is the use of intermediaries. For example, airlines use travel agencies to provide their booking and reservation services. This allows the airline to conserve resources and achieve more extensive coverage of the market. The second is the use of computer-based information systems and technology. For example, the increasingly extensive use of cash terminals by the major banks allows consumers to access core services without the involvement of staff.

Growth tends to be more difficult for service organizations. Services are time-bound – they can only produce and sell when customers want to buy the service. They are also place-bound – growth is limited by the number of people who can conveniently get to the location. Consequently, even a successful service formula at a single site has limited potential. A firm then has to choose from four growth directions:[9]

■ *Multisite strategy*. This strategy replicates the original service formula in multiple sites. It is the typical strategy employed by successful fast-food and retail chains. It is usually the most straightforward strategy. The key issues are finding managers, obtaining the right locations and administering the growing infrastructure. Franchising is often a means for rapidly exploiting a multisite strategy.

■ *Multiservice strategy*. Here the firm seeks to grow by capitalizing on its reputation and knowledge of its customers to sell new services. For example, many accounting firms have sought to grow by adding tax advice and management consulting to their basic accounting service. Here the organization maintains the simplicity of a single site and single customer base, but adds to the operational complexity of the business with its growing range of new services.

■ *Multisegment strategy*. Here the organization seeks to utilize its spare capacity by selling its service to new types of customer. For example, the railways seek to sell the spare capacity available outside peak times to shoppers and holiday-makers. The marketing problem is, of course, finding new segments that want to buy a bundle of services designed for another target market.

■ *Mixed strategies*. Many service organizations drift into combining strategies. For example, they not only add new locations, but also develop new services and even new segments. For example, fast-food firms attempt to broaden their menu (multiservice) while at the same time increasing the number of sites.

Many of the growth problems of service firms are caused by the adoption of these mixed strategies, which result in a loss of focus and an erosion of the original service concept. Some European banks illustrate the dangers of such mixed strategies. Bateson studied one bank which had 3,000 branches, was selling over 285 different services and was also seeking to move into new market segments. He found that the bank's staff lacked the knowledge to sell the array of services; service was deteriorating and the bank was being increasingly slow and bureaucratic as top management vainly tried to control the business's spiralling complexity.[10]

Such problems account for the comparative lack of success that service firms have had with international expansion. Retail firms, for example, have often seen internationalization as simply a multisite strategy. But often the foreign consumer attracted to the service concept is different from the one in the domestic market. These differences pull the organization into introducing new targeted products. What was originally a focused service concept then drifts into a multisite, multisegment, multiservice offer with all the attendant problems of managing such an extremely complex organization. Not surprisingly, such organizations frequently fail against more focused domestic competition.

Marketing within the service organization

There is no agreed view on how marketing should be organized in service businesses. Goods manufacturing companies are usually organized along functional lines – manufacturing is dealt with in one department, personnel issues in another, and marketing decisions by the marketing department. Such an approach has the advantage that it allows each group to develop its own specialist skills, organization and culture appropriate to the tasks that it faces. Integrating these separate organizations does, of course, create problems, but these can often be resolved at a higher level.

Fortunately, in manufacturing companies, the availability of inventory allows manufacturing and marketing to operate semi-autonomously, at least in the short term. Manufacturing needs to know the likely demand that marketing will create and the particular products that are required, but once these targets are agreed, the two departments can operate independently. Production can then be scheduled to create inventory as it is needed. Marketing does not need to know when or how production takes place.

However, in a service firm this dichotomy breaks down. There are no inventories, and production and consumption occur simultaneously. Production (producing the product) and marketing (satisfying the consumer) are one. The service operation has to be designed from the beginning to reconcile the trade-off between the operational need for high productivity and the marketing need to satisfy consumers. When short-term problems and trade-off decisions have to be made at the site or branch level, they are usually made by a manager, with simultaneous responsibility for operations, marketing and personnel.

For this reason it is crucial that a marketing orientation permeates all personnel within the service organization. Marketing cannot be separated. It has also led many experts to argue against separate marketing departments within service organizations. They argue that, if one creates a separate marketing function, the remainder of the staff will feel that marketing is not their responsibility, with disastrous consequences for service quality.

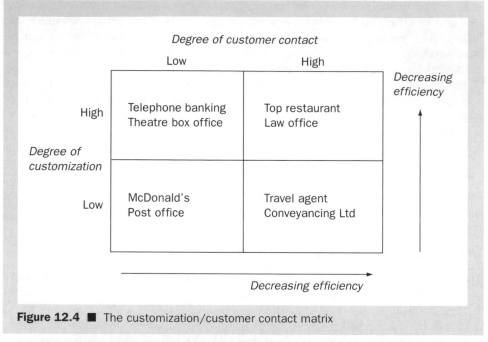

Figure 12.4 ■ The customization/customer contact matrix

Source: adapted from John E. G. Bateson, *Managing Services Marketing*, Orlando, FL: Dryden, 1992, p. 452

As with most complex organizational issues, there is no simple answer: a contingency approach is required. How you organize marketing departments depends upon several facets of the firm and its environment. The issues are represented in Figure 12.4. Most service firms can be described in two dimensions: the degree of customer contact and the degree of customization. The higher the customer contact, the more difficult it is to run a high-productivity organization. This is because the high involvement of consumers in the process slows down the system and prevents standardization. Similarly, the higher the degree of individual customization, the more difficult it is to run an efficient 'production line' service.

From an operations perspective, the low/low cell is the ideal. Customer contact and customization are minimized, so that the operation can be run almost like an efficient manufacturing plant with a narrow product range. However, from a marketing perspective the high/high cell might be ideal, since the customer is able to interact and a solution is designed exactly for him or her. The other two cells look for a trade-off between efficiency and effectiveness. For example, the firm Conveyancing Ltd offers the personal contact of a law firm, but simplifies its offer to routine house conveyancing which it can process with high efficiency.

The different cells suggest different roles and organizations for marketing. In the high/high cell there is little scope for centralized marketing departments or even specialized marketing personnel. Responsibility for the product and marketing lies with the professional operators (e.g. solicitors, accountants) who have intensive contact with the clients and customize the service client by client. By contrast, in the low/low cell (e.g. car rental) the business is offering highly standardized services and customer contact is limited. Such a situation makes for centralized marketing and brand development. Site personnel can be trained to follow simple routines and can be controlled by rules and systems.

In the other two cells, which mix the high and low dimensions, marketing tasks usually have to be shared. A central marketing department can help to achieve scale economies in advertising and brand-building. It can also act as a change agent in creating a stronger customer orientation in the business. But a marketing orientation is crucial among the frontline personnel who have key roles in either customizing the product or in interfacing with clients.

Marketing in the non-business sector

The previous sections have assumed that service organizations are being run with a view to making a profit for their owners. However, there are two major sectors of service where this is not true – private non-profit and public sector organizations. Public sector organizations account for well over half the service sector in most countries. Private non-profit organizations are smaller, accounting for perhaps 10 per cent of the sector.

Defining these organizations is not easy, since many non-profit organizations (e.g. Oxfam, trade unions) engage in activities such as retail shops and mail order catalogues which are clearly intended to make a profit. The distinction is that these profit-making activities are not their primary goal and any profits made are transferred into their real mission, which is alleviating poverty, protecting its membership's interests or some other worthy goal. Blois' definition is useful: 'A non-profit organisation is an organisation whose prime goal is non-economic. However, in pursuit of that goal it may undertake profit-making activities.'[11]

A public sector organization is one which is controlled by and responsible to a government body rather than to shareholders or members. Again such a definition is hardly watertight, since many public sector institutions (e.g. universities) engage in profit-making activities and rely on a mixture of financing from government, consumers and voluntary contributions from donors. Some public sector organizations the government would like to see making a surplus (e.g. the Post Office); others are inherently non-revenue generating (e.g. the police). Finally, with the 1980s movement towards 'privatizing' public sector organizations, many public bodies are shifting to become private, for-profit enterprises.

Criticisms of non-business organizations

Non-profit, and especially public sector, organizations are in most countries subject to considerable criticism and hostility. Criticisms focus on both their inefficiency and ineffectiveness. In terms of efficiency, most are visibly overstaffed. Both non-profit and public sector bodies have not had the same pressure to reduce overheads and administrative costs. In addition, the capital invested in them often appears to have had minimal effects on productivity. For example, before privatization, the railways came under public criticism when much of the network was closed down by a rather modest fall of snow. This was particularly surprising in that the organization had just completed a major investment programme to prevent this type of problem. British Rail's public response was bemusing. A spokesman blamed the problem on 'the wrong type of snow'.

Their ineffectiveness has been subject to even more criticism. These organizations have often been extremely slow in reacting to problems. Bureaucracy and over complex systems have often prevented even simple difficulties from being identified and quickly resolved. They have also often lacked any customer orientation. Few would put as a goal 'delighting the customer'. Many appear to be run for the convenience of the staff. Their primary aim often appears to be preserving the jobs of the people working there, discouraging change and avoiding increased effort.

A reporter investigated why a public hospital always woke its patients at 5.30 a.m. This seemed unnecessarily early, particularly since they had to wait until 8.00 a.m. before receiving breakfast. The reason discovered was that the staff changed shifts at 6.30 a.m. and staff had agreed that a 'fair' schedule for them was that the leaving shift should wake the patients, allowing the new shift an hour to 'settle in' before they had to deliver breakfasts.

Not only is the performance of so many of these organizations poor, but it appears to be getting worse. Services that fifty years ago were seen as efficient and effective are now visibly unable to perform. The postal service, education, hospitals, the police and railways are all perceived by the public to be deteriorating and often in critical condition. This lack of confidence has been the driving force behind the move to 'privatize' as many services as possible.

However, the causes of this crisis are not well understood. Many rationales appear to be unconvincing alibis rather than true explanations. Some of the more common ones are the following:

Multiple stakeholders

Some argue that achieving performance in non-business organizations is more difficult because they have multiple stakeholders. But, as shown in Chapter 1, it has never been true that effective businesses have only sought to maximize the profits of their shareholders. Successful companies have always sought to balance the partially conflicting goals of multiple stakeholder groups – shareholders, customers, employees, managers, suppliers, creditors and the communities in which they operate.

Ambiguous goals

Non-business organizations have multiple constituencies. For example, Professor Shapiro of Harvard saw the difference between a profit and a non-profit organization as being that the former has only one consistency – customers 'to which it provides products and from which it receives funds'.[12] By contrast, a non-profit organization has to market to two constituencies: 'clients to whom it provides products, and donors from whom it receives resources'. However, again such an explanation appears too simple. In fact many, if not most, businesses have multiple constituencies. For example, financial institutions have to appeal to both savers to obtain funds and investors to purchase their services. These constituencies have different and even conflicting requirements.

Poor-quality employees

Another common explanation is that these organizations do not attract good people. But again it is not obvious that those who hold managerial and professional jobs in hospitals, universities or other non-profit services are less qualified or honest than those in business. In America and Europe there are many examples of top business managers being put in control of public and non-profit organizations. Few have done better than the 'bureaucrats' they replaced. Indeed, most became bureaucrats themselves. The fault appears to be with the system rather than with the people.

Unmeasurable outputs

A common defence is that the objectives of a non-business organization are not quantifiable. Hence, the success or performance of such an organization cannot be easily judged. But once more this explanation appears unconvincing. Any mission, even that for a successful business, is intangible. Marks & Spencer, for example, defined its mission as 'to foster good human relations with customers, suppliers and staff'. Ciba-Geigy defines its mission as 'striking a balance between our economic, social, and environmental responsibilities'. These are equally as intangible as Oxfam's goal of 'alleviating hunger and poverty', that of the churches of 'saving souls' or the mission of the police to 'safeguard the community'.

However, what successful businesses do, but which few non-business organizations achieve, is to translate these broad missions into more specific, clearly defined targets which are measurable. 'Saving souls' is not measurable, but church attendance is. 'Alleviating poverty' is intangible, but delivering 1 million daily food equivalents or building 100 field hospitals is a very tangible target. Only if such output goals are defined can resources be allocated and performance improved. In contrast, many non-business organizations measure performance in terms of inputs rather than outputs. They use the money they receive or the size of the organization they build as a measure of performance. Of course, such measures contribute more to increasing bureaucracy than to the organization's efficiency and effectiveness.

Characteristics of non-business organizations

The real differences which account for the poor performance of most non-business organizations are three – the lack of a profit measure, funding being divorced from the market, and the monopoly power most possess.

Lack of profit measure

Profit is not the objective of business managers, but it is a requirement. Investors will not supply capital unless they see an adequate return. This requirement ensures that managers will normally seek to operate the business efficiently: that capital and people are not wasted.

Non-profit businesses are created because it is believed either that insufficient private capital would be attracted to do the 'necessary' job, or that a private solution would be unfair. The former occurs where there are 'externalities'. Individuals would not buy enough of the product or service because they are shortsighted or because they do not take into account the benefits received by others. For example, voluntary payments would not be likely to be sufficient for the defence budget or similar 'public goods'. Charities are needed because the poorest people cannot afford to buy food or healthcare. Hence reliance on the market would be socially unacceptable.

However, once the profit measure is taken away, there is no natural test of organizational efficiency. There is no measure of the return that managers are obtaining on the resources they have at their disposal. With no test of performance, not surprisingly, capital and people tend to be used inefficiently.

Funding divorced from the market

While some non-businesses obtain their revenues from customers, most do not. In the public sector, most receive all or a substantial part from taxation (e.g. the health service, education, police). In the private non-profit sector (e.g. AIDS research, Salvation Army) donors provide the majority of funding.

This is the most fundamental distinction between profit and non-business organizations. Businesses (in competitive markets) are paid only if they satisfy customers. Customer satisfaction is, therefore, the basis for achieving performance and results. By contrast, the revenues of non-businesses do not depend upon performance. They are paid out of taxation or from the generosity of donors who often do not consume the outputs of the organization. Such revenues depend more upon promises than deeds. Being paid out of taxes or donations changes what is meant by performance. Performance for a manager in a non-business is the ability to increase the budget or the staff. Satisfying customers inevitably becomes a secondary consideration because it does not determine the survival of the organization or the career prospects of the managers. This disconnection from the market has three consequences.

First, it discourages efficiency. Administrators know that not to spend every penny of the budget will only convince the sponsors that the budget for next year can be safely cut. Second, there is no pressure to set priorities and concentrate resources on them. The overstretched police force is a good example. All the crime statistics show that the police are increasingly unable to cope. Rather than focus on the obvious priorities of protecting citizens from serious crime, they divert efforts to the old lady who has lost her cat, or to help the householder who has locked himself out of his home or car. Resources are misallocated this way because the police do not want the local politicians who set their budgets receiving complaints from the voters. The result is that the proportion of serious unsolved crimes continues to escalate.

Finally, no institution likes to abandon anything that it does. In the profit sector, the choices of consumers kill off obsolete products or services. But in non-profit and public sector organizations no such discipline exists. Maintaining the past is regarded as virtuous and innovation is seen as a threat to jobs.

Monopoly power

Most non-business organizations have some form of monopoly power. In the public sector (e.g. railways, gas, electricity), it is usually a natural or legal monopoly. In the non-profit sector (e.g. charities), the power is generally based on demand substantially exceeding supply. In both situations the consumer lacks a choice. This, of course, amplifies the existing tendencies towards inefficiency and lack of customer orientation. Inefficiencies can be hidden in some organizations by raising prices (e.g. the telephone or electricity authority), and in others by allowing the service to deteriorate (e.g. schools). The lack of consumer choice means that there is no reason to satisfy consumers – they are obliged to use the service. The consequence is that non-business staff typically lack the courtesy and professionalism found in competitive, profit-oriented businesses. They usually believe that they know what is wanted better than the consumer. The service is run for the benefit of the people who work there rather than the customers they are meant to serve.

Striking evidence of these features is provided by the increasing number of public sector institutions which have moved to attract additional resources by setting up activities which compete in the private sector. State hospitals which compete for fee-paying patients or universities which introduce courses for executives are typical examples. To be successful, the organizations rapidly learn that they have to segment the customer base like an airline. The traditional, tied customers (e.g. National Health Service patients or undergraduate students) get 'economy class' treatment. The new, fee-paying customers, who have the power to choose, receive 'executive class' treatment: their needs are analyzed, their wants are quickly tended to, and they obtain upgraded facilities and the attention of the best staff. It is clear that non-business organizations can perform if the systems are right.

Systems for non-business organizations

The challenge for top managers in non-business organizations is to create the systems which will allow people to perform efficiently and effectively. Without the right systems, non-businesses will lack direction, will have no basis for rationally allocating resources, and will leave both staff and customers frustrated by the organization's failure to perform (see Box 12.1). In many ways, such systems are more important to the non-business sector than they are to the competitive profit-oriented firm. With the latter, the choices of customers and the pressure to meet the profit requirement force

BOX 12.1

Public sector mismanagement

Concerned people assume that more public investment means better public services – better roads, healthcare and education. But studies show that public sector mismanagement wastes much of the investment. Among the most shocking examples is investment in the developing countries. After investing $200 billion a year in infrastructure, the World Bank found that 1 billion people still have no clean water and over 2 billion are without sanitation and electricity.

The Bank found that resources were squandered in several ways. Facilities were not maintained. For example, an average 40 per cent of power-generating equipment was out of action. Infrastructure, roads and power stations were built in the wrong places. Services were run with woeful inefficiency. Two-thirds of rail staff in some countries were adding no value. Finally, prices were held below marginal costs, thus requiring large state subsidies.

Government involvement was found to be the root of the problem. The World Bank proposed a three-part solution: first, making the services run on clear business-like lines with professional managers or private sector firms contracted to run them; second, introducing more competition to break down their monopoly power; and third, involving consumers directly in planning, designing and paying for projects, especially at the local level. Many countries now think privatization is the most effective way of achieving the transformation.

Source: World Development Report 1994: Infrastructure for development (Oxford: Oxford University Press, 1994)

the firm towards adding value if it is to survive. But, as we have seen, for public sector and non-profit institutions such forces do not exist.

Making non-businesses perform requires five steps (see Box 12.2).[13]

Defining the mission

First, management need to define the mission of the organization. The mission statement, as in the private sector, should answer four questions.

■ Who are the 'customers' it aims to serve?

■ What is the vision of what it wants to accomplish?

■ What is its distinctive competence – what can it do better than other organizations?

■ Who are the stakeholders whose interests it must seek to satisfy?

Most non-business organizations have not thought through these questions. The alternative answers and conflicting interests have not been brought into the open, discussed and evaluated and the necessary trade-offs determined. As a result, management have no basis for getting agreement on priorities or for allocating resources and measuring performance. Activities are justified on vague 'public interest' arguments

BOX 12.2

Planning in the non-business sector

1 *Mission statement*
   - Customer scope
   - Vision of the organization
   - Distinctive competences
   - Key stakeholders

2 *Organizational objectives*
   - Customer
   - Innovation
   - Resources
   - Productivity
   - Regulatory

3 *Strategic plan*
   - Marketing audit
   - Priority setting

   - Marketing mix
   - Action plan

4 *Performance measures*
   - Customer satisfaction
   - Output measures

5 *Feedback on performance*
   - Self-control
   - Appraisal
   - Incentives

and good intentions. Failures are explained away as due to lack of resources or the results of mistaken political directives. In effect, managers abdicate responsibility for strategy in favour of administrative or bureaucratic work.

Setting measurable objectives

Once management have an agreed mission, this needs to be disaggregated into clear, specific, measurable objectives which people can commit to and which, if achieved, will progress the mission. Objectives should cover four fundamental areas. First, and most important, are the customer objectives. For a hospital one objective might be reduce waiting time for operations by 50 per cent in the next two years. For a police force, one could be increasing the detection rate for violent crime by 30 per cent. It is crucial that such objectives are relevant. Relevance means being based upon research into what needs customers most want satisfying.

Second, the organization should have innovation objectives which enable it to do new important things or to do existing things radically better. Third, it needs resource objectives. For a charity this may mean setting targets for donations and legacies that are necessary to achieve its mission. It may also mean attracting particular professional skills or obtaining specialized equipment to do a better job. Fourth, like any efficient organization it should have productivity objectives which indicate the outputs to be obtained. Finally, non-business organizations normally need regulatory objectives – goals set for them by governments or regulatory bodies.

Developing strategies

Next, management have to develop strategies to achieve their objectives and mission. This involves four tasks. First, there should be a thorough marketing audit to identify those activities within the organization's portfolio where it is doing well, meeting objectives and achieving results. It should also identify those areas where it could do well if resources were put there. For a charity like Christian Aid, these units of analysis might be countries. For a university, they might be programmes or departments. The organization should then identify those activities where it is doing poorly and where real results are never likely to be achieved.

This analysis should then allow the organization to set priorities. In which areas can it really add value and meet needs? These are the areas where resources should be concentrated. Which areas should be eliminated if stakeholders and regulators will permit this to happen? Which activities should be left on a 'care and maintenance' basis? Most organizations will then need to develop a marketing plan to implement these priorities. This will mean defining target markets. Often there will be two sets of customers to target – recipients and donors. It will also need a marketing mix: a communications programme, distribution channels, product policy and often pricing decisions.

For example, the Cancer Society will need to target selectively the types of men and women it can best help – its potential 'customers'. It will also need to analyze the market for potential donors – who are most likely to be willing to donate to this charity? It will then need to develop a communications programme to appeal to both groups. This will include setting a budget and choosing media and message: for example, 'Fight cancer with a check-up and a cheque'. It may also need a distribution policy – where should it locate offices for local fund raising and operations? It will have 'product' decisions too. In fighting cancer should it focus on cancer screening, research, informing the public or some other product option? Finally, there may be pricing decisions – should it ask people to contribute if they receive, say, a cancer test? If so, how much?

Finally, the organization should produce an action plan. This will detail what needs to be done over the coming year and who will be responsible for doing it.

Establishing performance measures

Next, management need to think through measures of performance. The question is: how can managers judge whether they are doing their jobs well? In profit-oriented firms this is usually a straightforward task. The main measures of performance are marketing and financial results. But in non-business organizations performance is different.

Management need two types of performance measure. The first, and most important, are customer satisfaction measures. Because the market does not work for these organizations, it is crucial to have direct, regular and systematic feedback from customers on how satisfied they are with the service and its major components – the core service, the behaviour and attitudes of the staff, the quality of the facilities, the pre- and post- delivery services, and so on. This is the key to shifting staff from a 'we know best' attitude to their clients.

Second, management need to think through the output measures which are relevant for calibrating performance. For a hospital these might be the number of operations it performs in a period, or the length of the waiting list. Output measures are essential to shift the organization away from an input focus, where the size of the budget or the number of staff acts as a measure of success.

Providing feedback

These performance measures should then be used to provide employees with feedback on their work. The customer satisfaction and output measures need to be highly and continuously visible in offices and newsletters, so that the staff can see how they are doing now. It is particularly valuable if league tables or comparisons can be made between units of the organization: for example between different schools in the area, between hospitals or between similar charities. However, given the resistance to performance evaluation which normally exists within non-business organizations, such changes need to be carefully and sympathetically prepared.

Feedback gives staff the information to manage themselves better. For example, in some university departments degree students now rate the performance of the professors teaching their courses and the results are published each term (a practice, incidentally, that has always existed on university 'for-profit' courses). The result is always a dramatic and speedy improvement in teaching performance. Before the feedback was provided, many professors had no idea how bad they were. Others did not care, since their poor performance was never revealed. Once comparative information is available, every professor wants to do good work.

A perspective

The failure of public sector organizations to manage themselves properly led, in the 1980s, to a revulsion against them and pressure to privatize as many as possible. In general, privatization brought substantial benefits in terms of greater customer orientation and higher productivity. However, there will always be a need for a public sector and for private non-profit organizations. Improving these organizations requires the government to introduce the right frameworks and managers more capable of providing vision, strategy and systems.

The right framework depends upon the type of organization. Drucker distinguished three types: natural monopolies, service institutions paid out of budgets, and policy areas.[14] Natural monopolies are those institutions which must have exclusive rights in a given area, such as the water authority or the electric power service. Without control, such monopolies, besides being inefficient and ineffective, will inevitably exploit the consumer. The question then is: should it be under public ownership or public regulation? The evidence is strongly in favour of private ownership with public regulation.

A government-owned monopoly of the telephone system or the railways, for example, may not exploit, but the customer has no redress against inefficiency, poor service, high prices and a general disregard of his or her wants. An independently managed monopoly under public regulation is likely to be far more responsive to customer dissatisfaction because this influences the public regulatory body which sets the organization's rates and hence its revenues and profits.

The second type are organizations paid out of governmental budgets, including universities, schools and hospitals. They have two significant characteristics. First, they supply a need rather than a want. Second, demand greatly exceeds supply, so there is little pressure to be responsive to the consumer or to improve efficiency and service. The answer most countries are edging towards to handle these organizations is to stimulate regulated competition. Parents can be given vouchers to equal the cost of tuition and they can then choose the school or university from a list of approved suppliers. This is also being introduced into health services, where doctors receive hospital vouchers on behalf of their patients. Competition will gradually lead to a shift of resources towards those organizations which are more efficient and responsive.

Finally, there are policy areas like the courts or defence ministries where managerial autonomy and competition are virtually impossible. Here the only external stimulus can be the periodic, independent audit of the purposes and performance of these institutions. Do they still have a purpose? Are they being run in a way which meets the expectations of the public?

Once the right frameworks are in place, they need to introduce the systems to shift from an administrative to a managerial focus. Administrators concern themselves with internal operations and procedures – with inputs – while managers concern themselves with outputs. The purpose of any public or non-profit organization is to serve certain publics – to meet the needs and wants of their 'customers'. The primary tasks of management are to define clearly what the organization's mission is and what its priorities are, and to plan how people can be motivated and measured to perform against these goals.

Summary

The service sector is the largest and most rapidly growing part of the modern economy. Even in the manufacturing sector most of the new jobs are 'service' jobs – research and development, marketing, information technology and so on, rather than 'making things'. The basic principles of marketing all apply in the service sector, but managers have to note differences in emphasis. These arise from the distinctive character of services – intangibility, inseparability, variability, perishability and the lack of ownership.

These characteristics create four special problems for managers in the service sector: managing quality, achieving high productivity, internal marketing and building a differentiated offer. Especially with high-contact services, marketing strategy must place much greater attention on integrating with an effective operating strategy. Marketing and operations cannot be separated in the way that they are in the goods sector. The key issue is building a positioning strategy that jointly leverages high value for customers with a manageable cost structure and break-even point.

A very large portion of the service sector consists of publicly owned and private non-profit organizations. While everyone recognizes that these are needed, the way most of them are run is heavily criticized. Most such non-business organizations are inefficient and unresponsive to their customers. The sources of these problems lie in the lack of profit measure, the lack of competition and the disconnection of their funding from the market. Non-businesses can be made to perform, but this requires managers rather than administrators. The task of management in these organizations is to develop an agreed mission, set the objectives and strategies, and establish performance measures which focus on customer satisfaction and outputs.

Questions

1. Why is the service sector growing more rapidly than the manufacturing sector?

2. The most fundamental distinguishing characteristic of services is intangibility. Discuss the implications of this with specific reference to marketing.

3. Give an example of a business which has substantially increased its service quality and analyze the reasons for the improvement.

4. Find and analyze a service organization which has a very high productivity. How is it achieved? What are the trade-offs against service quality?

5. Why do so many publicly owned organizations appear to perform so poorly?

6. Does marketing apply to the non-profit sector?

Notes

1. G. Lynn Shostack, 'Breaking free from product marketing', *Journal of Marketing*, April 1977, pp. 77–82.

2. Donald W. Cowell, 'Marketing Services', in Michael J. Baker (ed.), *The Marketing Book* (London: Heinemann, 1994), pp. 666–77.

3. Robert D. Buzzell and Bradley T. Gale, *The PIMS Principles: Linking strategy to performance* (New York: Free Press, 1987), pp. 103–34.

4. Philip B. Crosby, *Quality is Free: The art of making quality certain* (New York: New American Library, 1979).

5. David A. Garvin, 'Quality on the line', *Harvard Business Review*, September–October 1983, pp. 65–73.

6. A. Parasuraman, Valarie A. Zeithanel and Leonard L. Berry, 'A conceptual model of service quality and its implications for future research', *Journal of Marketing*, Fall 1985, pp. 41–50.

7. Theodore Levitt, 'Production-line approach to service', *Harvard Business Review*, September–October 1972, pp. 41–52.

8. James L. Heskett, 'Lessons in the service sector', *Harvard Business Review*, March–April 1987, pp. 51–61.

9. John E. G. Bateson, *Managing Services Marketing* (Orlando, FL: Dryden Press, 1992), pp. 389–94.

10. *Ibid.*, p. 394.

11. Keith J. Blois, 'Marketing for non-profit organisations', in Michael J. Baker (ed.), *The Marketing Book* (London: Heinemann, 1994), p. 405.

12. Benson P. Shapiro, 'Marketing for non-profit organisations', *Harvard Business Review*, September–October 1992, p. 124.

13. This section draws on Peter F. Drucker, *Management: Tasks, responsibilities, practices* (London: Heinemann, 1974), pp. 158–66.

14. *Ibid.*, pp. 154–60.

Chapter 13

Turnaround management

Decisive strategic change is required when an organization is in decline or its decline is anticipated. For a business the symptoms of decline are falling profitability, eroding market share and deteriorating liquidity. These are the *symptoms*, but the *causes* of decline are different. The fundamental problems are invariably caused by a transformation occurring in the industry: the emergence of new distribution channels, new technologies or new competitors with strategies or value chains that permit them to make superior offers to customers. Such changes make obsolete the strategies of the firms which have led the industry in the past.

Companies run into a crisis when organizational inertia prevents a sufficiently rapid and decisive change in strategy to meet the new industry environment (Figure 13.1). Rapid organizational response is always difficult – especially for a traditional market leader, because the leader normally has extensive financial assets which have to be written off, skills and distribution networks which no longer have value and a management culture which is not effective. Not surprisingly, most organizations find these barriers difficult to surmount. When such barriers to change are not overcome, the organization slips into crisis, exhibiting declining marketing and financial performance.

The tasks of the turnaround manager are to halt this erosion and then develop a programme of revitalization. The first task we call *consolidation*, which largely entails operational measures to restore profitability and cash flow. These consist of policies to cut costs, increase margins, remove redundant assets and control cash. The longer-term and more important strategic task is *transformation*. This consists of understanding how the industry is changing and forming a vision of the means by which the business can be revitalized to regain leadership. Such a vision entails deciding where the new market opportunities will be, what core competences are needed to capitalize on these opportunities, and what new supply networks and distribution channels will best create and deliver the new value that the company will provide.

The next section shows why consolidation and transformation need to be pursued in partnership. In a turnaround it is very easy to create a situation where these conflict. Worse, many managers confuse the two, thinking that short-term consolidation or a

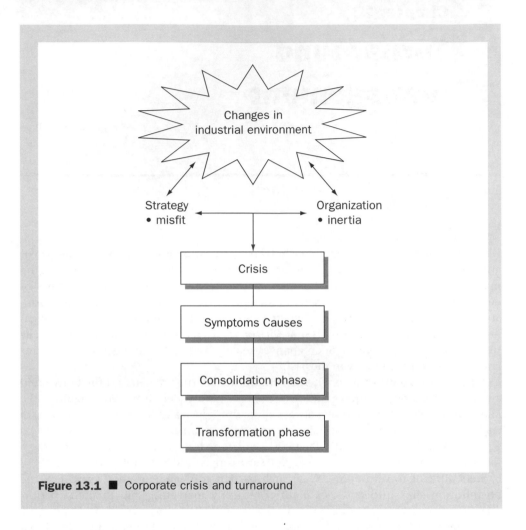

Figure 13.1 ■ Corporate crisis and turnaround

profit recovery is synonymous with the successful turnaround. In fact, engineering a short-term profit recovery is normally straightforward. However, such a recovery is never sustainable unless management proceed with the longer-term and more challenging task of dealing with the causes of the decline through a sustained programme of transformation.

Short- versus long-term improvements

Consolidation focuses on short-term profits; transformational change is directed at long-term market performance. The former views profit as an end in itself; the latter sees profits as the result of winning the loyalty of customers. Pressures on managers to achieve quick results frequently lead to an overemphasis on short-term profits and a neglect of transformational change. This often has a devastating effect on the firm's ability to achieve a long-term turnaround. To see why this occurs we need to look at the conflicting, time-dependent nature of profit improvement decisions. First, all decisions affecting the firm's value chain (i.e. the decisions about products, prices, promotion, service and distribution channels) have two *conflicting effects*. For example, a cut in price or an increase in the promotional budget will normally have a positive effect on sales, but can easily have a negative impact on current profits. Looking at this conflict from the other direction, short-term profitability can usually be increased by raising prices and reining back promotional spend, but this will normally involve some loss of market share.

Second, not only is there a directional conflict, but there is also a *timing difference*. The effect of decisions on profits usually occurs much faster than the impact on sales and market performance. For example, a decision to cut R & D or brand advertising will immediately boost cash flow and profits, but a negative effect on sales may not occur for several years. Looking at it the other way, a decision to boost research, advertising or service takes time before it is implemented, achieves positive recognition in the market and builds loyalty among customers. There is a delay – often a long delay – between expenditure and return. When profits come under serious pressure, not surprisingly few managers are willing to initiate longer-term, market-oriented spending programmes. They know that postponing such investments has a negligible effect on short-term sales, but a large and immediate positive impact on profits.

The implication of these two conflicts is that management have to choose how they balance short-term profit goals against long-term competitiveness in the market. If executives are solely financially oriented, then short-term profits can be quickly turned around by raising prices, slashing investment and pruning the business back to its

---

BOX 13.1

Hanson Trust

Hanson is a striking example of the results of a short-term profit focus. This huge Anglo-American conglomerate, built by Lords Hanson and White between 1965 and 1985, defined its aims solely as profits and cash generation. Companies were acquired and ruthlessly rationalized to maximize return on capital employed and avoid any investments which would not have a rapid payback. The concepts of vision and long-term strategy were ridiculed. The chairman and CEO made a point of never visiting the businesses. For a time, the cutbacks resulted in rapid earnings growth and a rising share price. Hanson and White became business heroes and were given lordships for their services to industry. Unfortunately, a decade later it became clear that the lack of investments and long-term vision had stunted the businesses, leaving them with eroding shares of declining markets. Hanson Trust went into a long period of decline and by 1996 it was decided to dismember the group.

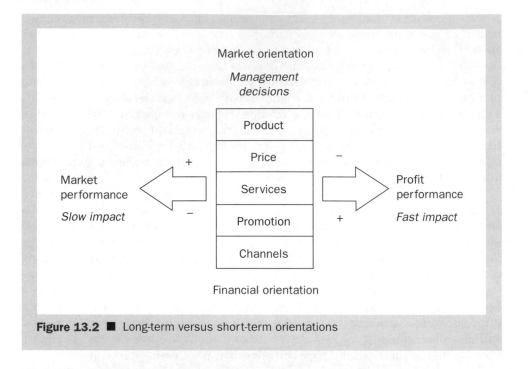

Figure 13.2 ■ Long-term versus short-term orientations

currently profitable core. Unfortunately, over a longer run, such policies destroy the competitiveness of the company. Box 13.1 illustrates how this occurred for one well-known company. On the other hand, a purely market orientation (Figure 13.2) which ignores an inadequate profit performance is equally vulnerable, especially in a western environment.

Turnaround management needs a three-pronged approach to resolving this dilemma. First, managers need to communicate a convincing, well-thought-out vision of where the company is heading, which will inspire the stakeholders to take a more sanguine view of the company's future. If management can impress with their long-run marketing strategy, then investors' views of the value of the business will not be dominated by its current profits travails. Second, management need to achieve a realistic balance between the short term and the long term. This is why a consolidation phase is important – to optimize the current businesses and strip out those that no longer fit the company's future. The consolidation phase provides time and resources for implementing the more fundamental changes that are necessary. Third, management need to develop a long-term revitalization plan which is lean on resources. Successful Japanese companies, in particular, have shown that long-term success is achieved not by outspending competitors in R & D, marketing or operations, but by using skills and finance more effectively. Competitive advantage is achieved by out-thinking not outspending rivals. This way long-term growth does not necessarily result in an inadequate return on investment.

Types of industry change

Change becomes necessary when a mismatch occurs between the firm and its environment. The consolidation phase of the change programme is tactical, focusing on the financial and operational symptoms of the malaise. The transformation stage is strategic, dealing with the root causes of the problem. *Strategic drift* is the term used to describe an increasing gap between what the market requires and what the organization is able to offer. Strategic drift is reflected in the company possessing products, processes or distribution channels which are no longer appropriate to achieve growth and profitability.

Two types of environmental change which trigger strategic drift can be distinguished. *Evolutionary change* occurs relatively slowly and should be predictable by an alert management. Examples include the drift of low-skill, labour-intensive manufacturing from high-cost to low-cost countries, the growth of out-of-town retailing and the growing application of electronics in engineering. *Radical change* is rapid and discontinuous change which is far more difficult to anticipate. Examples include dramatic technological breakthroughs (e.g. SmithKline's discovery of H2-antagonists), major economic or political changes (e.g. the sudden collapse of the Soviet empire in 1991) and significant innovations in the market or distribution channels. With this type of change, management have to grasp quickly the magnitude of the shift for the company's future, and prioritize forging a view about how the business must be transformed.

Faced with strategic drift, management have four options.[1]

Zero change

This occurs when an organization's historic strategy remains essentially constant over a long period of time. There is no substantial change in its market positioning, product portfolio or channels of distribution. In today's rapidly changing environment, zero change is always fatal. As Figure 13.3(a) illustrates, what may begin as a small mismatch with the market grows, through a process of strategic drift, into a disastrous strategic gap.

Woolworths was once the world's most successful international retailing group. But the company failed to adapt to evolutionary change as living standards rose, markets became increasingly segmented and consumer expectations for greater quality and fashion increased. What began as a small, solvable problem became, through management's reluctance to challenge their historic strategy, a gap which required the complete dismemberment of the group.

Gradual change

This occurs when the organization changes incrementally through small, piecemeal adaptations. Some products, markets and channels are changed, while other core areas remain constant. Most organizations that achieve long-run performance seek to adapt through a process of gradual change. It is like a process of experimentation: successful moves are built on; failures are abandoned. Over time, the accretion of these relatively small moves can be seen as substantial strategic change.

Such a process has many advantages. It builds on the organization's expertise and experience. It is relatively low risk. Managerial flexibility and creativity are encouraged. It avoids the trauma and resistance to change which normally occur with corporate transformation.

Flux

This is a period of indecision in which strategies change but in no clear direction. It is common where a substantial strategic gap has emerged and management are uncertain how to close it. Experiments might include new ventures to copy industry innovators or acquisitions seeking out new market opportunities. One danger in this period is responding too little, too late. The opposite danger is gambling on a major investment in which the company lacks the core capabilities or industry foresight to succeed.

Transformational change

This occurs when management radically change their view of opportunities in the industry and aggressively develop the new processes, products, channels and market positioning to capitalize on the new scenario. Transformational change involves acquiring new competences and resources, re-energizing the workforce to embrace the new direction enthusiastically, and the substantial reconfiguration of the business and its network of suppliers and distribution partners.

Transformational change may become necessary when there is a radical change in the company's environment. More commonly, it becomes necessary when management fail to respond over a long period to evolutionary changes (see Figure 13.3(c)). The strategic gap then becomes too great to be closed by gradual change. In the 1990s many major companies sought to produce transformational change to break their downward spiral. These include Philips, British Airways, AEG and IBM. All saw tough consolidation stages with huge reductions in workforces and major disinvestments, followed by efforts to re-energize the organization and culture, acquire new skills and set a new marketing direction.

Such a change is the focus of this chapter. Transformational change is difficult to initiate and even more difficult to sustain. It normally requires management to introduce initially a fairly ruthless programme of consolidation. For example, AEG, the German industrial company, cut its workforce from 150,000 to 40,000. Philips, IBM and BA lost similar numbers of jobs. Consolidation needs to be followed by a change in gear with top management painting a convincing and enthusiastic vision of the transformed company leading a much-changed industry. It also involves the patient build-up of new competences and the accomplishment of intermediate challenges which act as milestones marking the company's progress. Finally, it requires top management to

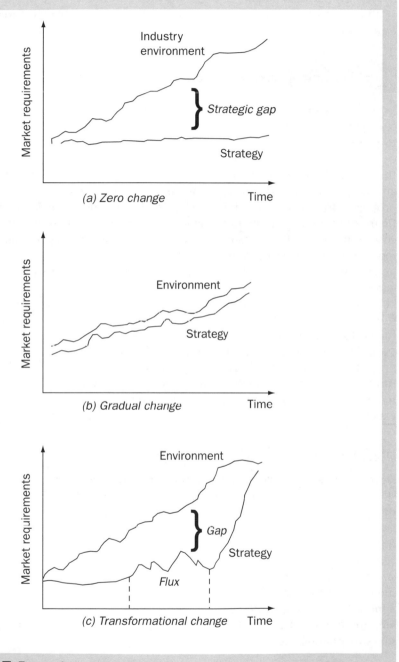

Figure 13.3 ■ Types of adaptive change

possess the persuasive ability to overcome the barriers to change which inevitably exist at all levels of the organization, and which represent the biggest threat to successful transformation.

Some financial concepts

When an organization is in serious trouble, the first stage of the turnaround is usually consolidation – halting the financial deterioration. To see how this is done, it is useful to present some basic financial concepts. Analyzing financial reports is unnecessarily complicated because accountants use different terms to describe the same concept; they use different methods and styles to present accounts, and employ different ratios and criteria to assess financial performance. However, with familiarity most of these problems do not cause too much difficulty. Deeper dilemmas lie in the valuation of financial assets and profits in a changing environment, the way accountants allocate costs and the 'window dressing' that companies often employ to make their accounts look more appealing to investors.[2]

The three key financial accounts are the income statement (or profit and loss account), the balance sheet and the cash flow statement. The income statement and balance sheet for Chemco are summarized in Table 13.1. The balance sheet shows, on the left side, the financial assets used to generate the company's sales and create value for customers: the year-end value of its plant and equipment, stocks, credit outstanding to customers, etc. The right side shows how these value-creating assets are financed: via short- and long-term borrowings and through equity or shareholder funds invested in the company. The income statement (or P & L account) shows how much profit was obtained from the sales produced over the year after all costs and expenses were deducted.

Objectives

Developing a financial plan for a company has two components: objectives and strategy. The most obvious financial objective is profit. Here Chemco has a *net profit* (before tax) of £13 million. But to compare and evaluate businesses of different sizes and characteristics, profits need to be analyzed in a relative way. A commonly used ratio for doing this is *return on sales* (ROS) – net profit divided by sales, which is 3.9 per cent (i.e. 13 ÷ 330). This figure is useful for comparing businesses which are different in size but similar in structure, but if companies require very different levels of investment it is less meaningful. Hence *return on investment* (ROI) is the most common approach to looking at financial performance – a ratio which compares profit with the amount of investment required to generate the profit. There are three ways of defining investment and hence ROI:

1. Return on equity (ROE) = $\dfrac{\text{Net profit}}{\text{Equity}}$

Table 13.1 ■ Chemco plc accounts

Profit and loss account	£m
Sales	330
Variable costs	235
Contribution	95
Fixed costs	
Manufacturing	28
Selling and administration	53
Operating profit	14
Net interest payable	1
Net profit before tax	13

Balance sheet	£m			£m
Current assets	200	Current liabilities		105
Stocks	80	Long-term debt		55
Debtors	70			
Other	50	Equity		150
Fixed assets	110			
Total assets	310	Total liabilities		310

This ROE figure is the most relevant measure for shareholders, since equity (share capital and reserves) represents their most obvious stake.

2. Return on assets (ROA) = $\dfrac{\text{Net profit}}{\text{Total assets}}$

ROA is relevant for the manager since he or she is expected to obtain an adequate return on *all* the funds invested in the business, whether provided by shareholders or borrowed from creditors.

3. Return on capital employed (ROCE) = $\dfrac{\text{Net profit}}{\text{Net assets}}$

Capital employed or net assets consists of fixed assets plus net current assets (i.e. current assets less current liabilities). Looking at the balance sheet, it can be seen that net assets is identically equal to equity plus long-term debt. Accountants often see capital employed as the best indicator of the amount of capital or assets employed in the business.

For Chemco these ratios are respectively: *ROE* = 8.7%, *ROA* = 4.2% and *ROCE* = 6.3%.

It should be emphasized that accountants have many slightly different variations of these ratios. Some will use operating profit rather than net profit, especially when calculating ROS, ROA and ROCE. Often tax is deducted from net profit to calculate ROE. Also rather than using year-end investment figures, some accountants calculate the average invested during the year, or even compare profit this year with last year's investment. While these variations produce different numbers, fortunately they do not in any way change the operational implications for management. They do not affect what managers should do to improve profitability.

Another important term is the *gearing ratio*, defined here as:

$$\text{Gearing ratio (GR)} = \frac{\text{Total liabilities} + \text{Equity}}{\text{Equity}}$$

$$= \frac{\text{Total assets}}{\text{Equity}}$$

For Chemco this is 2.1. The higher the GR, the greater the proportion of the assets that are financed by debt rather than shareholder funds.

Finally, we can introduce *asset turnover*:

$$\text{Asset turnover (AT)} = \frac{\text{Sales}}{\text{Total assets}}$$

which for Chemco is 1.06. This measures the effectiveness with which sales are generated from the company's assets. The greater the AT, the more sales are generated by the company's assets. Using these ratios, three important financial identities can be generated (the illustrative figures for Chemco are shown below the identities):

$ROE = ROA \times GR$
$8.7\% = 4.2\% \times 2.1$

This equation shows how, in good times, high gearing can give shareholders spectacular returns, by multiplying up the return on assets. However, in bad times, the need to meet high interest payments and possibly repay debt can put the whole company at risk.

The second equation dichotomizes the task of the manager in improving return on assets into two sets of activities:

$ROA = ROS \times AT$
$4.2\% = 3.9\% \times 1.06$

In other words, the manager can improve performance by achieving either a higher return on sales or higher asset turnover. ROS is increased by obtaining higher prices, more sales or lower costs. AT is increased by raising sales or cutting the level of current and fixed assets employed in the business.

Putting these two equations together gives the *basic financial planning equation*, which identifies the central financial objective (ROE) and the three dimensions of strategy which are required to achieve it:

$$ROE = ROS \times AT \times GR$$
$$8.7\% = 3.9\% \times 1.06 \times 2.1$$

It is commonly argued that the basic goal of a capitalist enterprise, if it is to survive, has to be achieving a satisfactory return on shareholder funds, i.e. ROE. The last equation shows that there are three, and only three, ways of achieving this. For example, comparing Chemco's ROE with other companies would show that 8.7 per cent is a very poor return. To improve this, management have to raise ROS, AT or GR, or some combination of these. The next section will show how this is done. The basic financial planning equation also interprets how the enterprise generates results. For example, for Chemco it reveals that, on average, for every £1 shareholders invest in the business, Chemco obtained £2.10 of assets; every £1 of its assets generated £1.06 of sales, and every £1 of sales generated 3.9 pence profit. The objective of an efficient management team is to make these numbers bigger. This is especially the case in the consolidation phase when the ratios are in, or moving towards, unsatisfactory levels.

Consolidation phase

A successful turnaround requires two types of decision: operational and strategic. *Operational decisions* are concerned with making the best use of resources to optimize the current business. These are essentially internal, about deploying the firm's financial and physical resources more profitably. *Strategic decisions* are concerned with deciding which markets, products and channels represent the best future for the company. Such decisions are primarily external: they are about seeking to foresee the emerging opportunities being created by changes in the environment, and choosing in which of these the company has the best potential competences to build competitive advantage.

The consolidation phase of the turnaround focuses on operational decisions, but it is crucial that these do not undermine the strategic task of transformation. This can easily happen because consolidation requires substantial disinvestment of yesterday's businesses. By contrast, transformation requires investment in tomorrow's businesses. Operational and strategic decisions need to be pursued in parallel. First, consolidation without a strategy for transformation is highly demoralizing for staff. Without the promise of a more successful future, the company will find its best managers drifting away, often to competition. Second, a strategic plan is necessary to ensure that cutbacks in the consolidation phase do not hit areas vital to the company's future. Hasty disposals of businesses or R & D skills where the company has core competences can prove extremely costly mistakes. Third, looking at both together also stimulates management to consider the conflicts between short-term profit and long-term market performance.

Selecting a focus

The basic financial planning equation $ROE = ROS \times AT \times GR$ provides a powerful framework for improving profitability and cash flow. Applying this systematically has a number of advantages. First, it ensures that management consider *all* the important profit levers. Second, by providing a clear path it allows the task to be done *quickly*. Third, because it is relatively simple it means that the chief executive can *delegate* to lower-level managers key areas for improvement. The system provides the less experienced manager with clear guidelines for analysis and action.

There are many levers for improving profitability and cash flow. The ones that should be the primary focus depend upon several factors:

■ *Speed*. Some profit levers work much faster than others. How urgent is the profit improvement requirement? For example, new products improve profits, but developing them can take years. By contrast, a price increase can offer very speedy results.

■ *Customer reaction*. Some financial levers can be negated by market responses. For example, price increases are likely to lose market share, whereas cost reductions are not. It is important for managers therefore to estimate the relevant demand elasticities.

■ *Competitor reaction*. Efforts to increase volume are likely to produce a competitor response, especially in mature markets. Therefore a head-on strategy to increase market share could be counterproductive.

■ *Upside potential*. Managers should generally focus on where the biggest numbers occur. For example, a food retailer has high variable costs and low fixed costs; a pharmaceutical company's cost structure is the reverse. Therefore in the former management may well see greater upside focusing on cutting variable costs, whereas in pharmaceuticals fixed costs are the key.

■ *Downside risk*. Some turnaround tactics carry higher risks. For example, investing £1 million on an advertising campaign to boost volume is fine if it works, but if the expenditure does not achieve the results expected, profits will be worse than before. Cost-cutting and asset reduction strategies, by contrast, usually carry little downside risk.

■ *Long-term damage*. Cutting R & D and disposing of key assets can impose disguised but deep long-term costs. For example, in the 1970s Motorola was forced to sell its loss-making television business to Matsushita. Subsequently, it discovered that its loss of core competences in video display technologies was handicapping many of its potential areas for growth.

■ *Legal and environmental constraints*. A company's options may be constrained by laws and regulations. For example, in ethical pharmaceuticals, prices are often regulated. In Italy and Germany it is very difficult for companies to lay off workers.

■ *Morale*. Cutting staff and closing factories generally have a very negative effect on motivation and morale. In contrast, cutting variable costs, which transfers the pain to the suppliers, usually gains more support.

Two examples

These techniques and constraints can be illustrated with Chemco (Table 13.1), a struggling industrial chemicals company, and Pharmco (Table 13.2), a highly profitable ethical pharmaceutical company. Chemco's problems are that new products and

Table 13.2 ■ Pharmco plc: impact of a predicted decline in prices and volume

	Current year	Predicted (£m)	Change required
Sales	400	320	320
Variable costs	44	40	30
Contribution	356	280	290
Fixed costs			
Manufacturing	44	44	33
Selling and administration	164	164	122
Research and development	52	52	39
Net profit	96	20	96

Faced with a predicted 10% decline in both volume and prices:
■ 25% across-the-board cost cuts needed to restore profits
■ 30% cost cuts needed to maintain R & D spending

aggressive competition have already eroded its market share and margins. Strategic drift has occurred as the company has failed to adapt to changes in its market environment. Pharmco's problem is different. Here management are more dynamic: they anticipate a deteriorating market environment and wish to prevent a future erosion of the company's profit and growth performance. Specifically, changes in the healthcare market lead Pharmco's management to anticipate a 10 per cent decline in both volume and prices over the next five years. Table 13.2 shows that, if they do not respond to these threats, profits will collapse from £96 million to £20 million. If they are unable to halt the erosion of volume and prices, then Pharmco will need a 25 per cent across-the-board cut in costs to maintain profits. If the company wants to maintain its level of R & D spend, the other costs would have to be cut by 30 per cent. Clearly the threats it faces are very serious. Pharmco needs a consolidation strategy to limit the short-term damage and a longer-term transformation strategy to find new areas for growth and profit margin enhancement.

Improving ROS

A turnaround management team must set new, satisfactory targets for return on investment, return on sales, asset turnover and gearing. These targets should be based upon benchmarking against high-performing companies in the sector. Management need to set clear dates and intermediate goals by which progress towards the goals are measured.

Of the three components of the basic financial planning equation, return on sales is usually the one which sees the biggest decline when a business runs into trouble. This therefore is normally the major focus of attention in a turnaround situation. There are six ways to improve return on sales in any company.

Table 13.3 ■ Effects of 5% changes on profitability

Variable	Chemco		Pharmco	
	£m	%	£m	%
Fixed costs	4.05	31	13.00	65
Variable costs	11.75	90	2.00	10
Volume	4.75	37	14.00	70
Price (elasticity = 0)	16.50	127	16.00	80
Price (elasticity = 1)	10.90	84	1.20	6

Cutting fixed costs

These are the costs which do not vary directly with volume and include indirect labour, management salaries, most of the selling and marketing expenses, administration, research and development, depreciation, heat and light, etc. Cuts here should be targeted to accelerate the long-term transformation process. Management should have first completed a portfolio analysis to identify the future core of the business. They should also have thought through the type of culture they want to create. Cutting bureaucracy, better systems, rationalizing facilities and eliminating non-value-adding work will further the transformation strategy and allow substantial savings in fixed costs. Even small cuts can have big effects on improving the return on sales. As Table 13.3 illustrates, a 5 per cent cut in fixed costs would raise net profit by over £4 million or 31 per cent at Chemco. Looking at Pharmco, for the predicted year where profits are set to fall to £20 million (Table 13.2), a 5 per cent cut in fixed costs would give £13 million or a 65 per cent profit improvement. Redundancy costs need to be considered, but taking out overhead costs can in practice go a long way to restoring profits to reasonable levels.

Cutting variable costs

These are costs which vary directly and proportionately with volume. Examples are materials, direct labour, lubricants, power and supplies. A thorough analysis of the supply chain can normally lead to significant opportunities to reduce variable costs. This may involve switching to lower-cost sources, value analysis, reducing the number of suppliers, and centralizing and more effectively negotiating over prices. For Chemco, where variable costs are a high proportion of total cost, the leverage of small cuts is great: a 5 per cent cut would boost profits by 90 per cent. For Pharmco, where variable costs are a small proportion, the leverage for cutting variable costs is much smaller. In poorly run businesses, variable cost reduction is generally a major source of potential profit improvement.

Raising volume

Sales people generally believe that increasing sales is the way to solve the company's profit problems. A 5 per cent volume increase would raise profits by 37 per cent at

Chemco and 70 per cent at Pharmco. The problem is: how would volume be increased without spending more on promotion or cutting prices? For example, at Chemco if prices were cut by as little as 2 per cent to achieve the 5 per cent boost in volume, it can be calculated (from Table 13.1) that profits would actually fall by 17 per cent. Especially in mature markets, management should be extremely cautious about volume strategies to boost short-term profits. Such policies can easily backfire. Volume is best thought of as a longer-term strategy based upon finding new market segments and developing products, services and distribution systems which offer real competitive advantages. If the company's offer does not possess any such advantage, then seeking to expand volume in current segments is likely to erode margins rather than to increase them.

Raising prices

Potentially at least, higher prices always have the greatest leverage on profits. Perhaps surprisingly, in practice, there is very often room for small price increases and such increases can have an enormous effect on the bottom line. For example, at Chemco a 5 per cent price increase would improve profits by £16.5 million if volume remained the same. If the elasticity is 1 (i.e. a 5 per cent price increase leads to a 5 per cent volume drop), profits still increase by £10.9 million (84 per cent). Note, however, that this depends upon the cost structure. If variable costs are low as at Pharmco, the loss of volume greatly reduces the advantage of the price increase if demand is price elastic. But certainly in mature industries, where contribution margins are typically low, better margins are generally the key to consolidating profits.

How can marginal price increases be obtained? Often the greatest pressure against raising prices comes not from customers, but from the firm's own sales department. Sales people invariably oppose price increases, since they believe it will make their own jobs more difficult. Generally, dealing with this problem requires basic commercial training which educates sales staff on the economics of business, and in particular on how price is the central determinant of return on investment. Price or gross margin attainment also needs to be structured into the incentive scheme to orient staff to achieve results on these dimensions. Good marketing training is also necessary to teach the basics of selling on value rather than price, market segmentation, creating and sustaining relationships and effective negotiating techniques. Marketing management also need to update the product line and how it is presented to customers. While customers resist price increases on current products, they are often willing to negotiate when the products or services appear new and improved.

It is also important to look at the discounts the firm is giving. In a recent report McKinsey & Company emphasized the dangers of businesses focusing on their list prices. Typically the price the company actually receives is 23 per cent less than the published list price. The difference disappears in numerous discounts for early payment, volume bonus, co-promotions, etc. Yet management often have a very poor understanding of these discounts: where they occur and whether they offer perceived value to customers.[3] Tying incentives for management and the sales team to realized prices will encourage them to focus on the most profitable customers and the importance of demonstrating value rather than selling on price.

Improving the customer mix

All suppliers face segmented markets. Companies vary in the volumes they purchase and in their sensitivities to price. As a result, some customers are much more profitable than others. Exploiting such differences is often the key to substantial short-term improvements in volumes and profitability. For example, a leading Paris department store found that Japanese tourists spent three times what the average American customer spent. By shifting its advertising and promotional budget towards Japanese visitors, it was able to improve profits significantly.

In both consumer and industrial markets, an identical product will typically have a price spread of over 80 per cent from the least to the most price-sensitive accounts. For example, while the average price the firm receives is £10, some aggressive customers will be paying only £7, while less price-sensitive accounts will be paying up to £13. Thus while the average gross margin might be 30 per cent, the spread could be between 0 and 46 per cent. A segmented approach to pricing is crucial. In practice, it is virtually impossible to raise prices by 5 per cent to *all* customers (i.e. the most price-sensitive customers would be alienated and the business lost altogether). But it is often not difficult to raise the price to *some* accounts by 10 or 20 per cent. In other words, any price increase should be seen as an average achieved from a segmented strategy. For example, if Chemco could get one-third of its customers to take a 6 per cent price increase, then its net profit would rise by over 50 per cent from £13 million to £19.6 million (from Table 13.1). To deploy a segmented pricing strategy, managers need a three-stage approach. First, they should analyze all their accounts and judge their price sensitivities. Which customers could stand a price increase? What could we offer to make such an increase acceptable? Second, marketing and sales should target customers at the high end of the price band for increased volume. Third, the clients in the bottom 20 per cent of the price band should be marked for action that will result in either improved price levels or their termination as customers.

Improving the product mix

Recognizing differences among customers is important, but there may be upper limits to its use. Wide price variations for the same product may not be sustainable if the differences are visible to customers paying the higher prices. One obvious solution is to introduce multiple brands so that customers can be encouraged to trade up to superior products. For example, most suppliers of both product and services offer de-luxe and cheaper standard models of their brands. Such product differentiation supports and enhances a company's ability to price discriminate among customers.

More generally, unless a company renews its product line, its prices will be under continuous pressure. Customers normally expect real prices to fall, and industry supply and demand conditions usually ensure that this occurs. The only way to main-

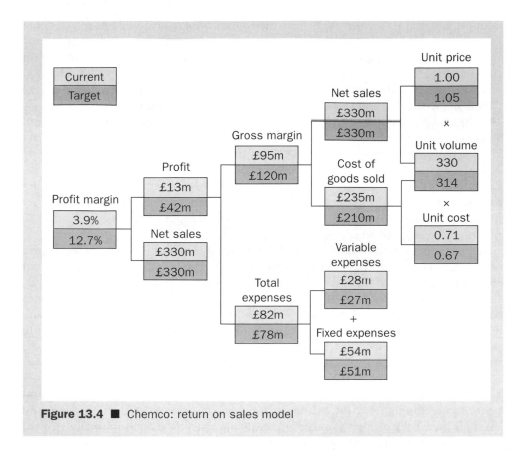

Figure 13.4 ■ Chemco: return on sales model

tain prices and margins in the longer run is to change and innovate continually with the aim of offering customers higher perceived value.

The results of the planned improvement in return on sales are summarized in Figure 13.4 for Chemco. As a result of the consolidation programme, the profit margin increases from 3.9 to 12.7 per cent and net profits more than treble. This is achieved by a 5 per cent average price increase and a 5 per cent decline in variable and fixed costs. Units sold drop by 5 per cent, but the price increase holds revenue in money terms to around the same figure.

Improving asset turnover

The second component of the basic financial planning equation is asset turnover or the ratio of net sales to total assets. When multiplied by the ROS, the AT ratio gives the firm's return on assets. By planning and controlling AT, the management can improve return on assets and return on equity. AT can be increased by raising sales in relation to assets or reducing assets in relation to sales. Again managers need to set targets. For example, the goal at Chemco might be to increase AT from the current 1.06 to 1.2. Other things being equal, this would increase return on investment by over 13 per cent.

Assets are divided into current and fixed. It is usually best to focus initially on current assets for two reasons. First, unlike fixed assets, current assets can be changed relatively easily in the short run. Second, for many businesses, current assets are the largest share of assets and therefore represent the greatest potential for improvement. The three major components of current assets are normally stock, debtors and cash. Stocks can be cut back by better forecasting of sales and encouraging suppliers to offer an effective just-in-time delivery system. In practice, stocks tend to be particularly excessive in slow-selling lines, so a rebalancing exercise is usually fruitful. For companies that have been loosely managed in the past, there is generally the opportunity to reduce stocks by eliminating fringe sizes, duplicate brands and perhaps some price lines. At Chemco such activities would be expected to produce savings of around £10 million in average investment in stocks.

Better management of debtors should also quickly improve the rate of asset turnover. Many companies have poorly organized collection programmes. Management should set up a high-level team to achieve targeted improvements. For example, Chemco sells primarily on a 30-day account, but in practice the average account is 45 days. An organized collection programme should be able to bring this down to around 36 days, which would result in savings of about £12 million in average investment in debtors. Cash is another costly investment to have if it is underutilized. Again targeted reductions in cash should produce important economies.

Turning to fixed assets, the major items will be plant, equipment, land, buildings and investments. Here the options are selling off surplus assets, disposing of poor-performing subsidiaries, consolidating manufacturing on one site, outsourcing, and sale and lease-back of high-value assets. Reducing fixed assets will normally also cut overhead costs, bringing a double benefit. The difficulties with fixed asset rationalizations are several. First, they take longer than with current assets. Second, there are various types of exit barrier. These include redundancy costs, difficulties in finding buyers for specialized assets, interrelatedness with other products and markets that the firm wishes to maintain (e.g. shared production facilities or salesforces), emotional attachments and government and social barriers to exit. Third, such fundamental restructuring is very dangerous without management first having a clear plan of where it wants to be in the future. It does not want to dispose of assets and capabilities which it will subsequently discover are vital to its long-run transformation strategy.

Nevertheless controlling fixed assets is crucial to any consolidation programme. If fixed assets could be cut by 15 per cent at Chemco over a two-year period, this would save £16 million, which together with current asset savings of, say, £30 million would raise asset turnover from 1.06 to 1.25 or 18 per cent (Figure 13.5).

Improving gearing

Return on assets ($ROA = ROS \times AT$) is a measure of *management's* financial performance, but it does not measure adequately the financial performance of the *firm*. In the private

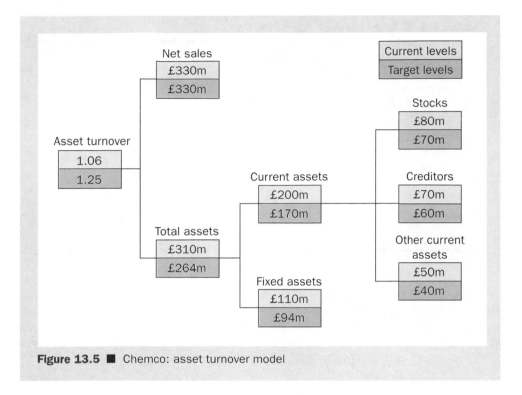

Figure 13.5 ■ Chemco: asset turnover model

enterprise system, the owner's viewpoint of financial performance is seen as primary. The key measure here is return on equity. The link between ROA and ROE is the gearing ratio. A higher gearing (i.e. more debt) allows shareholders to lever upwards the assets they control and the returns they receive. When a firm has exciting opportunities to profit, gearing allows the owners to obtain more assets and to appropriate the profits which are left after the due interest is paid to the creditors.

The firm has two types of debt available to it: short (due for repayment within one year) and longer term. Short-term debt usually consists of amounts owing to suppliers and the bank overdraft. Longer-term debt is negotiated loans from banks and other financial institutions. Higher gearing increases risks both to the firm and to the creditors. Debt levels much beyond the norm for the sector become difficult and expensive to increase. With a gearing ratio of over 2, Chemco would find it increasingly difficult to raise this further.

Higher leverage is encouraged by periods of rising sales and low interest rates. But when a company is in difficulty, when there is a recession or when interest rates are high, creditors become very nervous about their funds due from companies with high gearing.

To summarize for Chemco, the actions proposed should increase return on equity from below 9 per cent to 33 per cent and return on assets from 4 per cent to 16 per cent. This would result from a trebling in the ROS and an increase in AT. The GR would

Table 13.4 ■ Chemco: cash flow statement

	Current	(£m)	Target
Net profit	13		42
Tax	(5)		(16)
Depreciation	8		8
Trading cash flow	16		34
Capital expenditure	(10)		(2)
Change in working capital	(1)		6
Operating cash flow	5		38
Fixed asset disposals	0		4
Reorganization costs	0		(3)
Net cash flow	5		39
NCF/Sales (%)	1.5		11.8

not be expected to increase. Most of the substantial improvement would come from the higher ROS achieved by a 5 per cent average price increase spread tactically across customers and products according to price sensitivities. There would also be a 5 per cent cut in costs achieved through rationalization. The calculation allows for 5 per cent fall in volume. The results in summary are as follows:

$$
\begin{array}{ccccccl}
ROE & = & ROS & \times & AT & = & GR \\
8.7 & = & 3.9 & \times & 1.06 & \times & 2.1 \quad \text{Before} \\
33.3 & = & 12.7 & \times & 1.25 & \times & 2.1 \quad \text{After}
\end{array}
$$

Finally, the impact of the consolidation plan is shown on Chemco's cash flow statement (Table 13.4). Net cash flow is boosted from £5 million to £39 million annually. The major source of this improvement is the increase in net profit, but this is supported by the disposal of surplus assets and a reduction in both capital expenditure and working capital requirements. Net cash flow as a percentage of sales increases from 1.5 per cent to 11.8 per cent, representing a healthy surplus to satisfy shareholders and provide reasons for the revitalization programme which will create shareholder value in the future.

Transformation programme

The consolidation phase is usually a necessary part of the turnaround process, but it is never sufficient because it focuses on the symptoms of the problem rather than its true causes. At most it can temporarily halt the company's downward spiral, giving management two or three years' breathing space to develop and implement their blueprint for transformation.

Figure 13.6 contrasts the consolidation and the transformation stages of the turnaround. Consolidation can only produce short-term gains because it does not tackle

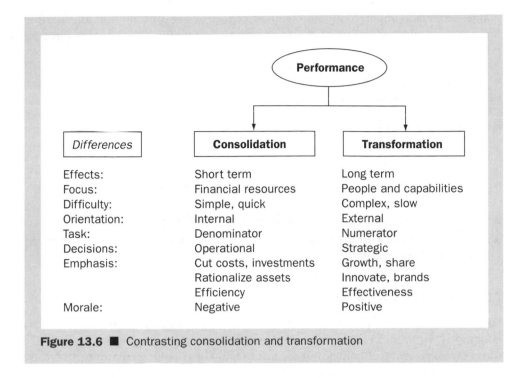

Differences	Consolidation	Transformation
Effects:	Short term	Long term
Focus:	Financial resources	People and capabilities
Difficulty:	Simple, quick	Complex, slow
Orientation:	Internal	External
Task:	Denominator	Numerator
Decisions:	Operational	Strategic
Emphasis:	Cut costs, investments	Growth, share
	Rationalize assets	Innovate, brands
	Efficiency	Effectiveness
Morale:	Negative	Positive

Figure 13.6 ■ Contrasting consolidation and transformation

the root causes of the company's declining competitiveness. It is a simple operation in denominator management: cutting inputs (costs, expenses and assets) in the output/input productivity formula. It is home ground for accountants because it is entirely inward focused on the company's internal financial resources, costs, margins and assets.

By contrast, transformation is about long-run competitiveness in the market. It focuses on acquiring the core competences and remotivating the staff to achieve industry leadership. It is slower and more difficult than consolidation because the challenges are external. Essentially it is about being better than competitors and winning the hearts and minds of customers. In today's international markets it means becoming a 'world-class' company. Decisions are about outputs rather than inputs: building market share, positioning brands and stimulating innovation in products, processes and marketing channels. It is definitely not the forte of accountants.

More generally, the skills required for transforming a company's competitive position are quite different from those of consolidation. Few chief executives have the ability to make the switch between the consolidation and transformation stages, between the internal and external focus, from denominator to numerator management, from emphasizing parsimony to communicating and inspiring vision. When the chief executive cannot make the transition, the company becomes immobilized in the consolidation phase, the fundamental causes of strategic drift are not tackled and continual cutbacks are required in a vain struggle to disguise the effects of declining market share and rapidly eroding competitiveness. A good example is the Hanson Trust case summarized in Box 13.1. To prevent this, a key task of the board of directors is to ask, during the latter stages of the consolidation phase: does the chief executive have the skills to carry us forward to the next stage?

To create a blueprint for the transformation, the chief executive and his or her team need to find answers to five questions:

■ What are the key external forces *transforming* our industry?

■ What is our *vision* for achieving industry leadership – what will be our differential advantage, core competences and new channels of distribution?

■ How will we build the *core competences* necessary to achieve our vision of world-class competitiveness?

■ What *strategies* must be developed to implement the vision?

■ What are the *leadership* qualities required from top management spearheading the transformation process?

Anticipating industry evolution

Strategic drift is caused by the organization's failure to adapt to changed industry conditions. To be successful in the future requires the organization to adapt, not to today's markets and technology, but to tomorrow's. The changing environment creates both new customer requirements and the new technological possibilities for meeting them. If the company does not adapt, it is replaced by new competitors which better match the requirements of the new industry environment.

Companies like 3M, Motorola and Unilever that have maintained a match to the changing environment do not depend upon luck or random innovations; instead they plan systematically for innovation. They recognize that few of today's really profitable innovative products created change; rather they responded to obvious environmental changes already taking place. The success of Unilever's low-fat spreads or of diet Coke were the result of effectively responding to the obvious demand for healthier eating and drinking. Peter Drucker accurately captured this when he defined the entrepreneurial organization as one which 'searches for change, responds to it and exploits it as an opportunity'.[4] In most of today's rapidly changing industries, once a firm ceases to be entrepreneurial, it quickly loses the ability to compete.

Transformation requires recapturing this entrepreneurial drive. To kick start this, the chief executive needs to set up a sequence of high-level, cross-functional taskforces whose objective is to analyze and project changes in the industry. The objectives of this process are to question comprehensively how the firm's markets will differ in the future, and what the key discontinuities will be in customer behaviour, technology, distribution channels, competition and products. This is not a quick and straightforward process. The results will provide the intellectual basis and psychological trigger for the whole transformation process. They are the elements on which top management will create a vision of what the revitalized company will be like, what accomplishments it will seek over the coming years, the core capabilities it will aim to build, and the strategies it will follow.

The review should consider at least the following areas:

- *Market and customers*. A taskforce needs to evaluate the key changes taking place in the company's markets: how customers and their expectations are changing. Areas to explore include the strengths and weaknesses of the company's position, the emergence of new market segments, changing customer buying patterns and potential new distribution channels.

- *Industry and competition*. Key competitors need to be identified and analyzed. What are their strengths and weaknesses, opportunities and threats? Can new competitors be expected to enter the market? If so, who are they and how should we prepare to respond? What is the trend and structure of the industry? Is it becoming more concentrated? What are the trends in backward and forward integration? How will these affect the business? Are competitors involved in strategic alliances that could be threatening? Does the trend of outsourcing or facilities management offer potential new customers or competitors?

- *Technology*. How aware is the organization of technological developments likely to shape the industry in the future? Does the company have any partnerships with customers, suppliers and other firms to advance its technological capabilities? Do other technologies threaten our existing skill base? How up to date are we in terms of product and process technologies? Have we benchmarked our technological capabilities against the emerging competitors?

- *Suppliers*. A taskforce should review the opportunities for closer partnerships with suppliers to accelerate change. It needs to check into new sources, options and partnerships, particularly in the newly industrialized countries. The advantages of contracting out non-core activities also should be evaluated. The risks and threats attached to current suppliers need to be considered. Alternative sources of finance for the business's future development can also be explored.

- *Demographic and economic changes*. A major source of opportunity is created by demographic, economic and consequential changes in lifestyles. Which markets are likely to offer the highest growth potential? How will movements in costs affect location decisions in the industry? How will changes in the European Union and other economic zones affect the industry? How are changes in lifestyles likely to influence buying decisions?

- *Political, legal and environmental*. What new laws or directives might affect the industry in the future? How are environmental issues shaping current market demands? How do we rate in our environmental performance?

- *Staff and skills*. Another taskforce needs to evaluate the company's human resources. Are the people working for the organization motivated and committed? How close to best practice are we in meeting the financial and other employment expectations of staff? What is their level of education, training, skills and qualifications? How do we compare with competitors? How do we compare in productivity and unit labour costs?

Developing the vision

This detailed review of the forces transforming the external environment should provide management with a perspective of the future. Of course, this will not be a detailed set of predictions: today, the levels of uncertainty are too great for that. It should, however, lead to a common view of the major trends in demand, competition and technology.

Management then need to formulate a vision of what the organization needs to achieve to be a winner in this new environment. This vision will reflect the results of the projections made of the environment and be constrained by the perception of the organization's own capabilities. The vision is likely to cover three areas. First, management will want to define the *target markets* it will seek to serve in the future. It will need to take a view of which customers represent the most attractive opportunities. Second, it will need to decide how it is going to gain *competitive advantage*. Sony, for example, decided on miniaturization; Federal Express on speed and service; Glaxo on innovative healthcare products. Third, management will need to be clear about which *core capabilities* they will require to create and sustain such competitive advantage.

For example, Hamel and Prahalad describe how in the mid-1990s Electronic Data Systems, the leading IT specialist, felt the need to redefine its business to maintain industry leadership. It recognized that new competition and rapid environmental change threatened, as it did for all successful companies, the viability of current strategies. EDS first created teams to forecast the major discontinuities likely to occur in the industry. This led to a new vision which the company termed 'globalize, informationalize and individualize'. It defined its primary customers as individuals and businesses which would want its key IT skills. EDS redefined its competitive advantage as being first and fastest to provide the new information services and products that would be the markets of the future. To do this it identified new core competences that it must acquire. These included genetic re-engineering, high-level strategic consulting skills, digital media and retail expertise.[5]

Building core competences

To have the capability to offer customers products and services which are superior to competitors requires the organization to possess unique core competences. It must have specialized skills which are difficult for competitors to copy. Such competences are usually built up over generations. They consist of knowledge and routines created from longstanding relationships among the organization's employees, suppliers, customers and other firms engaged in related activities. These core competences or 'organizational architecture'[6] allow the firm to respond flexibly to a changing environment and to achieve easy and open exchange of information.

Toyota, Marks & Spencer, Siemens, SKF and GE are examples of companies possessing such architecture. Companies in a turnaround situation need to build these capabilities. The problem is that the architecture cannot be built quickly; it can take a decade to create and consolidate these networks of knowledge. Companies that come, apparently from nowhere, to exhibit explosive growth in sales and profits rarely have staying power. They are usually shooting-stars, fuelled by windfall opportunities and gambles which beat the odds. Unless the company has built the networks of knowledge and trust, it will not be able to maintain the momentum once the windfalls are spent out and new opportunities have to be created.

All organizations have knowledge and skills, but for these to be valuable core competences for the future, they must meet three tests. First, they must enable the firm to offer benefits that customers will value. For example, Glaxo has a strong salesforce which is important to its sales process. But it is not a *core* competence because doctors do not prescribe Glaxo products because of its salesforce. Its real core competence is its R & D skills. Second, to be a core competence, the skills must be unique. If competitors have similar skills then the competency may be necessary, but it does not provide the basis of a competitive advantage. Third, the skills must provide access to new markets in the future. Managers must avoid defining their skills in terms of the specific product. Specific products generally become obsolete as technology progresses and needs change.

Management's perception of the future and vision will highlight what new core competences the organization needs to build. Hamel and Prahalad adapted the familiar Ansoff matrix to propose a competence-market model for identifying what new competences a business has to find (Figure 13.7). This identifies four types of opportunity:[7]

- *Fill in the blanks*. These are opportunities for new products in the company's existing markets which can be created from better utilization of the organization's current competences. Generally these competences have to be imported from another of the company's business units. For example, Burmah Castrol used the skills in brand building possessed by its auto lubricants business to create new branding opportunities in its speciality chemicals business. These opportunities are created by opening up the flow of ideas between business units. Because they are based upon current competences and the firm's existing markets, they are often the easiest and least risky opportunities to exploit.

- *Premier plus ten*. These are the new core competences that a business will need to build if it is to remain a leader in its current market for the future. For example, the pharmaceutical company Zeneca has been focusing on developing disease management consultancy skills because it believes that future national health services will not just demand drug products, but wish to find partners that will provide more effective disease management (e.g. for cancer, asthma care) by integrating diagnostic, medical and hospital cost components into a lower-cost, high-quality system for patients.

- *White spaces*. These are opportunities to create new products or services, and enter new markets by redeploying the business's current core competences in different ways. For example, the Walkman was a white space opportunity for Sony because it deployed the company's competences in the tape recorder and headphones business units.

- *Mega-opportunities*. These are the high-return, high-risk gambles of moving into completely new markets. To make such moves work, management have to ask what

	Market	
	Existing	New
New **Core competence** **Existing**	*Premier plus ten* *What new core competences will we need in our current markets?*	*Mega-opportunities* *What new core competences are needed for tomorrow's most exciting markets?*
	Fill in the blanks *What is the opportunity to improve in existing markets by better utilizing our current competences?*	*White spaces* *What new products or services could we create by redeploying current competences?*

Figure 13.7 ■ Identifying core competences

Source: adapted from Gary Hamel and C. K. Prahalad, *Competing for the Future*, Boston, MA: Harvard Business School Press, 1994, p. 227

new core competences they need to acquire to succeed. The company may then look for acquisitions or strategic alliances to gain access to, and learn about, the required competences. For example, the airline and retail company Virgin moved into the huge growing financial services market, forging a partnership with one of the established leaders, Norwich Union.

Once this strategic direction is defined and the core competences required are identified, management need to acquire these skills. Top companies may employ a variety of paths to build these competences:

- *Project teams*. Empowering teams to achieve ambitious strategic goals (e.g. develop a new product, launch into a new market) creates a learning environment. Properly motivated teams seek to acquire the skills and knowledge to make their projects successful.

- *Training and development*. If, for example, service or customer care are identified as desirable core skills, then the business unit must comprehensively train and develop its people in these capabilities to bring them to world-class standards.

- *Cross-deployment*. Companies often have people with scarce, world-class skills stuck in business units with little scope to create new market opportunities. It is headquarters' responsibility to deploy valuable core skills effectively by encouraging personnel to work across business unit boundaries on projects which are central to the transformation process.

- *Hiring.* Successful companies like Hewlett-Packard, McKinsey and Glaxo target to recruit the best graduates and postgraduates – individuals with the latest skills crucial to the company's future, and with the personalities, drive and ability to apply these skills.

- *External expertise.* The turnaround company's key need is normally to access and absorb skills and technologies from outside. Building close links to leading-edge university departments is a policy pursued by many top engineering and pharmaceutical companies.

- *Government research contracts.* Companies can seek to participate in governmental research contracts into new areas.

- *Partnerships with customers and suppliers.* Businesses can lever their resources through the common interests of customers and suppliers in developing new products and markets. Each can input and share specialist skills, market knowledge, technology and production capabilities.

- *Licensing.* Licensing agreements can bring new technology, processes and products to a company short of its own resources. Even companies with strong core skills increasingly augment them by licensing in outside ideas.

- *Equity stakes in emerging companies.* Taking equity positions in start-up companies has also often proved a fruitful means of investing in potentially important new areas and gaining new knowledge.

- *Strategic alliances.* Corporate alliances are increasingly becoming the pattern for adding and sharing competences. The need for speed, and for bringing in diverse knowledge about new technologies and markets, makes partnerships between companies often a flexible and effective way to exploit market opportunities. Success is increasingly about being part of a successful coalition of companies.

Formulating strategy

After the management team have taken a view of the future of the industry and formulated a vision of how the company will transform itself into a market leader, it needs a more detailed implementation strategy. This process can be divided into four stages:

Portfolio analysis

The change team needs to undertake a hard and fundamental review of the current businesses. The objective is to decide which are worth keeping and which should be divested. As described in Chapter 4, this means looking first at the relative current and potential strength of each of the businesses. Do they have the capabilities to be world class? Second, it involves looking at the future attractiveness of the market. Is this an industry which has a long-term future? From this analysis the strategic priorities should become clear – which businesses are going to be invested in and which harvested or divested.

For a faltering company, the key is to be decisive about divestment. Management have to be refocused on capitalizing on new emerging market opportunities, not wasting their time on problem businesses which have no potential to generate a future for the company. The team need to ask a simple question: 'If we were not in this business today, would we go into it now?' If the answer is no, then the business should be got rid of as quickly as possible. These portfolio decisions need to be taken early in the turnaround process because they have direct impact on the consolidation phase. Cash generation and rationalization should be targeted to those parts of the portfolio with least potential.

Separate the businesses

A major source of a failing company's problems is middle management lacking the power to take responsibility and make fast decisions. Instead managers are disempowered by head office committees, corporate infighting and general disillusionment about the company's inability to make decisive change. The only solution is to break the business down into independent SBUs. It is invariably a mistake to tie together, in the same business unit, businesses which are unalike. If businesses have separate markets, different core competences or different margin structures, they are better split and given autonomy.

As far as possible the units should be completely separated: they should have their own sites, salesforce, operating and support staff. When staff and facilities are shared, it almost always leads to compromise, delay, excuses for failure and unnecessary overheads. When a management team has profit responsibility and autonomy, the pressure is much stronger to eliminate unnecessary overhead costs. The paradox is that there are rarely real savings in practice in combining businesses which have distinctive market positions.

Role of headquarters

The head office of the new company should be very small. With the new autonomous business units, headquarters should keep out of operational decisions. Staff with operational responsibilities should be reassigned to the units – if they are wanted. The new headquarter team has three crucial roles. Richard Branson of Virgin, Bill Gates of Microsoft and Jack Welch of GE illustrate the first role – that of energizer of the company. Percy Barnevik of ABB is another example. He split the company into 5,000 individual profit centres and 1,300 separate companies. He sees his job as stimulating change, providing vision and encouraging unit managers to be aspirational about the future. He reckons to speak personally to 5,500 of his employees every year.

The second role is to be a catalyst for creating new businesses. The most obvious resource that headquarters normally controls is the company's cash. But the most important resource it should control are the people, particularly those with the most valuable skills. Top management have the responsibility for triggering new business opportunities which do not fit neatly within an individual business unit – the 'white spaces' and 'mega-opportunities' of Figure 13.7. These opportunities may be in exploiting new markets, developing new products or acquiring new technologies. To make these happen, top management need to assign key people from the business units to cross-disciplinary project teams. Management have the responsibility to ensure that the company's key resource – its people – are put into areas where their contribution is maximized.

The third role is the generation and allocation of resources. The allocation task is to ensure that the units and projects which have the potential to generate the greatest returns get the resources they require. Consistency and patience are important here – few of these opportunities will be achieved within the pay-off period normally assigned to routine investment projects. Resource allocation requires courage from management – they have to give the new projects the chance to develop properly and build a market position. The headquarters team also needs to take the lead in generating new resources. This involves blending skills, technologies and best practices across the company to help individual units achieve synergy. It also involves assisting the units to develop alliances, joint ventures, inward licensing, and supplier and customer partnerships to access new capabilities.

Business unit and project team strategies

The units and the teams need to be challenged to develop ambitious strategies which stretch the businesses. The components of the strategic plan have been detailed in Chapter 4. The unit first needs a vision – an inspirational statement which defines the positioning it wishes to capture in the minds of its target customers and how it is to achieve it. Each unit then requires a *strategic objective* which describes its strategic intent. It must define its *strategic focus* – whether its aim is to develop new markets or penetrate existing ones. Third, it needs clear thinking about its *target customers*. In particular, it should understand who its customers are *today* and ask who the target customers should be *tomorrow*. Changes in the industry and in the technology available create new opportunities for a fundamental reappraisal of the opportunities that different types of customers offer. For example, until the 1990s, most car and household insurance companies saw their key customers as the independent brokers and intermediaries who recommended insurance policies. Direct Line transformed the industry by perceiving that new information technology and rising service expectations permitted the insurer to cut out the broker and go directly to the final consumer – the car owner and householder. Such innovative thinking about paradigm shifts provides the basis for catapulting a business from the back to the very forefront of the industry.

The fourth step of the plan is the analysis of *competitor targets*. It means asking again who the competitors are today, and who they will be tomorrow. In the past Coca-Cola's major competitor in Europe was Pepsi Cola; today the real problem has become retailer private-label brands which compete at much lower prices and with assured shelf space.

Microsoft's real competition is no longer Lotus or similar software vendors, but rather the Internet. The Internet offers a radically different approach to computing, not reliant on powerful PCs, each with their own comprehensive packages of software.

The next step is the definition of the unit's *core strategy* – how it will offer superior value to customers. Again managers need to think through the dynamics – how will it change in the future. In the past, core strategies often focused on the performance of the company's products. But now service is increasingly the tool for the competitive advantage. Pharamceutical companies are generally shifting from selling drug products to the health services in favour of disease management services. Consumer goods companies shift their emphasis from product brands to offering supermarkets a cate-gory management service. Successful industrial companies are changing from supplying components to offering strategic partnerships to key customers. The focus on service reflects a greater emphasis on meeting the customer's needs rather than selling the firm's production capacity. Even more, it points to a focus on building long-term relationships with customers.

The final stage of the strategic marketing plan is the *marketing mix* – putting together an innovative set of products, services, communications and channels which implement the unit's new positioning strategy, meet the needs of the new target customers and form the basis for long-term relationships with them. This marketing mix needs to be co-ordinated to generate a consistent set of *brand values* which give customers confidence in and generate loyalty to the business.

Alongside the marketing plan should be a reassessment of the unit's operations and supply chain. Management will want to minimize the investment of people and finan-cial resources in low value-added activities and areas where it lacks competitive advan-tage. Outsourcing and partnerships offer the advantage of flexibility and access to top-class capabilities outside. It should evaluate whether its processes can be re-engi-neered to take out operations which slow activities down, add disproportionate over-heads or do not directly add value.

Leadership

Leadership plays a crucial role in the turnaround situation. In the consolidation phase, the primary requirements are a decisiveness and toughness in taking the unpopular decisions necessary to deal with the company's short-term profit and cash flow prob-lems. For the transformation phase, the leadership challenge is even greater. Management must be able to lead the reappraisal of the changing industry, forge a vision for the transformed company and catalyze the enthusiasm of its people to implement the strategies required. Equally important is the skill to overcome the resist-ance to change which inevitably occurs in the transformation process.

Leadership rests upon power. There are two fundamental sources of power. The first is *authority* – normally the chief executive will have been given the authority by the board to make changes. In extreme cases, when an outsider has been brought in with a record of expertise and charismatic leadership, he or she is often given a blank cheque to make the changes necessary.

But such power usually does not last unless positive results come rapidly, and one of the problems with transformational change is that the process is likely to take several years. New markets, new competences and new differential advantages are not achieved quickly. To keep shareholders, employees and colleagues on board, the leader needs to deploy certain personal traits which garner support, overcome obstacles to change and create enthusiasm among the people. There is substantial research of successful change agents and broad agreement about what the characteristics are.[8]

- *Clear vision*. Successful change agents need a clear vision of what the organization needs to accomplish if it is to be transformed into an industry leader. They must have formed firm ideas about where the market opportunities are, what new competences the organization must acquire and how the new strategies will be implemented.

- *Strong communications*. A vision achieves nothing if it rests only in the head of one person. The leader must be able to communicate his or her vision in such a way that it inspires the organization's stakeholders. The change agent needs to create enthusiasm and commitment to the goals and to the belief that all will share in the success once it is attained.

- *Decisive follow-up*. Organizational transformation takes place gradually via a series of incremental accomplishments. The leader needs to set monthly targets and challenges for the business units, which must be rigorously followed up. Successes have to be celebrated and failures overcome. Without a continual focus on results, the initial enthusiasm for change can drift away among the daily difficulties of running the business.

- *Stamina*. Organizational leadership today imposes incredible physical demands. The company's sites and customers are often dispersed around the world. Management not only have to develop the strategies for the organization, but have to circulate continually among the staff, customers and stakeholders, communicating, inspiring and networking. Eighty-hour working weeks are the norm for these leaders. Unfortunately, without such stamina and physical drive, it is very difficult for a top manager to be effective today. Transformational leadership can have an enormous personal cost.

- *Ethical standards*. People expect leaders to have high moral standards and to act in ways which are 'fair' to stakeholders. In the past, power, secrecy and lack of media attention made this less important. However, today managers who are seen as unfair or unethical lack the popular support to make the work sustainable over the long run.

- *Networking skills*. The leader of the change process must maintain effective personal relationships with others who control resources or influence which they may need. All change agents require support and an important task is to maintain good personal contacts with those whose endorsement may be critical when events take an unexpected turn.

Summary

A turnaround normally involves two phases: consolidation and transformation. The former is the easiest and quickest to accomplish. Here management focuses internally on cutting costs, reducing assets and enhancing profit margins. By such methods, profits and cash improvements can be rapidly realized. But consolidation alone does not revitalize a company. In fact, if continued for long, it can easily destroy the organization's base for long-run competitiveness.

The key to long-run success is the transformational process. This entails understanding how the industry environment is changing and forging a vision of what the organization needs to look like to become an industry leader. This means redefining the firm's markets and competitive advantages and identifying the core competences that the organization will need to revitalize itself. The role of the change agent is to see that these questions are decisively answered and to provide the leadership for the new strategy and the creation of the new organization.

Questions

1. Take a company you are familiar with which has experienced significant decline. Using what data are available, identify the symptoms and causes of such decline.

2. A company has net profits of £10 million, sales of £130 million, variable costs of £52 million, current assets of £50 million, fixed assets of £60 million and equity of £30 million. Calculate your basic financial planning equation. Estimate the effects of cutting costs by 4 per cent, increasing volume by 4 per cent and raising prices by 4 per cent.

3. Repeat the exercise on Chemco for 6 per cent changes.

4. A manufacturer of branded shirts wants to achieve higher prices from the independent outlets which market its products. Advise a strategy for implementing such a plan.

5. You are appointed a consultant to a large multinational which is seeking to develop a turnaround strategy. Outline the steps for such a strategy, suggest how they will be accomplished and estimate the time required for completing each of them.

6. Looking at the characteristics of leadership described in the chapter, develop a seven-point scale to rate the experience of the most successful manager you know. Then rate yourself against these criteria.

Notes

1. Andrew Pettigrew and Richard Whipp, *Managing Change for Competitive Success* (Oxford: Blackwell, 1991).

2. See, for example, Tony Hope and Jeremy Hope, *Transforming the Bottom Line* (Boston, MA: Harvard Business School Press, 1996).

3. Michael V. Marn and Robert L. Rosiello, 'Managing price, gaining profit', *Harvard Business Review*, September–October 1992, pp. 84–94.

4. Peter F. Drucker, *Innovation and Entrepreneurship* (London: Heinemann, 1985).

5. Gary Hamel and C. K. Prahalad, *Competing for the Future* (Boston, MA: Harvard Business School Press, 1994), pp. 115–22.

6. John Kay, *Foundations of Corporate Success* (Oxford: Oxford University Press, 1993), pp. 63–86.

7. Hamal and Prahalad, *op. cit.*, p. 227; H. Igor Ansoff, *Corporate Strategy* (Harmondsworth: Penguin, 1968), p. 99.

8. For example, Noel M. Tichy and Mary Anne Devanna, *The Transformational Leader* (New York: Wiley, 1986); Christopher Barlett and Sumantra Ghoshal, 'Changing the role of top management', *Harvard Business Review*, May–June 1995, pp. 132–42.

Chapter 14

Marketing in the twenty-first century

In this final chapter the focus is on two questions. First, how will marketing evolve in the years ahead? What changes are likely in the philosophy of marketing and in the strategic and organizational issues that managers will face? To answer this question, the major changes taking place in the marketing environment are explored and the implications of these forces for marketing strategy and organization are assessed. Second, what do we know about implementing marketing strategy? The difference between successful and unsuccessful companies is often due not so much to strategy, but to the effectiveness with which managers implement it. What skills do managers need to implement marketing strategy effectively?

Marketing: a recapitulation

Before an effort is made to forecast how marketing will change, it is useful to recapitulate the core concepts of marketing, marketing strategy and the organizational capabilities required for effective marketing performance. This is reviewed under four headings: the marketing concept, segmentation and positioning, planning and core capabilities.

The marketing concept

The marketing concept is at the heart of the free enterprise capitalist system. In a competitive economy, customers can choose from whom to buy. In today's global markets they are offered an increasing variety of choices by companies from around the world. Customers choose to buy from those companies that they perceive as offering the best value. Value is a function of the perceived quality and the price of the company's offer. Consequently, to succeed companies must be managed to offer superior value in terms of lower prices or higher quality. Unless they are competitive, they cannot generate the revenue from customers to survive.

Marketing – the task of seeking to provide customers with superior value – is so central that it cannot be seen as just another function alongside production, finance or

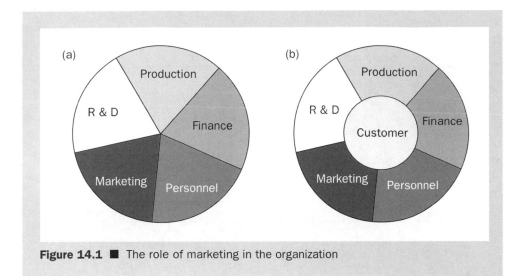

Figure 14.1 ■ The role of marketing in the organization

personnel (Figure 14.1(a)). The central task of management is finding better ways of meeting the needs of customers. This is illustrated in Figure 14.1(b). The central focus of the business has to be the customer. The marketing department has a role to play in helping create value, but is no more central than R & D, production, finance or personnel. The marketing specialist may take the lead in researching the customer and developing sales strategies, but the other functions play key roles in innovation, product development, quality and responsiveness. The marketing concept is the integrative outlook which should bind the separate activities together. Marketing is essentially a team effort and its accomplishment needs to be organized to reflect this fact.

How the firm should view the task of delivering value to customers is shown in Figure 14.2. The old-fashioned, production-oriented companies operate like Figure 14.2(a). Engineers develop a product that they think is attractive; the job of marketing people is then to sell the product that the company manufactures. Today, such an approach rarely works. Why should it? The engineers have not analyzed the market; they do not know what customers want or what competitors are offering. The consequences are that the sales people often do not believe in the product and the customers do not see any new value in it. The results are poor: sales and margins are inadequate and the company fails to build a viable market position.

The modern marketing-oriented approach operates as in Figure 14.2(b). It starts with managers segmenting the market and understanding the value needs of customers. They then develop positioning strategies for the segments upon which they decide to focus. After the opportunity is defined, a team-like approach across the functional areas is needed to develop and provide the fast, value solution to match the opportunity. Next, marketing and sales people have the task of communicating the value to the market. Finally, the organization seeks to obtain continuous feedback so that a long-term relationship with the customer can be built.

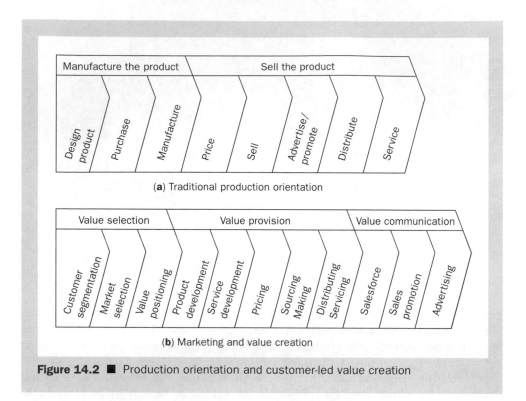

Figure 14.2 ■ Production orientation and customer-led value creation

Segmentation and positioning

Market segmentation and positioning are the two fundamental marketing tasks. Customers in any market are very heterogeneous. The first job of management is to find ways of effectively segmenting their markets. There are two principal criteria: differences between customers in their actual or potential needs, and differences between them in what they may be willing to pay for a solution to their needs. In consumer markets, such differences are often corrolated with income, age or lifestyle. In industrial markets, these differences are often associated with the industry of the end user and customer size. Only by segmenting markets are firms likely to be able to meet customers' needs effectively and profitably.

The identification of new market segments represents among the most powerful forces of innovation today. It offers growth and profit opportunities with minimal technical risk and investment. However, the company does have to position the product effectively both to the new consumer group and against current competitors. For example, Ciba-Geigy's Voltaren was among the world's top-selling pharmaceutical products with sales of almost £1 billion. Its primary use was as a pain-reliever for elderly rheumatic patients. However, by the late 1980s, profits and sales were flattening out as the product's patients expired and low-priced generics entered the field. But in the 1990s the company's marketing strategists identified a new target market – athletes and sports people who suffered muscle strains and bruises on the field. Voltaren was reformulated to be quicker acting and a rub version was sold alongside the original tablet form. Two new products, Voltaren Emulgel and Cataflan, created major new growth areas for the business, quite offsetting the predicted decline in Voltaren.

Successful marketing is essentially about strategies like that pursued by Ciba-Geigy. The major technological breakthroughs that create radically new markets or make current competition obsolete are too few and far between to be worth banking on in developing long-term strategies.

Many textbooks advance the thesis that positioning strategies can be divided into three types: differentiation, cost leadership and focus. A differentiation strategy is based upon achieving premium prices by offering unique value in one or more attributes desired by customers. This might be superior product performance, service or image. Cost leadership is based upon being the single, lowest-cost producer in the industry and using low price as a means of gaining market share. A focus strategy concentrates on serving a specific segment more effectively than broader-based competitors.

However, such generic strategies look too naïve in today's environment. Now successful companies need a combination of all three. Companies today cannot succeed without segmenting their market and focusing offers on each segment. Low prices rarely make a viable strategy: even the poorest customers seek a range of attributes besides price. Companies that focus solely on minimizing costs are invariably trumped by companies with innovative solutions that change the basis of competition and make the experience curves of competitors obsolete.

Marketing planning

Marketing planning should start with an analysis of the potential of the market. Professor Michael Porter's five-forces model provides a useful tool for assessing the overall attractiveness of the market.[1] This suggests that average profitability in an industry depends upon the following:

■ *Inter-industry rivalry*. The more fierce the competition between companies in the market, the greater the pressures on prices and profits.

■ *Power of buyers*. If the customers are powerful, then the profits that suppliers earn will be under continual pressure.

■ *Substitute products*. If there is a threat from substitute products or services, this again caps the price increases that suppliers can obtain.

■ *Potential entrants*. The lower the barriers to entry, the less likely it is that companies will be able to maintain a high level of profitability.

■ *Power of suppliers*. The bargaining power of suppliers affects the cost competitiveness of the companies.

Consequently, some markets are much easier than others in which to make adequate returns. Pharmaceuticals, soft drinks and cosmetics have had high average levels of profitability. Steel, personal computers and tyres have been very tough to operate in. In the latter industries, even innovative products often produce only modest and short-term profit improvements because the innovations are quickly copied, strong buyers pressure prices down, or new entrants erode margins. But while these five forces determine the average pattern of results, behind these averages there are often wide divergences of performance. Some companies can do exceptionally well in tough industries; others do poorly in industries with high average returns.

Planning to beat the odds and shift the balance of industry forces in the company's favour starts with *portfolio analysis*. Most companies operate in a range of markets with a range of products. Some of these have great potential; others are increasingly uncompetitive. The task of management is to identify appropriate marketing and financial objectives for each of these strategic business units. For some it will make sense to pursue aggressive market development strategies; for others, harvesting or cash flow management may be the goal.

Once the objectives for a market are defined, the marketing plan centres around understanding the target market segment and developing a differential advantage.

After the positioning strategy is formulated, the marketing mix is designed: product, price, promotion and distribution policies. Finally, an action plan has to be developed.

Core capabilities and strategic intent

What is clear is that clever strategies are not enough. There are two additional requirements for the strategies to be implemented successfully. The first is the commitment of the people in the organization to the success of the strategies. The second is the knowledge and skills to deliver superior value. The former is now commonly referred to as *strategic intent* – a goal, enthusiastically endorsed by managers and personnel, to make the organization the leader in its chosen market or channels. Such a commitment requires visible, consistent leadership from the top, creating an inspiring vision for the people who work in the organization.

The second requirement is for the company to possess *core capabilities*: to develop in its people the specialist technical or marketing skills to produce products and services of outstanding quality and value. Unless the company invests in its workforce and puts in the training programmes to enable them to achieve top-quality performance, the idea of creating a world-beating company is mere wishful thinking.

 ## Changing marketing environment

Professional marketing has become more important as advanced countries have shifted from a supply to a demand environment. For most of history the world has been characterized by insufficient supply: not enough food and material goods to meet human requirements. The key priority in the past has been improving production, purchasing and the finance of trade. Today this has all changed. Now, the advanced countries are characterized by excessive supply. The central problem is attracting demand, not meeting it. Faced with an array of alternatives, the customer is spoiled for choice. The priority in management is how to identify and develop goods and services which are more attractive to customers than those of competitors.

As the market environment changes, managers have to adapt their strategies and organization. Unless these changes are made, the business will no longer fit the needs of the moment – it will be made obsolete by changes in customer wants, new technologies and new competitors that have adapted more effectively. Looking ahead towards the year 2000, environmental changes appear to be accelerating. Ten such changes are discussed here. This is followed by an assessment of their strategic and organizational implications (see Table 14.1).

Fashionization

In the past fashion was identified with women's clothing. But today more and more markets – watches, motorcycles, beer, cars, pharmaceuticals, cinema, music, electronic goods, even management courses – are characterized by annual model changes, rapid obsolescence and an unpredictable and fickle demand. Companies that cannot handle novelty, rapid model replacement, fashion and style see their market shares slipping and their profit margins eroding as their products look increasingly dull and old-fashioned to customers. New models and new services have become the key to maintaining or enhancing prices or margins. Without novelty and continual feature enhancement, the company will see its prices and market share relentlessly chiselled away.

Micro-markets

The old textbooks used to postulate that a company could choose between a differentiated and an undifferentiated strategy. An undifferentiated strategy is where a company makes a single product for the whole market. The usual example was Coca-Cola, which, it was said, offered one product, in one bottle size, at one price and with one advertising message to all customers, everywhere in the world. No longer. Even Coca-Cola is today offered in an increasing and bewildering variety of forms – new Coke, classic and cherry, with or without caffeine, diet Cokes, in cans or in numerous bottle sizes, all advertised in various styles and formats. Today's customers expect the manufacturer to customize the product and service to their specific needs. Technology has made this variety expansion economically viable for companies. New flexible systems, like computer-aided design and manufacturing and customized software, permit ever-finer market segmentation and product range expansion.

Rising expectations

The success that high-performance companies have had in raising the quality of their products and services has led to continually rising customer expectations. Today's customers will no longer accept the delays, variations in product performance and sloppy service which were the norm a generation ago. Many companies see customers giving them poor ratings for performance, not because they are getting worse, but because they are not raising quality standards as fast as their competitors.

Technological change

Technology continues to advance at a very rapid rate in many industries. Successful companies do not need to be technological pioneers, but they do at least need to be fast followers. Companies that resist change in their products or processes risk faster obsolescence than in the past. Competition and rising customer expectations are shortening the time taken for new technologies to gain mass-market acceptance.

Competition

Competition is unquestionably getting tougher in most industries. Many of the weaker players have by now been already shaken out. Market barriers have fallen with declining tariffs, lower transport costs and the speed of real-time information about market opportunities. Eroding profit margins and pressures from shareholders are forcing all companies to sharpen their competitiveness and raise their levels of performance.

Globalization

Today we live in a 'global village'. Rising incomes and particularly access to information through television, travel and advertising messages have created common demands and expectations in all countries. Common demands have created the opportunities for common suppliers. Now, since every business faces global competitors, they all have to consider themselves as international businesses.

Software

Customers increasingly want a service rather than a product. Real product advantages are difficult to gain and even harder to maintain, so that differentiation is increasingly based upon how companies augment their products with additional services. Both BA and Virgin Airlines fly business people on Boeing 747s from London to Tokyo, but Virgin captured share by providing its business-class customers with a chauffeured car service to take them from the plane to their home or hotel when they arrived. Business schools differentiate themselves by services that augment their core products – residential facilities, spouses' clubs, crèches, career counselling, placement services, alumni associations and so on. Differentiation in services and software is a new competitive battleground.

Commoditization

Today's speciality products are tomorrow's commodities. Services which customers today regard as special, tomorrow will be seen as standard. Profitable products and market niches invariably attract new entrants which copy the successful innovators and compete for market share by lowering prices. As customers gain familiarity with using products and services, they look increasingly upon them as commodities and price becomes more and more important. Unless companies can keep moving the goalposts through faster innovation, profit margins invariably decline.

Erosion of brands

In most margins the mega-brands like Coca-Cola, Marlboro, IBM, Hertz, the BBC, Zantac and McDonald's are losing share. This is being caused first by the fractionalization of once homogeneous markets. Intensified competition and innovation and more options are leading to a changing diversity of micro-brands rather than a few mega-brands. Second, buying power, especially the power of the major retailers, is eroding manufacturer margins and hence their ability to put advertising support behind their brands. In the USA, for example, in the last ten years advertising has dropped from 70 per cent to 25 per cent of total market spending[2]. Most of the manufacturers' marketing spending now goes to providing promotions and discounts to get retailers to carry their brands.

New constraints

Changes in government, politics, the economy and society also bring new constraints which create both new threats and new opportunities. One is new regulations from governments and regional authorities such as the European Union. In particular, companies that produce products that are harmful to the environment face increasingly stringent constraints and outright bans. Another trend is the raising of ethical standards. Companies which pursue policies which look unfair, immoral or dangerous are coming under increasing scrutiny and criticism. Management are now facing new challenges to define their social and ethical standards.

Table 14.1 ■ The changing marketing environment and its implications

Changing environment	Marketing strategy	Organizing for marketing
Fashionization	Speed	Breaking hierarchies
Micro-markets	Customization	Small business units
Rising expectations	Quality	Self-managing teams
Technology	Information networks	Re-engineering
Competition	Core competences	Strategic alliances
Globalization	Think global	Transnational organization
Service	Software augmentation	Learning organizations
Commoditization	Partnerships	Account management
Erosion of brands	Innovation	Expeditionary marketing
New constraints	Stakeholders	Role of the board

Changing marketing strategies

Organizations succeed when they develop and implement strategies which fit the environment. As the environment changes – in the ways described above – companies must adapt or their market positions will rapidly erode. Each of the environmental changes is creating new priorities. Ten of these corresponding strategic priorities are discussed below.

Speed

The spread of fashion and the explosion of variety are forcing management to review their new product development and manufacturing operations to make speed and variety expansion top strategic priorities. AT & T Components, which supplies parts to PC manufacturers, has, for example, slashed its design-to-delivery cycle tenfold from 53 days to 5 days. IBM Credit has cut the time it takes to approve financial deals from 1 week to 4 hours. Managers are learning that, if they can take time out of internal processes, they can cut overhead costs, increase the number of new products offered, provide better customer service, boost market share and charge higher prices.

Customization

The splintering of mass markets means that, to succeed today, companies have to give customers exactly what they want. In industrial markets, they have to tailor strategies to individual accounts. In consumer markets, they need ever-finer segmentation. Mass-media advertising and broad pricing strategies have ceased to work effectively. Not surprisingly, direct response is the most rapidly growing promotional medium. Similarly, managers need to fine-tune pricing policies to differences between customers in perceptions of value. Undifferentiated strategies pull product appeal and profit margins down to the lowest common denominator.

Quality

Customers are no longer willing to accept the sloppy quality standards of products and services that they were offered in the past. Companies such as Toyota, Federal Express, Xerox, Hewlett-Packard and Club Med have shown that high quality can be provided consistently without the customer having to pay Rolls-Royce prices. A total quality management (TQM) programme has now become an essential ingredient for competitiveness. High quality is not a sufficient requirement for success – too many now offer it – but it is a necessary entrance ticket to the race.

Information

Technology and particularly information systems offer new sources of competitive advantage. Flexible manufacturing technologies now permit a company to offer customers more variety without adding to cost. Twenty years ago a telecommunications company like British Telecom or Bell provided one telephone – the standard black model – to everyone. There was no choice. Today these companies offer over one thousand to choose from, each variant differing in its combination of colour, size, features, programmability, services and price.

New technologies also allow companies to link up directly to customers and add value. For example, Coats Viyella is one of Europe's largest clothing manufacturers. In exploring the needs of their customers, management found that retailers were less worried about the cost of the items they sold than about the costs of too many unsold items at the end of the season. The conventional once-per-season ordering system often left retailers with substantial overstocks and required heavy discounting to get rid of the unsold stock. This critical discovery suggested a new source of differential advantage. Coats set up a new ordering system which allowed retailers to place a smaller order at the start of the season, then make the necessary top-ups during the season as the retailers monitored consumer off-take. To make the system work, Coats radically restructured its manufacturing to eliminate delays and increase responsiveness.

Core focus

The pace of competition in the past decade has forced companies to focus increasingly on their core businesses. In the boom years of the 1960s and 1970s, many companies diversified into totally unrelated industries. Oil companies moved into retailing, tobacco companies bought into insurance, grocery businesses acquired electronics companies. However, as competition hotted up and economic conditions toughened, the lack of core capabilities possessed by these companies was brutally exposed. Management have learned that sustainable competitive advantage depends on focusing upon core capabilities – building up real skills in a limited area of the market and technology.

Think global

The development of global markets and global competitors has meant that companies need to develop global strategies. There are three reasons for this. First, in many industries, global markets are necessary to spread the cost of research and development. Second, diverse markets allow a company to spread its risks – downturns in some markets can be offset by upturns in others. Finally, having all one's eggs in one basket leaves a company with a high level of strategic risk. A company with its entire sales in one country is hopelessly vulnerable in its margins if it comes under attack from a multinational using price as a weapon. The latter can cross-subsidize its low prices; the former has no other sources of high-margin business to rely on.

Software differentiation

In today's environment, managers – especially in industrial markets – have to get away from the idea of products as the basis for competitiveness. It is rare for a company to be able to maintain an advantage in product performance for very long. Management have to create a strategy built upon augmenting the product to build brands which can bond in distributors and customers. Increasingly, service and software are the key to maintaining these relationships when product differences dissolve.

General Electric's new strategy in the white goods industry is a good example. Historically, appliance manufacturers sought to incentivize retailers to load up with their range. However, this began to work less well as the big chains began to dictate trade terms and the small independents lacked the resources to carry the full product range. GE's response was its Direct Connect programme. Retailers ceased to have to invest in inventories. Instead they received a computer system which gave them instant access to GE's on-line order-processing system, 24 hours a day, 7 days a week. Customers use the system to check on model availability and place orders for next-day delivery. The benefits to the retailer are reduced working capital requirements and instant access to a much greater range of models. The benefits to GE are a stronger partnership with its dealers and, for the first time, on-line information about which of its models are proving most attractive to customers. In effect, GE is now manufacturing in response to consumer demand rather than to build inventory.[3]

Partnerships

Today's strategies place the highest priority on building partnerships with existing customers. New customers are difficult to win and often take years to break even. In contrast, satisfied customers are assets with years of income-generating potential. In addition, existing customers are invariably the easiest to interest in new products and extensions which offer the company additional opportunities for growth and profit.

Managers need to develop strategies which build partnerships with customers. This involves understanding their problems. Customers can also be involved in developing new products and services. The *Financial Times* noted one example:

> A cultural revolution is taking place at Boeing. It is encouraging airlines, suppliers and sub-contractors to participate actively in the design of its latest airliner, the 777 wide-bodied jet. In the past, Boeing felt it knew what was best for its airline customers. 'But with the 777, Boeing has for the first time given us direct access to the process of designing an aircraft,' says James O'Sullivan, BA's Chief Engineer on the 777 programme.[4]

Innovation

The erosion of traditional brands makes innovation a crucial strategic priority for companies. But innovation is less and less about investing vast sums in R & D in the hope of technical breakthroughs. Today's companies rarely make these blockbusters, and when they do occur, it is more often by chance than by investment and planning. Management have to prioritorize the small, incremental enhancements and extensions which keep their products fresh, add value for the customer and safeguard profit margins. These new product ideas are much more likely to come from the field – from the customer, the salesforce or the service engineer – than they are from the labs. Where the breakthroughs do occur, they are usually new ways of envisaging markets – new channels of distribution, new market segments or new presentational approaches – rather than radically new technologies.

Multiple stakeholders

Years ago entrepreneurs could pursue an almost unfettered capitalism in which their own interests predominated. But in today's complex environment, the long-term success of the firm depends upon satisfying a variety of stakeholders in addition to the shareholders. These include the professional managers who run the business, other employees, suppliers, customers and the communities in which the business operates. All provide valuable resources and all feel they have legitimate claims on the business. Furthermore, each of their claims partly conflict. The interests of the shareholders for profit may conflict with the interests of the employees for security. The goal of the community for a good environment may constrain management's drive for growth and profit. A key task of the board is to develop strategies that can reconcile these different groups.

 Changing organizations for marketing

The rapidly changing business environment makes existing products and marketing strategies obsolete. Companies have to become faster, more flexible, more innovative and capable of forging new partnerships with customers and suppliers. To put in place such strategies, however, requires sweeping organizational changes. Yesterday's giant organizations like IBM, General Motors, ICI, Midland Bank, Sears and Philips have proved to be too bureaucratic, slow moving and production oriented to adapt their strategies to the momentum of their markets. In this section, ten organizational implications for tomorrow's businesses are discussed.

Breaking hierarchies

Central requirements for effective marketing today are speed and flexibility. This means anticipating the ephemeral nature of current products and designs, and achieving a rapid response to new customer requirements and competitor initiatives. Organizationally, this entails sweeping away those restraints which put brakes on change and discourage initiative. The most important 'killer' of new initiatives and fast response is the large bureaucratic organization with its multiple hierarchy of managers and large head-office staff. These cripple fast decision making, disillusion front-line people and suck able managers into non-value-adding administrative work.

Today's high-performance businesses are dramatically delayering the hierarchy to a maximum of four or five levels. They are virtually eliminating head-office staff and are reassigning such people to line jobs. For example, Richard Branson runs his Virgin Group of entertainment, retail and airline businesses with a headquarters of five people. ABB cut its corporate staff by 95 per cent as part of its revitalization programme. BTR runs its £12 billion global manufacturing business with a headquarters of 47. The emphasis is now on empowering line managers, giving them the power and responsibility for achieving results.

Small business units

In the past, large organizations were regarded as necessary to achieve economies of scale. But today's priorities have shifted from scale to variety, customization and speed. Top companies are splitting themselves up into smaller units to achieve these goals. For example, ABB has splintered its 200,000 people into 5,000 largely independent profit centres that average only 50 people each. Small organizations can simulate the advantages of the entrepreneurial family business. People can totally identify with its success. Managers can understand its operations and do not need to hand over key tasks to distant functional experts. The unit can have a flat horizontal structure and avoid staff departments and the attendant bureaucracy.

Self-managing teams

A team is a small number of people with complementary skills who are committed to a common purpose, set of performance goals and approach for which they hold themselves mutually accountable.[5] With innovation, impermanence and change dominating the features of today's markets, temporary teams are likely to become the primary unit of performance in successful organizations. These teams will not eliminate existing structures, but they will encourage functional excellence to be channelled in a way which facilitates change and avoids the specialist bias in conventional functional structures. Such teams are purely horizontal: they possess at the same level all the skills necessary to do the job. There are no delays while waiting for permission or handing over tasks for working on by separate specialists.

Re-engineering

In the past, most organizational changes have been slow and incremental. But now some companies are seeking to totally reorganize from scratch, the objective being to produce a dramatic leap in productivity and competitiveness. Companies that have embraced this concept of re-engineering or 'process redesign' include AT & T, Texas Instruments, Reuters, Ford and Citicorp.[6] The stimulus has been the alarm at the threat they face from new competitors, especially from the Far East, which appear to possess both lower costs and dramatically faster innovation and manufacturing processes. The opportunity to restructure processes radically has now been provided by the rapid advances in computers and their plummeting prices.

Re-engineering is based upon two ideas. The first is to start with a clean sheet of paper and design all parts of the operations of the company in the best possible way. The second is to look on companies as performing a small number of continuing processes, rather than as collections of people performing hundreds of distinct, though related, functions.

It has proved easiest to configure and computerize new businesses. For example, Dell became one of the world's largest PC companies by using computers to avoid an expensive dealer network or salesforce and sell directly to customers. Similarly, the Midland Bank could start with a clean piece of paper when it established First Direct, Britain's first successful telephone-banking business.

But process redesign also offers vast opportunities for ongoing businesses. For example, Ford once employed 500 people shuffling papers among themselves in its accounts payable department. Then Ford asked whether any of these bits of paper were necessary. Now 125 people do the same job three times as fast. The clerk at the receiving dock, using a computer to reconcile deliveries with orders instantly, accepts goods on his or her own authority and issues payment. There are no bits of paper any longer to shuffle. Not surprisingly, re-engineering has become one of the major topics in top management.

Networks and alliances

To build sustainable differential advantages, management increasingly recognize that they have to identify and focus on their core capabilities. Glaxo, for example, defined its core as prescription pharmaceuticals. Marks & Spencer defines its core as retailing. But the core is never sufficient to build a dynamic and growing business. Marks & Spencer needs access to first-rate manufacturing skills. Glaxo will want to exploit opportunities in switching some of its prescription medicines into consumer markets. All successful companies search for innovations outside their own labs and want to draw on special skills in such areas as advertising, market research, information systems and financial instruments.

Vertical integration – possessing these skills internally – is too expensive and inflexible and rarely produces the levels of creativity and performance that dedicated professional organizations achieve. At the same time, buying in these skills in an ad-hoc manner fails to build a competitive advantage. High performance depends upon building networks and alliances with outside suppliers and sources of creativity which produce mutually beneficial partnerships. Companies like Marks & Spencer, Hewlett-Packard and Merck have been successful because they have incentivized outsiders to prioritize working with them, and to dedicate key personnel and specialized facilities. Building and managing such networks is becoming one of the most essential marketing skills.

Transnational organizations

Management must organize to optimize their opportunities and competitiveness internationally. Competing globally raises organizational complexity and the skills required from managers. The complexity arises from the need to reconcile three organizational criteria.[7] First, the company has to seek global cost efficiency. This criterion pushes the business towards centralized decision making, the pursuit of scale economies in manufacturing, and standardized products and strategies. The second criterion is the need for local adaptation. This pushes management in the opposite direction towards decentralizing, and tailoring products and strategies to the individual markets. The third criterion is the need to accelerate the rate of innovation. This leads to the development of global strategies and increasing co-ordination for local decision making.

Management have to seek a sensitive balance between these, at least partly conflicting, criteria. Too much centralization discourages local initiative and drive. Too little fails to lever the company's technological and marketing know-how. Formal structures can only poorly reconcile these objectives; real balance depends upon the personalities, styles and leadership of the international managers responsible for implementing these strategies.

The learning organization

The speed of environmental change is making obsolete the knowledge base of managers and employees at an accelerating rate. Degrees earned at universities quickly become historical mementoes. Similarly, in an age when companies are into re-engineering their organizations and processes, on-the-job training provides few bankable skills. Today managers have to build learning organizations which continually upgrade the skills and knowledge base of their people.

Nowadays this is becoming a crucial requirement if the firm wishes to hire good people. People know now that even the top companies cannot guarantee job security. The next best thing for them is to obtain from employers the training and the skills which will make them valued and employable elsewhere if they have to leave their current positions. For the firm, well-trained, up-to-date employees are its greatest asset.

Account management

Building partnerships means developing organizations that put the customer at the centre. More companies are now creating account managers whose job is to integrate the specialist expertise within the business around the task of adding value for individual or small groups of customers. Management consultants and advertising agencies have long found this to be the most effective way to serve clients, but now banks and manufacturers are discovering that it is a good way to keep their organization focused around what really counts – delivering value to the customer.

Expeditionary marketing

In the past, new product development was a carefully planned, slow process. The emphasis was on minimizing the risk of new product failure. Today the priorities are changing. Speed and being first to market is the new emphasis. The costs of being late exceed the costs of being wrong. In addition, the speed of change makes market research much more difficult. Customers cannot easily predict what products they will want: they cannot visualize technologies and solutions they have not seen.

Hamel and Prahalad called the new approach 'expeditionary marketing'.[8] Instead of planning for the blockbuster innovation that gets it right first time, they observed that companies like Canon, Toshiba and Motorola bring out a stream of low-cost, fast-paced innovative products. The variety allows the company to explore a range of niche markets and models, and then fine-tune and exploit those which catch on among customers. Those which do not take off are quickly discarded.

The role of the board

A board of directors should have three functions. First, it must review and evaluate the company's top managers. Second, it should advise on the broad strategic direction of the business. Third, it should provide access for the range of stakeholders – employees, customers, bankers, suppliers and local communities – who are concerned with the business. Too often boards do not fulfil these tasks properly. Frequently, they are dominated by the managers that they are expected to supervise. When this occurs the company's capacity to change and renew itself becomes threatened. Developing an objective and functioning board is a prerequisite for the organization's long-term success.

Towards a partnership mentality

These organizational changes imply new roles for marketing. The organizational changes that high-performing companies are introducing can be summarized along internal and external dimensions. Both are aimed at freeing up management to act faster and more decisively to seize market opportunities. Both also aim to do this in ways which economize on labour and capital resources.

The internal organizational restructuring focuses on destroying bureaucracy, delayering the organization, creating small business units and self-managing teams which aim at adding value for customers, and taking out unproductive overhead costs and investments.

The external organizational changes are parallel and aim at building partnerships not just with customers, but also with suppliers and distributors. Figure 14.3 shows how organizational thinking has changed over the last fifty years.[9] Organizational forms can be thought of as a continuum from pure transactions at one end to fully vertically integrated forms at the other. In the former, management negotiate one-off transactions with customers and suppliers. In the latter, the firm owns the whole supply chain from raw materials through manufacturing to the retailing of its products to the end customer. The epitomy of the fully integrated firm was Ford, and most notably its River Rouge plant, in the 1920s. It was a form that many firms sought to achieve or maintain right up to the 1960s.

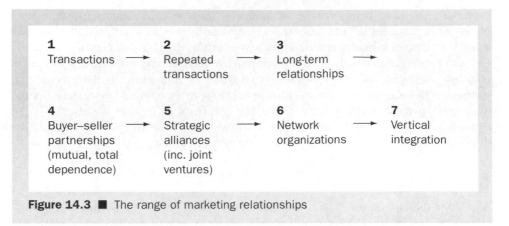

Figure 14.3 ■ The range of marketing relationships

Source: Frederick E. Webster, 'The changing role of marketing in the corporation', *Journal of Marketing*, October 1992, p. 5

Neither extreme works well today. *Vertical integration* creates an organization too inflexible to respond to rapidly changing markets and extends the firm's activities beyond its area of competence. Manufacturers, for example, rarely make good retailers. A focus on one-off *transactions*, on the other hand, ignores the value of relationships, trust and loyalty between the parties involved in the transaction. Short-term profit rarely builds a long-term business.

In fact a very high proportion of the firm's activities are typically based upon *repeated transactions*. Consumers buy grocery brands weekly and industrial buyers make similar repeated purchases of components and operating supplies. *Long-term relationships* increasingly mark successful suppliers, particularly in industrial markets. Nevertheless all three forms – transactions, repeated transactions and long-term relationships – reflect an adversarial connection. Both buyer and seller negotiate to get the best deal – albeit a long-term advantage.

Japanese *kanban* or just-in-time systems demonstrated the limitations of the western adversarial model. The Japanese approach to low cost with high quality depended heavily on a system of strategic *partnerships* with a small number of suppliers that are incorporated at an early stage of development. *Strategic alliances* take these partnerships into entirely new ventures. These focus on shared objectives and commitments with the aim of substantially enhancing their joint competitive positions in the industry. Finally, *networks* are the complex, multifaceted and evolving organizational structures that result from strategic alliances. These networks allow the company to focus on its core competences and use partnerships to lever these with complementary skills and resources.

To some managers today, joint ventures and strategic alliances are an early glimpse of the business organization of the future. The new concept is termed the *virtual corporation* – a temporary network of companies that come together quickly to exploit fast-changing opportunities. In the virtual corporation, companies share costs, skills and access to global markets, with each partner contributing what it is best at. These partnerships will be less permanent, less formal and more opportunistic. Companies will band together to meet a specific market opportunity and, more often than not, fall apart once the need evaporates.[10]

Such changes suggest new tasks for marketing. Managers have the task of not only forging partnerships with customers, but also creating new value-adding partnerships with suppliers and other parties which augment the company's core competences by integrating those of others to create new sources of competitive advantage.

Implementing marketing

Strategy focuses on *what* managers should do; implementation is about *how* it should be done. Success requires both good strategies and good implementation. Unfortunately, when things go wrong, it is often difficult to identify whether the problems are due to poor strategy or ineffective implementation. Making the wrong diagnosis can lead to unfortunate consequences. For example, a metallurgical company brought out a new filter for use in iron foundries which substantially cut the operating costs of customers. An average foundry was anticipated to save materials and labour of over £100 on a complex casting, potentially doubling the customer's profit. The company therefore wanted the sales people to sell the filters at premium prices, exploiting their high economic value to the customer. Unfortunately, the results were disappointing and sales only began to take off when the price was discounted, earning the company disappointing margins.

Reviewing the launch, managers differed on whether the problem was due to poor strategy or poor implementation. Some saw the price as too high for customers used to paying only half the price. Others saw the problem as due to an inadequately trained salesforce and a sales culture based around achieving volume through low prices rather than demonstrating economic value to customers and seeking high margins.

The alternatives are illustrated in Figure 14.4. Success is most likely to be achieved by an appropriate strategy and effective implementation. But the other three cells in the figure are problematical. The failure of the new filter to generate expected returns may be due to poor strategy (the roulette position), poor implementation (trouble) or both (failure). In fact, management acted as though the strategy was incorrect and changed this, perhaps hastening the failure to hit profit targets. If they had struggled to improve implementation, the strategy might well have moved to a success position.

Bonoma identifies four levels of implementation:[11]

■ *Marketing actions*. These involve handling effectively the individual elements of the marketing mix, such as pricing, promotions, selling and distributor management.

■ *Marketing programmes*. These involve integrating the separate marketing mix elements into a coherent whole.

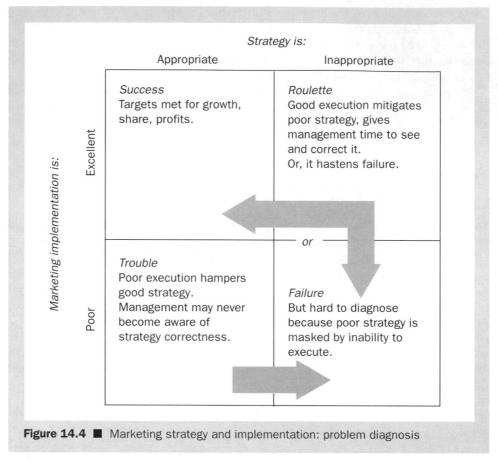

Figure 14.4 ■ Marketing strategy and implementation: problem diagnosis

Source: reprinted with the permission of The Free Press, a division of Macmillan, Inc., from *Managing Marketing: Text, cases and readings* by Thomas V. Bonoma, p. 13. Copyright © 1984 by The Free Press

■ *Marketing systems.* These are the organizational structures, monitoring and budgeting systems which control and facilitate activities.

■ *Marketing policies.* These are the interpretation of the corporate policies by marketing managers.

How effectively these activities are performed determines how successfully the firm's marketing strategies are implemented. To be effective implementers, marketing managers need four skills:

■ *Interacting.* This is the skill that marketing people need to persuade others to follow the policies they are seeking to implement. It involves influencing both insiders such as R & D personnel and sales people, and outside partners such as customers and suppliers. These interface or communication skills are crucial to the successful implementation of all marketing activities.

- *Allocating*. Managers need the skill to allocate time, money and people to the right customers and products. They must be able to shift resources out of problem areas into areas which represent future opportunities for the business.

- *Monitoring*. This is the skill required to construct and maintain feedback mechanisms which measure and control the results of the marketing activities. Managers must be able to identify when problems are occurring and to intervene to put things back on track when necessary.

- *Organizing*. This is the managerial skill of developing informal marketing networks which can overcome the resistance and barriers implicit in the formal organization. Managers need to know whom to contact to get things moving fast and how to work around problems.

Summary

The principles of marketing – being customer led, effective segmentation and positioning, and sound planning – will remain fundamental to the successful firm in the years ahead. In fact, the changing environment will test these skills as never before. The pace of change – splintering markets, fashion and variety, together with ever-increasing competition – is making past strategies and organizations obsolete at breathtaking speed.

The emerging strategic priorities for tomorrow's firms focus on speed of response, customizing products and services, enhanced information networks and the search for higher standards of quality. The organizational pyramids with their multiple layers of management and enormous head offices are being blown away by the winds of competition. Such organizations are too slow, too costly and insufficiently motivating for the front-line managers to be successful in today's markets.

The new organizations are global and made up of small business units, linked together by networks communicating via sophisticated electronic information systems. Most of all these businesses will be knowledge organizations – run by people with the skills to master core technologies and key markets, and with the ability to communicate with partners both inside and outside.

Questions

1. What are the core concepts of marketing? Are they likely to change in the future?
2. Is 'marketing' primarily a function or a philosophy?
3. Take an industry familiar to you and analyze the key environmental changes taking place. Then identify how top-performing companies are adjusting their strategies and organizations to gain competitive advantage.

4. What are the organizational blocks to faster response to market demands, and how are they being overcome by fast-track companies?

5. Peter Drucker recently wrote that capitalism is giving way to the 'knowledge society'. Knowledge is replacing capital as the basic resource of economies. What does this mean and what are its implications for management?

6. Discuss the problems that are likely to occur in implementing marketing strategies.

Notes

1. Michael E. Porter, *Competitive Strategy: Techniques for analysing industries and competitors* (New York: Free Press, 1980).

2. 'Brands on the run', *Business Week*, 14 April 1993, pp. 26–9.

3. Michael Treacy and Fred Wiersema, 'Customer intimacy and other value disciplines', *Harvard Business Review*, January–February 1993, pp. 84–93.

4. 'Boeing's culture revolution', *Financial Times*, 7 May 1993, p. 8.

5. Jon R. Katzenback and Douglas K. Smith, *The Wisdom of Teams: Creating the high-performance organisation* (Boston, MA: Harvard Business School Press, 1993).

6. Michael Hammer and James Champy, *Re-engineering the Corporation* (London: Brealey, 1993).

7. Christopher A. Barlett and Sumantra Ghoshal, *Managing Across Borders: The transnational solution* (London: Hutchinson, 1989).

8. Gary Hamel and C. K. Prahalad, 'Corporate imagination and expeditionary marketing', *Harvard Business Review*, July–August 1991, pp. 81–92.

9. Frederick E. Webster, 'The changing role of marketing in the corporation', *Journal of Marketing*, October 1992, pp. 1–17.

10. 'The virtual corporation', *Business Week*, 8 February 1993, pp. 36–41.

11. Thomas V. Bonoma, *Managing Marketing: Text, cases and readings* (New York: Free Press, 1984).

Further reading

This chapter looks at the most important tasks of senior managers in today's environment. By far the most influential and accessible author on these topics is Peter F. Drucker. His authoritative *Management: Tasks, responsibilities, practices* (London: Heinemann, 1973) is essential reading. Among his more recent books, *The New Realities* (London: Heinemann, 1989) is a fascinating review of the impact of changes in government, economics and society on business.

Tom Peters and Robert H. Waterman's *In Search of Excellence* (New York: Harper & Row, 1982) triggered a new interest in the management literature and, in particular, the characteristics of successful companies. Several more recent best sellers by Peters have modified and developed the original themes. A recent European perspective covering parallel topics is Hermann Simon, *Hidden Champions* (Boston, MA: Harvard Business School Press, 1996).

Much of the corporate strategy literature touches on these topics. Among the best are Gerry Johnson and Kevan Scholes, *Exploring Corporate Strategy* (Hemel Hempstead: Prentice Hall, 1993); Richard Whittington, *What is Strategy and does it Matter?* (London: Routledge, 1993); Peter McKiernan, *Strategies for Growth* (London: Routledge, 1992) and Richard P. Rumelt, *Fundamental Issues in Strategy* (Boston, MA: Harvard Business School Press, 1995).

The issue of stakeholder constraints is discussed in G. E. Greenley and G. R. Foxall, 'Consumer or nonconsumer stakeholder orientation in UK companies', *Journal of Business Research*, July 1996, pp. 433–43; Nigel Piercy, *Market-Led Strategic Change* (Oxford: Butterworth-Heinemann, 1992) and J. S. Harrison and C. H. St John, *Strategic Management of Organisations and Stakeholders* (St. Paul, MN: West, 1994).

A comprehensive approach to the financial view of strategy is Richard A. Brealey and Stewart C. Myers, *Principles of Corporate Finance* (New York: McGraw-Hill, 1994). International aspects are covered in Stefan H. Robock and Kenneth Simmonds, *International Business and Multinational Enterprises* (Homewood, IL: Irwin, 1988) and

C. K. Prahalad and Yves L. Doz, *The Multinational Mission* (New York: Macmillan, 1987). Current thinking on diversified companies is reflected in Michael Gold and Kathleen Summers Luchs, *Managing the Multibusiness Company* (London: Routledge, 1996).

Chapter 2: The customer-led business

This introduces the marketing concept and the issues in creating a customer-led business.

In modern times the best-selling and most influential graduate textbook on marketing has been Philip Kotler, *Marketing Management: Analysis, planning, implementation and control*, 9th edn (Englewood Cliffs, NJ: Prentice Hall, 1996). A compendium of essays on the current state-of-the-art by European academics is Michael J. Baker (ed.), *The Marketing Book*, 3rd edn (Oxford: Butterworth-Heinemann, 1997).

A considerable literature has arisen seeking to define the precise organizational and behavioural characteristics of a market-oriented business. Among the most influential contributions are G. S. Day, 'The capabilities of market driven organisations', *Journal of Marketing*, October 1994, pp. 37–52; B. Jaworski and A. Kohli, 'Market orientation: antecedents and consequences', *Journal of Marketing*, July 1993, pp. 53–71, and J. C. Narver and S. F. Slater, 'The effect of a market orientation on business performance', *Journal of Marketing*, October 1990, pp. 20–35. How to create a marketing culture is well presented in Nigel Piercy, *Market-Led Strategic Change* (Oxford: Butterworth-Heinemann, 1992). Relationship marketing is covered in Frederick F. Reichheld, *The Loyalty Effect: The hidden force behind growth, profits and lasting value* (Boston, MA: Harvard Business School Press, 1996). The origins of relationship marketing lie in European and particularly Scandinavian research into business markets. For a good review see David Ford, *Understanding Business Markets*, 2nd edn (London: Dryden, 1997) and D. Ford, L. E. Gadde, A. Lundgren, H. Hakansson, I. Snehota, P. Turnbull and D. Wilson, *Managing Business Relationships* (Chichester: Wiley, 1996).

Chapter 3: Segmentation, positioning and the marketing mix

The central technical skills of the marketing manager are in segmentation and positioning.

Marketing planning is well covered in Sally Dibb, Lyndon Simkin and John Bradley, *The Marketing Planning Workbook* (London: Routledge, 1996). Most of the marketing textbooks also cover the subject.

The techniques of market segmentation are presented in detail in Malcolm McDonald and Ian Dunbar, *Market Segmentation* (London: Macmillan, 1995). Presentation of the techniques of segmentation are in Philippe Naert and Peter Leeflang, *Building Implementable Marketing Movers* (Leiden: Martin Nijhoff, 1978) and Gary L. Lilien and Philip Kotler, *Marketing Decision-Making: A model-building approach* (New York: Harper & Row, 1983).

Positioning and competitive advantage are discussed in Michael Porter's influential book *Competitive Advantage* (New York: Free Press, 1985). Also see George S. Day and Robin Wensley, 'Assessing advantage: a framework for diagnosing competitive superiority', *Journal of Marketing*, April 1988, pp. 1–20. Positioning from an advertising perspective is in Al Ries and Jack Trout, *Positioning: The battle for your mind* (New York: Warner, 1982).

The broader issues of organizing the supply chain to target different market segments are discussed in J. P. Womack and D. T. Jones, 'From lean production to the lean enterprise', *Harvard Business Review*, March–April 1994, pp. 93–105, and B. J. Pine, *Mass Customisation* (Boston, MA: Harvard Business School Press, 1993).

Chapter 4: Strategic market planning

The fundamentals of modern strategic market planning were first comprehensively presented by Igor Ansoff. See his *Corporate Strategy*, revised edn (Harmondsworth: Penguin, 1987). The next key works are Michael Porter's *Competitive Strategy: Techniques for analysing industries and competitors* (New York: Free Press, 1980) and his *Competitive Advantages: Creating and sustaining superior performance* (New York: Free Press, 1985).

An excellent collection of papers on strategic marketing is H. I. Costin and H. A. Vanolli, *Classic Readings in Strategy* (London: Dryden, 1997). Graham J. Hooley and John Saunders, *Competitive Positioning* (Hemel Hempstead: Prentice Hall, 1993) is also strongly recommended.

Besides the familiar Harvard-type case studies, there are now some excellent computer simulations which permit managers to practise strategic market planning. The best of these is Jean-Claude Larreche and Hubert Gatignon, *Markstrat: A marketing strategy game* (Palo Alto: Scientific Press, 1995).

There are some good studies of marketing strategy in particular industries: for example, Marcel Corstjen's excellent *Marketing Strategy in the Pharmaceutical Industry* (London: Chapman & Hall, 1991). Hugh Davidson, *Offensive Marketing* (Harmondsworth: Penguin, 1997) is a good practical work, particularly aimed at consumer markets.

Chapter 5: Market dynamics and competitive strategy

There have been numerous articles about the product life cycle. A well-known one is Theodore Levitt, 'Exploit the product life cycle', *Harvard Business Review*, October–November 1965, pp. 81–94. Some others are cited in the references to the chapter.

The most important treatment of the more general concept of market dynamics is in Michael E. Porter, *Competitive Strategy* (New York: Free Press, 1980). Many of the issues are also covered in George S. Day, *Analysis for Strategic Market Decisions* (St Paul, MN: West, 1986).

A good review of the competitive strategy and warfare literature is John Saunders, 'Marketing and competitive success', in Michael J. Baker (ed.), *The Marketing Book*

(Oxford: Butterworth-Heinemann, 1994). Robert D. Buzzell and Bradley T. Gale, *The PIMS Principles: Linking strategy to performance* (New York: Free Press, 1987) has some fascinating and influential data on how different competitive strategies affect the financial performance of the company.

Chapter 6: Building successful brands

The literature on brands has grown rapidly in recent years. Probably the most comprehensive work is David A. Aaker, *Building Strong Brands* (New York: Free Press, 1995). Another review, focused particularly on advertising and fast-moving grocery products, is John Philip Jones, *What's in a Name? Advertising and the Concept of Brands* (Lexington, MA: Lexington Books, 1986). J.-N. Kapferer's *Strategic Brand Management* (New York: Free Press, 1994) has some real insights into brands.

An interesting collection of papers on branding by European contributors is in a special issue of the *International Journal of Research in Marketing*, March 1993, edited by Patrick Barwise. Leslie de Chernatony's paper 'Categorizing brands: evolution processes underpinned by two key dimensions', *Journal of Marketing Management*, April 1993, pp. 173–88, provides an interesting perspective again using European examples.

There have also been some sceptical assessments of the value of brands. A. S. C. Ehrenberg, *Repeat Buying: Theory and applications* (London: North Holland, 1972) presents the theoretical reservations. A review in *Business Week*, 'Brands on the run', 19 April 1993, pp. 26–9, suggests that loyalty to the mega-brands may be eroding. This is discussed further in Chapter 13 of this book.

Chapter 7: Innovation and new product development

Most of the textbooks have a chapter on innovation, although many of them look a bit old-fashioned for today's fast-pace environment. The new emphasis is well described by George Stalk and Thomas M. Hout, *Competing Against Time* (New York: Free Press, 1990). A broad perspective is contained in Peter Drucker, *Innovation and Entrepreneurship* (London: Heinemann, 1985).

Good comprehensive discussions of the literature are available in J. Tidd, J. Bessant and K. Pavitt, *Managing Innovation* (London: Wiley, 1997) and Michael J. Thomas, 'Product development and management', in M. J. Baker (ed.), *The Marketing Book* (Oxford: Butterworth-Heinemann, 1994).

More recent reviews are Veronica Wong, *Innovation: Identifying and exploiting new market opportunities* (London, Department of Trade and Industry, 1993) and Susan Hart, *New Product Development* (London: Dryden, 1996).

An interesting discussion of the significance of innovation to marketing strategy is in Kenneth Simmonds, 'Marketing as innovation: the eighth paradigm', *Journal of Management Studies*, September 1986, pp. 479–500. The creative process in innovation is presented in Simon Majaro, *The Creative Process* (London: Allen & Unwin, 1991). The role of employees is discussed in Hirotaka Takeuchi and Ikujiro Nonaka, *The Knowledge Creating Company* (Oxford: Oxford University Press, 1996).

Chapter 8: Pricing policy: delivering value

One of the most comprehensive reviews of pricing issues and techniques is N. Henna and R. Dodge, *Pricing: Policies and procedures* (London: Macmillan, 1996). Another insightful and practical approach to common pricing problems is Thomas T. Nagle, *The Strategy and Tactics of Pricing* (Englewood Cliffs, NJ: Prentice Hall, 1987).

Some good articles by European authors are Martin Christopher, 'Value-in-use pricing', *European Journal of Marketing*, November 1982, pp. 35–47, Gordon R. Foxall, 'The logic of price decision-making', *Management Decision*, November 1980, pp. 235–45, and Herman Simon, 'Pricing opportunities: how to exploit them', *Sloan Management Review*, Winter 1992, pp. 55–65.

The mathematical techniques that can be used for estimating price elasticities are presented in Leonard J. Parsons and Randall L. Schultz, *Marketing Models and Econometric Research* (New York: North Holland, 1976). A simpler version is G. L. Lilien, P. Kotler and S. Moorthy, *Marketing Models* (Englewood Cliffs, NJ: Prentice Hall, 1992).

Chapter 9: Communications strategy

A good MBA-type text is David A. Aaker and John G. Myers, *Advertising Management* (Englewood Cliffs, NJ: Prentice Hall, 1994).

Three excellent books by practitioners which give a feeling of how the top companies and agencies plan advertising and communications in practice are: Judith Corstjens, *Strategic Advertising: A practitioner's handbook* (Oxford: Heinemann, 1990); Simon Broadbent, *Spending Advertising Money* (London: Business Books, 1985); David Ogilvy, *Ogilvy on Advertising* (London: Pan, 1983).

On other forms of promotion and communications, the best analytical treatment is Robert C. Blattberg and Scott A. Neslin, *Sales Promotion: Concepts, methods and strategies* (Englewood Cliffs, NJ: Prentice Hall, 1990). On direct marketing see Stan Rapp and Tom Collins, *The Great Marketing Turnaround* (Englewood Cliffs, NJ: Prentice Hall, 1990). On the Internet some current leading-edge insights appear in Mary J. Cronin, *The Internet Strategy Handbook* (Boston, MA: Harvard Business School Press, 1996) and J. Hagel and A. G. Armstrong, *Net Gain: Expanding markets through virtual communities* (Boston, MA: Harvard Business School, 1997).

Chapter 10: Managing personal selling

Two good and comprehensive textbooks are D. J. Dalrymple and L. J. Parsons, *Sales Management* (New York: Wiley, 1995) and T. N. Ingram, R. W. LaForge and

C. H. Schwepker, *Sales Management: Analysis and decision-making* (New York: Dryden 1997).

More complex selling is well treated in Robert B. Miller and Stephen E. Heiman, *Strategic Selling* (New York: William Morrow, 1985) and also in David Mercer, *The Sales Professional* (London: Kogan Page, 1988).

The best book on negotiation is Roger Fisher and William Ury, *Getting to Yes: Negotiating agreement without giving in*, 2nd edn (Boston, MA: Houghton Mifflin, 1992).

Chapter 11: Managing marketing channels

The most widely used textbook is Louis W. Stern and Adel I. El-Ansary, *Marketing Channels* (Englewood Cliffs, NJ: Prentice Hall, 1996). Another good managerially oriented work is Bert G. Rosenbloom, *Marketing Channels* (New York: Dryden, 1994).

A useful European perspective is James Cooper, Michael Browne and Melvyn Peters, *European Logistics* (Oxford: Blackwell, 1991). Also on logistics R. H. Ballou, *Business Logistics Management* (Englewood Cliffs, NJ: Prentice Hall, 1993) is a well-regarded text.

The trend towards strategic alliances, partnerships and more complex channels is discussed in R. T. Moriarty and U. Moran, 'Marketing hybrid marketing systems', *Harvard Business Review*, November–December 1990, pp. 146–57, and R.S. Achrol, 'Evolution of the marketing organisation', *Journal of Marketing*, October 1991, pp. 77–87.

Chapter 12: Marketing in service businesses

There is a great deal now being written about the service sector. An up-to-date and stimulating review of the key issues is John E. G. Bateson, *Managing Services Marketing* (New York: Dryden, 1992). Another useful guide is Jeffrey Pfeffer, *Competitive Advantage through People* (Boston, MA: Harvard University Press, 1996). Some innovative insights about building high-powered service organizations are in Leonard L. Berry and A. Parasuraman, *Marketing Services: Competing through quality* (New York: Free Press, 1991).

On non-profit organizations, two good books are Philip Kotler, *Marketing for Non-Profit Organisations* (Englewood Cliffs, NJ: Prentice Hall, 1988) and D. Z. Rodos, *Marketing for Non-Profit Organisations* (New York: Random House, 1981). A good review article is Keith J. Blois, 'Non-profit organisations and marketing', in Michael J. Baker, *The Marketing Book* (Oxford: Butterworth-Heinemann, 1994).

Chapter 13: Turnaround management

In today's rapidly changing environment, many firms fail to adapt decisively and pay the penalty in terms of declining sales and profit performance. New management are then brought in to produce a turnaround.

The accounting principles are covered in C. T. Horngren, G. Foster and S. M. Daton, *Cost Accounting: A management emphasis* (Englewood Cliffs, NJ: Prentice Hall, 1994) and C. Drury, *Management and Cost Accounting for Non-Accounting Students* (London: Pitman, 1994).

A real insight into how some companies manipulate their accounts to disguise growing financial problems is given in Terry Smith, *Accounting for Growth: Stripping the camouflage from company accounts* (London: Century Business, 1996). For modern approaches to using management accounting information for strategic decision making, see Tony Hope and Jeremy Hope, *Transforming the Bottom Line* (Boston, MA: Harvard Business School Press, 1996) and R. S. Kaplan and D. P. Norton, *The Balanced Scorecard* (Boston, MA: Harvard Business School Press, 1996).

Turning to transformation, recent research is reviewed in Thomas E. Vollman, *The Transformation Imperative: Achieving market dominance through radical change* (Boston, MA: Harvard University Press, 1996). Other useful insights are John P. Kotter, *Leading Change* (Boston, MA: Harvard University Press, 1996), R. M. Kanter, B. A. Stein and T. D. Jick, *The Challenge of Organisational Change: How companies experience it and leaders guide it* (New York: Free Press, 1992) and R. M. Kanter, *When Giants Learn to Dance: Mastering the challenges of strategy, management and careers in the 1990s* (London: Unwin, 1990).

Chapter 14: Marketing in the twenty-first century

This chapter looks at the changing marketing environment and how it is likely to influence marketing strategy and actions in the future.

There are many books that aim to predict trends. Perhaps not surprisingly this is an area of fads and fashions, so the reader is advised to get the latest editions! Tom Peters' latest blockbuster *Liberation Management: Necessary disorganisation for the nanosecond nineties* (London, Macmillan, 1992) is an effort to cover the subject in a comprehensive way. It has hundreds of mini-case studies and recommendations on how to reorganize the company. Hamish McRae's *The World in 2020* (Boston, MA: Harvard Business School Press, 1996) has some insightful views about trends.

Another influential book on shaking up big companies is Rosabeth Kanter's *When Giants Learn to Dance* (New York: Simon & Schuster, 1989). More technical books which have had a big impact are Michael Hammer and James Champy, *Re-engineering the Corporation* (London: Brealey, 1993) and George Stalk and Thomas M. Hout, *Competing Against Time* (New York: Free Press, 1990). The human implications of these changes are brilliantly analyzed in Charles Handy, *The Age of Unreason* (Boston, MA: Harvard Business School Press, 1990). More of an economist's approach to these issues is interestingly presented by Michael J. Mandel, *The High Risk Society: Peril and promise in the new economy* (New York: Times Business Books, 1996).

Turning more specifically to marketing, a good review is Frederick E. Webster, 'The changing role of marketing in the corporation', *Journal of Marketing*, October 1992, pp. 1–17.

Index of authors and firms

Index of subjects